TOURISM MANAGEMENT

TOURISM MANAGEMENT

Editor

P. C. SINHA

ANMOL PUBLICATIONS PVT. LTD.
NEW DELHI-110002 (INDIA)

ANMOL PUBLICATIONS PVT. LTD.
4374/4B, Ansari Road, Daryaganj
New Delhi - 110 002
Ph.: 23261597, 23278000
Visit us at: www.anmolpublications.com

Tourism Management
© 2005

ISBN 81-7488-627-3

[All rights reserved. No part of this publication may be reproduced, stored in a retrieval system or transmitted, in any form or by any means, mechanical, photocopying, recording or otherwise, without prior written permission of the Author/Publisher.]

PRINTED IN INDIA

Published by J.L. Kumar for Anmol Publications Pvt. Ltd., New Delhi and Printed at Mehra Offset Press, Delhi.

Contents

	Preface	vii
1.	Planning Tourism	1
2.	Goals and Methods	40
3.	Essentials of Tourism Planning	51
4.	Purpose and Approaches of Tourism Planning	66
5.	Tourism as System	92
6.	Tourism Planning Process	110
7.	Elements in Tourism	116
8.	Regional Planning Concepts	136
9.	Implementing and Monitoring Tourist Plans	170
10.	Destination and Site Planning	176
11.	Cost-benefit Analysis	243
12.	Tourism Planning Principles	252

Preface

TOURISM IS recognised as a major global industry today. It is a sizeable and complex service industry. In last 40 years, tourism has seen rapid and continuous growth. The desirability of tourism has seldom been questioned by governments mostly due to profit motives. However, local communities, due to some negative social and environ-mental impacts of tourism have voiced their concern against it. Therefore, tourism development strategy must get defined in different regional contexts. Policy initiatives towards undertaking corrective actions must be applied.

This work focuses on all aspects of tourism development viz. social, economic, cultural, physical, anthro-political, spatial, environmental and overall recreational. This work has been undertaken with the aim that it could provide in detail the possible ways and means for sustainable development of tourism and addresses itself to a much wider audience, particularly those involved in the planning and management of the tourism industry at different levels. Emphasis has been thereon the integrated approach and the techniques that need to be applied in implementing tourism approaches and plans.

This work aims at providing a basic reference text on the subject, details about various concepts, principles and nature of tourism industry, and a supportive literature on various facets.

Attempts have been made to cultivate global interest towards an integrated development of tourism. It makes a comprehensive analysis and evaluation of the process of tourism development and various strategies put forward for its uninterrupted growth and development. Issue identification and planning strategies in the sphere of travel and tourism is well covered and described in detail. Also sufficient focus is there on the potentials and problems involved in the development of tourism at global level. Based on different situations and development plagiarism, attempts have been made towards evolving other forms of alternative tourism and their feasibility in present day context. A detailed reference has been provided to encoverage further research.

P.C. SINHA

1. Introduction

IN ALL societies, the transformation of leisure from an activity to industry has taken place. Tourism being concrete form of recreation available to man best exemplifies and explains this change. In the per-industrial area, tourism emerged as a cultural practice amongst the elite sections of the society the transformation of this elite practice into a phenomena cutting across social class line took place during Industrial Revolution and subsequently in the nineteenth century when a host of factors led to a "democratisation of travel". Mass Tourism commenced only in 1920s, firstly in USA, when science and innovative technology made possible the mass production of vehicles and then in 1930s when due to greater availability of leisure time the system of paid holidays was introduced. In advanced industrial societies in general and Europe in particular, tourist became a mass phenomena after the end of Second World War. With time, the nature and geographical horizons of mass tourism changed from domestic holiday-making to international travel over long-haul destinations. The second half of the twentieth century has witnessed the mushrooming of tourist space everywhere and sociologically a distinct tourist type has emerged. In this era of mass tourism a leisure ethic has taken root where Right to leisure is seen as basic human right. Tourism as an Industry, has made governments conscious of its value as an item of world trade and in order to keep the trade in surplus governments have devised Tourism Policies to regulate, promote and managed the tourist product. The Economic factor has gradually taken precedence over environmental and cultural factors in the growth and regulation of International Tourism. An interesting feature accompanying the contemporary tourist boom is the proliferation of diverse forms of Tourism ranging from short excursions to round the world trips, from beach tourism to mountaineering expeditions, from organized mass travel to individual exploration. John Urry argues that there is a discernible shift in tourism with post-modernist concern with more importance placed on play, pleasure and pastiche than standardized and regulated kind of tourism sees the presentday tourist developments as "multiplying with an amazing inventiveness" where all nations are trying to gain the benefits from tourism. Societies in the west regard tourism as a industry for the future. Tourism in the Third World is seem as a panacea for economic ills, like rising foreign debt and poverty. Tourism promotion is an important part of the Structural-Readjustment Pro-grammes of the World Bank in many of these countries.

The United Nations has already, in 1963, recognized the importance of tourism to the economies of Third World. In the 1980 Conference on World Tourism, held at Manila (27 September-10 October 1980), it was accepted by the participating countries that Tourism could be a vital force for peace and could contribute to the establishment of a New International Economic Order.

However, Tourism is beset with many problems relating to its environment and cultural resource base and social and economic values of its market. Tourism induced change is inevitable and it is not always with positive consequences for the host communities. It has been suggested by many studies that Tourism Impacts are not always sustainable. It is the endeavour of this study to explore this vary dimension of tourism, in an international context.

International Tourism through its evolution from the era of Grand Tour to the present-day Mass International Tourism has brought about changes in all the spheres of life. The factors that led to the world-wide expansion and growth of tourism can help us to analyse the implications of certain issue areas that result from it. It is appropriate, therefore, to review the factors that led to its growth and development in order to understand its operation mechanism and issues resulting from it.

Increasing opportunities to travel coupled with increasing safety and speed of long-distance travel are some of the important factors responsible for the growth of tourism. In the pre-industrial era pleasure travel was limited to the wealthy few and the privileged explorers who combined business interests with explorations. Pilgrimage was the most popular form of domestic travel which combined social, recreational and religious components in the world. In Europe, Spas, seaside resorts, hot springs etc. were popular amongst those who could afford them. Long tours like the "Grand Tour" could be undertaken only by the wealthy few who could afford to take a "year off" to travel to the European continent, between leaving school and starting a job or their business. Industrial Revolution brought about increases in productivity, regular employment and greater urbanization which together gave more people the opportunity and motivation to travel. Now, tourism could cover a larger and a broader social spectrum. The working class and the newly emerging middle class were new actors on the tourism scene.

Technological Innovations like the Steamers increased the potential geographical mobility of the population. With the coming of Railways, tourism as an Industry began to dig roots as the factor of "rail-tourism symbiosis" became important. Both railways and tourism were seen as new busineses with immense scope and potential as companies competed with each other for developing a resort and linking it with rail-roads. Hotels mushroomed everywhere and entertainment facilities grew in variety and number, as more and more tourists came to visit these places. Thomas Cook, in 1841, became the first Professional Consultant and Travel Organizer in the newly developing tourism industry. The concept of the "Package-Tour" was his brain-child.

The gradual development of tourism continued till the end of Second World War, when a host of factors led to acceleration in its pace of growth. Technological advances such as the Jet Engine coupled with post-war economic recovery in the western countries made possible the long distance travel. The economies of the West became increasingly consumerist. The well entrenched Work Ethic and a increase in available leisure time motivated the people to travel over long distances. As the competition over markets, within the tourist industry grew, the trips became more economical.

The boom period of tourism industry coincides with the Expansionary period of capitalism, immediately after the Second World War. In the Post-Industrial Phase of consumption the tourist production mechanism has taken the dimensions of multinational corporation completely integrated in the world economy. One feature that sets it apart from capitalism is that unlike capitalism Tourism has always responded quickly to crisis situations. The crisis generated by the rise in energy prices led to a downturn for tourism but for a very short time. The economic crisis in the affluent societies in the early 1980s and the worldwide recession initially hit the tourism industry but it quickly stablized. The decline in International Tourism recently due to the Gulf War and the trouble in Arabian countries was quickly overcome by the Industry because of its ability to control demand and market.

"The Growth of Tourism has become increasingly supply driven" (Lanfant, 1989). Tourist Industry Multinationals which are vertically and horizontally integrated in the world economy have come to weild enormous power in the industry. Decision making which concerns regions, and whole countries are taken at International level by the Multinational corporations, which ruthlessly pursue the interests of the tourist industry rather than the host population.

Another discernible feature is the emphasis put by the host governments to promote the "unique", "out of ordinary landscapes" (Urry, 1990) and "mega-events" (Maurice Roche, 1992) such as Olympics and carnivals in order to attract tourist attraction which in result yields economic benefits. Tourism in the advanced countries, according to Roche, is linked to the post-industrial information society where the foreign cultures—as seen through the eyes of the tourists and governmental and private promotion agencies—are reduced to a few instantly recognisable characteristics. This results in distortion of reality and an increasing commercialization of environments and cultures. KLEIN (1993) shows how the Arizona State National Park Service in USA has constructed an abstract image of Western Landscape and a glorious past where, the "Frontier", although it has long been declared "closed", has been preserved as something sacred and which every tourist must visit.

In the present day Tourism, many strategies of tourism development run contrary to each other. The goal of preservation of landscapes and people is pursued side by side with building alien facilities like ski-resorts with mechanized lifts and artificial slopes. Tourism has been termed as a "two-sided entity", which can fulfil the related expectations of the visitors and the societies that welcome them. The reason why International Tourism continues to grow is because it has the ability to invent new resources for promotion which the market, must consume because of his mounting leisure needs and recklessness.

The issues arising from the growth and development of International Tourism concern the disparties in tourism development and the social, economic and environmental costs and benefits of tourism. The issues are of, both international as well as national, regional and local significance and raise questions regarding the ethics of development.

(a) Problems in under-developed countries due to international tourist flow from the more developed countries

As a worldwide industry tourism has grown so quickly but haphazardly during the last quarter of a century that it has become a problem for both industrialized and developing world. Tourism despite its phenomenal growth remains a first world phenomena. Two-third of all International Visitor arrivals are concentrated in 20 most industrialized countries and 90 per cent of the world travel market is in the developed countries. The Industrial World, due to its economic prosperity has a very strong tradition of tourism. In the early years, after the war, the Europeans and the North Americans preferred to travel within their continents but due to the growth of tourism and the resulting overcrowding and pollution of many of the resorts led to a decrease in their popularity. Due to the decline of the attractive value of many of these resorts, long-haul destinations in the developing countries became more popular.

As the developing countries haven't had any significant amount of domestic tourism, the prospects of earning foreign exchange from international tourism has forced many of these countries to promote International Tourism without developing sufficient infrastructure and taking precautions. The basic problem is that Third World countries have been compelled to make a "leap from predominantly rural based economies into service oriented tourist economies without passing through the inter-mediary stage of industrialization". The needs of the international tourists are at odds with the needs of the local population. In some cases the host countries look towards the tourist-generating countries for investment in tourist infrastructure development. Third World Tourism problems highlight many social economic and environmental issues. These issues are discussed in the following sub-section:

(b) Social and Economic issues

The Social Impact of tourism varies according to the difference between the visitors and the hosts in terms of numbers, race, culture or social outlook. To the International Tourist, tourism brings benefits like relaxation, recuperation, recreation, change of environment, widening of horizons and social contacts. To the hosts the impacts are not always positive, although tourism is promoted as a major force in up-grading the standard of living; the values; fostering international understanding and preservation of cultural heritage, among the host population. The issue of social costs vs. benefits becomes even more pronounced when the traditional cultures of underdeveloped countries come into contact with affluent societies of the advanced countries. Social tensions, distortion of lifestyles and cultural decay are some of the costs that host destinations might have to pay for haphazard and unregulated tourist development.

The inevitable commercialization, due to International tourism, of ethnic arts and crafts, can lead to development of "shoddy replicas and fakes" and can have a "corrupting influence" by "cheapening" the artistic values. The commercialization brought about by International tourists tends to change the patterns of consumption in the host population through "demonstration effect".

There are also doubts as to whether International Tourism improves International understanding. It is impossible to believe that it does so, when examined through evidence of Prostitution, Immoral traffic, Gambling casinos and rising crime rates in destinations like Thailand, Fiji and Philippines. The very demand of many international tourists to stay in Tourist Enclaves away from contact with locals, suggests not much improvement in international understanding.

The World Council of churches in its report "Leisure Tourism: Threat and Promise" (1970) examined the issue of tourism induced social stress in the pilgrimage places and put forward recommendations calling upon both tourists as well as local population to fulfil their role more responsibly. The rising numbers of tourists interested in visiting such sites which gave rise to problems of religious nature, necessitated such an international response.

Another social cost of tourism is that it tends to change the indigenous languages. This change is brought about through three ways:

(i) through immigrants who come to fill new jobs.

(ii) through demonstration effect of the outsiders.

(iii) through direct social contact with the tourists.

Much of the tourism literature since 1970s has been concerned with conflictual tendencies that result from International Tourism in areas where the hosts are confronted with "comparatively wealthier and culturally different" guests. These conflictual tendencies might lead to latent or actual hostility in the destination area. The greater the cultural and economic distance between the hosts and the guests greater the probability of attitudes of the hosts becoming antagonistic. The more rapid and intense the growth of International Tourism at a destination greater the degree of conflict between the hosts and the guests. The lure of money and better life to the rural migrants plays an important role in breaking down traditional social and cultural values.

Although these conflictual tendencies are not unavoidable but they usually arise due to uncontrolled influx of tourist traffic into the area. High tourist densities can cause tensions between holiday-makers and the local communities and these tendencies are compounded especially if tourists are concentrated into a few pockets.

(c) Economic Issues

Much of the motivation for development of International Tourism in the Third World comes from the perceived economic benefits that it brings, through foreign exchange earnings and employment and income generation, to destinations and regions. Flow of tourists and their revenue to peripheral regions has been seen as a counterbalance to the economic pull of urban industrial core in the West.

However, many studies point out that a considerable amount of the generated tourism revenue returns to the tourist-generating core. The money thus leaked goes to travel companies, for buying consumer goods to satisfy tourist needs, and for repaying of loans and dividends on foreign investments.

Another major reason for the tourist money leaking back to the advanced countries is that many of the leading hotel chains providing room accommodation to the tourists are based in the advanced countries. For instance, Multinational Hotel Corporations like the Holiday Inns, Marriot Corp., ITT Sheraton Corp., Hilton Hotels Corp. and Hyatt International have their headquarters in the USA. Some other problems related to the change economic impact of International tourism are:

(i) International Tourism causes Inflation. It causes the rise in prices of commodities and land in the destinations.

(ii) International Tourism due to its dependence on Foreign Capital makes the economies of the host countries over dependent on tourism industry which is prone to fluctuations in demand and operates under uncertain conditions.

(iii) International Tourism in many developing countries results in foreign control and dominance because the industry, basically, is supply driven. Foreign control and dominance might lead to greater amount of leakages and hence the industry's diminishing role in clearing the balance of payments deficits.

(iv) "The foreign Exchange cost of overseas promotion, advertising and other development programmes by a nation and its tourist industry is yet another Foreign Exchange cost."

(v) Most of the employment generated in the wake of International tourism is seasonal. The hotel building is capital intensive and if the same money is spent on agriculture proportionally more employment opportunities can be created.

(vi) Although International Tourism has the potential for regional economic growth, it can also create pockets of development and thereby further increase development disparities.

(d) Issues of Natural Environment

One of the major criticism of Tourism is that it is self-destructive i.e. it destroys the very resource that feeds it. Natural Environment as a tourism resource needs to be preserved because an increase in number of tourists leads to a greater possibility of tourist induced stress on the environment. While the overall environmental impact of the "Smokeless Industry" called Tourism is probably less than that of most other industries developed on a similar scale, the significance of its impact lies in the fact that it frequently impinges upon the fragile, sensitive and interesting segments of landscape. Activities like the construction of roads, buildings, ski-resorts etc. lead to permanent restructuring of the landscape. Tourist activities like walking, skiing, hunting etc. can result in trampling of vegetation and destruction of species. Increasing International Tourism at a place leads to increasing population densities and greater transportation activities which cause pollution is of the environment. According to a Botanical, both the Dal lake and Nagin lake in Srinagar may disapear within 80 years if the present rate of pollution is not arrested. The issues outlined above indicate the limitations of the present path of tourism development and call for radical reorientation of the planning process and strategy formulation. The issues are not merely of national level but are also international and local. Any response to these issues must be co-ordinated at International level and an integrated strategy must be developed keeping in mind all the dimensions of tourism impacts.

Introduction

Sustainable Development

The concept of development grew out of the ideology of nineteenth century Western Industrial Society and was rooted in the belief that technological innovation and industrialization will inevitably lead to human improvement. This belief was best realized in North America where settlers rushed to "transform wilderness into a domesticated environment". The Spanish and Portuguese colonizers exploited the vast store of natural resources in Latin America and rationalized their actions as a march from primitive towards civilized way of life. Colonialists with their superior technology and skilled manpower progressed at the cost of the natives who remained impoverished.

Development understood purely in terms of the goal of economic growth through industrialization and technological innovation is misleading as concept and has many drawbacks. Development strategies based on economic indicators like the Gross Domestic Product camouflage the social inequalities that economic growth brings. Factors like family, work attitudes, social ethics, authority structure, content and quality of scientific education and degree of domestic tranquillity are some of the factors determining the success of development efforts.

At a global level, the economic growth model has failed to bring about economic justice to all. The Global Economy has developed structural inequalities leading to disproportionate distribution of income, technological development and degrees of human well-being. It has widened the economic and social gap between the under-developed and the developed countries. The Unequal Exchange between the two has further marginalized the improverished majority in the underdeveloped countries. The rapid strides of the developed nations in industrialization is matched by a threatening pace of population growth and increasing poverty in the underdeveloped countries. In a way, both, rapid industrialization in developed countries and rising populations in the underdeveloped countries prove taxing on the environment. All the factors, combine to paint a picture of earth as being more unjust, less secure, more polluted and with ever depleting resources.

Sustainable development has been suggested as the only way out of the present state of affairs. The concept of sustainable development emerged out of the ever increasing concern and awareness among the governments for the environmental decay, depleting natural resources and increasing poverty that threatens the very survival of man and other living beings. The concept has developed through the various United Nations conferences over the years. It was implicit in the Bio-sphere Conference held in Paris in 1968. The concept of "ecologically sustainable development" was given shape by the United Nations Conference on Human Environment, held in Stockholm in June 1972. In 1974 the UNEP/UNCTAD Symposium on Patterns of Resource use, Environment and Development held in Cocoyou, Mexico, called for a new approach to development keeping in view "Imaginative Research in alternative consumption patterns, technological lifestyles, landuse strategies, as well as institutional frameworks and educational requirements to sustain them". The 1987 report of United Nations Commission on Environment and Development, titled "Our Common Future" concluded that the "human survival and well-being could depend on success in elevating sustainable development to a global ethic". It was felt that "real world of interlocked economic and ecological systems will not change" but the policies and institutions concerned must change by the way of greater international co-operation in formulating and imple-menting policy changes concerning the problems of environment and development.

Sustainable development was defined as "development that meets the needs of the present without compromising the ability of future generation to meet their own needs". A sustainable path of development implies an idea of equity—both inter-generational and intra-generational. The satisfaction of basic human needs and aspirations of an improved quality of life by extending to all the opportunities rank among the important goals of sustainable development.

The sustainable development policies must be based on the following objectives:

1. revival of growth,
2. a change in the quality of growth,
3. meeting essential needs for jobs, foods, energy, water and sanitation,
4. ensuring a sustainable level of population,
5. conserving and enhancing the resource base,
6. reorienting technology and managing risks, and
7. merging environment and economics in decision making.

Redclift (1989) thinks the term sustainable development refers to "sustainable levels of both production and consumption". It denotes both "the resource base itself and livelihoods which are derived from it" (Goodman & Redclift, 1991). The concept is riddled with disciplinary biases and two sets of contradictions are evident in it.

Firstly, the intellectual divide over the emphasis to be given to Nature and Human Progress in conceptualization of sustainable development. Some scholars believe nature to be a major constraint on further human progress and suggest its conservative use. Other writers think that Human Progress carries implications for nature itself because the industrial society has failed to come to terms with implications of capitalist economic development.

Secondly, considering sustainable development in a North-South Framework the structural inequalities of the global system have resulted in contradictory approaches. Perceptions in the North i.e. environment must be valued and preserved can be inverted in the South where it is considered to be vital subsistance and therefore must be exploited. None of these approaches can be lauded or derided because both are right as per there respective position in the world economy. Goodman and Redclift suggest that the environmental agenda and the issue of sustainable development should be oriented towards the local level situations by providing realistic options keeping in mind the regional and national political economy of resource use and dimensions of social justice. In the local level situations, the assessment of environmental and economic "trade offs" necessary for any sustainable policy must be made.

Writers have pointed out the difficulties encountered in conceptu-alization and measurement of sustainable development (Hahn, 1993), while others see in sustainable development a moral challenge to bring advocates of varying opinions on a common platform (Engel & Engel, 1990). Three conditions, according to Caldwell (1984) are vital for the success of the paradigm:

1. There must be a seizable politically effective constituency in favour of the sustainable policies.
2. Governments should have "incentive" to favour long range objectives of sustainable development over short-term considerations.
3. There must be an ethical ideology of development with explicit political expression.

Although most of the countries are in favour of Environmental protection and Sustainable Development Paradigm, it remains to be seen how it is translated into Practice. As an international response, the Agenda 21, adopted by the United Nations Conference on Environment and Development on June 14, 1992, in Rio de Janerio has outlined a comprehensive programme of action to be implemented during 1993-2000 with the help of governments, development agencies, United Nation organizations and non-governmental organizations. It covers a wide range of issues extending over Poverty, underdevelopment, consumption patterns, health, human settlements, Atmospheric protection, biological diverty, hazardous wastes, desertification, deforestation, toxic chemicals, biotechnology and women development besides suggesting means of implementation and financial assistance.

It has been suggested by many studies the haphazard tourism development in many parts of the world can be socially and ecologically damaging to the host communities and environments and that tourism development for economic benefits is unsustainable as it exercises strees on Human and Natural Resources. This criticism arises from a shift of paradigm from a growth oriented tourism development towards more sustainable forms of development, in Tourism Research in tune with a general shift in other social sciences.

For Tourism Industry, sustainability is a new world, which is often missing or rarely used. But it is not difficult to identify what is not sustainable about Tourism Development. The Unsustainable effects can be categorized into Economic, Social, Environmental, Political and Administrative.

1. *Economic*
   (a) Tourism causes rise in prices of essential items.
   (b) Increase in land prices.
   (c) Economic marginalisation of the poorer sections of the society.
   (d) Overdependence on foreign capital.
   (e) Requires foreign investment and causes "Leakages" of revenue from host countries to tourism generating countries.
   (f) Makes the destination populations consumerist through the demonstration effect.
   (g) Incurs losses due to fluctuations in foreign currency exchange rates which might result in reduction in demand.
   (h) If fails to bring about equitable distribution of economic benefits among the host Population thus maintaining the gap between the rich and the poor.
   (i) Its seasonal nature results in

only part-time economic benefits.

2. *Social*
   (a) Growth of population at the destination due to in-migration of workers and tourists.
   (b) Brings occupational mobility which in many cases leads to breakdown of the extended family system.
   (c) Change in vernacular language through contact.
   (d) Loss of privacy of the hosts.
   (e) Seasonal influx of workers might affect social stability.
   (f) Increase in social ills like Gambling, Prostitution, Drug use, etc.
   (g) Changes in values through contact with outsiders.
   (h) Increase in inter-generational gap of young and old.
   (i) Commercialization of arts and crafts.
   (j) Loss of freedom and opportunity to enjoy the local tourist resource.
   (k) Decrease in the availability of water, electricity etc.

3. *Environmental*
   (a) Alternation of Habitat through construction activity.
   (b) Encroachment over agricultural land.
   (c) Pollution through effluents, solid wastes, noise, etc.
   (d) Trampling of vegetation and destruction of species.
   (e) Destruction of fragile ecosystem like islands, mountains etc.
   (h) Depreciating aesthetic values due to unsympathetic architecture.

4. *Political*
   (a) Hurdles in the path of promoting environmental and develop-mental awareness due to lack of support from certain vested interests.
   (b) Non-involvement of host populations in the planning decisions that affect them.
   (c) Non-integration of environmental and developmental issues in tourism policy decisions.
   (d) Short-sighted tourism policies.
   (e) Lack of government initiative to involve non-governmental organizations into planning decisions.

5. *International*
   (a) Disproportionate growth of international tourism worldwide
   (b) Lack of representation of local communities at international flora.
   (c) Lack of measures to implement and monitor International Agreements concerning tourism.
   (d) Theft and Smuggling of Antiques for sale in international markets.
   (e) Lack of consideration for the requirements of developing countries by the tourism multinationals.
   (f) Selective kidnapping and killing of international tourists in trouble torn areas of underdeveloped nations.
   (g) Adverse impact of international

conflicts on international tourism in Border and other regions in conflict.

6. *Administrative*
   (a) Lack of integration of tourism policy with the general planning process.
   (b) Lack of efficient measures to educate the local population, hotel owners, resource managers and the tourists about their respective obligations and duties towards local environment and culture.
   (c) Lack of trained personnel.
   (d) Inadequate and unreliable data on tourism which has serious implications for its management.

As there are many economic, social, ecological and political limits of tourism development, sustainable strategies are necessary to eradicate these problems. Tourism, being a consumptive resource, with short-term cycles of booms and busts, can be, both, a powerful force or a scourge for Environmental protection and preservation of cultural heritage. It therefore, demands that if steps are not taken tourist destination areas and resources become over used, unattractive and eventually decline. Sustainable Tourism, calls for development of a more positive and symbiotic relationship between Environment and Tourism, which would give importance to the leisure needs of the tourists on one hand and Environmental Resource use, its protection and preservation for the future generations on the other. Co-ordination of policies, practiceable planning, acceptance of limitations on growth, education of all parties concerned and commitment to long-term objectives are pre-requisite to the successful planning for sustainable Tourism.

Since, it is unrealistic to believe the population of the tourist-generating countries will dispense with their leisure needs and destination countries will ever want not to promote tourism, international understanding and cognizances over the issue of Sustainable Tourism is of paramount importance. The Manila Declaration, adopted the World Tourism Conference in October 1980, agrees that "there are many constraints on the development of tourism" and suggested that nations and groups of nations should "determine and study these constraints and adopt measures aims at attenuating their negative influence". It was also recognized by the conference that "International co-operation in the field of tourism is an endeavor in which the characteristics of people and basic interests of individual states must be respected." The 1989 Hague Declaration on Tourism called for its promotion in terms of sustainable development and sought to encourage "alternative forms which favour closer contact and understanding between tourists and receiving population, preserve cultural identity and offer distinctive and original tourist products and facilities." The 1989, Inter-Parliamentary Conference on Tourism, held at The Hague, also recommended that the States should position tourism clearly within the framework of national priorities and assess the impact of any legislation on the facilitation and liberalization on tourism to ensure that this does not impede flow of international tourism. Proper steps should be taken for the protection and security of tourists, sites and facilities.

Sustainable Tourism

Butler, suggests the following possible solutions for tourism problems to pave the way for more sustainable forms of tourism:

1. Curbing tourist numbers to a level which allows the environment to function without being under pressure and to sustain itself.
2. Changing the type of tourism by attracting a different type of tourists.
3. Changing the resource base itself to resist the pressure of tourism.
4. Educating all parties concerned.

Although these strategies do cure tourism industry from some of its ills they are not sure antidotes to all its ills. Studies have pointed out the Lacunae in even some of the alternative strategies like Eco-tourism, Ethno-tourism, Anthro-tourism etc. Jacobson and Robles (1992) point out that sustainable tourism strategies are not environmently benign and need highly efficient and innovative management. In their study they found that there were some negative impacts of Eco-tourism and there was a need to develop a training programme for tour-guides. In their survey they collected data regarding the resourcement management and information needs of scientists, National Park managers, current and potential tour guides, the tourists and the hotel owners. As a second step they conducted a pilot training course for twelve local residents. The results showed that the Tour Guide Programme helps to mitigate negative impacts upon resources, provided environmental education to locals, apart from providing information for tourists and bringing local economic benefits. Gorden (1992) illustrates the negative impacts of Anthro-tourism on primitive culture of the Bushmen in the Kalahari. Bushmen have been at the receiving end of the government tourism policy and vested interests in advanced countries because Anthro-tourism further isolated them by cashing upon their poverty, vulnerability and powerlessness. Dearden (1991) points out that various forms of Sustainable Tourism Schemes are of different suitability in different contexts. Zurick (1992) proposes the alternative strategies alone do not mean anything and important structural changes must accompany alternative strategies like Adventure Tourism for tourism impacts to be sustainable.

For any strategy of sustainable International tourism to succeed in the objective of maximum benefits at a minimum cost, the following are necessary:

1. International consensus and co-operation about the strategy adopted.
2. Initiative in the tourist-generating countries (the market) aimed at increasing the environmental and cultural awareness of the tourists and developing consciousness about their duties and role towards the environment and culture of the host regions.
3. Placing tourism within the framework of national priorities and according a place to tourism in the general planning process.
4. Framing policies keeping in mind the resource management, information needs and economic conditions of the local populations.

Introduction

5. Implementing the policies, plans and strategies as Pilot Projects at selected destinations first and then implementation of the revised plans at all the destinations.
6. Ensuring public participation.

In real situations, trade-offs will have to be made between protecting environments and culture and economic benefits; between protecting the product and the markets, between planning for long-term gains and short-term benefits; between conservation and rampant depletion and between ethics and selfishness, in planning for Sustainable Tourism.

A Case Study

When compared to other parts of the Indian-Subcontinent, Himalayas are as unique entity. The Himalayas are a world in itself. The Environment of the Himalayas in all its variety and internal complexity is very fragile. Culturally, the inhabitants of Himalayas have evolved a distinct way of life. Throughout the march of history, Western Himalayas have been subjected to many kinds of external influences from the people of diverse religious, cultural and ethnic stocks. The Cultural-Ecology of the Himalayas has evolved through modifica-tions of the Ecological settings by diverse cultural groups in different ecological contexts by Adaptation and Adoption of resources. When compared to other parts of India it has its own peculiar features and problems. Its strengths—namely the environmental richness and strong commitment of people to traditions-are also its biggest weak—nesses.

Developmental change in Western Himalayas is an post-independence phenomena. The entire process of development has been geared towards improving the socio-economic conditions of the inhabitants. Development was also sought to be a vehicle for bringing the hitherto isolated regions into the political mainstream of national life. The strategic and military significance of the region necessitated that political stabiligy and economic development be accorded maximum priority. In this regard, planning strategies have aimed at fulfilling the basic human needs of the people and encouraging economic development.

Though the economic development of Himalayas is of key importance, but there are certain constraints to its realization. The fragile nature of ecosystem, difficulty of access and cultural difference of its people from the other parts of the country are constraints to Himalayan Development. The Development Process as it has unfolded has resulted in disparities among people and regions. The benefits of the development process have not trickled down to all sections of the population and are not distributed judiciously over space. The Trans-himalayan Region stands in sharp contrast to the lower and middle Himalayas in terms of development benefits according to people and places. An important effect of development has been the permanent restructuring of the environment through deforestation, soil erosion, Landslides and building activity. Increasing population and greater urbanization beyond the environmental carrying capacity combined with migration from other regions have put severe strees on Himalayan Resources. Cultural change resulting from contact with outsiders—trades, tourists, workers, etc. and the values of modernization have brought about far reaching changes in work, food and clothing habits apart from distortion of environmental sensibilities of the people by the Environmentally Unsympathetic Architecture—in gross imitation of alien fads and fashions.

Although the Western Himalayas have a long tradition of pilgrimages, Mass-tourism started only in the colonial period when the British rulers patronized the Hill Stations and Cantonement Towns. Developments since Indepe-ndence has been marked by a lack of integration of tourism into general developmental process. In Himachal Pradesh, little was done to develop facilities and other infrastructure important to tourists. Development was restricted to a few scenic beauty and popular colonial resorts like Shimla, Dalhousie, Manali, Dharamshala etc. Political restrictions like the requirement of an Inner Line Permit in the trans-himalayan region further discouraged Tourism in the region.

The governmental approach to Tourism Development in Himachal Pradesh changed only in the mid 1980s when it realized the role tourism—especially International Tourism—could play in economic development of the state. HIMTAB (Himalayan Tourism Advisory Board) was set up in 1987 as a "voluntary, consultative mechanism for greater inter-state co-operation in publicity, promotion and marketing of tourism facilities" for the Western Himalayan Region. It has advised standardized inter-state taxation, better management of leisure facilities, popularization of local festivities, preservation of ecology, architectural design concepts and alternative tourism as essential part of the tourism policies in the region. The 1991 Tourism Policy document of the Himachal Pradesh Government declared tourism as an Industry and accorded it a high priority for "accelerating economic development of the state". In 1992, the Government of India, amended the Foreigner (Protected Area) Order, 1958 by considerably relaxing the conditions of travel within the Inner Line.

The changed attitude towards tourism development has much to promise through increase in tourist volume but it also has its dangers because it is feared that the tragedy of tourism industry in Himachal is due to the targedy of the general development processes which are not sustainable. The lack of sustainability arises from aggressive development at the cost of natural and cultural landscape. Tourism Development in Himachal Pradesh suffers from some contradictory processes where the need to protect and preserve environment and culture is at odds with the political and economic aspirations. The challenge before the sustainable development of tourism in Himalayas is that the goals of economic development, political and strategic stability, social well being, environmental protection and cultural preservation should not be compromised. Recognizing that these are in contradiction at various points, the only viable solution may be to promote sustainable tourism development by trading-off and not compromising environmental, political, economic and cultural concerns. The success of the sustainable solution will ultimately depend on efficient management, and participation and education of tourists, hosts, traders and decision makers.

The Organization of the present study derives from the social and environment impacts in the wake of international tourism in developing countries like India and the need for "sustainable development" paradigm to its study.

Tourism as a phenomenon, has over

Introduction

the last 200 years become increasingly diversified and even more fuzzy as a concept of academic treatment. Significant changes since World War II in tourism has resulted in mushrooming of tourist spaces everywhere and sociologically a distinct tourist type has emerged. Economically, the increasing significance of tourism as a item of world trade has made governments conscious of its monetary value and the tourist resources have been commercialized and marketed as attractive products.

Global Trends of International Tourism, demonstrate that it reinforces the existing structural inequalities between the developed and the developing nations. Developed countries are the major tourist generating and tourist receiving countries of the world. Recently, the developing countries have become the destinations of the affluent tourists from the advanced nations. In dire need of foreign exchange, many of the developing countries have recklessly promoted tourism. Apart from the problem of leakages, international tourism has made developing countries dependent on the developed countries for the supply of tourists. The economic advantages of international tourism to Third World countries are part of a package deal which also consists of social, economic and environmental disadvantages. The type and intensity of social, economic and environmental impacts, in these countries, depends on factors such as, the nature and the carrying capacity of the destination; the type, intensity and pattern of tourist development; the approach to planning, design and management and the ideology of the tourists. The presence of traditional lifestyles, fragile environments coupled with haphazard tourist development for economic ends and a culture shock resulting from affluent tourist—traditional host contact; all combine to produce, tourism impacts, not always sympathetic but instead potentially threatening to the local setting. Such a incompatibility situation is counter-productive to the growth of tourism industry.

International Tourism has grown at a rapid pace since the World War II and it has in its wake given rise to many social, economic and environmental problems. Cumulatively these problems have a devastating effect on the settings of underdeveloped countries whose cultural and ecological fabrics are fragile.

Tourism has remained a first world phenomena in terms of market and economic benefits, whereas the costs of international tourism are being borne by underdeveloped countries which haphazardly promote tourism for short-term economic gains. It is suggested that the future of international tourism in countries like India depends on the manner in which the tourist product is developed, promoted and marketed and to that effect the domestic political stability and economic atmosphere will be the pertinent factors.

Picking up the thread from here it has been shown they how Western Himalayas despite their rich tourism resource potential have inefficient infrastructure to match the rising demands of tourists on one hand and environment on the other. The general economic backwardness and environmental fragility coupled with mismanagement and selfishness of entrepreneurs are the major hurdles for the tourism industry's inability to balance economic benefits and environmental stress.

The perceptions of the local population at Shimla and Keylong tourist destinations were more or less homogeneous regarding the social and environmental impacts of international tourism. Majority opinion indicates that international tourism is promising for local communities and much more careful planning needs to be done in the development of tourist infrastructure and provision of better living conditions in the destinations.

The problems of international tourism in developing countries are an ideal case for understanding the general development process in these countries, which is beset with contradictions. The goals of environmental preservation and conservation are at logger-heads with the objective of fulfilling the basic subsistance needs of the population. Environmental Protection, though necessary, can not be carried out in the face of starvation of the populace. Similarly in the case of tourism, environmental degradation takes place because of the interests of tourism industry and needs of the government.

Since development by means of industrialization is not possible in the hilly terrain of Western Himalayas, the government is left with a few alternatives to usher in economic change. Whatever development initiative that has been taken has led to permanent damage to environment through deforestation, soil erosion, landslides and construction projects. Cultural change resulting from contact with outsiders are interface with modern values have brought about for reaching changes in work, food and clothing habits. In such a situation tourism was promoted as a vehicle for accelerating economic development of the state. Tourism, like other constituents of development necessarily produces a difference in attitudes and perceptions of the people. People who economically benefit from it are usually more tolerable of any negative consequences of tourism than others. Also tourism like other facets of development increases the social and economic dispatities among population, giving rise to class/group formation in the destination. The increasing differentiation of population produces more class and group differentiated responses to the negative consequences of tourism. A high level of class and/or group—differentiation is an unsustainable impact of tourism in the sense that it affects the fabric of society. More tourist means more tourist business and more migrants. Cumulative increase in the tourist volume, tourist business and in-migration creates more imbalances in the shape of: 1. Inqual distribution of economic benefits among the population. 2. Invasion of alien values and displacement of existing value system. 3. Greater potentiality of intra-group and inter-group conflicts of attitudes. People no longer have a shared meaning of tourism. Group Homogenity is necessary because in its absence, Differentiation of perceptions amongst community members becomes a threat to the social solidarity. Conflicting perceptions are highly damaging at the local level as such a cultural and social change is difficult to correct because cultures unlike eco-systems do not have the capacity to recover from the damage.

Although the perceptions in Shimla were not differentiated on the basis of groups at the time the present study was carried but the very fact that perceptions are stronger in Shimla than Keylong indicate that in future the degree of group-differentiation of perceptions of tourism impacts might increase.

The challenge for "sustainable development" paradigm in the third world generally and Western Himalays, particularly is to devise strategies for minimising the tourising impacts. For this, the environmental agenda and the strategies of the sustainable development must focus attention on the local level situations by providing realistic options. Recognizing the fact, that there are many social, economic and environmental limits to tourism development, sustainable tourism policies need to be framed for developing a more symbiotic relationship between environment and tourism.

There is also need to globalize sustainable tourism concept through various international fora such as United Nations. The recent Rio-Summit on Environment and Development by discussing the problems of Hill Areas Development has initiated a step in this direction.

Tourism in Third World

Socrates had the inconvenient habit of insisting on defining the meaning of words before starting a dialogue. Of course his dissertations were about philosophic concepts like the good and the beautiful which defy precise definitions. The phrase Third World is not a philosophic concept but over the last decade it seems to have assumed several connotations. In tourism terms I would like to equate it with the concept of developing countries because it conforms to the pattern of international tourist movements. Depending on certain political affiliations this concept would apply to the non-aligned group as well, because most of its members can be described as developing countries.

During the last five years, 1977-81, out of the aggregate of 1329 million international movements Western Europe accounted for 751 million and USSR and other East European countries received 183 million. North America and Mexico received 187 million visitors during this period. So the two high concentration areas, Europe and the USA, Canada and Mexico accounted for nearly 84.7 per cent of world movements. The Caribbean has traditionally been the playground of North America and Western Europe and tourist arrivals averaged close to 7.5 million a year, which outnumbered the local populations in several island countries. Its share of world tourism in the last five years was 2.47 per cent. The new growth area of the last four years was Southeast Asia (ASEAN group) and East Asia which together claimed more than 15 million visitors a year or 4.4 per cent of world tourism. The Middle East including Egypt, despite political disruptions, maintained its hsare of world tourism at 1.8 per cent, the arrivals amounting to 24.56 millions. The total for Africa despite the high figures of Morocco and Tunisia totalled 27 million or two per cent of the global figures. South Asia which according to WTO's definition is comprised of the five countries of the Indian subcontinent plus Afghanistan and Iran received only 10.3 million visitors, 0.8 per cent of world movements.

But the arrival figures are somewhat deceptive in the sense that a majority of European tourists just criss-cross within Europe and much of tourism in North America is cross-border traffic between the USA and Canada or between USA and Mexico. For instance, in 1980 out of 280 million international visitors Europe received 196 million but more than 80 per cent of them travelled within Europe, while there was an exchange of about 20 million visitors between the USA and Canada. That to some extent is now also true of tourism among four countries of Southeast Asia, Malaysia, Thailand, Singapore and Indonesia and more so in the Middle East. The largest single contributor to Singapore arrivals in Indonesia and not Japan and of the one and a half million annual visitors to

Jordan nearly 80 per cent are from neighbouring countries.

In order to analyse the character of world tourism one should, therefore, break down the arrival figures between long-haul and medium or short-haul movements. This is particularly important for assessing the economic value of tourism. The per capita expenditure of long-haul visitors is as a rule somewhat higher than that of short-haul. Since much of tourism in the Third World countries consists of long-haul tourists this is reflected in the share of receipts from tourism as against its share of arrivals. The arrivals share during the five year period was 13.3 per cent while that of receipts was 21.9 per cent. Of course a more important factor is that because of inflationary trends resulting in extraordinary escalation in prices the increases in receipts has been much higher than the increase in arrivals though not necessarily in real terms. Part of the increase in receipts is due to variations in exchange rate of the US dollar in various markets.

During the last three years the continued economic recession in the industrialised countries which generate more than 80 per cent of world tourism is adversely affecting long-haul travel. There is considerable evidence that because of a perceptible decline in discretionary incomes and ten per cent unemployment in North America and Western Europe, comparatively more people are taking shorter vacations within their own countries or nearby countries. The earlier trend of the sixties and seventies of high growth rate of long-haul travel to Third World destinations is being reversed. For instance, the West Germans who have been the highest spenders on foreign travel since 1977 spent US$ 19.7 billion in 1980 on foreign travel, contributing nearly 21 per cent of the total global receipts from tourism, but US$ 3 billion less in 1981. There have been similar, though proportionately less marked declines in foreign expenditure on travel by other developed countries like France, Italy, UK, Netherlands, Japan etc. This would partly explain the rapid growth of intra-regional tourism is Southeast and East Asian regions. But in South Asia there has been marked growth in exchange of visitors only among three countries, India, Sri Lanka and Nepal. Because of political and other extraneous factors this region as a whole with a population of 950 million has shown little growth in intra-regional tourism.

The four-fold escalation in fuel prices towards the end of 1973 did hurt world economy considerably but it bounced back by the year 1975-76. It did hurt tourism too but only temporarily. 1974 was the first year in the post-war era when international tourism showed an actual decline albeit of only 2.5 per cent. On the whole, tourism demonstrated greater resilience than many other industries usually regarded as more stable. The general price level rose to higher plateau but it was remarkable that the cost of travel in real terms was less in 1976-78 than in 1973. After all, the Freddie Laker phenomenon resulting in low basement fares offered by both scheduled carriers and charters over the Atlantic happened in 1977. As was to be expected the Laker phenomenon gradually spread over other routes as well.

But all predictions by economists and others that the recession would start bottoming out by 1982 have proved to be wrong. In fact 1982 was a worse year than 1981. The fuel prices have remained stable for the last one year and in fact are likely to show a downward trend. However, other adverse factors have emerged and the general recession is likely to continue for some time, may be until 1984. It has led to protectionist policies by highly industrialised countries which are likely to cause further imbalance in the balance of payments between. North and South. The South is already reeling under unprecedented heavy debts of US$ 700 billion. The great saving grace of tourism is that even though most of the developed countries have an adverse balance of payments on travel account, which means that their receipts from tourism are less than the expenditure on travel by their citizens, most of them have not imposed currency restrictions on travel abroad. That makes tourism a very important factor in redressing the balance of payments situations of the Third World countries. In terms of US dollars international trade in 1982 fell by five per cent but WTO's preliminary estimate is that world receipts from tourism grew by four per cent. But arrival figures declined by 1.3 per cent and were 279.9 million in 1982 as against 283.6 million in 1981. There was a decline in numbers in Africa, North America, Latin America and the Middle East while Asia and the Pacific were still on the upswing redressing the overall deficit.

Forecasting for the next ten years one can assume that tourist movements from the industrial countries to the Third World, from the North to the South, would continue in a rising curve, that there is no long-term prospect of the flattening out of this curve and that there is a reasonably good prospect for the growth of tourism among developing countries themselves, at any rate among those showing comparatively high rates of economic growth. But the fundamental question is to determine the extent of benefits derived by the Third World from international tourism, or rather to assess the nature of the economic and social impact of international tourism on developing countries. Because the visitor spends large amounts of money in foreign currency in the countries visited, it is assumed that tourism is an excellent means of transfer of wealth from the richer to the poorer countries. After all a good part of the money is paid for services and not for consumption of resources. The tourist is paying for an experience and the resources of the country are not transferred by way of exports. A closer study would, however, show that these assumptions are not altogether correct.

How much of the money spent by the visitor is retained in the destination country? There is no simple answer to this question because present-day tourism consists of a complicated set of alternative arrangements. A comprehensive study called 'The Economic and Social Impact of International Tourism on the Developing Countries' undertaken by IUOTO (now WTO) in 1974-75 on behalf of ECOSOC (Economic and Social Council) describes one of the usual arrangements as follows:

> A group of European tourists may buy a 'package' for US $ 2,000 apiece for an Asian country from a retailer; the retailer may have to pay 20 per cent to the wholesaler in the originating country who took the initial risk of promoting a variety of such package tours; 30 to 35 per cent of the balance of US $ 1,600 may go to the foreign carrier, scheduled airline or charter operator; 40 per cent of the balance US$ 1,000 may be charged by the hotel for board and lodging. It means that only the remaining US $ 600 would be spent on internal transport, sightseeing, entertainment, beverages, tips and sundry expenses.

The carrier in most cases will be foreign, the hotel may be partly financed by external investors and operated by a multinational hotel group or owned by a local company but operated by a foreign hotel chain. In the first case the likely share of the destination country may be $500 to $600 plus part of the hotel charges, or approximately 30 to 35 per cent of what the visitor originally paid; in the second case it may be 45 per cent after the hotel owning company has paid management fees to the foreign hotel chain and external debt service charges. In some cases, if the carrier belonged to the receiving country, the net benefit may be as high as 75 per cent. Additionally, the host country has also to incur foreign exchange expenditure on publicity, promotion and maintenance of sales promotion offices overseas; and also to pay for the imports of aircraft for domestic air services, of machinery and equipment for hotels, of motor vehicles, food and beverages required by visitors, and so on. Depending on how much of the sophisticated goods required the host country can produce indigenously, the foreign exchange component may be as high as 70 per cent as in some developing African and Caribbean countries or as low as 10 to 12 per cent as in India. But despite such leakages it has been established that the overall benefit: cost ratio of tourism, taking into account foreign exchange earnings and their multiplier effect, and the tax revenue and employment they generate, is higher than that of many other industries.

It needs to be explained that the estimates of receipts from tourism computed by the WTO and IMF or regional organisations like OECD and PATA are usually based on the foreign exchange expendtious in the destination area. They exclude payments made to international carriers and the commissions deducted at source by travel agents. Hence the 'leakage' of foreign exchange receipts in certain situations would be considerably less than those indicated in the foregoing paragraph. To makes a fairly precise assessment it would be necessary to make an input-output analysis of the various countries individually. Several case studies of the real economic benefits have been made in the last ten years by the European Community, Kenya, Sri Lanka and the Bahamas. Sri Lanka is a typical case of a developing country which depends on considerable imports for tourism infrastructure, does not own a sizeable national airline and owns but does not operate some of its large hotels. A study of the economic contribution of tourism made by the German Development Institute in 1973 estimated that only 52 to 53 cents out of every dollar spent by tourists were retained in the country of origin. As there has been considerable development of indigenous industries in the last ten years it may be assumed that the leakage has correspondingly decreased.

There is no doubt that the international hotel chains and tour operators have played a significant part in promoting tourist traffic to the developing countries. To achieve this there has been considerable vertical integration whereby one organisation, a carrier or a big tour operator may assume a large measure of control of accommodation and other facilities of a resort. It is true that foreign operators have helped in opening up new areas and but for them tourism would not have developed so rapidly all over the world. They had the expertise and could muster sufficient risk capital for development from international financial institutions and commercial banks. In this context a significant development has been that hotel groups and tour operators of some of the developing countries have emerged on the international scene. For instance, some Indian hotel groups such as the Oberois and the Taj operate hotels overseas. Others are following the trail and so are some of the financiers of Hong Kong and Singapore.

A recent study on the role of transnationals in tourism published by the UN Centre of Transnationals Operations has argued that in the tourism field they have been able to siphon off large parts of their earnings, they have not made enough use of indigenous materials and have created highly expensive facilities which are not usable by the local people. They have also been accused of not investing their own capital and thus not having a stake in the enterprise. Some of these accusations are perhaps exaggerated because, after all, the multinationals take considerable risks and expect a fair return.

A more important complaint against them is that their plans do not necessarily conform to the national goals of the Third World. They developed and promote resorts which are marketable and commercially viable, but may not fit in with the development plans of the country concerned. Futhermore, they are not sensitive enough to the traditions and sentiments of the local people. partly this is inherent in the situation because for eign visitors must bring in new social and cultural patterns which are bound to have a disrupting effect on the indigenous way of life. This is particularly so in areas where the cultural tradition is not strong enough to withstand the onslaught of a foreign culture, as in the South Pacific Islands, or where the onrush of visitors is too large to be absorbed by the local population. An obvious example of this is the Caribbean where the number of visitors exceeds the total population. In the extreme case of the Bahamas and Bermuda the visitors each year outnumber the total population in the ratio of eight to one.

But this has happened, historically, whenever there is interaction between two cultures. In the modern age of fast communications and jet travel the process of acculturation resulting from interaction is more pervasive. But its effects are not altogether negative. In many counteries the tourists have created among the local people a new awareness of their own heritage and environment. The revival of traditional handicrafts, folklore, dance and drama is to some extent sustained by the income derived from tourists. It has happened even in a country like Britain. But for the Americans and other English-speaking visitors, some of the theatres in London would have closed by now. Coming from a more affluent and permissive society they no doubt introduce new lifestyles, more expensive habits and a free and easy way of life; but they also stimulate fresh thinking and a less inhibited oulook. Many new approaches and technologies introduced in the last 25 years in developing countries can be traced back to the influence of visitors.

Tourism has often been blamed for polluting the environment, in fact, damaging the ecosystem of the world. It is true that mass tourism has polluted beaches in the Mediterranean, Canary Islands, Florida and several other areas. The extinction of wildlife in certain countries and the pollution of mountain resorts in the Alps, the Himalayas and the Andes have also been attributed to the influx of tourists. But a close look at the causes of pollution would show that far more damage has been done by unregulated industrial development and, of course, the growth of population. More often it is the lack of planning of the tourist infrastructure that has generally caused the deterioration in the character of resorts.

In recent years, tourist executives have been in the vanguard of protest against environmental pollution, because they have realised that this is the main tourist asset and its loss would be irreversible. Fortunately there is now a new generation of planners and architects who attach immense value to environment. The high rise hotel buildings which stood like a sore thumb in some beach resorts are a story of the past. The presentday hotels and other structures are being planned to merge with the environment. For instance, a sound planning principle in Sri Lanka is that no building on the beaches will stand higher than the top of the coconut trees.

So long as the flow of tourist movements will continue from the North to the South, international hotel chains, wholesale tour operators and some other interests are likely to expand their operations in the Third World, as in fact they are doing now. Despite the healthy trend noticied earlier of a larger tourist movement being generated by the developing countries the fact remains that their share of the world tourism markets is still quite small. In fact a majority of the developing countries are in need of foreign investment for their tourism infrastructure, and generally welcome international participation. The right approach for the Third World, therefore, would not be to turn its back on transnationals but to develop its own resources, particularly human resources. Even the UN study has recommended a more pragmatic and flexible approach.

Unfortunately most of the developing countries seem to believe that the answer to the problem is to establish public sector tourist enterprises. Tourism being a service industry, the key to its success is good management. This is precisely the area where public sector tourist establishments have generally proved to be less efficient. Part of the reason is that, historically, tourism in the Third World has not grown from grass roots as it did in Europe. In the developing countries, the process was reversed from the top downwards. The government, generally at the federal or central level, took the initiative in promoting tourism, and its base gradually widened embracing the provincial and muncipal administrations. Private enterprise was associated with government efforts somewhat grudgingly, or was allowed to play a subservient role. However, with the growth of international and even the domestic holiday market the tourist industry, e.g. hoteliers, travel agents and ground tour operators have started asserting themselves, though not quite successfully because the carriers, airlines, railwlays and road transport services are usually owned and operated by the state. In some relatively less developed countries presumably the state had no alternative but to develop tourism in the public sector or invite foreign investors and operators to do the job. But in countries with a mixed economy and an enterprising and relatively well-developed private sector, governments had the alternative of allowing private enterprise to play its role by creating a favourable environment for investment and management. The more far-seeing governments saw the wisdom of collaboration with the industry, in partnership as it were.

Another fundamental question to which each developing country must find its own answer is: how much and what sort of tourism should a developing country cater for? The answer would be that for all developing countries some international tourism is desirable. Countries with large natural resources may have other equally viable alternatives available to them, but for those which have poor resources for economic development a high level of international tourism may be the best option.

"Tourism is the temporary movement of people to destinations outside their normal place of residence and work the destinations, and the facilities created to cater to their needs." The movement of tourist, from origin to destination includes a minimum trip distance and stay component, the interplay of these two elements give rise to demand of various services and other physical and cultural infrastructure which may be provided by different sectors of the tourist industry. In a spatial perspective, tourist movement is an interacting force which interweave various elements in the place of origin and destinations.

International tourism is a spatial process which primarily acts across the national boundaries thereby providing enough space or extending the scale of interaction between innumerable attributes of touristic nature. However, the degree to which the system operators to a large extent could be explained by distance. Historically international tourism first arose in the cultural centres like Venice. Forence or Paris and in the poorer or marginal areas of the industrialised hinterland, like the Alps, the Mediterranean littoral, Scotland and Egypt. It was designed to bring visitors to there places for specific purposes. viz., sightseeing, to enjoy the climate, sport, health and so on in limited numbers, usually in a particular season and as conditions clearly defined at the outset.

Conversely, today travel for any purpose has become markedly homogenised. Different type of tourists are mingled tougher not only at airports, railway stations or bus terminals, but also often at accommodation offered at common places of destinations. This undoubtedly, resembles to a demo-cratisation of travel. The people and expectations interact with each other and avail the same facilities but are differentiated principally by price levels ratha then by inherent heterogeneity.

Today tourism has emerged as the fastest growing industry in the world. In the present context, it can no longer be viewed as peripheral or a luxury oriented activity. The ramifications of tourism reach out to many sector of the economy, the great age of automation industry has made this rapid progress possible by providing people with more leisure time and money. The rapid growth of tourism industry makes its study important because of its impact, changing trends and directions.

Infact tourism as a significant activity, existed long before it was actually identified. In ancient times the main motivations were trade, pilgrimage and conquest, for instance, there was considerable interchange of ideas and knowledge between India and West Asia, while Romans and Greeks people had history of pilgrimages. Within India religion was the dominent motivation for travel with indigenous concept of "Chardam" Badrinath, Puri, Dwarka and Rameshwaram ensured travel through the country. Tourism had transformed considerably from its earlier motivation, i.e. mainly baseness and religion by the ninteenth century.

The major age of travel started in eighteenth century when the concept of annual holidays was introduced in Europe, with the development of industrial society of western Europe and northern America in the second half of ninteenth century, modern tourism took birth. The concept of mas tourism emerged in the post war era. This was because of increasing income, holiday entitlements and technology promoted it. It was for the first time that tourism was viewed as an emergence of a number of international organisations concerned with travel and tourism. Among them were the International Union of Official Travel Organisation (IUOTO), now an intergovernment agency called the Internationatal Air Association (IATA) etc. India became a member of IUOTO in 1951 and same time Air-India joined IATA.

In the 1960s the post economic boom begin to speed much more widely and international tourism began to reach mass markets around the globe. A key role in this movement was played by the jet aircraft. By the 1970s wide bodied its with a capacity of 400 passengers reduced the cost of air travel and the mass tourist emerged at resorts all over the world. In Europe and America it is now a part of life-style of not only the aristocracy but also the merchants and the professionals class. It has within the reach of the industrial workforce as well.

The world 'Tourism' has its roots in the word 'tour' which means a circulative trip or journey. The origin of the word tourist dates back to the year 1292. It has come from the word, 'tornus' meaning a tool for describing a circle or a turner's wheel.

One of the pioneers definition of tourism was given by Hermann V. Schullard, an Australian Economist in year of 1910. He defined it as, "The sum total of the operators, mainly of an economic nature, which directly relates to the entry, stay and movement of foreigners inside and outside a certain country, city or region."

A second definition was given by Professor Hunziker and Krapt Berne University in 1942. They defined, "Tourism is totality of the relationship and phenomena arising from the travel and stay of strangers, provided the stay does not imply the establishment of a permanent residence and is not connected with a remunerated activity."

Over the years the definition of tourism has undergone a change alongwith the historical changes. Dr. Zivadin Joviac defined "tourism as a social movement with a view to rest, division and satisfaction of cultural curiosity of a tourist."

The definition by Malthieson and Wall differs fromnabove definitions they through light on the significant of requirement of tourists. The Tourism Society of Britain in 1976 proposed to clarify the concept of tourism by saying that "tourism is the temporary, short term movement of people to destinations outside the places where normally live and work and their activities during their stay at these destinations, including day visits and excursions." Adding to it, it has been said, "tourism is the business of providing accommodation and other facilities for people who are travelling through or visiting a locality for pleasure." It, therefore, can be said that, tourism has expanded in its ranges and scope, which includes spatial interaction arising out of temporary movement of people to a destinations and facilities created to cater to the needs of tourists. Today tourism is no longer the prerogative of a few but it is an accepted and accustomed even expected part of life-style of a large and growing number of people.

Nevertheless, definitions are not the statement of absolute truth, but instruments for demarcating an area of investigation. The main objective of defining international tourism in this study is to understand clearly the attributes and then measure the activity.

According to World Tourism Organisation, the trend in international tourism growth continues to be positive, the sluggish increase in arrivals of 38 per cent in 1995 to 567 million tourists after a promising 5.4 per cent increase in 1994, reflects the slowdown in the trace of economic expansion and persistence of unemployment in major industrialized canters. However, the impact of this recessionary environment on consumer confidence has affected primarily tangible goods while spending on travel abroad has held remarkably well. In 1995 international tourism receipts rose by 7.2 per cent to almost US $372 billion. The more rapid increase of receipts over arrivals follows a relatively constant trend established since 1985.

The pattern of international tourist flows reveals first and foremost a heavy geographical concentration to tourist arrivals. Top ten leading destinations infact, account for 54 per cent of the world volume of tourist flows. Moreover, the past five year have witnessed a gradual diversification of tourist markets with the emergence of new destinations, especially in the East Asia and the pacific region, such as Hong Kong and Singapore. The same phenomenon is observed in central and Eastern Europe where such destinations as Hungry, Poland and the Czech Republic have all chocked up sizable gains in the world ranking. Spain has overtaken the United States as the second most important distinctions after France. China's position in this regard comes top of the five club from 12th in 1990 to 5th in 1995.

In terms of per cent change by Region of destination shows the Middle East is the fastest growing tourism region oF the world, both for tourist arrivals and receipts. South Asia comes second with 17.3 per cent then East Asia/pacific with 11.1 per cent of receipts. In case of total's both arrivals and receipts Europe occupies the first position, then comes the Americans.

South Asia was the second fastest growing tourism region of the world both for the tourist arrivals and tourist receipts. The entire South Asian Region which accounts for over a third of the world population does not receive even 2 per cent of the total foreign tourist arrivals. India's share has come down from 53.2 per cent in 1994 to 48.40 per cent in 1995. WTO has predicted that the total volume of tourist taddic by year 2000 will be 660 million number of arrivals in South Asia projected as 6 million. International tourism in the region was inspired by strong increase in tourism flow to India and a sustained growth of long haul leisure travel from traditional European markets and new emerging markets of the Middle East and East Asia to major destinations in the region.

According to the Department of Tourism, India receives 2,123 million foreign tourists in 1995 with growth rate of 12.5 per cent. The tourists coming to India are only 0.4 per cent of world arrivals and receipts are 0.51 per cent of the world receipts. Major receipts comes from Europe and South Asian countries with more then 10 per cent of growth rate. In case of percentage change Central and South America and Africa are main leading regions. While arrivals from Eastern European countries shows negative change, rest of the blocks shows positive change in tourists arrivals to India.

2. Environmental Tourism Management

IN CONTEMPORARY world, polarized approaches to land development and management are reducing the potential of both the environment and public benefits from leisure land use. Instead of collaborating, the three forces (of tourism, recreation and conservation) are forcing greater conflict and spawning greater bigotry between and among themselves. This is a conclusion one can reach if the present action of leaders of conservation, tourism and recreation are analyzed.

APPROACHES

Conservation

The concept of conservation grew from several independent and even conflicting roots. An understanding of these roots is essential to modern planning of parks and areas for tourists.

The park movement grew out of a *social concern*. The ills of expanding industrialization and industrial cities gave rise to a demand for park and open space. The dedication of public land was (and still is) seen as an antidote to delinquency, crime, illness, and the drudgery of work. Moral and ethical values are strong components of conservation in the eyes of many.

Early conservation efforts, both in the United States and Canada, were expressions of *efficiency* of resource use. It was less 'wasteful' of resources to consider long-range programmes, especially those for renewable resources, such as timber. But emphasis was on utilisation, not preservation. Water resources were to be harnessed and soils were to be made more productive. Much of modern agricultural production is based upon this concept of conservation.

The idea of land conservation in an *aesthetic* sense came relatively late, historically. The defence of conservation areas today on the grounds of scenic beauty is a complete capitulation of the frontier master of nature. The most popular recreation activity today, sightseeing, depends heavily upon a strong contemporary definition of conservation. Wilderness beauty is described as timeless, dimensionless, all-encompassing, dynamic, uncluttered by the artist's conception and a form of beauty that gratifies all the senses.

A modern concept of conservation is that of *science* and *ecology*. The premise is that of man-environmental balance. The only way of striking this balance is to define conservation as protection of natural resources. Conservation, to the exponents of 'ecology' means the exercise of rigid controls to prevent habitat destruction, habitat homogenization, reduction of species and natural resource pollution.

Conservation, in the sense of preservation of the cultural heritage is popularly supported today. Many manmade artifacts have a scarcity value that becomes as important to society's wellbeing as do the natural resources. Therefore, conservation means their protection, restoration and interpretation.

Tourism

Currently well accepted into the language is a term that grew out of nineteenth century society and technology—tourism. A though definitions vary, most include components such as pleasure travel, expenditures of money and more than a short stay.

Certainly, the element of travel is an important one and was perhaps the main one to give the phenomenon its foundation. The new mobility of people, dropping the slow, tedious, undependable and costly forms of travel, revolutionized both society and economics. The era of steamboats and railroads catapulated remote regions into the tourists business. But, it took the automobile and jet plane to compress the entire world into tourist destination.

Tourism is now of such economic impact that states, provinces and countries cherish it and undeveloped nations seek it. Not only does it affect the more conspicuous commercial enterprises, such as hotels, restaurants and airlines, but thousands of supporting manufacturers and services as well. Some cities derive their total support from tourism and millions of people depend upon it for their livelihood.

A large proportion of this impact is created and managed by profit making private enterprise. While certain subsidies assist greatly, such as highways and parks, each enterprise must make profits. The failure of many farm recreation programs in the United States and Canada is due to misunderstanding this fundamental.

Another, and equally important segment of tourism is carried on by governments and non-profit organisations. Much of what tourists see and do is sponsored by the non-for-profit sector.

Tourism derives ultimately from personal satisfactions. These satisfactions range from the most lofty to the most crass, depending upon your value system. The same traveller may, at one moment, derive great inspiration from a mountain 'lookout' and soon thereafter may be thrilled in a strip joint or by an exotic alcoholic beverage. Sometimes satisfaction comes as much from the purchase of a souvenir as from an interpretative tour of an historic site.

Governments as well as businesses take tourism promotion seriously, spending millions of dollars directly for its support. Every state in the U.S., all provinces of Canada and many nations spend enormous sums on colourful, stimulating and informative material.

Recreation

Recreation, as pleasurable diversionary activity, has been practised by man for centuries. Although it has met with varying social acceptance throughout history, it has been practised by all people everywhere.

Recreation is defined in many ways but most definitions include such terms as activity engaged in during leisure, activity for pleasure and enjoyment or activity engaged in during leisure, activity for pleasure and enjoyment or activity that enriches the lives of people. But, in many countries the word does not even exist. Instead, the several components, such as sports, physical training dance, hunting, and fishing are actively engaged in but are not under control of recreation agencies.

In north America, as recreation became a role of government, definitions became more important. As it was formalised and institutionalized, recreation became whatever the proponents created as policy.

Some recreation professionals draw a strong distinction between that which is an end in itself and that which is purposeful. They say that the former is negative while the latter is positive. Leisure, engaged in for its own sake, provides no focus whereas those recreation activities accepted by society as wholesome, creative and uplifting and worthy of public support.

Recreation agencies, having land, facilities and programmes are now well institutionalised at all levels of government in both Canada and the United States. They vary from those that are resource-oriented (extensive parks that accept a minimum of people-use) to those that are user-oriented (marinas, beaches, picnic areas and playgrounds).

FACTORS OF RELATIONSHIPS

Coexistence

For many years, the three separate forces, with their three separate leaderships and following, functioned independently and without much conflict. Recreation exponents were preoccupied with programme emphasis and were busy promoting the establishment of playgrounds, parks and their staffs. Recreation became a motherhood goal that never failed for public support.

Conservation, even with its many meanings, retained its popularity and support primarily from its soil-erosion control and reforestation origins.

Tourism was seen as strictly as promotional programme. It appeared that greater enticement was the only element lacking for the development and support of tourism. Therefore, the first expression was that of providing money for advertising.

During this stage, there was little contact between the agencies, organizations and individuals from these three groups. Whatever contact that did take place was casual, polite and tended to support their independence. Each saw his role as well defined and clearly separate from the others. In many countries this is even true today.

Conflict

As all three elements (conservation, tourism, recreation) grew in stature and in total public awareness, the next expression was that of conflict.

Park departments in cities, especially in the United States, saw their roles as clearly separate from those of recreation departments and opposed overtures toward amalgamation. Each saw the other as competing for public funds, public support and in some instances competing for the same lands.

As mass recreation expanded and congestion at camp-grounds and beaches became the rule in parks, conservation interests cried 'rape'. In spite of the fact that early park policies in Canada, the United States, and several other countries supported and promoted visitor use and visitor facilities, the exponents of conservation (meaning resource protection) believed people were ruining the parks.

With the promotion and increase of tourist travel, parks were included as attractions. As the masses of recreationists and tourists increased, the need for commercial tourist facilities and services increased. The manner in which these were located, built and managed were not always to the liking of those who created and managed the parks.

Park and conservation exponents couched their goals in social welfare terms and justified land expropriation and entrance into commercial operation as for the good of society. Tourism exponents, as champions of private enterprise, called this unfair competition.

Further conflict came between all three of these forces and outside interests. Competition for land occurred between tourism-recreation conservation forces and other developers for manufacturing, housing and agriculture. Sometimes tourism, with the use of 'outside' capital and labour disrupted both the social and economic order of a locality.

Symboisis

In spite of continuing issues of conflict, the three forces of tourism, conservation and recreation have developed many symbiotic characteristics—mutual benefit by functioning together.

Tourism interests complement conservation and recreation efforts in many ways. Tourist literature expounds the virtues of recreation activities in the out-of-doors—swimming, fishing, hunting, hiking, boating and a host of others. Furthermore, it emphasises the social and personal values of recreation, such as family togetherness, individual well-being and, freedom from stress. The commercial enterprises of tourism—hotels, restaurants, entertainment—offer much needed and heavily patronised services and products that recreationists seek. Furthermore, tourist elements—transportation, guided tours, literature—stimulate interest in the landscape, heightening access to and understandings of the environment, an important component of conservation.

It seems quite obvious that much of conservation ideology and practice fosters tourism and recreation. Conservation, as a social value is supported by the popularisation of the landscape by tourism and recreation interests. Conservation, in the sense of efficiency, is fostered by the geographic clustering tendencies of business enterprise, especially at transportation nodes. Conservation, in its concern over aesthetics, plays directly into the hands of recreation and tourism, especially in support of protecting and making accessible both vast and intimate areas of outstanding scenic beauty. Conservation of plant and animal life is providing basic appeal to society to view and understand biology. Concerns over species elimination and pollution are highly complementary to the interests of tourism and recreation. Certainly, conservation, in the sense of cultural and heritage protection, restoration and interpretation, heightens people's interest—hence complements this form of recreation and tourism.

Recreation, stemming from a social good is the very foundation for many of the functions now practised in both tourism and conservation. The multiplicity of federal, provincial, state and municipal agencies in Canada, the United States and elsewhere is solid evidence of social and political acceptance of recreation. Recreation principles and philosophies are fundamental to tourism activities engaged in by people.

Synergism

Although each force would deny it, tourism, recreation and conservation are abstractions that have greater total impact and interdependencies that their sums would imply; hence, strong synergistic characteristics.

Tourism, for example, is not only completed by the addition of commercialism to recreation and conservation. It is different, stronger and more penetrating because of the conservation and recreational components within its makeup. It could not survive without them.

Yet, seldom do institutions of (tourist bureaus, agencies, organi-zations) included any consideration of conservation or recreation in their policies and scope of activities. Seldom are there joint projects of planning and development.

Recreation is more than social concern over physical fitness or mental enrichment. Much of the participation would not take place if it were not for the components of tourism, such as travel, lodging, food service the sale of products. Further more, elements of conservation, such as aesthetics, resource protection, environmental education and heritage interpretation are included in definitions of recreation.

Yet, most conservation institutions today have taken a swing away from recreation and condemn it in all forms as destructive.

It would appear that the functions within the realms of conservation, tourism and recreation have outrun their organizations and policies. It would seem that the time is long overdue for greater understanding of the inter-relatedness, even synergism, of these forces among the land owners, planners, policy-makers and managers.

Institutional Policy-Making

Policy-making in the area of synergism between tourism, conservation and recreation virtually does not exist today. Institutional boundaries do not generally allow interlacings between institutions. While each one has primary roles that are bound by custom and even by law, there is need today for much broader policy-making.

The purests, for example, who wish to designate parks for specific purposes are ignorings between institution. While each one has primary roles that are bound by function, by custom and even by law, there is need today for much broader policy-making.

The purests, for example, who wish to designate parks for specific purposes are ignoring the facts of both environment and behaviour. No piece of land is completely homogeneous and people are not singular in their behaviour. Only parts of parks may, at certain times, provide only parts of people's interests and activities.

An excellent example of multi-purpose policy is included in the new master plan for Algonquin Provincial Park, Ontario, Canada. Included in the policies are forest production, economic viability of nearby communities, recreation, tourism and protection of special primitive areas. These show the influence of many institutions and outside factors as well as internal policies of the parks branch of the Ontario government.

Institutional Planning

Institutional planning, primarily at the site scale, by park agencies, by conservation authorities and by private enterprise, is not enough. It does not reach the modern scope of interlaced functions of tourism, recreation and conservation.

Park are part of a large tourism-recreation-conservation system. Each park succeeds or fails as much as it relates to nearby community services, transportation and surrounding land uses as it does to internal factors.

Tourism development also is part of a larger tourism-recreation-conservation system. Tourism depends as much on the identification and protection of natural and cultural resources as it does upon the building of facilities. A rare and exemplary case is that of a one resort complex business organisation that operates in South Carolina, Puerto Rico, and Florida. It not only is an integral part of tourism but includes recreation and conservation. A major division deals only with 'environmental systems development'.

Conservation areas are established for the good of man—the protection and management of resources to prevent abuses that would destroy them. Because they are a social good, they are supported by the public. Neither political nor social forces will allow restrictions that will prevent their use. Integral to their use are many tourism and recreation components.

Rarely is an integrated large-scale tourism-conservation-recreation plan developed. Such a case is the current 'CORTS' (Canada-Ontario Rideau Trent-Severn) programme designed to analyse, plan, develop and manage two huge waterway corridors in Ontario. The agreement board includes officials representing agencies within all three sectors—conservation, tourism and recreation.

Need for Coordination

Both within institutions and between them, the roles of policy-making, planning and management have become isolated.

For example, the input of neither National Park managers or potential users is made (except as tokenism) upon the creation of a new National Park in both Canada and the United States.

A new breed of park managers see operational problems daily that they cannot solve because they are hamstrung by isolated boards or administrative units. Parks are social places and reflect the changing interests, attitudes and activities of people. Resistance to nudity, group use, and unisex toilets exemplify the inability to inject new use practises into policy and planning.

Most of the design and planning is taught in highly specialized schools in universities, isolated form both the policy-making and managerial realms. Schools of landscape architecture and park planning seldom include in their curricula on park planning and design courses in political decision-making or behavioural uses of parks.

Even within the field of planning, the relationships with policy-making and behaviour are often weak. There are many instances where regional planners, country planners, tourism planners and recreation and park planners, have virtually no communication with each other. Furthermore, their understandings of both the environment and people's interests and activities are frequently in direct conflict.

Striking forward steps are the Federal-Provincial Park Conference held annually in Canada and the World Conference on National Parks. Each of these offers a forum for policy, planning and managerial discussions about parks. However, even these are closed conferences and have not as yet been opened up to tourism, recreation and other outside interests.

Protecting the Environment

Agencies, organizations and other institutions are essential. These are the mechanisms through which we operate. No one would suggest their abolition. However, when their vision and their mandates, and therefore their programmes and accomplishments, are kept within constrained boundaries, the result is fragmentation and lack of integration. Both the environment and society suffer as a consequence.

If each tourism, recreation and conservation entity saw, as part of its role, its interface with the other segments, there would be great progress toward improved environmental protection and use for society.

At present, there appears to be no world-code mechanism that can freely allow discussion and exchange of view on the interface of the three approaches of truism, recreation and conservation.

Internationally and nationally there are separate organizations that identify with each of these fields. Occasionally, their scope includes discussion of the other approaches. Mainly, however, conservation and park organizations do not include the very important topics of recreation and tourism except in a negative manner. The same can be said for recreation and tourism organizations.

For the sake of improved physical environment and improved value to society, it seems imperative that some means be created for greater collaboration and cooperation between international forces of tourism, recreation and conservation.

Ecotourism Management

Ecotourism can be defined as travel to natural attractions that contributes to their conservation, respects the integrity of local communities, and enhances the tourist's understanding of the natural attraction, its conservation, and the local community. It should have a minimum impact on soil, water, air, flora, fauna, and biophysical processes; use little energy; cause little pollution; educate the tourist; and contribute to the welfare of local and indigenous populations.

Ecotourism can be beneficial. It can help to justify nature protection, enable public enjoyment and understanding, and provide income and employment contributing to development. Ecotourism can also become problematic if it involves activities, transport, facilities, or levels of visitation that have major environmental impacts, or if it occurs in areas that are environmentally fragile, or with vulnerable communities. Accordingly, while there are reasons to encourage ecotourism, it must be controlled so that it is ecologically and socially sustainable. There must be controls on tour operators, tourist behaviour, and tourism development in natural areas, as well as enforcement of regulations, and monitoring of impacts.

While ecotourism has been around since the nineteenth century, it has grown considerably in popularity and commercial significance in just the past ten years in response to interest in the environment and exotic and adventure holidays, increases in leisure time and personal incomes, the improved accessibility of many natural attractions, promotion by selected countries and businesses for economic benefits, and a belief that ecotourism will build support for conservation.

Ecotourism has been developed particularly in East Africa, Central America, North America, Antarctica, the Himalayas, New Zealand, Australia, and parts of Europe. Costa Rica's national parks now receive over 300,000 visitor-days of use per year; over 40,000 tourists now visit the Galapagos Islands each year, and even Antarctica attracts over

5,000 tourists annually. Ecotourism is a major source of foreign exchange for countries such as Kenya and Costa Rica. The estimated gross value of Tourism on the Galapagos Islands in 1991 was $33 million. It should be noted, however, that there must be a considerably initial and continuing investment in nature protection, facilities, services, promotion, and training to earn such revenues.

To ensure that ecotourism is environmentally and culturally sustainable, standards for tour operators and guidelines for tourist behaviour are being developed, while managers of protected areas are studying the impacts and introducing measures, such as permits, quotas, guiding, and inter-pretation. There have been numerous conferences, training courses, and publications dealing with ecotourism, and the Ecotourism Society has been established in the United States. Located in North Bennington, Vermont, the Ecotourism Society recently provided a special library collection on the subject to George Washington University (Washington, D.C.). The Society is "...dedicated to finding the resources and building the expertise to make tourism a viable tool for conservation and sustainable development."

Challenges and Pitfalls

Basically, ecotourism means linking environmental awareness with people's vacations. Whether the aim is to revel in natural beauty or simply to lie on the beach, awarness of the environment will add a new dimension to any holiday.

There is no ecotourism blueprint, every project is different. But in designing an ecotourism programme, the first step is always to define what is needs to achieve. The second is to assess the impact (positive and negative) it will have on the local economy and people. If promoting environmental protection undercuts the livelihoods of local people, the project will never work.

So it is very important that local hotel owner and tour operators be brought on board. They are normally more than happy to help raise tourists' awarness of the local environment, organize trips with an environmental flavour, and devise activities such as talks and nature walks. But it is important to member that people on holiday may resist the "missionary" approach to environmental protection.

A successful ecotourism programme finds common ground between tourism professionals, local communities, and conservation groups—no mean feat. There are confidences to win, compromises to make, apathy (or worse) to overcome, and meeting after meeting to attend.

It sounds frustrating. Sometimes it is. But when a consensus is reached, it provides ecotourism planners with a solid basis to build on.

The pitfalls? The worse thing ecotourism developers can do is build up unrealistic expectations. Project beginnings should be modest and transparent. Better to aim low and minimize the risk of failure.

Another danger is assuming that because an idea sounds good, it will work. As foreigners in Madagacar, we are often unaware of the subtle social and cultural implications of our well-meaning interventions. This, of course, is another reason why it is so important to involve local residents in development plans. The key to success is teamwork and communication to assure that the issues addressed and the approach being used are not only technically sound but also culturally appropriate.

Whether Ecological Imperialism

'Ecotourism' is the buzz word in tourism. Exciting industry, government and conservationists alike, it has come to embrace 'environment-friendly', 'community-friendly' and 'market-friendly' tourism. But despite its value in raising awareness of the relationship between tourism and the environment, the term has become so abused and misused that it is little more than a worthless cliche which is probably at least as harmful as conventional forms of tourism.

Ecotourism products have become a major selling point of tourism destinations and specific tourist packages. It has a lot going for it: tourists are made to feel that they are contributing to saving the planet while having a good time in the process. And who can argue with a concept that simultaneously promotes economic development and helps to preserve the environment?

The problem, however, is that the concept of ecotourism reflects western ideas about environmental conservation which tend to separate humankind from nature. In traditional societies, there is no division between the natural and cultural components of the landscape—the physical environment is an everyday lived-in experience. However, many advocates of tourism either ignore or fail to understand the relationship of indigenous people to their environment.

Tourism is an environmentally-dependent industry. And ecotourism is only the latest expression of this relationship. In many developing countries, western supporters of ecotoursm have focused on species preservation at the expense of indigenous peoples. Since the natural environment is a cultural resource, we should be talking of 'sustainable' tourism with its emphasis on the interrelationship between ecology, society and economy, and the role of local people in making decisions which affect their land. Any form of tourism development needs to be based not on the culture of the tourists, but on the valuers and culture of the host community.

In his book Ecological Imperialism: The Biological Expansion of Europe, 900-1900, Alfred Crosby describes the sometimes forced Europeanisation of the global environment through the spread of the plant and animal species most-desired by Europeans. Today, many Europeans are seeking ways to restrain gene, species and ecosystem loss and preserve biodiversity. Ecotourism is one way of doing it.

Undoubtedly, the maintenance of biodiversity is a critical component of sustainability. But sustainable development also teaches us that the environment and the economy are integrated with society and culture. Many promoters of ecotourism have either forgotten or ignored this lesson. Perhaps, therefore, we are facing a new form of ecological imperialism in which Western cultural values are being impressed on indigenous cultures through ecotourism. To neglect the socio-cultural dimensions of development, is to completely oppose the principles of sustainability which ecotourism claims to support.

Mass Tourism

Before going to trace the growth and direction of mass tourism, let us first look at the long-term trends in demographic movements of human history in a nutshell. Pre-historic man was nomadic by nature. Being an agent of collecting economy he was by occupation a hunter as well as gatherer of vegetables and fruits in those early days. Earliest type of agriculture was perhaps shifting agriculture. Woods and other forest products were burnt for the supply of fuel and warmth. The burnt ashes were used as fertiliser after putting the seed into holes made by hoes. With an increase in population and the consequent reduction in the time for rotation, forest fallows did not get a chance to grow into a forest again and grass and weeds encroached on what would have been formerly afforested region with a long fallow period. Soon pastoralism based on grass land became a way of life. Moreover, with further growth of population, available supply of food fell short of requirement. Consequently, the situation forced the people to rush elsewhere in search of food. As a result, in the next phase, we see, human habitation began to settle near river and water sources leading to sedentary agriculture. Gradually, the primitive collecting economy gave room for a production mechanism based on settled agriculture and the habitation pattern of man on land became stable over time. In the next stage, urban centre grew up surrounded by rural hinterland.

Since then, throughout history, people travelled for various reason, Apart form the exploration of unknown or the satisfaction of curiosity the major motivation for travel in the past included trade, pilgrimage to holy places, education and cultural or religious missions. However, only since 1950, mass tourism has come of age drawing its tourists largely from the middle income groups.

Strictly speaking, mass tourism is not a recent phenomenon for a large and populous country like India, where pilgrimage to a holy place on the auspicious day (say like Kumbha Mela) always had been on a massive scale because of the heavy rush of the pilgrims drawn from a broad section of the society. The same is true of local market fairs (like one that is annually held near Hajipur in Bihar) where traders, merchants and would-be buyers meet together. But such tourism was mostly, occasional in nature. The term 'mass tourism' acquires significance if and only if tourism is defined in its narrow (and perhaps its more conventional) sense. So far as pleasure travel (the largest and the most dynamic component of tourism) is concerned, it is not at all difficult to discern its two phases. In the earlier phase, tourism for pleasure was in most cases infrequent or occasional but even when it assumed a steady flow (as in the case of European travellers going to the Mediterranean shore), it was the privilege of the 'leisure' class. In this aristocratic phase, the flow of tourist traffic to a tourist site never assumed a massive proportion. In the latter phase of tourism, tourism for pleasure (like for recreation, holiday-making, sport, game-hunting) whether it assumed massive proportion or not has definitely lost its 'elitist' character drawing its tourists from the broad spectrum of society. As a result, being limit less in its expansion-possibility, it has laid the foundation of tourism industry producing tourist oriented facilities and services (inclusive of promotional services) on a mass-scale. In this chapter, we therefore, try to explain how this transition came about.

Factors Responsible

Mass tourism has been fuelled by nine basic factors:

1. Sustained prosperity and consequent rise in the level of income of a wide section of society.
2. Monotony of work and life in an industrialised society.
3. Increase in paid leisure time of the working class/employees.

4. The growing number of the self-employed professionals.
5. Rise in the average educational standard of general population and rise in the expectation of life and improved health care.
6. The reduction in the average family size.
7. Development of an efficient communication net work and a mass transport system.
8. A change in the attitude of the policy-makers towards tourism.
9. The growth of travel agents, tour promoters and cooperative holiday associations of workers.

One major outcome of the industrial revolution is the emergence of a growing affluent consumer society particularly in the western industrial world. The susceptibility of the demand for tourism to the growth of income has been established empirically on the basis of available data for various countries. In some studies it was found that one per cent rise in real income results in 1.5 to 1.8 times increase in propensity for travel. In many industrial societies, tourism enjoys the highest preference in the use of supernumerary income, that is income left after satisfying the fixed consumption requirement. While, the major factor for the rise in super-numerary income in real terms must be ascribed to the diversification and overall growth of the economy, rise in per-capita real income of an average household in the last quarter of the present century is partly due to the preponderance of double income families with fewer children. The travel for pleasure is no longer a previlege of a small segment of society.

With the advent of the factory system, workers became engaged in more specific jobs in comparison with those in the domestic production system. While in earlier days artisans or cultivators were involved in the production process from start to the end and were psychologically tied with creation of a finished product, in the new situation of large scale production, a factory worker's involvement is reduced to a fractional monotonic fragmentary job of a mechanical type. In conse-quence, such routine job breeds boredom and fatigue. So, it is not at all surprising if the workers sometimes want to break the monotony of work and as a way of escape choose to travel as a form or recreation.

The third important factor influencing travel motivation is an increase in paid leisure time from around two weeks to four or five weeks. Paid holidays and weekends, which were introduced as a social welfare measure some 50 years back have now become an accepted feature not only in industrialised countries but also in many developing societies. In many countries there is a single (double) annual vacation(s) for law court etc. time of major festivals, while three is a double or sometimes triple a year vacations for schools, colleges and universities. With an increase in the holiday period, working week has come down to 40 hours or even less. Another novel feature that has been introduced is the reimbursement of the cost of travel in the form of Leave Travel Concession (LTC) for those who do not enjoy a long vacation. According to one estimate of the WTO, the total number of people entitled to paid holiday and LTC or Leave Fare Concession (LFC) is today 600 million.

Another feature of the post-industrial society is the phenomenal growth of the service sector with a consequent growth in the number of self-employed professional people like managers and business executives, doctors, engineers, lawyers and advocates, actors, writers, journalists etc. Once you become successful in a profession, people flock around you and you find it difficult to delegate the work to your juniors and therefore, you become too busy. It is difficult to carry such a heavy work load without a period of rest. (Americans call this 'taking a vacation' and they often taken it more than once in a year and usually away from home i.e., a travelling vacation).

The rise in literacy and the educational standard of the general population have widened the mental horizon of people and led to the increasing popularity of cultural tourism and of outdoor recreations like trekking, mountaineering, skiing and river rafting among the younger generation. On the other hand, a rise in the expectation of life, improvement in health care has given rise to increasing popularity of tourism among older generation, particularly, after retirement.

Industrialisation and urbanisation have also led to the replacement of the joint-family system by the nuclear family. Moreover, the reduction in family size and the delayed birth of the first child also have contributed to the increased popularity of family-tourism by married couples. The increased popularity of resort-tourism (say, for health or a favourable climate) could not have been possible for a middle income household if a joint family system had been the most prevalent form of family organisation.

The strongest force leading to the emergence of mass tourism has been the technological breakthrough in the transport technology. The replacement of slower and less capacious sailing vessels by steam shipping accompanied by a rapid expansion of the world railway network resulted in a sharp decline in railway and shipping rates, travel time during last part of the nineteenth century. The discovery of internal combustion engine lead to the phenomenal growth of the automobile industry in the twentieth century. Lastly, the introduction of ject-propulsion technology has led to a remarkable growth of cruising speed and seating capacity of a modern jumbo-jet. As a result, air travel has not only lured passengers away from ocean liners but also enlarged the flow of tourist traffic. A parallel technological development in the construction of roads like all-weather metalled (or gravel) roads, highways or expressways took place. It has not only shifted passengers away from railway and river steamer based transport system but through a co-ordination among rail, road, river and air transport has reduced the time and inconvenience of travelling over the same distance. The institution of car-rental service and the improvement of tele-communication system (like telex and microwave computer system) have strengthened the above co-ordination process.

During the aristocratic phase of tourism, the demand for tourism had either an elitist or an off-beat image and it was therefore, looked down upon by the policy makers as a non-priority good. Recently, the drug abuse problem and the increasing crime rate among the urban youth have changed the above value system. Nowadays, as David Sernoff comments, 'not labour but leisure will be the great problem in the decade ahead'. It is now felt that to cope with the steadily worsening law-order situation in the urban conglomerations, we require not only preventive but also directive measures. The young generation is therefore encouraged to travel in order to promote better understanding of a different culture, way of life etc. The favourable impact of tourism on regional development and foreign exchange receipts are also factors that led the policy makers to follow a more active policy to promote domestic as well as international tourism.

As against the above favourable factors for the growth of D T or I T, several difficulties in the way of tourism (especially I T) have also emerged since the second world war. In the first place, visa or permit system has been introduced. The difficulty or delay in getting customs clearance, foreign exchange and even getting railway reservation at a short notice are some of the extra hardships that have been imposed on a modern tourist. Such difficulties were not there even in the nineteenth century. To meet these difficulties, the tour agents, tour promoters and tourist offices either in the private or public sector, have sprung up. The reduction in cold war tensions between the great powers have considerably helped the formidable task of the tour promoters.

Thus, it follows that the psychological forces like monotony of work and changing value system of the general population leading to high income elasticity of the demand for tourism on the one head and economic forces arising out of substained prosperity and larger paid leisure time create an atmosphere which, being coupled with improved transportation system and change in attitude of the policy-makers towards tourism in general give birth to mass tourism. The interaction process is shown in the following chart.

A viewpoint that has often been expressed is the tourism based on wanderlust is likely to be elitist in nature while resort tourism can only develop into mass tourism at a later stage of development with the develop-ment of mass transit system and the user oriented facilities for recreations like casinos. In the incipient stage, even resort tourism is likely to be elitist in nature. But there seems to little empirical foundation for such a supposition. For instance, all the visitors to Tajmahal or Konarak do not come from the affluent section. At this place, it may be helpful to draw a distinction between two distinct senses in which the term 'mass tourism' has been used.

(a) In its usual meaning, mass tourism like mass consumption goods means that type of tourism which is not restricted to a small segment of the society.

(b) Mass tourism is also designed as a phase in the development of tourist site (usually a resort site) when tourists start coming to the site in a massive wave requiring mass production of tourist oriented facilities. While, mass tourism in the first sense, is logically a necessary condition for a mass tourism phase of a tourist site, it is not a sufficient condition if the tourists could be widely dispersed to different destinations.

A related question that has been raised in relation to the developing countries in general is, what is the more appropriate form of tourism in these countries, elite tourism or mass tourism. In some tourist sites, mass tourism is responsible for the degradation of environment through the congestion of the tourist spot and by the unplanned ribbon development near the main thoroughfare due to the concentration of tourist oriented commercial facilities in the favoured location. So long as the developers of a tourist site, is aware of its 'capacity constraints' of the tourist site, deleterious effects of mass tourism could be avoided by developing alternative tourist sites etc. On the other hand, elite or off beat tourism may also have some deleterious effects. Demonstration effect of 'consumerism' of a more affluent section of the people and their uninhibited life-style not only raise the marginal propensity to consume of local residents in favour of luxury goods but also may have other corrupting influence on the local population.

So far, we have concentrated on tourism in its more restricted sense of recreational tourism and have tried to explore the factors for its growing popularity. Some of the factors discussed above must have also a favourable impact on other types of tourism like social tourism that is tourism with a view to visiting friends and relatives or one's native village or home town (for one who have settled elsewhere in connection with his job or employment), ethnic tourism to visit one's place of origin (for migrants to other countries) and long haul pilgrimage to holy places by air or surface transport. For instance, the break-up of joint family system and the growth of nuclear family organisation had contributed to the rise in the demand for social tourism (to meet one's parents or near relatives). Industrialisation has led to increased mobility and migration of rural population to distant urban areas in search of job. The rise in the educational standard has opened up the prospect of more lucrative foreign service in a more technologically advanced economy. This, in turn, along with the growing affluence of those settled abroad gave an upward thrust towards the growth of ethnic tourism. Lastly, the growth in aircraft technology (more cruising speed, seating capacity, safety) has contributed to the growth of the number of pilgrims coming from abroad. Reduction in cold war tension and prosperity phase of 60's and 70's have helped the process in every possible way to promote tourism for better international understanding and the exchange of knowledge across the countries by holding international seminars, conferences etc. The phenomenal growth of business tourism in the world since 1945 is however, mainly due to the growth of international trade and the flowering of the multinational corporate form of organization.

Mass tourism was the logical outcome of key social, economic, political and technological influences after the Second World War. Mass tourism took off with the 'jet aircraft in 1958. Post-war peace and prosperity, paid holidays, charter flights and cheap oil lubricated the wheels of tourism change. Sun-lust and inexperienced tourist, together with the availability of cheap package tours to sun destinations and the diffusion of 'plastic' cards ensured the demand for mass tourism. Tech-nology also facilitated the development of mass tourism for it made possible the standardization, management and distribution of mass tourism services on a global scale.

By the mid-1970s, mass tourism was the order of the day. Mimicking mass production in the manufacturing sector, tourism was developed along assembly-line principles: holidays were standardized and inflexible; identical holidays were mass produced; and economy of scale was the driving force of production. Likewise, holidays were consumed *en masse* in a similar, robot-like and routine manner, with a lack of consideration for the norms, culture and environment of host countries visited.

Within two short decades, the tourism industry became mass, standardized and rigidly packaged. The industry offered a limited range of inflexible travel and holiday options to a seemingly identical group of mass travellers. By the 1970s and early 1980s, mass tourism was 'best practice'. In other words, mass tourism became the organizational and managerial common sense for best productivity and most profits in the industry.

So pervasive was the tendency toward mass production, standardization and rigid packaging that not even *sex tourism* could escape its overwhelming impact. Of the Japanese all-male tour party in the Philippines, for example, it is documented that:

> ...there are a number of private houses which cater to Japanese tourists. In this case the tourist bus travel around the sites of the city and at some stage calls in at the private house through a back door. The group troops into the building and are told that they have an hour. Behind closed doors and windows they choose a girl. An hour later the bell rings, they march out to the bus and continue their tour of the city.
>
> (O'Grady, 1981)

Several key forces were responsible for the spread of mass, standardized and rigidly packaged tourisms.

1. *Consumers:* sun-lust, sex-starved and inexperienced mass consumers.
2. *Technology:* jet aircraft, automobile, computer reservations and accounting systems, credit cards.
3. *Production:* cheap oil, charter flights, packaged tours, hotel over-building, mass production.
4. *Management: economies* of scale, hotel and holiday branding; promotional air fares, mass marketing.
5. *Frame conditions:* post-war peace and prosperity, paid holidays, regulation of air transportation, incentives to attract hotel chains to establish operations in many 'sun' destinations and the world over.

In North America and Europe, different agents facilitated the development and spread of mass tourism. In the USA, multinational hotel chains, airlines and automobiles, were the main vehicles driving the tourism industry. In Europe, by comparison, tour operators, charter flights and package tours to Mediterranean 'sun' destination, were the key agents in the rapid growth of mass tourism. With growth came much destruction: destruction to the ecology, the environment, the compro-mising of indigenous cultures, the 'flesh trade' crime, deviance, new diseases and a whole lot more.

One of the key questions today is: 'will mass tourism continue its socially, culturally and environmentally destructive patterns of growth or are the days of mass tourism numbered?

Travel Agencies

The importance of travel agency reservations, ticketing the client advice functions are all expected to grow in importance. Already travel agencies handle a large and growing proportion of airline bookings. In creating more value form these activities, travel agencies will have to use their CRSs creatively and provide the information that consumers want.

It is to ensuring the satisfaction of the travel consumers that agencies must give priority in order to ensure their own long-term survival and competitiveness. *The ability of travel agents to acqurie, provide and transmit unbiased information in a courteous, efficient and timely manner will be key to their competitive success.* Indeed, a competitor agency will be able to copy a convenient 'high-street' location, subscribe to the same airline reservation system and place satellite printers in their corporate clients' offices. However, a competitor will have tremendous difficulty in copying travel agency personnel who place the interest of the consumers first, causing them to be loyal.

New opportunities for travel agencies to create value will emerge in the areas of packaging and in the representation of services other than those of tour operators. Travel agencies will have the information at their finger-tips to provide flexible itineraries. Strategically, through cooperation with other agencies, agents can increase buying power with airlines and other suppliers in order to obtain competitive prices for package components. This will allow travel agencies the avenue to provide competitively priced, flexible holiday packages. Travel agencies will also find it profitable to represent other services such as cruise ships, pleasure boats, car-rental companies, hotels spas and other segments that will grow in importance in the travel and leisure industry.

Hotels

Hotels will no longer be able to leave their marketing to tour operators or their reservation systems. They will have to get closer to their consumers and to travel agents in the market place. This is the only way that hotels will be able to adjust effectively their products to suit their changing clients. Being close to consumers and supplying the experiences they want have become so important that hotels can no longer simply sit back and expect their rooms to be sold.

One of the key ingredients in the success of Sandals and Super Club all-inclusive hotels in the Caribbean, for example, is the strong links they have established with travel agents in the marketplace. Nothing is left to chance. Sandals and Super Club employ sales agents in the marketplace whose business it is to travel the length and bredth of the USA (and increasingly European) markets to educate travel agents about their product, new services, new properties and new experiences being offered.

Hotels will have to work more closely with their guests, *listen* to them and modify the services they offer to meet the new demands. Hotels will also have to identify market niches, segment the market and provide the experiences that consumers want and for which they are willing to pay.

The Winners and the Losers

Although travel agents, hotels and cruise ships are closest to the consumer and are thus expected to increase their influence on the industry's valuecreation, this will not happen automatically. The current dominance of airlines over the industry's CRSs is no accident. CRSs are the results of strategic decisions and continuous investments initiated by US airlines beginning more than a decade ago. Similarly, cruise ships, hotels, resorts, theme parks, travel agencies and suppliers on site will all have to make strategic moves and undertake strategic investments and build strategic alliances in order to ensure their own competitive success.

The very same logic holds for tour operators. Although the role of the tour operator is expected to decline, this will not be the case for all operators. While the role of the tour operators in their conventional roles of 'middle men', capacity buying and holiday packaging are likely to decline, their role could increase as they seek to control other wealth-creating activities within the industry (*e.g.* CRSs, flexible holidays, on-lone holiday packaging, hotels and travel agency operations). Competitive strategies are key determinants of competitive success-for industry players and for tourism destinations.

The End of Mass Tourism?

Mass tourism will not disappear altogether or be completely replaced by the new tourism. However, the *rate of growth* of new tourism will rapidly outplace that of the old. The future growth prospects of old and new tourism can be compared with *typewriters* and *computers*. While there will continue to be a market for typewriters (mass tourism), the growth of new computers (new tourism) will be far greater. Having used typewriters and then been exposed to the power of computers, users will be unwilling to go back to the old way. This exact logic holds for old and new tourism.

Also as new demand is fuelled by population growth and the opening up of new markets in Eastern Europe, Asia, the Pacific and Africa, the demand for rigidly packaged holidays to sun destinations could surge. In time, these consumers will become more experienced, more mature, more green, more flexible and more discerning. They will advance to higher levels of consumption, as signified by flexible, independent and more environmentally sound vacations. And, of course, once bitten, there will be no turning back.

Moreover, there is growing evidence that new consumers are quick to learn and they will not necessarily have to pass through the era of rigidity and mass environmental destruction before they are 'born again'. The sheer fragility of the environment will not tolerate it. New markets, for example, the Eastern European countries and Japan, will not first have to re-invent the wheel—in other words to make their experiences with mass tourism before they move on to the new. In fact, first-timers provide some of the best markets for the new tourism. The mass search for the sun is neither a driving factor in the vacation pursuit of the Japanese nor the former East Germans. Rather, sightseeing, relaxation and sport, on the part of the Japanese, and the need to visit friends and relatives and to experience nature, on the part of the former East Germans, are the prime motives of travel by these new groups of travellers.

Computers, like the new tourism, signal the beginning of a new paradigm—a new best practice and new opportunities for consumption. Computers allow for flexibility and make it possible for flexibility to be obtained at prices that are cost-competitive with mass, standardized and rigidly packaged options. Growth in the new flexible options will be tremendous.

Companies and countries dependent on tourism will have to take strategic decisions as to which route they pursue or what combinations of the old and new tourism they choose to develop. Taking a conscious strategic decision to develop a new tourism is critically important for industry players and for destinations. As a tourism destination, the Commonwealth of the Bahamas provides an excellent example of the importance and benefits of new tourism (the Family islands), when compared with old tourism (Nassau). The Bahamas offers important lessons both for old tourism destinations as well as would-be or soon-to be new tourism destinations.

Corporate entities and countries cannot afford to let the new tourism happen to them. They must make it happen. They must be leaders in the new tourism. Otherwise, they will be left behind.

MASS TOURISM

Introduction

Tourism was brought sharply into international focus at the end of the Second World War. Within a mere 20 years of the industry's take-off, international tourism displayed nearly all the characteristics of its manufacturing counterpart—it was *mass, standardized* and *rigidly packaged*. By the mid-1970s, tourism was being produced along assembly-line principles, similar to the automobile industry, with tourists consuming travel and leisure services in a similar robot-like and routine manner.

Today mass tourism is no longer common sense. The factors that caused mass tourism (*e.g.* frame conditions such as cheap oil and paid holidays, mass consumers, computer technology and standardized production and management practices) are themselves changing. Understanding the evolution of mass tourism, and the factors that created it, are key to understanding the industry's transformation. Building a capacity to respond to the changes taking place in the international tourism industry and to play a lead role in the creation of a new best practice, will be key determinants of competitive success in tourism—for regions, for countries, and for industry players.

This chapter will demonstrate that mass tourism was the logical outcome of key social and economic influences at the time. It will show how and why post-war prosperity, together with paid holidays, the jet aircraft, packaged tours, sun-lust tourists and other developments gave birth to mass tourism. It will also be shown how the forces of mass tourism took on different roles and significance in the USA and Europe.

The Historical Setting

Tourism harks back to the conquests of Alexander the Great (356-323 BC) and the subsequent development of the Hellenistic urban system (Turner and Ash, 1975, p. 20). It is argued that tourism requires both large claustrophobic cities and the means to escape from them, both of which were present in Greece during this period. With modern times, the notion of tourism is closely linked to the idea of the 'Grand Tour', which spanned the 16th to 19th Centuries. The Grand Tour is 'a tour of certain cities in Western Europe undertaken primarily, but not exclusively, for education and pleasure' (Towner, 1985, p. 301). This later era of grand tourism was typified by long, expensive, 'classical' and 'romantic' visits, mainly by the British aristocracy, to France, Italy, Germany, Switzerland and the Low Countries. Over time, and with the rise of the middle professional class, the Grand Tour was patronized by a wider segment of the population. Nonetheless, only 3-4 per cent of the population represented the nucleus from which Grand Tourists might have been drawn (Towner, 1985, p. 306). the golden age of the Grand Tour was the 18th Century, particularly the 30 years before the outbreak of the French Revolution in 1789. By the 1830s, the length of the Grand Tour fell from an average of 40 months in the mid-16th Century to an average of only four months (Towner, 1985, p. 316).

The growth of tourism to 'mass' proportions as it known today, has its foundation in several timely innovations: technologically in the field of transportation; and in the existence of a critical facilitating force, entrepreneurship—in the person of Thomas Cook.

In 1815, one year after the Battle of Waterloo ended the Napoleonic wars, the first channel crossing by steamer was made (the site of the battle itself becoming a major tourist attraction). By 1821, a regular service was operated between the ports of Dover and Calais. In 1828 the first railways were laid in France and Austria, and in 1844 the railway reached Switzerland. 'This revolution in Transport technology and the low cost, speed and efficiency that it provided, led to an immediate expansion of European tourism' (Turner and Ash, 1975, p. 52).

Complementing transportation technology was the existence of entrepreneurial talent, 'initiative' and 'organizing genius' in the person of Thomas Cook. 'His originality lay in his methods, his almost infinite capacity for taking trouble, his acute sense of the needs of his clients, his power of invention and his bold imagination' (Young, 1973, p. 21). It has been written that 'the father of modern tourism was unquestionably Thomas Cook' (English, 1986, p.3). 'Cook was the perfect entrepreneur, a brilliant opportunist, quick to sense the need of his clientele...' (Turner and Ash, 1975, p. 52). He was a true Schumpeterian entrepreneur—a leader, a 'disturber of the peace', who had the initiative, authority, foresight, intuition and psyche to carryout innovations.

Thomas Cook organized travel on a scale that had never been seen before. He heralded an era of organized, large-scale, relatively cheap tourism, spread across national, regional and international destinations. If Europe had the 'hot spots' for the Grand Tourists, the opening of the Far East, India and America, were the hallmarks of the Cook era. Until the early 1860s, Britain remained the main field of Cook's activities; in 1862 he moved into Europe; he moved into America in 1866; took his first round-the-world trip in 1872; reached India and the Far East by the 1880s; and the first Cook hotel was established at Luxor (Egypt) in 1887.

In 1862, the first true package tours were provided by Cook—all the details of transport and accommodation were pre-arranged for tourists who were, generally, of modest means. Spurred on by his example and the profits made by this entrepreneur, many imitators entered the fray. Turner and Ash write, for example, that 'it was not long before his example was imitated; in 1863, the Stangen Travel Agency was established in Breslau. Stangen soon moved his centre of operation to Berlin and became a successful rival to Cook' (Turner and Ash, 1975, p. 54). By taking advantage of 19th-Century advances in transport technology, Thomas Cook and Son had effected a revolution in tourism by the end of the century. No longer the preserve of the wealthy and the leisured, tourism was now an industry. While an average of 257 people per annum took part in Grand tourism during the 1547-1840 period (Towner, 1985), Cook had taken 20000 people to the *Paris Exhibition* of 1897—such was the magnitude of his entrepreneurial prowess.

Despite the leaps and bounds that the industry experienced, tourism, until the 1930s, was still a matter of trains, boats and coaches. Travel by water transportation was a very important form of tourism during the 1920s and 1930s. The ships themselves were a form of floating hotel, where the act of travel was equated with tourism. Travel was seen as an end in itself. As if the industry has gone full circle, today, cruise tourism is one of the fastest growing segments of the international tourism industry.

It was in 1950 that the first package holiday built around air transport was organized. This was undertaken by Vladimir Raitz, a Russian 'emigre' educated at the London School of Economics. His successful company, Horizon Holidays (now merged with Thomson, the largest UK operator) was one of the top three tour operators in Britain. By the 1960s, the package holiday business began to use air transport in a major way as Raitz's competitors, spurred on by his success, also betan using the aircraft.

Still, foreign travel in the 1930s remained a luxury commodity within the reach of only a privileged few having both plenty of free time and considerable purchasing power. This picture was to change when, coupled with post-war peace and prosperity, came innovations in aircraft technology and changes in labour legislation, which provided paid holidays, and the development of the package tour. Aided by these innovations, mass tourism had arrived.

Mass tourism is a phenomenon of large-scale packaging of standardized leisure services at fixed prices for sale to a mass clientele. Mass tourism refers to key characteristics that the international tourism industry displayed during the 1960s, 1970s and 1980s. Mass tourism exists if the following conditions hold.

1. The holiday is standardized, rigidly packaged and inflexible. No part of the holiday could be altered except by paying higher prices.
2. The holiday is produced through the mass replication of identical units, with scale economies as the driving force.
3. The holiday is mass marketed to an undifferentiated clientele.
4. The holiday is consumed *en masse*, with a lack of consideration by tourists for local norms, culture, people or the environments of tourist-receiving destinations.

Standardization and rigidity are very clear characteristics of package tours offered on a large scale. An inclusive charter tour provides the same level of transportation, accommodation, meal and transfer services to all clients who pay the same price, visit the same sun destination, sunbathe on the same beaches, sleep in the same high-rise hotels and in the same type of beds, read the same tourist brochures, visit the same sites, stay the same length of time, take the same kinds of photographs and even buy the same souvenirs.

Within the confines of mass, standardized and rigidly packaged tourism, choice, individuality, personalized services and flexibility are just not possible (or where possible, it is at horrendous prices compared with the package price). There is little place within mass tourism for the individual who wishes to be different from the crowd, who wishes to use different accommodation or participate in different holiday activities. It is true that many tourists have avoided the 'mass' tourist holidays and many have used the relatively cheap services of mass tourism as launching pads for their own vacations. However, in the 1960s and the 1970s, these were the exceptions rather than the common trend.

Commenting on the trend mass tourism, Turner and Ash wrote:

The people-processors hate individual tourists, especially those with quirks and idiosyncrasies (though the computer is helping the industry handle such non-conformists). The individual needs as much attention as a flock of mass tourists, so he offers disappointing returns.

(Turner and Ash; 1975, p. 108)

Mass tourism certainly had its time and place. Today the tourism industry is in crisis. Mass tourism is no longer best practice. Conditions that gave birth to it—the frame conditions, consumers, technology, production and management practices—are themselves changing. Understanding how mass tourism came about and why it was best practice at the time are key to understanding why the international tourism industry is being transformed and the shape that the new best practice is taking.

Evolution of Mass Tourism

Mass tourism is a product of the late 1960s and early 1970s. Several factors came together to create mass tourism.

It can be seen that several inter-related developments in the world economy produced mass tourism. Important circumstances (e.g. post-war peace and prosperity, paid holidays, governments' promotion of tourism and generous incentives offered by developing countries to attract international hotel chains) provided the necessary conditions within which mass tourism flourished. Sun-lust and inexperienced mass consumers also aided the creation of mass tourism. While on the technology front, the jet aircraft, computers and reservations systems facilitated its development. In the area of production, cheap oil, charter flights, package tours, standardization, economies of scale and mass production helped in its maturation. Management practices of franchising mass marketing and vertical and horizontal integration also played their role in the creation and spread of mass tourism.

None of these conditions on its own could have produced mass, standardized and rigidly packaged (MSRP) tourism. However, the combination of these factors, together with the timing of their respective developments, provided both necessary and sufficient conditions for MSRP tourism to take off.

Different factors played relatively different roles in producing mass tourism. In the USA, for example, international hotel chains, airline oligopolies, business travel, the car, domestic tourism, short breaks and travel and entertainment cards were important forces for mass tourism. In Europe, tour operators, charter flights, holiday travel (as opposed to business), intra-European travel to Mediterranean sun destinations and long-stay holidays were the driving forces.

Frame Conditions

'Frame conditions' refer to factors within the social, economic and institutional framework of the world environment that are conducive to the development of tourism. Frame conditions normally lie outside the control of the tourism industry but have tremendous impacts on the industry's growth and development. Frame conditions that facilitated the growth of tourism include post-war peace and prosperity, paid holidays, increased leisure time, and a governmental framework of incentive legislation, tourism promotion boards and ministries of tourism.

Post-war Peace and Prosperity

A major impetus to tourism's growth was provided by a very congenial sociopolitical framework that delivered peace and prosperity to the world economy. The world economy recovered from the major depression of the 1930s, and sustained peace finally returned at the end of the Second World War in 1945. The stability and growth of the world economy were additionally promoted by the Marshall Plan, Keynesian-inspired economic policies and the strength of the American economy. At this time, oil, the main source of industrial energy, was cheap and plentiful. Energy at the right price was abundantly available to meet all the transportation requirements of a growing industry. As a result, industries flouri-shed, economies grew and affluence increased. This opened up new travel possibilities for many citizens of the world.

Labour Legislation/Paid Holidays

In the field of labour legislation, two important advances were made: paid annual holidays and the 40-hour working week. In 1936, at the instigation of its trade union representative, the International Labour Organization (ILO) adopted the first convention that was to promote paid holidays and later on, paid, annual vacations. The French government in 1936-37 instituted annual paid holidays. After the First World War, starting in the 1930s and gathering force in the 1940s, 2-3 weeks annual paid holidays became the norm. It was the coming of paid annual holidays that has had the real impact on the development of long-haul vacation trips such as exist between Europe and the Caribbean and Pacific islands. The introduction of paid holidays and paid annual vacations were important innovations in labour Law, since by the 1940s only 14 countries had enacted general legislation on paid holidays (World Tourism Organizations 1978, p. 31).

Then in 1938, the Fair Labour Standards Act in the USA mandated the working week to be 40 hours. These two significant social innovations provided more time for non-work leisure activities as well as the necessary incomes with which to spend in the pursuit of them.

Government Promotion of Tourism

In the inter-war years, governments of developed countries began to recognize the importance of tourism to the economy—particularly as an item in the balance of payments. This recognition of the importance of tourism was stimulated in the period of post-war reconstruction in the 1950s. Promotional activities of European national tourist offices were at the time directed mainly towards the North American market.

By the 1960s, many developing countries had come to the realization that tourism could help them to generate much-needed income, employment and foreign exchange. For example, in Indonesia's first 5-year development plan (1968-1973) tourism was adopted as a strategy for economic development (Noronha, 1979, p. 180). tourism was considered a welcome saviour in these economies at a time when:

- primary commodity exports were declining;
- many governments were eager to diversify their skewed baskets of primary exports (e.g. sugar, cocoa, coffee, citrus, bananas); and
- disillusionment with attempts at import substitution and industrialization in Latin America and the Carbbean was beginning to set in.

This conviction was not at all surprising at a time when tourism was, as it still is, considered 'a promising new resource for economic development' (Organization for Economic Corporation and Development, 1966, p.7).

Based on this view, the 1960s became a time when many developing countries rushed to establish boards and ministries of tourism. Young (1973, p.1) observes that 'the importance of tourism is gradually being recognized and, in many countries, particularly in developing ones, it now warrants a ministry all to itself'. Development corporations for the promotion of hotel and other infrastructure investments and generous tax incentives to foster and induce foreign capital to develop tourism, were the order of the day. These policies very naturally complemented the globalization drives of multinational corporations in the hotel sector.

The very nature and emphasis on tourism development in developing countries' reinforced the trend toward mass, standardized and rigidly packaged tourism. It should be considered that, at the time, governments and private sectors, were often firmly wedded to the equation: *volume-benefits*. The more flights, the more hotels, the more tourists, the more advertising, the more promotions and the more public relations there were, the more profits, incomes, employment and foreign exchanges would accrue to the country.

The institutional framework within which governments and companies operated in the development of their tourism sectors was also conducive to the development of an industry oriented along mass-production lines. For example, a hotel of 'international standard' by definition cannot be less than 100 rooms, it must have air conditioning, a lift and a swimming pool. Many governments and companies contemplating entry into the tourist business, hardly considered anything less then the international standard. It should also be considered that large projects (be they iron and steel mills, airports or large tourist resorts) were always safe investments for governments in political terms. It is within this context of 'the more the merrier', 'more is better', and the idea of attracting 'plenty' tourists, that mass tourism, with its standardized and inflexible consequences, was allowed to flourish.

Generous Incentives for Hotel Chains

Another important frame condition in the making of mass tourism was the existence in developing countries of several generous incentives that encouraged multinational hotel chains to invest in the replication of their standardized facilities throughout the developing world. This included repatriation of profits, cash grants, assistance with project financing, equity participation, loan guarantees, tax-free bonds, underwriting share issues, tax holidays, investment and other tax credits, accelerated depreciation, double taxation relief, special currency exchange rates, infrastructure cons-truction, leasing of properties, marketing support, development of amenities, training and the development of special institutions. By 1978, multinational corporations accounted for 4.3.9 per cent of total hotel rooms in the Philippines; 61.0 per cent in the Seychelles; 49.7 per cent in the Senegal; 33.4 per cent in Venezuela; 31.0 per cent in Jamaica; and 42.6 per cent in Trinidad and Tobago (United Nations Centre on Transnational Corporations, 1982).

The importance of multinational hotels in different parts of the world. It can be seen that multinational corporations played a major role in the hotel industry of developing region. MNCs accounted for 16 per cent of the hotel stock in the Middle East, and 16.6 per cent and 17.7 per cent of total hotel rooms in Asia and Africa respectively. Particularly because of its proximity to the USA (the franchising and MNCs capital of the world) the Caribbean region had the highest penetration (35.6 per cent) of multinational hotel rooms. When it is considered that hotel chains (*e.g.* Club Mediterranee, Hilton Hotel, Holiday Inn and others) built identical hotels worldwide, developing 'sun' countries were initiated into mass tourism with large, standardized, hotels. Mass, standardized and rigidly packaged tour operators and tourists were soon to follow.

Consumers

In any industry, consumers are supposed to be the most important consideration—virtually the *raison d'etre* for the industry's existence. In the period after the war, however, it was not the consumers, but rather, mass production, scale economies, product standardization and cheap prices that dictated the pace and direction of the growth of tourism, and indeed of all other industries. In other words, *mass tourism was producer-rather than consumer-driven.*

At the time, however, key characteristics of tourism's consumers allowed mass tourism to flourish on a global scale. Tourist's common search for the sun and their consumption of travel *en masse* played an important role in the development of mass, standardized and rigidly packaged tourism the world over. It is not that consumers were naturally undifferentiated and identical human beings. However, whatever individuality they possessed was simply subordinated to the greater logic of mass production and the new travel possibilities that cheap packaged holidays made possible.

Sun-lust Tourists

The fashion for the suntan was one the profound changes in the attitude of tourism's pioneering elite—an attitude that was a complete reversal of the old (Turner and Ash, 1975, p.78). By the 1920s, the leisured class deliberately began to cultivate a darkened skin tone. commenting on this redical transformation of ideals, Turner and Ash wrote:

> In Roman times ladies of refinement had swathed themselves in the fine silks of the Kos to filter the coarsening rays; gardens and parks were provided with elaborately shaded walks, pergolas and colonnades...Any deliberate cultivation of a tan would have savoured too much of identification with lower (largely rural) classes and coloured subject people. Thus the ladies of the British Empire in India did not relax the cumbersome properties of victorian dress to suit the climate. Similarly, for the females of the landed aristocracy in Europe, a pale complexion was the symbol of their superior delicacy.

(Turner and Ash, 1975, p. 79)

By the 1920s, the sun was not only an element of high fashion, but it was now sought after for precisely the reason it had been avoided—its simple virtues and its closeness—to the soil.

Today, industry observers agree that 'the most significant impulse in the development of tourism since the Second World War has been the search for the sun' (OECD, 1966, p. 12; Peters, 1969). This can be readily seen when one considers that the movement of leisure travel has mainly been from the cold northern countries to the warm southern countries. It is also not surprising that Spain and Hawaii have become mass tourism destinations, rather than Norway and Alaska.

Mass Consumption

While the industry was not directly consumer-driven, a critical ingredient in the making of mass, standardized and rigidly packaged tourism, had to be the tourists—the ultimate consumer. This was because, ultimately, hotels, travel agencies, tour operators, airlines and governments were satisfying what became *effective demand* for this type of tourism—effective demand being the demand or desire for something, a demand backed by money and followed through with purchase.

The sociopsychological make-up of the consumer a generation ago was largely receptive to mass, standardized and inflexible tourism. This is largely due to the fact that workplaces and everything consumed by mass consumers—were already 'infected' by decades of mass production, mass marketing and mass consumption. Tourists logically followed in the footsteps of mass production in the manufacturing sector. As a result, 25 years ago or thereabouts, many tourists did not mind being like everyone else: having the same washing machines or cars as others; eating cornflakes and drinking coca cola like everyone else; being on vacation in the same places as other tourists; or being part of the crowded tourism landscape-on the motorways, on the ski slopes or the beaches. After all, at the time, 'living up to the Jones's' was the consumers' best practice at the time. Copying other vacationers was natural.

If, 25 years ago, one went to a beach, a party or a social gathering, and it was not well partonized, 'crowded' or 'swinging', then one would immediately think that this was not the place to be; or the 'in place' to be; or the place where it was 'happening. This was precisely the sociopsychological atmosphere of the time that allowed mass, inflexible and standardized tourism to flourish the world over.

This is not to say that international tourism before the 1980s was completely inflexible. Naturally, the more independent, educated and well-to-do citizens of the world took exceptions to this trend. However, what little flexibility did exist, was submitted to the greater logic of the mass production paradigm. The economics of large-scale mass production produced cheaper and more affordable holiday prices—and this made good economic sense. Thus cheap, standardized, affordable holidays were as much a part of the logic of the time as were the forces (*e.g.* economies of scale and profit) that drove producers to produce fixed, low-priced, affordable, holiday packages. It should also be remembered that after the Second World War holiday-making was just getting within reach of wider segments of the population.

Inexperienced Travellers

The existence of an inexperienced clientele also allowed mass tourism to flourish. Consumers often were more taken up with the novelty and excitement of travel to foreign destinations rather than which destinations they visited, the type of plane seats they had, the hotels they stayed at or the quality of services they received. Since there was no previous experience, consumers had nothing to go by—no real yardstick with which to measure quality. The inexperience of consumers thus provided fertile ground for the replication of standardized hotels across of globe. These hotels provided familiarity, safety and reassurance to consumers who were often visiting foreign land for the first time. Identical hotels replicated across the globe virtually allowed mass tourist to feel 'at home'.

Inexperienced travellers, fearful of adventure, also encouraged the emergence of tour operators who mass-produced, standardized and rigidly packaged tours, removing any element of consumer risk. The tour operator would pre-test and pre-visit the destination and would normally have a hired representative in the destination—someone with a familiar face who spoke the same language and who could relate to the fears and anxiety of the inexperienced—providing an additional sense of security and an added incentive for mass tourism.

Inexperience, and the sense of insecurity bred by it, also complemented the phenomenon of group affinity, where one feels safer in an unfamiliar environment as a member of a group rather than as an individual traveller. In this respect it might be said that the mass tourists certainly tested the validity of the old saying that: 'there is safety in numbers'. It is therefore not surprising to find that the Japanese—the major new leisure class of the 1980s—began their penetration of new destinations in groups. Groups of camera-toting Japanese tourists may seem odd today to many Westerners who, as Western tourists, passed that stage 1-2 decades before. If the camera-toting Japanese tourists seem strange in the 1980s and 1990s, one can only wonder what perceptions the population of many developing sun-destinations had of masses of Western tourists in the 1960s and 1970s.

Technology

What the consumers perceived they wanted or needed at the time, on the demand side, were richly facilitated by technological possibilities on the supply side.

Important technological advances have had a very profound impact on the development of mass tourism. The development of the jet aircraft, plastic cards, and the applications of new computer technology facilitated the growth of mass tourism in no small measure. However, the technology did not create mass tourism; rather, technologies—the jet aircraft and computers—were the main instruments for the provision of mass tourism services. Computers were not developed because of the travel and tourism industry; rather, this industry became an essential user of technologies that were designed and developed for other sectors of the economy.

The application of computer technologies to the international tourism industry in the 1960s and 1970s had mainly the impact of improving the *efficiency* of production of mass tourism services. To some extent, technology applications also had the effect of improving the *quality* of tourism services provided. The impact of information technology in generating completely new services (e.g. airline computerized reservation systems and frequent flyer programmes) and in transforming the entire best practice of the tourism industry was to come in 1978 when the US government made considerable strides in deregulating the airline industry.

The role of technology in mass tourism was considerably different from its role today. In the 1960s and 1970s, tourism technologies were stand-alone items, incapable of interacting with human beings or with one another. Today, computers and communications technologies created by airlines are systems of wealth creation in themselves. They have now become indispensable to the industry.

A very important impetus for the creation of modern-day mass tourism phenomenon was the advancement in air transportation technologies. Rapid advances were being made in the technologies of land and sea transport as well. However, in air-transport technology, 1958 was the turning point. The year 1958 ushered in a new era—the jet age—which revolutionized transportation the world over and changed long-held perceptions of time and space' (Robinson, 1983, p. 17).

Until 1958, the fastest commercial aeroplane in the US scheduled Service was the Douglas DC-7, which averaged a 350 m.p.h. crusing speed. At that rate, it took the whole day to fly across the Atlantic. The introduction of jet aircraft—the Boeing 707 and the Douglas DC-8—the following year changed all that. Cruise speed went up to 590 m.p.h. and travel time over long distances fell by 40 per cent. The jet aircraft was not only almost twice as fast, it also offered *double the capacity* of the earlier piston-engine aircraft.

In 1958, both BOAC (now British Airways) and Pan Am began trans-atlantic jet services between new York and London and National Airlines launched the first domestic jet service between New York and Miami. By 1964, 72 per cent of ail air services were operated with jet aircraft (World Tourism Organization, 1966-86, p. 29).

The efficiency of jets produced lower fares. The idea of the 'economy fare' was introduced in 1958 and this made travel available to more people. In addition, a wider range of routes was made possible. Accordingly, 'the jet was the catalyst for a prolonged travel boom' (Feldman, 1983, p. 124).

The average annual rate of growth of air transportation was 11.9 per cent between 1958 and 1961 and 13.6 per cent over the 1961-1964 period (figures for 1966 in World Tourism Organization, 1966-1986, p. 29). By 1966, it had been observed that international air traffic was growing faster than the rate of tourism movements itself. World tourist arrivals increased by 259 per cent from 1950-1963 while the number of passengers carried on air services increased by 330 per cent in the same period (World Tourism Organization, 1966-1986, p. 29).

The 1970s was the decade of the wide-bodied jets. Pan Am (no longer in operation) put the first B-747 in scheduled air service in 1970. The aircraft was certified to carry 490 passengers, weighed 710000 pounds (322340 kg), had a wing span of 195 feet (59.44m), a length of 231 feet (70.41m) and a height of 63 feet (19.20m). It was the largest commercial transport in the world at the time of its introduction and carried a crew of 20.

In 1975, British Airways and Air France acquired their first faster-than-sound Concordes and sought to introduce them into the transatlantic market. In 1972, the US certificate carriers boarded more than 195 million passengers, and all the major carriers in the country were flying jets. There were 2239 jets in the airlines' fleets in 1968. By 1983, there were 10472 jets in service. Commenting on 25 years of the jet age, *Travel Weekly* concluded that: 'for better or worse, air travel now catered to the mass market' (*Travel Weekly* 25th Anniversary Issue, 1983). And so it did.

Air travel played a critically important role in opening up tourism to developing countries. Indeed, it played a more vital role in the creation of international tourism in developing countries than in developed countries mainly because of the great distances of most developing countries from their developed-country tourists. The share of air travel in international tourist arrivals was 65.2 per cent for the Bahamas; 83.1 per cent for Barbados; 89.3 per cent for

Kenya; 97.9 per cent for the Philippines; but as little as 10.9T for Italy and 25.8 per cent for Spain (World Tourism Organization figures for 1977; see World Tourism Organization, 1966-86).

While the jet aircraft changed long-held perceptions of time and place and was the catalyst for a prolonged travel boom, advances in micro-electronics and computers and communications technologies provided the wherewithal to manage this travel boom. Computers and communications technologies facilitated the globalization of the international tourism industry and greatly facilitated the distribution, control, management and coordination of tourism services across the globe. Plastic cards and other forms of electronic payment also facilitated the rapid growth and development of travel and related services.

Plastic Money

The year 1958 was significant for the travel and tourism industry not only because it was the year of the jet. It was the year that American Express launched its credit card. Diners Club was founded in 1950 and Carte Blanche (which with Diners Club is now owned by Citicorp) was created in 1959 by the Hilton Hotel Corporation. Around 1969 the bank cards entered the travel and entertainment arena. Bank America card (now Visa) and Master Charge (now Master Card) had been in existence for nearly a decade but had served almost exclusively as cards for small retail purchases.

Americans who travelled has to carry 'huge rolls of money', which was felt to be risky (Brower, 1983, P. 284). It was found that credit cards provided a safe, easy, convenient and reliable method of facilitating travel and related payments before, during and after the journey.

Credit cards have since grown in importance over time and are now a permanent fixture in the tourism landscape as travellers are increasingly urged not to leave home without them. The plastic card has created 'a revolution in payments for those on the move' (Cullen, 1988, p.65).

Credit cards got off to a slow start in the travel and tourism industry as major airlines were not convinced that the cards would generate more business. It was a major breakthrough in 1964 when American Express won acceptance by American Airlines. By February 1965, it was reported that air travel was the fastest growing segment of the credit-card business. Today, credit-card payment is one of the fastest if not the fastest growing sector of the payment business, especially among the higher spending business travellers who use plastic to pay for about two-thirds of business expenditure at hotels and restaurants.

The use of plastic cards in travel payments differs across regions and within individual countries. Europe lags behind the USA in credit card ownership. Within Europe, the UK has the highest concentration of credit cards per head of poulation (a total of about 25 million cards), while in West Germany, Eurocheque is the most popular form of payment (Cockrell, 1987, p. 33)—Germans use credit cards to pay for only 5 per cent of costs when on holiday (de Coster, 1990, p.56).

Information technology lies at the basis of other payment systems such as electronic funds transfer, the validation and authorization of credit-card transactions, cash-dispensing machines, travellers cheques and the myriad of consumer services related to lost or stolen cards and cheques. All of these services and the technology on which they are based facilitate payment transactions in the travel and tourism industry. They play an important role in the rapid growth and development of the industry.

Computer Technology

There are fundamental differences in the role that technologies play in the old tourism and in the new.

In the 'old' mass standardized and rigidly packaged (MSRP) tourism, technologies are used to facilitate the mass production of tourism services and to control the production process. Computer also assist with internal management functions of accounting, financial control and payroll. In the 'new' flexible, segmented and diagonally integrated (FSDI) tourism, technology takes on an entirely different role. Technologies in the new tourism are used to manage capacity, optimize yield and get closer to clients. The focus of technology applications and value creation.

From the 1960s to the early 1980s, technology usage by the tourist industry was principally aimed at *facilitation—facilitating* the rapid growth of mass tourism on a global scale. The use of technology by the tourism industry before 1978 was therefore limited. The technology users in the old tourism were limited to airlines, hotel chains, car-rental companies and tour operators (mainly, European).

By comparison, in the new tourism, travel agents are major users of technology (*e.g.* for computerized reservations terminals) and play an even more important role in the value chain of the travel industry. In addition other service providers such as cruise ships, car-rental companies and pleasure boats are users of the industry's computerized reservations technologies. Even champagne and flower services, tourist boards, independent resorts, theme parks and other suppliers are represented on CRSs.

Technologies used in the old tourism were embodied in stand-alone delinked equipment such as telephones, computers, telex back office accounting and management systems. The reservation systems used by the industry at the time were also limited in their ability to communicate with each other as well as their inability to operate in real time. It meant that if a booking for 20 rooms was made with Hotel X this information was not automatically reflected in Hotel X's room inventory; that information was relayed from the agency's CRS to the hotel at some later point.

Typically, airlines, hotels and tour operators developed their own dedicated systems. One airline system, for example, could not 'talk' to another airline system, far less to hotels and tour operators' systems. The carriers communicated with each other trhough Arnic and Sita, but this was not on a real-time basis. From one airline or hotel reservation system, one had only limited capability of checking availability on other airlines or hotel properties. This could make the job of the travel agent unnecessarily cumbersome because several telephone calls might be to be made for a single enquiry, booking or sale, if the CRS showed that products were sold out when in fact they were still available directly from the supplier.

In the 1960s and 1970s, information technologies mainly played a facilitating role in the international tourism industry. It allowed the tourism industry to reap tremendous productivity increases within the confines of the mass. Standardized production practices—a production practice that was the industry's best practice at the time. The technology itself did not create mass, standardized and rigidly packed tourism, it merely facilitated its development.

Technology applications in the old tourism (1960s and 1970s) had the effect mainly of improving the efficiency of tourism services and facilitating mass production, scale economies and low costs of production. Computer technologies facilitated the mass production of tourism services. Technology allowed tourism producers to plan better, manage and control their activities at a global level. Technology facilitated the standardization and replication of facilities and services on a global scale. Technology facilitated the distribution of product in international markets and was used to improve the efficiency of services provided to consumers.

Technology made it relatively easy, for example, for major international hotel chains to manage information to disaggregate in detail all aspects of the operation of a hotel, franchise the concept, mass produce indentical hotel rooms across the globe and yet succeed in achieving identical services, standards, facilities, fixtures, fittings and amenities and all affiliated properties. At the same time, functions such as buying, reservations, training, accounting, planning and marketing were centralized, allowing hotel chains to reap enormous economies of scale through their operations.

To some extent, the development of information technologies also increased the quality of services. One must remember that the rationale for mass production was not the improvement of quality, but lowering the costs of production, reaping economies of scale and offering low prices to an inexperienced clientele. It is only with the entry of competitiors where low costs are no longer sufficient to generate a competitive edge, that attention to quality, product differentiation, innovation, the generation of new services and paying attention to the consumer become critical to the competitive process. This was not to happen until the early 1980s.

The year 1978 was a major turning point for the tourism industry. In a very real sense, airline deregulation created the imperative for the extensive development of CRSs by airlines. Before deregulation, airlines, fares route structures were generally fixed, regulated, predetermined and largely predictable. Deregulation spawned increased competition that resulted in several new routes, new services, new schedules, new destinations, new fares and even new airlines. Moreover, the travel environment became more flexible and unpredicatable with mergers, bankrupticies and take-overs, airlines adding and dropping routes, frequent price changes, frequent flyer programmes, last-minute discounted seats becoming quite prevalent.

After 1978, the international tourism industry needed something as powerful as computerized reservation systems simply to keep track of all the new information and to satisfy consumers. Since 1979, technology diffusion in tourism has been rapid. Nearly all of travel agencies in the USA are now linked to airlines' computerized reservations systems (CRSs). CRSs provided by the airline industry, especially since deregulation, have dramatically improved matters. Travel agents can now look, book and sell at the CRS terminal without making a telephone call. They can check inventories of more suppliers, they can book more hotels, car rental and other services required by the modern traveller as well as more 'tailormade' holidays.

The impact of technology applications in the new tourism has also been tremendous. Improvements have been made on all fronts—improvements in the efficiency of production and the quality of services provided as well as the generation of completely new services. CRSs today allow airlines and other users more directly to monitor, manage and control their capacity (yield management) and their clients (frequent flyer programmes). Tourism suppliers are now better able to match their output with the needs of their ever-changing clientele—a marriage that has increasingly become a critical success factor in tourism.

It is the diffusion of a system of information technologies throughout the international tourism system that, on the supply side, is driving the transformation of the international tourism industry. The mass globalization of the tourism industry would not have taken place at the speed and intensity that it did were it not for the technologies to facilitate and control it.

Case in Europe and The USA

The USA and Europe accounted for a significant proportion (96 per cent) of world tourism arrivals in 960 (World Tourism Organization, 1966-1986). There are fundamental differences in the way in which mass tourism was developed in the USA and Europe: hotels and tour operators, for example, played different roles and assumed varying levels of importance in the shaping of mass tourism.

In the USA, the major players in the creation of mass tourism were hotel chains and airlines. US hotel chains, through branding and the replication of a standard product across of globe, provided consumers with the safety and confidence for them to travel *en masse*. The brand name provided the assurance and familiarity in a 'home away from home' atmosphere.

Tour operators played a similar role in the development of mass tourism in Europe to that played by hotel chains in the USA. In Europe, tour operators, by creating cheap package tours using charter air services, were the main instrument of mass tourism. They were able to offer similar levels of security and certainty that US hotel chains offered. This they achieved through the branding of holidays, selecting hotels and destinations, guaranteeing stan-dards and taking the risks and responsibility for delivering the holiday promised.

The European packaged holidays invariably included charter flights. This was another major difference between the mass tourism forces in the USA and Europe. Travel in Europe was mainly intra-European in nature, often involving air transportation to the Mediterranean sun destinations. In the USA, by contrast, it was domestic holiday travel and business travel that were the industry's driving force. It was therefore the car, rather than charter flights, that provided the impetus to North America's tourism industry. The car still dominates travel in the USA today. Over three-quarters of all personal trips taken in 1987 were by car, truck or recreational vehicle (US Travel Data Centre, 1989). As such, hotels did not take on a tour packaging function as the tour operators did in Europe. Instead, they set up roadside motels and city hotels, many of which could be reached by car. As a result, the tour operator industry in North America has been nowhere near as active as its European counterparts.

Another difference in the way in which mass tourism developed between Europe and North America is in the area of paid holidays. American employers continued to offer fewer vacation days than was typical in Europe. While many Europeans enjoyed between 3-5 weeks holiday during the 1960s and the 1970s (and today many more enjoy 6-8 weeks paid holidays plus a 13thy salary) in the USA, 2 weeks of paid holiday is still the norm for many workers. As such, the travel focus of North Americans was mainly on weekend travel and the short breaks. By contrast, European travel was for much longer periods, although today short breaks are a growing feature of European travel.

However, while there were differences in the way mass tourism developed in North America and Europe, the management of mass tourism was similar on both continents. Both engaged in mass marketing. In their respective markets, they mass produced identical tourism services for an undifferentiated group of mass tourists.

Economies of scale and standardization were achieved through *hotel branding* in the USA and *holiday* branding in Europe. In the USA, hotel brands such as Holiday Inn and Hilton Hotel were developed, while in Europe holiday brands included, for example: Club Mediterranee and Nouvelle Frontiers in France; Holland International in Holland; Thomson Holidays, International Leisure Group and Horizon Holidays in the UK; and NUR, Dr Tigges, Trans Europa, Meyers Welt Reisen and John Reisen in Germany.

Mass production was achieved through large, concentrated and integrated airline and hotel structures in North America and in Europe mainly by the tour operators' tremendous airline and hotel-buying power. International hotel franchising in North America was paralleled by the development of Mediterranean destinations for mass travellers in Europe. The tendency toward and over-building of hotels was prevalent both in North America and Europe.

It is very important to grasp the differences between the American and European travel market and the different forces that led to the old mass, standardized and rigidly packaged tourism. Fundamental differences also exist between both continents in the development of the new flexible, segmented, environmentally friendly and diagonally integrated tourism.

A number of production and management imperatives in the USA gave birth to mass tourism in America. These included the dominant position of airlines and multinational hotel chains, promotional air fares, mass marketing, hotel branding and hotel franchising. All of these factors played significant roles in determining the rate and direction of growth of the international tourism industry. In the case of franchises, for example, they facilitated the standardization and assembly line production of hotels, thereby allowing hotel chains to project a brand image, while obtaining tremendous economies of scale in advertising identical outlets around the world.

Airlines

In the airline industry, antitrust immunity preserved an oligopolistically structured industry from the Chicago Convention until deregulation in 1978. There has been a great deal of concentration of airline operations since the arrival of the jet aircraft in 1958. In

1961, the merger of United (with a 14000-mile route system) and capital (with a route system of 7000 miles) made the surviving carrier, United, the largest air carrier in terms of route miles, aircraft, personnel and potential passenger traffic (Travel Weekly, 1983). Northeast merged into Delta in 1972, and the American/Trans-Caribbean merger took place in 1970 giving American Airlines its first access to the Caribbean, then controlled by Eastern. Delta also merged with Western and Northwestern with Republic and Pan American Airways with National. Several other mergers also took place. This produced a concentrated airline industry, with carriers exercising a great deal of control over the rate and direction of growth of the tourism industry. An analysis of the patterns of related activities of selected airlines concluded that 'airlines have become the driving force in tourist activities', with the majority of them exercising varying degrees of control over tour operators and hotels (Clairmonte and Cavannah, 1984, pp. 250-254).

It was found, moreover, that airlines have very diversified portfolios of activities. Of 22 major airlines analysed in 1984, 72.7 per cent were involved in tour operations; 86.3 per cent had hotel interests; 13.6 per cent had interests in car rentals; 68.1 per cent were associated with other airlines; and all of them (100 per cent) had other related interests (Clairmonte and Cavannah, 1984). Such related interests included miscellaneous activities such as catering, international merchant banking, worldwide aviation insurance and re-insurance.

Airlines were instrumental in the vertical and horizontal integration of the travel and tourism industry. They provided the services for mass tourism and exercised a great deal of control over the rate and direction of growth of the industry. That airlines today dominate the CRSs of the travel industry is certainly no surprise—it is a reflection of the historical dominance of air transportation in the development of the tourism industry. The power of the airlines in the USA paralleled the power of tour operators in Europe.

Promotional Fares

Apart from the purely technological advances in aircraft design and operations, innovative pricing was an important ingredient in the creation of mass travel. The World Tourism Organization observed that 'the volume of air traffic passengers is closely related to the total cost of the holiday' (figures for 1972 in World Tourism Organization, 1966-1989, p.46).

Tourism is a luxury item that responds very well to price. It is both price and income elastic. This means that a marginal change in consumer's incomes or the price of a holiday will result in a more than proportionate change in their effective desire to consume travel. In his econometric analysis of international travel, Arts (1972, pp. 579-614) estimate price elasticities for expenditures on foreign travel by Europeans at between—3.58 and—2.61; while income elasticities were estimated between 2.30 and 1.16. This means that a unit rise in the price of travel will bring about a decrease in the quantity of travel demanded by a factor of between twice or three times as much travel. In other words, cheaper prices for travel bring forth proportionately greater travel demand by consumers.

The economy fare was introduced in 1958 and the fare structure has constantly been modified to attract a wider proportion of the population. A number of promotional fares were introduced to encourage tourist traffic.

Besides the normal first-class and economy fares, there were excursion rates, such as the advance purchase excursion (APEX) fare, group fares and the inclusive tour excursion (ITX) fare. These promotional traiffs had a very important effect on the number of travellers and, consequently, the load factors that these airlines were able to obtain.

Inclusive tours have thus made international travel accessible to an increasing range of socio-economic groups. 'The relatively low fares of inclusive tour charters have been a major factor influencing the growth of tourism' (World Tourism Organizaion, 1966-1986). This organizational innovation (inclusive tours), together with the emergence of charter-class fares (ITX), charter carriers and tour operators, ensured the services for mass tourism.

The objective of promotional fares was not to reduce the cost of travel to those who could already afford to buy travel (e.g. business travellers). Rather, they aimed at making travel available to more people. An APEX fare, for example, is a restrictive fare: tickets for travel have to be bought in advance, they are not subject to change, have limited availability, and can incur the penalty of no refund. By its very restrictive terms, the APEX fare ensures that the business clientele are largely unable to benefit from the low fare. This is due to the fact that business trips usually require more flexibility and are subject to short planning horizons. For vacation travel, the reverse may be true.

The ITX far was also a very important innovation. The ITX fare is a charter-class rate offered to tour operators who organized inclusive tours and it was very important for the tourist industry at the time. These special tour-basing fares made it possible for tour operators to offer inclusive tours. Before 1962 the North Atlantic charter market was dominated by International Air Transportation Association (IATA) scheduled airlines. These scheduled airlines performed the dual role of providing scheduled and non-scheduled (charter) services. It was only during 1963-1968 that charter (non-schedule, non-IATA) carriers entered the air transportation market, opening up the new possibility of inclusive tours which tour operators quickly seized.

Technological changes in air transportation as well as marketing innovations in the promotion and pricing of air travel, laid the foundation for mass, large-scale transportation and tourism. Jet aircraft and jumbo jets made it physically possibly to transport larger numbers of passengers. Innovative pricing policies made it possible for ordinary people to buy air transportation and to travel *en masse* to an increasing number of distant destinations. These air components of mass tourism were implemented by developments in the hotel industry—specifically the emergence of multinational chains.

Multinational Hotel Chains

Multinational hotel chains were important agents for the delivery of mass, standardized and rigidly packaged hotel bed-nights across the globe. They emerged primarily to satisfy the global demand that mass tourism fuelled. Hotel chains expanded rapidly and built thousands of properties all over the world. The case of the Holiday Inn hotel chain clearly demonstrates this.

In 1952 Holiday Inn built its first unit. In 1964 number 500 was completed, and in 1968 number 1000 appeared. In 1968, Holiday Inn opened its first European motel in Holland. The company invaded Japan in 1973, and the following year reached South America. By 1981, the chain had 212 motels overseas in 58 countries (Luxenberg, 1985, pp. 112 and 210). Holiday Inn is the largest corporate hotel chain in the world with 370081 rooms in 1900 hotels worldwide (*Travel Industry World Year-Book, 1991*). In 1988, Holiday Inn generated system wide sales of US$5.4 billion.

At the end of 1978, it is estimated that 81 multinational hotel chains from 22 countries were associated with 1025 hotels abroad and 270646 rooms. The USA was the clear leader in the development of international hotel brands. Europe lagged behind. Thus while the USA accounted for 56.2 per cent of all rooms in multinational hotel companies outside the chains' home countries, Europe accounted for 32.6 per cent of all rooms of leading hotel chains outside the chains' homeland.

Multinational hotel chains were a phenomenon not only of the developed countries. Many countries in the developing world had their own multinational hotel companies operating in other parts of the world. They included India, Colombia, Mexico and Guatemala. However, these accounted for a mere 4 per cent of total hotel rooms in multinational corporations' affiliated hotels overseas.

Up to the early 1960s, the developed countries and the higher-income developing areas attracted most of the activities of multinational hotel chains, but in the following decade there was a remarkable growth of new associations in Africa, Asia and Oceana (UNCTC, 1982, p.24) In developed countries, ownership or part ownership accounted for 47.8 per cent of multinational hotel involvement; leasing 11.9 per cent; manage-ment contracts, 23.5 per cent; and franchising, 16.8 per cent. After 1975, 65.4 per cent of all multinational hotel involvement in the hotel sector in developed countries were through management contract (UNCTC, 1982, p. 24).

Through their operations on a global scale, multinational hotel chains were able to achieve considerable scale economies in three critical areas of operation:

- mass marketing;
- buying power; and
- distribution and reservations systems.

Emulating mass production in the manufacturing sector, multinational hotel chains standardized, mass-produced and mass-marketed tourism on a global scale. Franchises were the main instruments used by multinational hotels to mass-produced standardized (branded) hotel bed-nights across the globe.

Hotel Branding/Franchising

Franchises allowed hotel chains to produce and to standardize hotel products by replicating details of site, layout of buildings, furnishings, fixtures, price, the quality of service, management, food, and other areas. The details of the hotel and its service are disaggregated and very well defined so that each segment could be measured and regulated. This definition, measurement and regulation formed the basis of the franchise and the standardization procedures contained therein.

Since the franchise system is based upon the replication of near-identical hotels the world over, the franchiser obtained considerable benefits from marketing the same standard principle worldwide. In addition, the need for standardized facilities, equipment and materials meant that purchasing power was consolidated on a global level, with the benefit of lower average costs, lower prices to consumers and complete control.

In a detailed cost-benefit analysis of the Trinidad Hilton Hotel, it was observed that:

> The hotel is run on a standardized system that has been developed by the company; most of the furnishings, operating equipment, china, glass, etc., are purchase through the central purchasing office in New York; some food is obtained locally and some flown in from the USA.
>
> (Forbes, 1977, p. 17)

This franchising mechanism, together with the availability of electronically powered communications equipment to link the worldwide chain of franchises, provided the basis for standardization and mass production of tourist accommodation the world over. The rapid expansion of these chains and their franchising principle was a major force in the development of a mass-tourism industry. The impact of franchises on a global scale was overwhelming and, while they satisfied the needs of mass tourism, their impact upon the communal environment was far from satisfactory. As one observed puts it, the growth of these chains resulted in:

> stultifying homogenization of products and communities. They destroy a sense of community by mass-producing environments that minimize personal contact. Moreover, since employees and managers are forced to operate inside a straitjacket of corporate regulations, franchisees have little chance to tailor their units to their own taste or local preference.
>
> (Luxenberg, 1985)

Mass Marketing

Mass marketing involves the sale of identical goods and services to a seemingly identical group of consumers. Two key factors are usualy present in mass marketing. These are:

- large numbers of identical consumers; and
- large-scale production of identical units.

Both of these factors were present in the development of the tourism industry in the post-war period leading up to the 1980s. Hotel and holiday branding by multinational hotel chains in the USA and tour operators in Europe, respectively, allowed for the replication of standardized holidays internationally. Mass, inexperienced sun-lust tourists, together with paid holidays and post-war prosperity, produced large numbers of apparently identical consumers ready and willing to buy standardized travel options. Tourism services were thus mass marketed both in Europe and the USA as a result of these two essential mass-marketing factors.

A number of production and management imperatives gave birth to mass tourism in Europe. These included the role and importance of tour operators, the development of charter flights, package tours, holiday branding, mass marketing, hotel *over-construction* and the development of Mediterranean sun destinations for mass consumption.

All of these factors played significant roles in determining the rate and direction of growth of the international tourism industry. Tour operators, for example, were very instrumental in the transmission of mass tourism. In the case of charter flights in Europe, there exists a direct correlation between the destination's popularity with the mass market and the percentage of charter flights to the total air traffic of that destination. On the other hand, promotional fares, mass production and packaged tours were important factors in democratising travel, bringing it within the reach of wider, mass segments of the poulation. The package tour itself removed the risks associated with travel to distant and foreign lands and encouraged the increased consumption of travel.

Tour Operators and Package Tours

Tour operators are essentially wholesalers who put together the separate elements that normally make up a tour or travel package. Includes air transportation, accommodation, board, and ground transfers, with sightseeing tours and other destination services as optional extras. The tour operator 'package' these services and sells them to the consumer for a single inclusive price. The tour organizer obtains considerable savings on each element of the package because these services must be procured and paid for in advance and they are usually bulk purchases (*e.g.* the special ITX fare from the airline). Some of these savings are passed on, in the form of lower prices, to consumer. The price of a package tour is usually considerably less than buying and packaging the elements of a vacation for oneself. Tour operators were key agents in the transmission of mass, standardized and rigidly packaged tourism.

The idea of buying a package of transportation, accommodation, and perhaps some ancillary services such as ground tours, became established in Western Europe in the 1960s. Package holidays were extensively used by tourists from the Northern industrial countries of Scandinavia, West Germany and the UK. These packages concluded at resorts in the Mediterranean. By the late 1960s, the emergence of the inclusive tour as a principal medium in holiday travel in Europe had been established. Thus by 1965, just over one million holiday visits to Western Europe from the UK were inclusive tours by charter—already twice the number of independent air holidays. By 1970, while the number of independent holidays by air remained at just over half a million, inclusive tours by air had doubled to two million in number (Burkart and Medlik, 1974, p. 32).

Tour operators, spurred on by success over time, amassed considerable buying power over air seats and hotel capacity. Most European tour operators also had their own charter airlines and considerable interests in hotel properties in the Mediterranean. Their advanced purchases of tourism services have considerably improved cash flow and planning by many suppliers, particularly hotels. Many operators also had substantial financial assets in the tourism industry and were able to accumulate considerably more economic power through their idle cash balances accruing from pre-paid holidays.

There were several incentives for tourists to buy these package tours rather than incur the higher risks and costs of doing it for themselves. With the package tour, the risks associated with travel (*i.e.* uncertain accommodation on arrival in a tourist destination, unknown terrain and disaster) as well as the cost of travel were considerably less to the consumer. Tour operators were the true risk brokers and price setters of the travel industry. The package tour has brought travel within the reach of many who could normally not afford to take vacations abroad. By organizing large groups of tourists and transporting them from the tourist-generating country to a single destination in a host country and back again, tour operators have had a great impact on the volume of tourist traffic:

> The tour operators in the late 1970s were able to charter planes and guarantee more than 90 per cent of capacity—compared with the average passenger load factor of 55 per cent of capacity on scheduled flights in the 1960s.
>
> (UNCTC, 1982, p. 31)

Charter Flights

With the arrival of the jet aircraft, promotional fares, charter flights and inclusive tours, the novelty of air travel and tourism had begun to wear off. According to Burkat and Medlik (1974, p. 187), 'within the last 10 years, a holiday abroad has become as much a feature of the good life as a refrigerator or washing machine'. If innovations in air transportation (*i.e.* jet aircraft), marketing (*i.e.* promotional fares) and organization (*e.g.* inclusive tours) came together to create the phenomenon of mass, standardized and rigidly packaged tourism. Charter flights sealed the fate of tourism in Europe.

The very nature of a charter flight is that it is non-scheduled and lowcost and it operates on a limited and inflexible route structure. Thus charter flights differ from ordinary air services with their schedule, route structure and price. The purpose of a charter is to provide low-cost transportation to and from a tourist destination for holiday-makers. The idea is to obtain as high a load factor as possible (*i.e.* get as many people on the aircraft as possible) to benefit from scale economies and therefore lower prices per passenger. It is the achievement of high load factors (*e.g.* a full plane load) that makes it possible to lower the average price paid per consumer for a return flight.

Charter flights are a logical development of the mass air-transportation market. With the advent of the jet aircraft and the development of strategies by tour operators, the expansion of the charter market in the 1960s was very rapid. By 1967, charter operators had the same amount of the charter market as the scheduled operators, with each group carrying about 200000 passengers (figures for 1974 in World Tourism Organization, 1966-1986, p. 50). By 1969, for the first time, the share of charter traffic exceeded 25 per cent of the air transportation market in the USA.

In Europe, revenue passenger kilometres form charter operations increased nearly six-fold between 1963 and 1969, at an average annual rate of 35 per cent per year (figures for 1976 in world Tourism Organization, 1966-1986, p.45). In 1971, charter carriers accounted for 32.2 per cent of total air traffic, with Europe taking 63.4 per cent of the total and North America accounting for the remaining 36.6 per cent. The tendency of Europe to dominate the charter market continues to persist to the present. The availability of charter flights played an important role in the development of mass tourism in Europe.

That the jet aircraft was a progenitor of the mass tourism era can readily be understood when one examines the critical role that air charter flights played in the development of mass tourism destinations such as Spain. The importance of charter flights to the emergence of mass tourist destinations can be readily seen in this example. Spain was the first Mediterranean country to exploit its tourism resources in a major way, taking advantage of an increasingly wealthy Northern European population who were beginning to travel southward in search of the sun. Over the period 1964-1974, the percentage of charter traffic in the total air traffic to spain averaged 69.5 per cent. This percentage was even higher for individual resorts: 92.6 per cent for Tenerife; 90.2 per cent for Majorca; and 92.2 per cent for Alicante (world Tourism Organization, 1978, pp. 88-90).

Post-war prosperity, the arrival of the jet age (with the development of the jumbo jets in particular) brought developing countries, particularly Africa, Asia, the Caribbean and Pacific islands sharply into the international tourism focus. Relatively cheap long-distance travel, together with the incomes and desire to penetrate and explore new regions brought places like Bermuda, Bali, Acapulco and Jamaica onto the tourism map. At the same time, there was an annual flood of North Americans across the Atlantic, traditional destinations such as France and Italy became more widely visited, and the Mediterranean coast of Spain soon became a mass tourist destination for Northern Europeans.

Over the past three decades, international tourism has generally displayed all the features of mass production: (i) holidays were standardized, rigidly packaged and inflexible; (ii) identical holidays were mass produced with scale economies as the driving force; (iii) holidays were mass marketed to an undifferentiated clientele; and (iv) holidays were consumed *en masse* with a lack of consideration for the norms, culture and environment of the host countries. Mass, standardized and rigidly packaged tourism (MSRP) became a key feature of the international tourism industry during the 1960s, 1970s and early 1980s. MSRP tourism was 'best practice'. It was organizational and managerial common sense for best productivity and most profits.

Important frame conditions created MSRP tourism: post-war peace and prosperity together with the emergence of paid holidays provided the atmosphere, income, time and inclination to travel.

Consumers themselves helped to create mass tourism. Inexperienced post-war tourists attracted by the idea and novelty of air travel and a common search for the sun ensured the effective demand for mass-tourism services. Many tourists at the time were more taken up with the novelty and excitement of travel rather than with the quality of the destination or where they went, the hotels they slept in, or the quality of services they received.

Indentical hotel chains' strategy of franchising and international branding replication of hotels across the globe, provided familiarity, safety and reassurance to mass tourists-virtually allowing them to feel 'at home.'

Technology also facilitated the creation of MSRP tourism:

1. The year 1958 ushered in the jet age. The jet aircraft changed long-held perceptions of time and place and was the catalyst for a prolonged travel boom.
2. The development of plastic cards and other electronic methods of payment facilitated rapid growth and development of travel and related services.
3. Computer technology allowed tourism suppliers to better plan, manage and control their activities at a global level and facilitated the standardization, replication and management of facilities and services on a global scale.
4. Technology enabled the distri-bution

of services in international markets and improved the efficiency of services provided to consumers.

5. The role of information technologies in transforming the tourism industry and in generating completely new services was to become more important in 1978, when an important frame condition changed—i.e when the US government formally deregulated its airline industry.

Different management and production imperatives drove mass tourism in Europe and North America:

1. In the USA, international hotel chains branded hotels and mass-produced standardized accommodation the world over, while airlines, exercising oligopolistic power, controlled the rate and direction of tourism growth.

2. In Europe, tour operators branded holidays, controlled charter flights and, beginning with Spain, succeeded in making the Mediterranean the first mass tourism region in the world.

Mass tourism certainly had its time and place. Mass tourism was 'common sense'. It was the industry's and indeed the world's best practice'. Today, the tourism industry is in crisis. Mass tourism is no longer 'best practice'. Conditions that gave birth to mass tourism—the frame conditions, consumers, technology, and production and management practices—are changing.

Today, one is already witnessing a transformation toward new organizational and managerial principles for the best productivity and most profitable practice in the travel and tourism industry. Such new principle include quality, flexibility, environmentally sound, customization, innovation and diagonal integration.

Forces directing the transformation of travel and tourism stem not only form the industry's internal frame conditions such as its consumers and the management and production imperatives of its suppliers. Fundamental imperatives at the global level are also engineering the transformation of the travel and tourism industry. As these global imperatives are examined, it will be shown that the travel and tourism industry was not alone in the adoption of mass-production principles. Neither will the industry be alone in the adoption of the new 'best practice' of flexible production. Flexible production is rapidly becoming the global 'best practice'. Flexible production is already common practice in the same industry that perfected mass production—the car industry. It has been perfected by the Japanese and remains a key source of their compe-titiveness. The Japanese experience in the automobile industry holds some key lessons for travel and tourism suppliers.

3. Tourism Impact Assessment

TOURISM IS a luxury. Until recently, participation was restricted to the select few who could afford both the time and money to travel. Increased leisure, higher incomes and greatly enhanced mobility have combined to enable more people to partake of tourism. Improvements in transportation, the proliferation of accommodation, and the growth of inclusive tours and other forms of relatively cheap vacation travel, have further extended the opportunity to travel for pleasure. Today the majority of people in the developed world and increasing numbers in developing countries are tourists at some time in their lives. Tourism is no longer the prerogative of a few but is an accepted and accustomed, even expected, part of the lifestyles of a large and growing number of people.

Tourism is of major economic and social significance. More than 270 million tourists spend $92 billion (US) annually in places outside their own countries. This is one of the largest items in the world's foreign trade. With a world growth in visitor arrivals rate of approximately 6 per cent per annum, tourism is also one of the fastest growing economic activities. It is the most important export industry and earner of foreign exchange in many countries.

The significance of tourism has been recognised in both developed and developing countries. This can be seen in the establishment of government departments of tourism, widespread encouragement and sponsorship of tourist developments, and the proliferation of small businesses and multinational corporations contributing to and deriving benefits from the tourism industry. There is widespread optimism that tourism might be a powerful and beneficial agent of both economic and social change. Indeed, tourism has stimulated employment and investment, modified land use and economic structure, and made a positive contribution to the balance of payments in many countries throughout the world.

At the same time, the growth of tourism has prompted perceptive observers to raise many questions concerning the social and environmental desirability of encouraging further expansion. Do the expenditures of tourists benefit the residents of destination areas? Is tourism encouraging prostitution, crime and gambling? Does tourism rejuvenate the traditional arts and crafts of host cultures? Do governments direct their development priorities to satisfy the needs of tourists rather than residents? Are residents financing expensive tourist facilities through their taxes? Is tourism contributing to the destruction of the very resources which initially attracted the tourists? Are there saturation levels beyond which further growth in tourist arrivals creates more problems than benefits? What is being done to calculate these levels and to ensure that they are not exceeded?

The unprecedented growth of tourism has prompted a host of such questions, and answers and are only now beginning to emerge. As tourism continues to expand, questions concerning associated economic, environmental and social effects will become more pressing. Adequate answers to such questions are predicated upon systematic and rigorous research which, until recently, has been almost totally lacking.

Research on tourism has been highly fragmented, with researchers following separate and often divergent paths. For example, there have been studies of the history of tourism (Sigaux 1966; White 1967), the development of seaside resorts (Gilbert 1939; Wall 1975), and the role of tourism in international trade (Peters 1969; Gray 1970). Impact-oriented research has been equally specialized, emphasizing specific types of impact to the exclusionof thers. For instance, Doxey (1976) and Smith (1977) examined the resentments which may result from tourist—host interactions; the World Bank (1972) and Peters (1969) treated tourism as an economic phenemenon; and Hall (1970) and Cohen (1978) documented some of the efforts of tourism on the physical environment. The value of such studies would be enhanced if they could be placed in a broader context.

There have been few attempts to integrate the findings of the diverse studies of the impacts of tourism, yet any assessment of the costs and benefits of tourism requires a full consideration of all the likely impacts. The volume is an attempt to synthesize the findings of research on the impacts of tourism, and to present them to the reader in a systematic fashion. The strengths and weaknesses of existing approaches will be identified, and topics which have yet to receive detailed examination in the literature will be pointed out. The materials assembled in this book are largely taken from published sources and emphasise the impacts of mass tourism in resort areas as opposed to the less apparent, scattered effects of individuals travelling in areas lacking a reputation of tourism. The value of this book will not lie in the originally of the ideas which are presented, for it will be necessary to draw heavily upon the work of others. Rather, as one of the earliest attempts to collate and access the numerous studies of impacts of tourism, it is hoped that this work will provide a balanced introduction to the topic. By drawing attention to the diversity and complexity of these impacts, conceptual and methodological difficulties will be highlighted which may be avoided in future research. An objective evaluation of the impacts of tourism is required if government agencies, planners, developers and businessmen are to appreciate the full implications of their actions. If some of the myths concerning the nature of tourist impact can be dispelled, then the way should be open for a re-examination of the true potential of tourism as a contributor to the economic, environmental and social well-being of reception areas. Thus, it should be possible to encourage types of development which confer many of the 'blessings' of tourism without the associated 'blights'.

Organisation

Widely-accepted procedures for investigating the impacts of tourism have yet to be established and few studies attempt a comprehensive examination of a broad range of types of impact. For the purposes of this work, impacts of tourism are grouped into three major categories: economic, physical and social. This distinction is somewhat artificial for, in reality, the boundries between the categories are indistinct and their contents merge. For example, money may be spent in an attempt to reduce unacceptable environmental change. This, in turn, may have repercussions for the availability of jobs and, hence, on social well-being. Similarly, tax revenues earned as a by-product of tourism expenditures may be spent to promote more tourism, to clean up the environment or to improve social services. Ultimately, therefore, this threefold division must be justified pragmatically. However, most studies of the consequences of tourism focus primarily on only one of these three types of impact so that the organisation into three major impact domains reflects the present status of research.

Just as there is overlap between the impact domains, there is also little consensus as to what should be included within them. For example, some economic studies focus upon income generation, others stress the creation of employment, whereas many reports are devoted to balance of payments questions. Such variations in emphasis hamper the comparison of findings of different investigations, frustrate the establishment of a body of theory, and contribute to inconsistency and contradiction of study conclusions.

For this study, environmental impact assessment checklists and social and economic indicator tables were consulted as a guide to the allocation of subject-matter to each impact domain. This procedure also enabled topics favoured by researchers to be distinguished from those which are largely unstudied. However, while a threefold division into economic, physical and social impacts constitutes the major organising framework of this book, it is not rigidly imposed. There are occasions when, for the sake of clarity and in tune with the multifaceted nature of tourist phenomena, aspects of one type of impact will be mentioned in conjunction with those of another impact domain.

Research issues

Rapid growth of tourism has given rise to increasingly pronounced economic, environmental and social effects. However, until recently, attention has concentrated on the more obvious economic impacts with comparatively little consideration being given to the environmental and social consequences of tourism. The relative neglect of these topics has occurred in spite of increasing anxiety about environmental problems evolving from man's continued manipulation of his environment, and in spite of expanding awareness of the increasing significance of tourism. The economic emphasis of much research is a reflection of the optimism with which tourism was generally viewed in the 1960s. Great interest was expressed in the potential of tourism to contribute to economic development. Tourism was widely acclaimed as generating a multitude of beneficial effects upon such economic indicators as balance of payments, income, employment and tax revenues. While there is an element of truth in this perspective, and some types of tourism may stimulate environmental preservation and benefit residents of destination areas, contemporary tourism is on a massive scale which may pose substantial environmental and social risks.

Recognition of the size of the impacts of modern tourism has prompted a reorientation of tourism research. There has been a noticeable shift towards a more balanced perspective incorporating a critical examination of the costs, or negative impacts, of tourism. An increasing number of such studies adopt an environmental or a social perspective but the majority of such investigations are of recent vintage. The potentially serious psychological, social and cultural effects of tourism were given prominence in the seminal works of Young (1973) and Turner and Ash (1975). Following these pioneering statements, a number of authors have illuminated some of the more alarming, negative impacts of tourism (Graburn 1976; Smith 1977; Cohen 1978; Pizam 1978). These have included the modification of traditional cultures, increases in prostitution and crime, and the pollution of beaches.

The consequences of tourism have become increasingly complex and contradictory. For example, the commercialisation of culture, through the marketing and sale of artefacts, may revive traditional art forms or modify them so that they are scarcely recognisable. The associated influx of money into a local economy may distort occupational stability and contribute to a breakdown in family and community cohesion. On the other hand, the commercialisation of culture may lead to the creation of a 'phony folk culture' but, at the same time, create jobs and thereby alleviate existing unemployment problems. Assessments of tourism must increase in breadth and sophistication as the industry expands, and as the diversity and intricacy of impacts is magnified.

Impact studies

Evaluations of the impacts of tourism reflect the status of impact research in general. Recent environmental legislation, and demands by society for environmental impact statements for projects which significantly affect the environment, have stimulated interest in impact research, and emphasised the need for the development of sound analytical procedures. Given the varied requirements of impact assessments and the recency of their rise to prominence, it should not be surprising that there is a paucity of methodological guidelines for undertaking investigations of the impacts of tourism.

Environmental impact statements of any kind are extremely difficult to make (Wall and Wright 1977: 3-5). Five reasons for this can be highlighted. Firstly, man has been living on and modifying the earth for thousands of years so that it is extremely difficult to reconstruct the environment before the intervention of man and, hence, to establish a base level against which to measure changes. In many tourist destination areas public use has existed for long periods of time so that it is now almost impossible to reconstruct the environment minus the effects induced by tourism. However, failure to establish baseline data will mean that it will be impossible to fully assess the magnitude of changes brought about by tourism.

A second difficulty concerns the problem of disentangling the role of man from the role of nature. Even without the intervention of man, the environment would not be unchanging, but would be in a perpetual state of flux. This leads to further difficulties in defining a base level. The problem is compounded because many impacts of tourism result from normal environmental processes whose actions are speeded up by the intervention of man. For instance, weathering and erosion are natural processes but they can become major problems when exacerbated by man. The processes remain unchanged but the flows of energy are radically altered.

A related problem is the difficulty of differentiating between changes attributable to pre-existing processes and changes induced by the influx of tourists. Tourism has emerged as a forceful agent of change and creates impacts which are clearly the product of tourist developments: resort landscapes, the construction of theme parks and the generation of employment and income are obvious examples. In many cases, however, it is exceedingly difficult to isolate the principal causes of change. It may be difficult to determine whether changes are directly attributable to tourist development or whether tourism is only one among a number of agents of change. In Tonga, for example, the increased demand for imported foodstuffs has resulted from an increasing population, inadequate agricultural production to feed the people, and demands imposed by international tourism. The extent to which tourism has contributed to the deep-seated social and economic problems emanating from this situation is not accurately known. Tourism, undoubtedly, has been one important contributing factor but it may also be a highly visible scapegoat for problems which already existed prior to the advent of modern tourism. It certainly is easier to blame tourism than it is to address the conditions of society and environ-ment.

Thirdly, the complex interactions of tourism phenomena make total impact almost impossible to measure. Many of the impacts of tourism are manifested in subtle and often unexpected ways. In other words, primary impacts give rise to secondary and tertiary impacts and generate a myriad of successive repercussions which it is usually impracticable to trace and monitor. Cross impacts are a direct result of the interactive nature of economic, environmental and social phenomena. Interactions between components of each of these impact domains induce further changes which reverberate through the system, creating a complex array of impact flows. For example, organised safaris to national parks in Africa can modify the feeding and breeding habits of wildlife. Preservation of wildlife may be in the interests of tourist developers and may have economic benefits to countries endowed with this resource. However, the establishment of national parks has forced the rapidly growing African population to farm in areas of low fertility where agricultural production may be barely sufficient to feed the population. Special impacts occur to particular groups of people, such as racial or cultural minorities, or to unique types of wildlife or vegetation. The distinctive characteristics of such groups can make them extremely attractive to the tourist but also highly vulnerable to impacts from tourist activity.

A fourth obstacle stems from spatial and temporal discontinuities between cause and effect. For instance, erosion in one location may result in deposition elsewhere, destruction of key elements of an animal's habitat may lead to population declines throughout its range, or development of new facilities may divert tourist traffic away from existing locations. A considerable time may elapse before the full implications of an activity are apparent. Thus, there are great difficulties in establishing both temporal and spatial constraints for undertaking impact studies.

A fifth methodological issue is the selection of impact indicators. What indicators should be used and what do they really mean? For example, what is the significance of prostitution and an increased crime rate when compared with traffic congestion or an expanded tax base? In other words, there is a problem in the identification of which variables best indicate the changing situation and, in consequence, of what to measure. A related problem is the assigning of weights to the selected indicators, as indicators of impact vary in their significance to the impacted system, and devising means of combining disparate measures into a composite index of the magnitude of impact.

Problems, such as those which have been discussed above, have restricted the scope and accuracy of research results and have encouraged inves-tigation to narrow the focus of their research. There has been a tendency to examine impacts from selected, specific developments or projects in isolation from the broader tourist phenomena of which they are a part; to concentrate on primary impacts to the exclusion of secondary and tertiary impacts; to measure the more tangible, quantifiable impacts, such as economic impacts, to the neglect of the less readily measured social and environmental impacts; and to stress positive impacts or benefits, and to overlook undesirable consequence or costs. Future examinations of the consequences of tourism for host communities will continue to be concerned with the types and magnitude of impact and whether they are predominantly beneficial or costly to the destination area. In addition, it will be necessary to give greater attention to the scale of impact for the spheres of influence of tourist development vary and their consequences may be viewed differently depending upon whether they are assessed from a local, regional, national or international perspective. At the same time, it will be appropriate to give greater attention to the assessment of who gains and who loses. Costs and benefits of tourism are not evenly distributed. What may be a benefit to one group or individual within community may be a cost to the neighbours. Investors in tourist developments and associated service industries may gain at the expense of other residents of the destination area who may suffer increased crowding, congestion, noise, pollution and modified lifestyles. Furthermore, tourism is dynamic and impacts and their significance are constantly changing due to modifications of the goals of both the tourists and their hosts, fluctuations in the processes shaping the economic and physical environments, and techno-logical changes and other developments in the tourist industry itself. This implies that impacts will change through time and periodic monitoring may be desirable.

Relationships

Discussions of recreation and tourism are plagued by imprecise terminology. Although there is a considerable body of literature which attempts to clarify the meanings of such terms as recreation and leisure, universally acceptable definitions have yet to be derived. The problem is compounded by the indiscriminate use of words such as pleasure, fun, spare time and enjoyment which are often used as synonyms for recreation and leisure and as substitutes for each other. In the interests of clear thinking it is desirable to make a distinction between the meanings of leisure and recreation. Leisure can be regarded as a measure of time: it is the time remaining after work, sleep and necessary personal and households chores have been completed. It is the time available for doing as one chooses. Leisure may thus be defined as 'discretionary time'. Recreation embraces the wide variety of activities which are undertaken during leisure. Outside of professional circles, there has probably never been one word or phrase in common circulation to describe that time which we think of as leisure. People talk about concrete, discrete activities, such as watching television, skiing or going to the cottage, and not about tourism, recreation or leisure. Leisure, recreation and tourism are abstractions from common experience, abstractions which only those who stand aside from that experience can perceive. The language is that of the academic and the planner rather than the participant (Cunningham 1980).

The simple distinction between leisure as discretionary time and recreation as activity is difficult to implement, for many activities include both obligatory and discretionary components. For instance, without food we would die and eating is a necessity; it is also a popular form of recreation from which many people derive great pleasure. Similarly, gardening and attending conventions are activities which can be both enjoyable and a chore. Such difficulties have prompted some authors to argue that leisure and recreation are states of mind and that they are best defined in psychological terms (Driver and Tocher 1974). While one can be sympathetic to this viewpoint and can acknowledge that individuals recreate for a wide variety of reasons and may even derive different satisfactions from the same activity, psychological definitions have their own inherent difficulties. The designation of areas of excitement, danger or relaxation is uncommon among recreation and tourism planners and site managers who usually operate on the basis of activities, designating areas for camping, skiing or hunting. However, the psychological definitions do serve to remind us that opportunities to recreate are not provided in and for themselves; they are made available to enable participants to achieve a wide range of satisfactions.

Tourism, recreation and leisure are not the prerogative of any one discipline. Recreations in the home, such as reading and watching television, are probably best studied by sociologists and psychologists, although economists may be interested in associated spending patterns. While recognising that other disciplines have important roles to play, it is suggested that the geographer is in a position to make a distinct and significant contribution to the understanding of tourism and outdoor recreation. Tourism and outdoor recreation are land uses. They are in competition with agriculture, forestry, mining, housing, industry and a variety of other functions for the same scarce resources of land and water. Tourist and recreation facilities such as ski areas, resorts, parks and swimming pools have service areas comparable to those of stores or ports, and tourism and recreation create patterns of movement analogous to those associated with commuting or migration and susceptible to analysis by similar methods. From these examples alone it should be evident that the concepts and methods of the geographer are appropriate to analyses of recreation and have the potential to further the understanding or recreational phenomena.

Tourism and outdoor recreation have two basic aspects: the supply of facilities and the demand for participation. Supply and demand interact to produce the pattern of tourism and outdoor recreation, which may be defined as the spatial and temporal incidence of tourism and outdoor recreation. These patterns have associated economic, environmental and social impacts and give rise to planning and management problems and opportunities.

Interactions between supply and demand occur at a variety of scales reflecting the time available for outdoor recreation and the distances that can be traversed during that time. When only short periods of time are available, as, for example, in the evening, recreation, of necessity, takes place in or relatively close to the home. In contrast, during vacations, when several days of leisure may be juxtaposed, it is possible to travel long distances. There is thus a continuum from recreation in the home to recreation at considerable distances from the home base, the latter often being associated with the acquisition of temporary accommodation. It follows that tourism can be regarded as an extreme form of recreation which is distinguished by relatively long lengths of stay away from home and relatively large distances travelled (Britton 1979). The literature generally focusses on either recreation or tourism but, it is argued, they are aspects of the same phenomenon which can usefully be considered together: after all, requisi-tionists and tourists may be found together at the same sites doing similar things.

The existence of the recreational time-distance continuum draws attention to the fact that the temporal distribution of leisure may be as significant as its quantity. If, for example, the working week were reduced by several hours, it would make a great deal of difference to patterns of recreation if these hour were distributed evenly across the week, added to the weekend, or accumulated towards a longer vacation. Other things being equal, the larger the size of the unit of leisure, the smaller are the distance constraints, and the greater is the freedom of locational choice of the potential participant. However, such time-distance relationships are further modified, particularly on long journeys, by the availability of money, for wealthy travellers may increase their time at a destination by substituting fast but expensive air travel for cheaper but slower ground transportation.

The difficulties of distinguishing between tourism and other forms of recreation have been recognised by most recreation and tourism texts. It is difficult to isolate the activities and demands of tourists as opposed to those of participants in other forms of recreation. Tourism and recreation often share the same facilities and compete for space and finance: facilities, such as theme parks, may be established to attract tourists and also to cater for recreationists; local demand for new recreational facilities (for example, artificial ski slopes) may be prompted by experiences gained as tourists abroad; measures adopted to improve the environment and to conserve and restore national park landscapes and historic monuments benefit both recreation and tourism. The demands and effects of recreation and tourism are, therefore, closely interrelated. Burkart and Medlik (1974: 10) described the confusing situation as follows:

> tourism represents a particular use of leisure time and a particular form of recreation but does not include all uses of leisure time nor all forms of recreation. It includes much travel but not all travel. Conceptually tourism is, therefore, distinguished in particular from related concepts of leisure and recreation on the one hand, and from travel and migration on the other.

Attempts to differentiate between recreation and tourism on the basis of motivations, activity types, modes of travel and distances travelled have met with mixed success. One way of classifying tourism and recreations is through the examination of the availability and use of leisure. According to Lawson and Baud-Bovy (1977:4) leisure is of four types:

1. Daily recreation uses facilities in close proximity to one's home or place of work and for short periods during the day;
2. One-day recreation encompasses excursions to the fringes of urban areas or further into the countrywide but within easy reach of home. No overnight stay is required;
3. Weekends and short holidays may be spent with some frequency relatively close to one's residence in second homes or other temporary accommodation;
4. Long holidays involve fewer distance constraints and may be taken in one's own country or abroad.

From this perspective, tourists would be included in the 'long holiday' and weekends and short holiday' classifications, although not all people assigned to these groups would, of necessity, be tourists.

Tourism, then, is but one of a range of choices or styles of recreation expressed either through travel or a temporary short term change of residence. Tourism, on its modern scale, is a relatively new use of leisure. Marked and rapid changes in technology and in social, political and economic systems have enabled people to pursue new and different forms of recreation and have magnified the importance of tourism. Tourism is an evolutionary development in the use of leisure and represents an expanded opportunity for the exercise of choice in the selection of recreational activities.

Before one can examine tourist phenomena and assess their effects on economic, physical and social environments it is necessary to devise appropriate definitions. Frechtling (1976: 59) stated that definitions for travel research should:

1. Be discrete and unambiguous and must clearly define one activity or entity as distinct from all others, i.e. there should be no confusion over what is included in or excluded from a category;
2. Facilitate measurement as much as is consistent with other objectives;
3. Follow established usuage as closely as possible. In other words, in developing definitions reference should be made both to major travel studies and to everyday language. This should facilitate comparison of results with those of other studies, aid continuity in research and permit a cumulative body of knowledge to be developed.

The above principle have been poorly adhered to in the research which has been undertaken to date. In fact, there are almost as many definitions of tourism as there are studies of the phenomenon (Cohen 1974). A survey of eighty travel and tourism studies conducted by Frenchtling (1976) yielded forty-three different definitions for the three terms of traveller, tourist and visitor. Such results indicate the lack of coordination in travel research and hamper comparisons between travel research data.

In assessing the impacts of tourism, it is fundamental to define the major components of tourism: the tourist. 'Tourist' is derived from the term 'tour' which, according to *Webster's International Dictionary* (1961: 2417), means: 'a journey at which one returns to the starting point; a circular trip usually for business, pleasure or education during which various places are visited and for which an itinerary is usually planned'. Accordingly, the *Oxford English Dictionary* (1933: 190) defines the tourist as: 'one who makes a tour or tours; especially one who does this for recreation; one who travel for pleasure or culture, one who visits a number of places for their objects of interest, scenery or the like.'

Dictionary meanings of the term 'tourist' have been expanded and complicated with the rise of tourism research. Ogilive (1933) was one of the first to incorporate additional meaning through use in social science research. He described a tourist as any person whose movements fulfil two conditions:

1. That the person's absense from home was for a relatively short period;
2. That money spent during absence is money derived from home and not earned in the destination visited.

Cohen (1974: 529) commented that Ogilvie's definition: 'translates the contention found in other definitions, namely that the tourist is a traveller for recreation or pleasure, into economic terms: the tourist is, economically speaking, a consumer and not a producer.'

In his analysis of definitions, Frechtling (1976: 60) outlined four basic criteria used in their formulation:

1. Purpose of trip;
2. Mode of transportation used;
3. Length of stay;
4. Distance travelled.

It is generally agreed that the former two criteria are insufficient for practical contemporary definitions and attention has been concentrated on the latter two criteria. Length of stay is a principal component of the United Nations definition which requires that tourists stay in excess of twenty-four hours but less than twelve months. The United Nations definition will be discussed in more detail below. Some definitions are dominated by a distance criterion. For example, the National Tourism Resources Review Commission (NTRRC) defined a tourist as: 'one who travels away from his home for a distance of at least 50 miles (one way) for business, pleasure, personal affairs or any other purpose except to commute to work.' The US Census Bureau has settled for a similar definition but has extended the minimum distance to 100 miles.

Cohen (1974) has also reviewed the literature which attempted to define the 'tourist'. He identified six major dimensions: permanency, voluntariness, direction, distance, recurrency, and purpose. He defined the tourist as: 'a volutionary, temporary, traveller, travelling in the expectation of pleasure from the novelty and change experienced on a relatively long and non-recurrent round-trip' (Cohen 1974: 533). This definition has the merits of being both concise and comprehensive but for the collection of data it is necessary to be even more explicit and precise time and distance constraints must be established.

In 1963 the United Nations sponsored a conference on travel and tourism in Rome. The conference recommended definitions of 'visitor' and 'tourist' for use in compiling international statistics. For statistical purposes the term 'visitor' describes any person visiting a country other than that in which he has his usual place of residence, for any reason other than following an occupation remunerated from within the country visited. This definition covers:

1. Tourists who are temporary visitors staying at least 24 hours in the country visited and the purpose of whose journey can be classified under one of the following headings;
   (a) leisure (recreation, holiday, health, study, religion and sport);
   (b) business, family, mission, meeting;
2. Excursionists who are temporary visitors staying less than 24 hours in the country visited, including travellers on cruise ships (International Union of Official Travel Organizations [IUOTO] 1963: 14).

In 1968 IUOTO (now the World Tourism Organisation) approved the 1963 definition and has encouraged countries to use it. Leiper (1979: 393) has noted that one consequence of this definition is that statistical data on international tourists include trips for purposes beyond the popular use of the word. For example, most people do not consider business trips as tourism. Nevertheless, the United Nations terminology has received widespread acceptance and, in the context of this book, it has proved useful in locating literature specifically pertaining to tourism. According to the United Nations definition, a tourist may be classified, in the terminology of Lawson and Baud-Bovy, in both 'weekend and short holiday' and 'long holiday' recreation. 'Daily' and 'one day recreation' participants can be grouped under the 'excursionist' category. However, this differentiation fails to distinguish between impacts of tourism as opposed to impacts of other forms of recreation because both leisure groups may be participating in similar activities at the same locations. As contemporary tourism is a mass phenomenon and is highly concentrated in particular destinations, its effects are likely to be more pronounced than those of excursionists, although the impacts of the latter are likely to be very similar in kind.

Other terms which require definition are 'international tourist' which include those individuals travelling across an international border and who remain away from home for at least twenty-four hours, and domestic tourists who are those individuals travelling within their own country but who remain away home in excess of twenty-four hours. Statistical definitions of the tourist in a domestic setting (travelling within the country of residence) have varied among countries and regions, but have generally included three major elements: distance, purpose of travel, and length of stay.

Since the focus of this book is on the impacts of tourism which accrue to destination areas, it is necessary to define the domain in which impacts occur. A 'destination area' is a place having characteristics which are known to a sufficient number of potential visitors to justify its consideration as an entity, attracting travel to itself, independent of the attractions of other locations. The natural and man-made features, infrastructural charcteristics, economic structures, and the attributes of the host populations of destination areas are of interest here.

Economic Impacts

Several standard types of economic measurements are made in tourism. Tourism is still not usually listed as a separate sector in national economic tables but is included in the service sector. (The WTO has developed the Standard International Classification of Tourism Activities (SICTA) which has been provisionally approved by the

Tourism Impact Assessment

United Nations Statistical Commission.) Therefore, it is more difficult to measure the economic contribution of tourism. But, by drawing on various information sources, tourism economists can make calculations sufficient to indicate the general extent of tourism's economic impact. The standard economic measurements are as follows:

Income generated and contribution to Gross National or Domestic Product. This indicates the relative importance of tourism in the total economy.

Foreign exchange earned from international tourism. This includes calculation of both the gross foreign exchange earnings—the total expenditure of foreign tourists, and net foreign exchange earnings—the foreign exchange remaining in the country after deducting the foreign exchange leakage factor. This leakage is the foreign exchange spent for imported goods and services used in tourism—food items and hotel equipment and supplies; expatriation of salaries of foreign workers and of profits of foreign-owned facilities; payments made to foreign hotel management companies; and other leakages. At the regional level, the gross and net money earned from outside the region can be calculated.

- Local employment generated by tourism. Employment is calculated by type:
  - direct employment—the persons who work in tourism enterprises such as hotels, restaurants, tourist shops and tour and travel agencies;
  - indirect employment—jobs generated in the supplying sectors such as agriculture, fisheries and manufacturing;
  - induced employment—additional persons supported by the spending of income made by the direct and indirect employees;
  - construction employment—jobs generated in the construction of tourism facilities and infrastructure (this is usually temporary but may be places with continuing development of tourism).
- The multiplier effect. This refers to the stimulus that an external source of income has on an economy. It is the number of rounds of spending in the local economy of the initial tourist spending. This effect measures the way in which tourist expenditures filter through the economy and generate other economiy activities.
- Contribution to government revenues. This includes hotel and other types of tourist user taxes, airport departure taxes, customs duties on imported goods used in tourism, income taxes on tourism enterprises and employees and property taxes on tourism establishments.

Although not as quantifiable, a benefit of tourism is that it helps justify and pay for transportation facilities and services and other infrastructure that are used by the entire community. Also an important general benefit is that tourism can serve as a catalyst for expansion of other economic sectors.

If not carefully controlled, tourism can generate some economic problems. Loss of economic benefits can occur if there is a high import content of goods and services used in tourism, and if many tourist facilities are owned and managed by outsiders. This situation reduces the net income and foreign exchange earned from tourism, and may lead to resentment by residents of the tourism area. For certain types of tourism development, however, there may be few alternative to outside ownership and management. This can be the case especially during the initial stages of development when local capital and managerial capabilities are limited. In small island economies with little local production of goods, it may be difficult to greatly reduce the import content of tourism. But the employment and income generated is still usually considered worth the investment in tourism.

Economic distortions can take place geographically to tourism is concentrated in only one or a few areas of a country or region, without corresponding development in the other places. Employment distortions may be created if tourism attracts too many employees from other economic sectors, because of its higher wages and better working conditions. Inflation of local prices of land and certain goods and services may take place in rapidly developing tourism areas. This places a financial burden on residents.

Economic Benefits

There are several techniques that can be applied to enhance the economic benefits of tourism. These should be incorporated into the planning process so that possible problems are prevented or reduced before they occur.

Strengthening the linkages between tourism and other economic sectors is a very important technique. This reduces the import content of tourism and provides more local employment—the indirect and induced employment—and income from tourism. Opportunities often exist, for example, to increase the locally produced food items used in tourism. Also, the tourism industry should be encouraged (or required) to utilise more local items, including building materials and interior decoration, in its development and operation of hotels and other facilities.

Encouraging in-country, in-region and local ownership of tourist facilities and services is also important so that more of the profits from tourism are retained. This can be done in various ways—providing investment incentives; organiing stock companies with sale of shares to the general public; and requiring joint ventures of local and foreign companies. Certain forms of tourism can be encouraged which will provide opportunities for local small business enterprises. If local capital is very limited, then a policy can be taken of initially allowing foreign ownership, but requiring purchases by local owners when capital is available.

Foreign hotel management by transnational hotel companies of large hotel properties results in a loss of some income to countries. However, it also offers the advantages of professional management and international marketing and reservation services. Whether to allow transnational management must be decided based on the circumstances of each particular country. It is also important that local tour operators be given the opportunity to handle foreign tour groups, and that local ground handling operations are not pre-empted by foreign tour operators.

Maximising local employment in tourism can be encouraged by proper training of persons to work in tourism. In some places, there may be some social resistance to service employment. It will be necessary to educate local people to understand that employment in tourism is a respected and worthwhile type of occupation. Training should be extended to the supervisory and management levels, so that these higher level positions can also eventually be filled by local staff.

When a trained pool of employees exists, then tourist facility and service establishments can be required to employ local persons. For the higher level positions, replacement of foreign employees by local ones can be phased in over a period of time.

Tourist expenditures can be increased in various ways. Most shopping opportunities, especially of local arts and crafts, can be provided in many places. Tourist activities can be expanded, for example by organising more attractions and tours, which will induce tourists to stay longer. Tourism product enrichment and diversification is becoming an important aspect of expanding and upgrading tourism in many already developed tourism areas.

By developing tourism in a gradual manner, the problems of inflated prices for land and goods can often be reduced because the economy has more time to adjust to new development. This also provides local residents with more opportunity to adapt to and be trained to participate in the benefits of tourism.

Environmental Impacts

Tourism and the environment are inter-dependent. The physical (natural and man-made) environment provides many of the attractions for tourists, and the development of tourism can generate both positive and negative environmental impacts. Developing and managing tourism so that it is compatible with the environment, and does not degrade it, is a major factor in achieving sustainable development. In order to plan tourism environmentally, it is first important to understand the possible impacts of tourism on the environment.

If tourism is well planned, developed and managed, it can generate important positive environmental impacts. These include the following:

- Helps justify and pay for conservation of important natural areas and wildlife, including marine environments, and development of national and regional parks and reserves, because these are major attractions for tourists. This is an especially significant benefit in countries with limited resources for undertaking environmental conservation.

- Helps justify and pay for the conservation of archaeological and historic sites as attractions for tourists. Otherwise many of these sites would be allowed to deteriorate or disappear. Even entire historic districts in towns and cities are being conserved and developed for tourism.

- Helps improve the environmental quality of areas because tourists like to visit places that are attractive, clean and not polluted. Tourism provides the incentive to clean up environments through controlling air, water, noise and visual pollution, reducing congestion and upgrading overall appearance with suitable landscaping and building design. Also, well sited and designed tourist facilities themselves can contribute to the attractive appearance of both urban and rural environments. Improvement of infrastructure, especially of water supply and sewage and solid waste disposal, also contributes to improved environmental quality.

- Increases local environmental awareness when residents, and especially young people, observe tourists' interest in conservation. They then begin to realise the importance of conservation in their areas.

If tourism is not well planned, developed and managed, it can generate several types of negative environmental impacts. These include the following:

- Water pollution resulting from improper development of sewage and solid waste disposal systems for hotels and other facilities. There can be pollution of river, lake and coastal waters from sewage outfall lines, and of groundwater by seepage of waste material.
- Air pollution resulting from excessive use of internal combustion vehicles (cars, taxis, buses, motorcycles, etc.) in tourism areas. Airplanes, used by many tourists for longer-distance travel and for local air tours generate some air (and noise) pollution.
- Noise pollution generated by a concentration of tourists and tourist vehicles.
- Visual pollution resulting from several factors—poorly designed hotels and other tourist facilities; badly planned layout of facilities; inadequate landscaping of facilities; use of large and ugly advertising signs; and obstruction of scenic views by tourism development.
- Waste disposal problems of littering the landscape by tourists, and improper disposal of waste generated by tourist facilities.
- Ecological disruption of natural areas by overuse and misuse by tourists and inappropriate tourism development. Coastal, marine, mountain and desert environments, all important types of tourism areas, are particularly vulnerable to ecological damage.
- Damage to archaeological and historic sites by overuse or misuse by tourists and inappropriate tourism development.
- Environmental hazards and land use problems resulting from poor planning, siting and engineering of tourist attractions and facilities.

Ecological Measures

Concern with environmental protection should be an integral part of the planning process. Application of the environmental planning and sustainable development approach is essential, including establishing and staying within the carrying capacities of tourism areas. Selecting the forms of tourism development that are most suitable for the environment also greatly help limit negative environmental impacts. Application of sound principles, such as concentration of facilities in certain zones with provision of adequate infrastructure, a very important in maintaining environmental protection. More generally development of tourism on a gradual basis allows for sufficient time to monitor its environmental impacts, and make changes in the development approach if any problems have arisen.

Adopting techniques of reducing the seasonality of tourism, especially peak season use or tourism areas, is another very useful technique. Environmental problems often occur only during the peak season when overloading of the infrastructure and overuse of attractions, facilities and services take place.

In addition to these general approaches, specific environmental impact control measures should be applied. These include the following:

- Install properly designed utility systems of water supply, electric power, sewage and solid waste disposal and drainage for tourist facilities. Conservation techniques should be applied—such as treatment and recycling of waste water and use of solar heating devices. Often these systems can be extended to serve general development in the tourism area, thus benefiting local communities.

- Develop adequate road and other transportation systems, with emphasis on development of public transit and non-polluting forms of transportation of tourists. Electric shuttle buses, for example, can be used in resorts. Proper maintenance of tourist vehicles is important.
- Provide open space, parks and suitable landscaping in tourism areas.
- Apply environmentally suitable land use and site planning principles, zoning regulations, development standards and architectural design in tourism areas. Control of advertising signs is also important.
- Carefully manage visitor flows at tourists attraction features. At fragile sites, the number of visitors may need to be limited or completely prohibited at certain times, or even year-round. For some important sites, the technique of modelling can be used—building a replica of the feature for tourists to visit, with prohibition of tourists at the original site.
- Prohibit tourists to cut trees in camping and trekking areas, to collect rare plant and animal species, and to disturb the natural behavioural patterns of wild animals. Hunting and fishing should be allowed only under carefully controlled conditions.
- In marine areas, several types of controls are necessary—operations related to ship bulge cleaning and ballast dumping; use of motorised boats in environmentally sensitive areas; collection of live sea shells, coral and endangered sea life; spear fishing; disturbance of nesting turtles; use of boat anchors in coral-bottom bays; and mining of beach, sand and coral for construction purposes. Boat piers should be properly designed so that they do not lead to erosion or other problems.
- Maintain environmental health and safety standards for the benefit of both tourists and residents.

There may be other control measures which should be applied in particular tourism areas depending on their characteristics. With respect to visitor use controls, it is important to inform tourists about the controls and why they must be applied. If tourists understand why the controls are necessary, they will more likely abide by them.

Socio-cultural Impacts

Tourism can bring both benefits and problems to the local society and its cultural patterns. Although more difficult to measure than economic or environmental impacts, socio-cultural impacts are major considerations in developing tourism in any place. These impacts can be especially critical in countries that still have strongly traditional societies and economies. Although tourism can generate socio-cultural impacts, it should be kept in mind that any type of new development brings changes. Tourism is only one source of change in a society.

If tourism is well planned, developed and managed in a socially responsible manner, it can bring several types of socio-cultural benefits. These include the following:

- Improves the living standards of people and helps pay for improvements to community facilities and services, if the economic benefits of tourism are well distributed.

- Conserves the cultural heritage of an area which otherwise might be lost as a result of general development taking place. Conservation of archaeological and historic sites was referred to under environmental impacts. Cultural patterns of music, dance, drama, dress, arts and crafts, customs, ceremonies, life-styles, traditional economic activities and architectural styles are also important attractions for tourists. If these are lost, cultural tourism will not be successful in the area. Tourism helps justify their conservation. In some places, tourism can be the impetus for revitalising cultural patterns which might be disappearing.

- Helps develop and maintain museums, theatres and other cultural facilities. Many are, in part, supported by tourism but are also enjoyed by residents. Many major museums and theatres in the world receive much financial support from the admission fees paid by tourists.

- Reinforces or even renews a sense of pride by residents in their culture, when they observe tourists appreciating it. This is especially true of some traditional societies which are undergoing rapid change and losing their sense of cultural self-confidence.

- Provides the opportunity for cross-cultural exchange between tourists and residents who learn about, and come to respect, one another's cultures. This exchange can best be achieved through certain forms of tourism—educational and other types of special interest tours; village tourism; and home visit programmes whereby tourists can arrange to visit local families.

Tourism can generate some socio-cultural problems if not well planned, developed and managed. A common problem is overcrowding by tourists and loss of convenience for residents, which leads to their resentment and sense of hostility toward tourism. If there are too many tourists in an area—which can happen particularly at peak season periods—attraction and features, and restaurant, shopping and transportation facilities can become so overcrowded by tourists that residents cannot easily use them. If residents are completely prohibited from access to amenity features such as hotel beaches, they may become even more resentful. Large numbers of tourists can be especially disruptive in small rural communities. Resentment particularly arise if residents perceive that they are not receiving many economic benefits from tourism, and that tourism development is controlled by outside interests.

Some problems can lead to cultural degradation and lessening of a sense of cultural identity. Deterioration of important archaeological and historic sites can result from overuse by tourists. There can be excessive commercialization and loss of authenticity of local customs, ceremonies, music, dance, crafts and other cultural patterns when these are inappropriately presented as tourist attractions. There can be a 'demonstration effect' of residents, especially young people, imitating the behavioural patterns and dress of tourists. This is done without understanding the different cultural backgrounds and socio-economic status of the tourists. Also, misunderstandings and conflicts may arise between tourists and residents because of different languages and customs.

Social problems of drug abuse, alcoholism, crime and prostitution may be worsened by tourism. The research conducted on these problems indicates that tourism is seldom their basic cause, but it may provide the opportunity to expand them.

Socio-cultural Problems

Some of the general policies that are applicable to economic and environmental considerations are also appropriate for socio-cultural reasons. An important general policy is to develop tourism on a gradual basis so that the society has time to adapt to it, be educated about it, and learn how to participate in its benefits. This approach also gives the government sufficient time to monitor the socio-cultural impacts of tourism, and remedy any problems before they become serious. As has been emphasised, residents should be involved in the planning and development process of tourism so that they can influence its decision-making and feel that they are part of tourism. Suitable forms of tourism must be selected that are compatible with the local societies. Also, selective marketing can attract the types of tourists who will respect the local social customs and cultural traditions.

As a policy, deliberate use of tourism as a technique of cultural conservation can greatly help in reducing its negative impacts on the culture. At the same time, many societies want to experience some positive change and participate in the benefits of modern development. The approach that they often wish to take is to be culturally selective. They want to keep the best of their traditions that give them a distinctive cultural character, but adopt the best of the changes that will make their lives more comfortable and interesting. Each society must decide on what approach is most suitable for their people when making choices about their tourism development patterns.

Several more specific socio-cultural impact control measures can be applied in tourism areas. These include the following:

- Maintain the authenticity of local dance, music, drama, arts, crafts and dress, even though they are somewhat adapted for presentation to tourists. This may require special training programmes being organised and quality controls being applied. However, certain types of ceremonies and rituals such as religious ones should not be modified for tourism, and tourist viewing of them must be carefully controlled.

- Preserve existing distinctive local architectural styles and encourage new development, including tourist facilities, to use local architectural motifs.

- Make certain that residents have convenient access to tourist attractions, amenity features and other facilities, and apply visitor control measures to prevent overcrowding.

- If residents cannot afford to use existing commercial tourist facilities, provide inexpensive or subsidized facilities for them to use. It is also common practice to allow residents to pay lower admission fees to attraction features than those paid by foreign tourists.

- Educate residents about tourism— its concepts, benefits and problems, the local tourism development policy and programme, how they can personally participate in tourism, and the social patterns of tourists visiting the area. Public awareness programmes about tourism can be organised, utilising radio, television, newspapers, magazines and public meetings. Education about tourism should be included in the public and private school system.

- Inform tourists about the local society—its customs, dress codes, acceptable behaviour in religious and other places, courtesies to observe in taking photographs, tipping policies, and any local problems such as crime. If tourists understand these matters, they will be more likely to respect them.
- Train employees to work in tourism effectively, including language and social sensitivity training where needed. In addition to providing better services, this will reduce any possible misunderstandings between tourists and employees.
- Apply strict controls on drugs, crime and prostitution if these are considered to be problems in the tourism areas.

Other types of controls may be appropriate in particular tourism areas.

Environmental Impact Assessment

Application of the environmental planning approach and incorporation of environmental protection measures into the planning process will prevent many environmental problems from arising. However, it is still important that an environmental impact assessment (EIA) be carried out for each specific tourism development project (as well as for all types of major projects). This procedure ensures that specific projects will not generate any serious environmental problems. If it appears that a proposed project will cause problems, then it should not be approved unless it is modified to be made acceptable. The EIA procedure is established at the national and regional levels. Many countries have adopted environmental protection legislation and the EIA procedure, but others have not yet done so.

The EIA should include all types of impacts—environmental, economic and socio-cultural. Even though a project may generate substantial economic benefits, for example, it may result in unacceptable environmental or social problems. It should not, therefore, be approved without modifications.

Tourism has become a high-profile activity in a number of economies. Increasingly, policy-makers and planners are turning to tourism development as a mechanism to restructure economies or to generate jobs. Such policies are found worldwide and are variable in their achievement of objectives. Tourism developments are accompanied by positive and negative effects, both economic and environ-mental. While the procedures for assessing economic costs and benefits are relatively well known, the potential environmental costs and benefits of tourism developments have tended to be left out of the appraisal of tourism projects, policies and programmes.

This chapter reviews the previous research concerned with tourism and the environment, particularly that relating to environmental impacts. It emphasizes the importance of the environment as a tourism resource before going on to discuss the importance of, and methodological issues raised by the assessment of environmental impacts. The chapter concludes with a discussion of the application of the Delphi technique to environmental impact assessment.

Tourism and the Environment—The Literature on Impacts

The growing volume of literature on the environmental impacts of tourism emphasizes the importance of the environment to the encouragement and development of tourist activity (Latimer, 1985). Equally it expresses concern about the potential adverse effects of tourism on the environment (Edington and Edington, 1986). The environment is a key tourism resource and consequently its conservation and management are vital both to the future of the tourism industry and to society as a whole.

Generally, research in this area is still relatively immature. The subject area concerned with the assessment of the environmental effects of development is characterised by a potentially extremely complex set of impact interactions. Mainly because of this complexity and the relative immaturity of the discipline, the research literature is fragmentary. Work has tended to concentrate on the classification of impacts, taking the form of either detailed studies of selected impacts or more general broadly based work (see, for example, Bodowski, 1976; Cohen, 1978; Krol, 1986). Case studies are a common feature of the literature, in which island ecosystems and new tourist areas are the centre of interest (Camhis, 1980; Pluss, 1987). Contributions have originated from a number of disciplinary perspectives, including ecological, geographic and socio-environmental, but there has been little evidence of the emergence of a true multi-disciplinary perspective.

The literature has concentrated largely on the negative impacts of tourism development and the potentially destructive force which poorly managed tourism developments can create. The improvements and environmental benefits that tourism can bring have largely been ignored (Hall, 1974; Haulot, 1985). This focus on negative impacts is closely linked to the environments that have received the most attention. Studies of environmental impact have been almost exclusively concerned with rural areas and in particular natural or semi-natural ecosystems (Hall, 1974; Cook and Wells, 1983; Dupuy, 1987).

This concern may reflect the fact that the impacts of tourist activity on the natural environment—footpath erosion and fire damage, for example—are often easily seen, and specific impacts are more easily measured. It may also reflect the greater importance placed on the natural environment, its vulnerability and need for protection (Pivert, 1987). Where discussion is directed to urban areas, it is often superficial and descriptive in nature and frequently avoids the issue of assessment. The urban literature does, however, recognise the potential benefits of tourism (Beioley, 1981; McNulty, 1985). The urban environment, its improvement and maintenance, has been the concern of recent work. Tiard (1987), for example, describes the positive impacts of tourism on buildings in Norway.

It is only in the consideration of adverse impacts of tourism in rural areas that serious attention has been given to the methodological issues of conceptualisation and measurement. Much of the work, however, has consisted of detailed measurement of very specific impacts, with little attempt to orientate the results in a form useful to policy-makers (Green et al., 1990).

More recently, there has been explicit discussion of the importance of the environment as a tourism resource and the need to consider the sustainability of that resource

(Papadopoulas, 1987). These issues have been developed by Romeril (1989), who argues that it is imperative to reconcile the need for an enduring and sustainable environmental tourism resource with a continuing pursuit of social and economic goals. As the tourist becomes more discri-minating and has a greater awareness of the impact of tourism in the physical and aesthetic environment, environ-mental management and careful design will be key attributes of successful projects (McNeely and Thorsell, 1989).

In a discussion of the importance of maintaining a high-quality environment in sustaining tourism activity it is appropriate to consider 'thresholds' of tourism activity. A given environmental impact (or combination of impacts) can be tolerated up to a point beyond which the environmental resource (e.g. clean bathing water) ceases to be a positive attraction and the tourism activity that relies on it has to substitute other resources or decline. Tourism development on the North Sea coast in the UK, for example, places great pressure on sewage treatment infrastructure, with the result that, in some cases, raw (or only slightly treated) sewage is discharged directly into the sea. However, the sea is a significant tourism resource, being used for swimming, paddling, boating and as a source of aesthetic pleasure. Increasing sewage pollution progressively decreases the attraction of the sea to tourists, either through a decline in the sea's aesthetic attraction or through the public's perception of an increased health risk. Ultimately, pollution levels may reach a threshold of acceptability (e.g. by contravening water quality standards), access to the sea is withdrawn and the resource is no longer available.

What is Meant by Environment?

As noted earlier, recent work on the environmental impact of tourism has been relatively unstructured and unquantitative. It does, however, provide a typology for the 'classification' of environment, which is a necessary precursor for a more systematic and comprehensive assessment of potential impacts. If the maintenance or enhancement of environment quality is to become a major element of tourism impact assessments, such a typology and structure is vital.

The literature suggests that a holistic approach to the definition of environment is necessary for a full appreciation of the complete range of potential impacts that may result from development projects or policies (e.g. OECD, 1991). However, for the sake of convenience, and to aid the discussion and understanding of potential impacts, the environment is often conceptualised as being composed of three components: natural, built and cultural environments (OECD, 1981). Although here defined as three discrete elements, the three components are interrelated and there will be cross-component effects associated with tourism developments.

The natural environment is perhaps the best documented and the component on which tourism impact research has concentrated. The natural environment may be seen to include air, land, clear light, climate, flora and fauna. The built environment encompasses the urban fabric, infrastructure, open space and elements of townscape. The cultural environment forms the third element of the typology. It is an area that has received increasing research attention during the 1980s, as the importance of culture as a tourism resource and the impact of tourism developments on culture become recognised (Meyer, 1988; Garrison, 1989). The cultural environment includes the values, beliefs, behaviours, morals, arts, law and history of communities. The cultural environment will include 'high' culture, such as opera and ballet, and popular culture, including elements such as folk, popular, contemporary and native expression, including folk music and craft work (OECD, 1981).

Although this typology is a useful starting point for a structured approach to recognising and assessing potential tourism impacts, it is only a rudimentary initial framework. It is limited to the consideration of potential impacts on the natural and built environments. However, it must be emphasised that the notion of environmental impact is of equal relevance in the cultural environment. Although it is possiby more difficult to isolate in causal terms because of more general influences, such as mass communications, it is important to realise the potential that exists for tourism developments to impact both positively and negatively on the resource of the cultural environment.

Assessing Impacts

Having introduced the importance of taking environmental considerations into account in the development of tourism projects and policies, we can raise an intriguing question: how can the potential environmental impacts of tourism be assessed and included in a project 'balance sheet', in order to prevent unacceptable environmental degradation and, indeed, to maximise the potential benefits of tourism? The short, and partial, answer to this question is that some form of environmental impact assessment (EIA) should be carried out before the commencement of a tourism project. It should be noted that the great majority of work on the assessment of environmental impacts of development has generally been concentrated at the level of the individual project, whether for tourism or other types of development (Wathern, 1988). However, an EIA can be applied to the assessment of different, area-based policies, plans or strategies (Wood, 1988).

What is EIA?

EIA has been described as the embodiment of the preventive or precautionary approach to environmental management (Haigh, 1984), and is one manifestation of the much quoted and lauded 'prevention is better than cur' principle so prevalent in environmental policy documents (see, for example, Haigh, 1984: OECD, 1991). Recently, EIA has been defined as:

> A process for identifying the likely consequences for the bio-geophysical environment and for man's health and welfare of implementing particular activities and for conveying this information, at a stage when it can materially affect their decision, to those responsible for sanctioning the proposals. (Wathern, 1988, p. 17).

It is apparent from this widely accepted definition that the primary concern of EIA is with potential impacts on the biological and physical components of the *natural* environment. Although some researchers argue for the extension of this definition to encompass potential socio-economic impacts (e.g. Davies and Muller, 1983), it is clear that EIA, as implemented, has largely remained 'loyal to its roots'. EIA has its origins in the USA, where it formed (initially a very small) part of the cost-benefit analysis procedures of the early 1960s. Its primary function then, as now, was to indicate the impacts whose significance could not be measured in monetary terms. While some socio-economic impact data are usually included in EIA, as developers are often very keen to stress aspects such as job creation and the possible upgrading of infrastructure under the guise of human welfare, and the more comprehensive cost-benefit analyses often include some information on environmental 'unquantifiables' (Wathern, 1988), the approach is still very far from the situation where environmental and socio-economic analyses are fully integrated into project appraisal. In this respect, the work of Nijkamp (1980) may provide the basis for much-needed research.

Potential Benefits of EIA for the Developer

Apart from indirect potential benefits associated with being seen to be 'environment friendly' by an increasingly sophisticated and environmentally aware public, there are a number of direct benefits that may accrue from the full integration of EIA into the project formulation process. It has been suggested that the inclusion of EIA at the earliest possible stage in project formulation results in a number of potential benefits, including: more effective compliance with environmental standards; improvements in the design and siting of plant; savings in capital and operating costs; spedieer approval of development applications; and the avoidance of costly adaptations to plants once in operation (Cook, 1979; Dean, 1979; Canter, 1983; Lee, 1988). Htun (1988, p. 225) suggests that:

> The concept that the environment and development can be mutually enhancing and do not inherently conflict is beginning to gain ground. In this context, the EIA process is seen as a means not only of identifying potential impacts, but also of enabling the integration of the environment and development.

Tourism Projects and EIA

A high quality environment is often the key tourism resource. Tourism projects are almost unique in their unusually close relationship with, and dependency on, the quality of the environment. EIA, if used properly, could help to avoid a situation of unfulfilled potential, or even collapse, of a tourism development owing to unforeseen environmental degradation. The remainder of this chapter is devoted to the description and discussion of the Delphi technique, which, if used properly, offers a progressive and very cost-effective way of assessing and anticipating environmental change resulting from tourism investment.

EIA Techniques

If the use of EIA is to be encouraged for tourism projects, an environmental impact assessment technique that fulfils a number of criteria must be found. Although many tourism projects have the potential to generate significant and wide-ranging environmental impacts, they are often relatively small scale and lack the financial resources of large infrastructure or industrial developments. It is critical, therefore, that a cost-effective and efficient EIA technique is used to assess potential environ-mental impacts. Much of the cost of an EIA is normally taken up with the collection and analysis of large quantities of 'hard' environmental data. A technique should be used which rapidly identifies the potential impacts that are going to be significant before the collection of 'hard' environmental data begins. The resources available for the EIA can then be better targeted on the potential impacts causing the greatest concern. The early identification of significant potential impacts is known as 'scoping', and the Delphi technique is well suited to this process. Additionally, the EIA technique should be capable of assessing both positive and negative potential environmental impacts, across both the built and natural environments. Furthermore, in order to ensure that the findings of the EIA are of maximum benefit to policy-makers and decision-takers, the EIA technique should include an element of subjective assessment of potential impacts by the local community.

The above requirements suggest the use of judgemental techniques. These techniques avoid the collection of 'hard' environmental data, can be tailored to indicate the relative importance of potential impacts using a dimensionless measure of significance (a score which can be either positive or negative) and are flexible in terms of the range and type of opinion sought on a particular matter (e.g. judgements can be sought from local residents, as well as from recognised environmental specialists). The Delphi technique is a well established judgemental technique used as a means of collecting expert or informed opinion and of working towards consensus between experts on a given issue. Linstone and Turoff (1975, p.3) have defined Delphi as: 'A method of structuring a group communication process so that the process is effective in allowing a group of individuals as a whole to deal with a complex problem.'

The Delphi technique achieves this goal by allowing a group of individuals to approach a consensus of opinion on the problem under consideration, without actually meeting face to face. This gives the Delphi technique two major advantages over other means of obtaining expert opinion. Firstly, the expert opinion expressed stems from the individual, not from a group of individuals in constant contact with each other, where peer pressure and the desire to conform may greatly alter any views expressed. Secondly, because the Delphi technique provides anonymity, more candid responses can be expected from the experts involved (a less personal, more corporate opinion may be given if responses are publicly attributed to the individual, as is often the case in a conference situation).

Any Delphi study falls into three distinct stages:

1. The preliminary questionnaire asks the experts to identify what they feel to be the most important considerations associated with the issue in question.

2. A second questionnaire is compiled based on the issues identified by the preliminary stage. This is the first-round questionnaire, which is circulated to the experts, who are asked to indicate which issues identified in the preliminary stage they feel to be most important. It may be necessary to enlarge this questionnaire, basing additions on information gained from the literature or other sources.

3. The second-round questionnaire is essentially the same as the first-round, except that it includes a feedback element in which experts are asked to modify their opinion if they so wish in the light of the overall expert response to the first round. The feedback element is designed to move the experts towards consensus.

Questionnaire rounds can be repeated as many times as is thought necessary until a sufficient level of consensus is reached. Each new questionnaire round will include the overall expert response to the previous round. The remainder of this chapter reports the findings of a Delphi study, the objective of which was to identify the potential major environmental impacts associated with the redevelopment of Salts mill, in Saltaire near Bradford, for tourism. This is not the first time that Delphi has made a contribution to EIA (see, for example, Richey et al., 1985), but this is the first time that Delphi has been used to identify environmental impact in both the natural and built environments.

The Salts Mill Redevelopment Project

The mill complex is situated on the north-east side of Bradford Metropolitan District's built-up area, half a mile from Shipley town centre. Illingworth Morris plc ceased all operations in the mill complex in 1986, after 130 years of textile manufacturing on the site. The mill was purchased in 1987 by Salts Estates Limited, a private concern which proposed to redevelop and reorientate the mill towards a visitor market. The Salts Mill site is being turned into a major tourist attraction, potentially generating identifiable environmental impacts, both positive and negative. A gallery has already been opened and is currently attracting 3,000 visitors per week, on average (Green et al., 1990). This seems a good indication of the potential overall economic success of the project.

Panel Selection

Panel size is a key issue in any Delphi study. Successful Delphi studies have been carried out in the past using only 20 initial respondents (Masser and Foley, 1987). In this case, it was decided to use 40 panel members to compensate for some expected initial non-response to the first-round Delphi questionnaire and for panel members dropping out between rounds. For the preliminary stage of the study a panel of 40 was seen as sufficient to obtain a balanced and broad cross-section of opinion on the environmental implications of the Salts Mill redevelopment proposals.

It was seen as important that the Delphi panel should include people with a working knowledge of the project, such as planners, tourism officers and economic development unit personnel. However, to achieve a better balance, the definition of expert was broadened to include residents and traders (local experts) living and operating in Saltair Village. This ensured that all interested parties could be involved and a wide range of opinion incorporated into the study.

Implementation

The panel was assembled following door-to-door visits in the case of residents and traders, and as a result of telephone calls to targeted individuals. Many of the latter group were employees of Bradford City Council. It consisted of three local planners, working out of both Shipley Town Hall and Jacobs Well in Bradford city centre, and personnel working within Bradford's Economic Development Unit, including an economic development officer, a land evaluation officer and a tourism officer. Other employees of the City Council were the conservation officer, two local civil engineers and two environmental health officers. The panel also included three local councillors, the political representatives for the Saltaire area. An employee from the British Waterways Board was included on the panel because of the proximity of Salts Mill to the Leeds–Liverpool Canal. Two academics (both environmental scientists), and three individuals directly involved with the Salts Mill redevelopment scheme were also included. The remaining 20 places on the panel were shared equally between residents and traders in the Saltaire area.

As already mentioned, the preliminary stage of the study involved the use of a general questionnaire, which introduced the study, and asked each panel member simply to state what he or she felt to be the main impacts, both positive and negative, of the Salts Mill redevelopment project. The use of this general questionnaire ensured that any potential environmental impacts which had not already been envisaged by the team could be incorporated into the first-round questionnaire.

After completion of the preliminary stage the first-round postal questionnaire was drawn up. The basis for this questionnaire was the extensive checklist of potential impacts stemming from tourism, supplemented by new impacts identified from the preliminary stage. The latter, however, identified only a small number of the more obvious potential impacts in this case and did not bring to light any information that had not already been considered as a result of the literature search.

The first-round questionnaire thus consisted of a comprehensive list of potential impacts on the natural and built environments. For each aspect of the environment panel members were asked to:

1. Indicate whether or not they felt that the redevelopment of Salts Mill would have a significant impact on the environmental aspect under consideration. If the panel member decided that the impact was not significant, then he or she could proceed to the next potential impact. A score of zero was recorded against each such response when questionnaires were analysed.
2. State whether the nature of this impact was positive or negative (i.e. beneficial or detrimental to the environment).
3. Rate the significance of the impact on a scale of one to seven.

Once the first round had been completed and the questionnaires analysed, the second-round questionnaires were despatched. The aim of the second round was to encourage the panel towards a greater degree of consensus. A feedback element was included next to each potential impact. Each panel member received a second-round questionnaire which showed the overall mean score found for each potential impact after the first round, alongside the score that he or she gave in the first round. Panel members were then asked if they would like to modify their initial response in the light of this information.

Study

Of the 40 first-round questionnaires, 28 were returned fully completed, with a further three returned only partially answered. At the end of the second round, 21 questionnaires had been returned, giving an overall drop-out rate of nearly 50 per cent. This shows the aggregate responses to each of the individual environmental impacts listed on the Delphi questionnaire sent out to the panel members. For the sake of brevity, only the ten most significant impacts identified by the Delphi study. The decision to give an analysis and comment on only the ten most significant impacts is arbitrary, but also reflected the very low overall scores for the remaining aspects of the environment of Saltaire.

The impacts identified by the study showed a marked tendency towards the built environment. In both rounds, the reuse of disused buildings and the restoration and preservation of historic sites and buildings were identified as the most significant potential impacts. Roads and car parking were identified as being important issues (ranked 3 and 5 respectively in the final results). There was some degree of disagreement between panel members as to the nature of the impact on infrastructure. It is probable that those panel members who thought that the redevelopment of the mill would have a negative impact on infrastructure (as a result of traffic congestion), were unaware of the proposed improvements, which included a new access road linking the mill to Otley Road, a new bridge over the canal and the development of vacant land to provide car parking for 1,180 cars. This issue of information levels among panel members should be addressed in future Delphi studies.

An increase in retailing within the area (ranked 4 in the final results) was identified as major potential impact of the mill redevelopment, as traders take advantage of the influx of tourists into the Saltaire area. The fact that retailing was seen to be such a significant positive impact may have been a reflection of the number of retailers included on the panel. If slightly fewer retailers had been included, opinion may have been more evenly split as to the nature of the impact. It could be argued that an increase in the number and size of retail outlets is not always a positive impact as the new shops may be oriented towards the visitor and not the local market. The question of panel composition is an area that should be addressed by future work on the application of Delphi to EIA.

The panel felt that the redevelopment of Salts Mill would generally cause beneficial environmental effects within its surrounding area. However, two negative potential impacts were identified, the first being litter and the second being noise generated by the visitors and their vehicles (ranked 6 and 7 respectively in the final results). Identifying these two negative impacts early on in the life cycle of the project eases the implementation of counter measures. As a condition of allowing the development to proceed the policy-maker could ensure that the problem of litter was partly or entirely met out of profits generated by the facility.

Identifying the potential negative impact of litter gives the policy-maker a clear indication of an area that may have to be subject to detailed monitoring in the future to ensure that the impact stays below acceptable levels. Similarly, the Delphi study indicated that noise pollution should be a topic for scientific, quantitative analysis and evaluation in the subsequent stages of any EIA investigation.

Review

The results above indicate that the Delphi technique, as applied in the Salts Mill study, offers a relatively quick and cost-effective means of identifying potentially significant impacts associated with tourism development projects. It is capable of identifying potential impacts across the natural and built environments, whether these are positive or negative and provides for local community involvement and the qualitative assessment of impact magnitude. The results are in a form that is useful to policy-makers interested in weighing up the environmental costs and benefits of a tourism project alongside economic costs and benefits

Tourism Impact Assessment

of a tourism project alongside economic costs and benefits. The results would also enable the developer to concentrate resources efficiently on only those potential impacts identified as being significant, in subsequent stages of the EIA process. Furthermore, the information provided by a Delphi study can be used, at a very early stage, by the developer and policy-maker to minimise adverse environmental impacts and thus to achieve a tourism development that is sustainable in the long term.

Future research on the application of the Delphi technique should investigate the influence of panel composition and size on results, particularly the balance between experts with a working knowledge of the project and those with good knowledge of the area in which the project is located. It should also be possible to provide each panel member with a more detailed description of the project and associated attributes (e.g. changes to infrastructure provisions in the local area) to enable more informed judgements to be made concerning the environmental implications of the project. There is also the possibility of widening the Delphi questionnaire to include the explicit consideration of potential cultural and economic impacts, thus allowing all aspects of the effect of a project on 'quality of life' to be recognised and assessed.

Although this discussion has concentrated on the application of EIA generally and the Delphi technique specifically at the level of the individual tourism project, there is great scope for the use of EIA in the assessment of area-based tourism programmes and policies. An approach based on the Delphi technique for such assessments would appear to be of particular potential benefit, given Delphi's ability to assess alternatives without large inputs of 'hard' environmental data. Finally, it should be stressed that community involvement in the EIA process should not begin and end with a Delphi study. The results of the Delphi stage, and the subsequent stages of the EIA process, should be made public via, for example, a mediated public meeting. In this respect, significant advances are being made in the USA, Canada and the Netherlands, and continued research is needed in the UK to allow for a greater involvement of the local community in EIA.

Findings

The quality of the environment is a key tourism resource. No matter what the short- or medium-term economic benefits of tourism development appear to be, tourism cannot be sustained at the optimal level if the environmental resource base is degraded beyond a threshold capacity. An understanding of the potentially very complex relationship between tourism development and the maintenance of environmental quality (itself a multi-faceted concept) is crucial to the success of tourism projects, programmes and policies.

It must be recognised that tourism can have profound impacts (both positive and negative) on many aspects of the environment and future research should address the need for a more holistic and systematic approach to the identification and assessment of potential environmental and economic impacts. Tourism projects should be subject to EIA in order to ensure that, in the interests of their long-term success, they do not cause unforeseen and unacceptable environmental degradation.

It is very important that EIA procedures and methods are made as efficient as possible, and as useful as possible to policy-makers. This will involve continued research into 'scoping' techniques for rapid critical appraisal, the use of qualitative judgements by the local community and the integration of economic and environmental considerations, among other issues. The Delphi technique has much to offer in overcoming some of the problems currently associated with EIA, whether at the scale of the individual project or in the appraisal of area-based tourism policies.

4. Geography and Tourism Management

TOURISM CAN be considered at different scales. In this chapter broad global patterns are first identified then attention focuses on the nature and extent of international circuit tourism and the spatial evolution of flows from the world's four leading markets. At all scales, however, analysis is limited and complicated by the data available. Major data sources are therefore reviewed at the outset with more specific types of statistics being considered in subsequent sections.

Data Sources

It is important to recall that what constitutes international tourism is movement across international frontiers while domestic tourism concerns travel within national boundaries. This distinction may be especially significant at a national level, for example in terms of foreign exchange earnings, social impact and immigration control. Clearly too, the fact of being in a foreign country may add something to the appeal of the trip for the individuals concerned, with the differences in culture, customs and so on being a major attraction for many tourists, especially the wanderlust travellers. In such cases, international tourism constitutes a particular form of tourism and the distinction made by official statistics between international and domestic tourists is an especially useful one. In other instances, as with much sunlust tourism, the reason for and nature of the holiday may be essentially the same whether it involves a German travelling to the Mediterranean coast of France (international tourism) or a New Yorker holidaying in Florida (domestic tourism). With this type of tourism, the distinction between domestic and international tourist flows is perhaps more official than functional. Whatever the nature of the travel, greater distances will in fact be covered by many domestic vacationers in the United States and other large countries such as Canada and Australia than international travellers in Europe. In 1990 the average round trip distance covered by domestic travellers in the United States (on trips of 100 miles or more) was 839 miles (Waters 1992).

The most comprehensive body of international tourism statistics readily available is that published annually by the World Tourism Organization (WTO) in their series World Tourism Statistics. Other international organizations such as the Pacific Asia Travel Association (PATA) and the Organization for Economic Cooperation and Development (OECD) also collate and publish statistics concerning tourism in their member countries. In their series the WTO, an intergovernmental organization, compiles and distributes travel statistics furnished by members and some non-member states. While the WTO provides technical guidelines for the collection of these statistics in an attempt to provide internationally uniform and accurate figures (WTO 1978, 1981), it remains dependent on the respective national tourist organizations, immigration or statistics departments for the nature and quality of the data received. These bodies collect travel data in a variety of ways and for a range of purposes. Consequently the type of information and its reliability varies considerably from country to country. Researchers must therefore view the published data carefully, particularly when making comparisons among countries.

Travel statistics worldwide are most frequently expressed in terms of 'frontier arrivals', that is the number of visitors entering a country as determined by some form of frontier check and irrespective of purpose of visit and length of stay; excursionists, that is visitors staying less than 24 hours, are usually included. 'Tourist arrivals' refer to visitors staying at least this minimum length of time. Where the majority of arrivals are, by air through a limited number of points of entry, as is the case for example in island states such as Japan, Australia and New Zealand, then the degree of control is usually very high and most related statistics can normally be considered reliable. Where immigration procedures require the completion of an arrival/departure (A/D) card, a range of information is usually obtained including, for example, details on nationality, age, occupation, purpose of visit (however defined) and intended length of stay. In other instances, where there is a large volume of traffic arriving overland through a number of entry points, as is the case in much of Europe, the degree of control is much less and some form of estimate may be used. Not all countries require the completion of an A/D card and, in these cases, periodic surveys may be employed to provide additional information.

A second common source of international travel statistics is that based on accommodation returns. Many countries require international visitors to complete registration cards in hotels and other forms of accommodation, which are then collated and analysed. A number of problems arise here, not the least of which is that the cards are often associated with some form of taxation so that a degree of underestimation might be expected. Conversely, visitors moving around the country would be recorded more than once, thus inflating the figures. Visitors staying in any form of non-commercial accommodation would not be recorded at all.

The WTO statistics do not usually take into account purpose of visit as all foreigners are usually recorded under 'frontier arrivals' and no distinctions are made in the accommodation figures. International comparisons are therefore limited essentially to studies of 'all travellers'. The originating national body, however, usually does provide some breakdown, for instance into 'holiday and vacation', 'business', 'visiting friends and relations (VFR)', 'education', 'sport' and so on. A more detailed study by the WTO of variations in purpose of visit by major regions in 1979 showed vacation travel accounted for almost three-quarters of all international movements. Only in the Middle East, where a large pilgrimage traffic was included in the 'other' category and where business traffic is more significant, did holidaymakers account for less than a half of all visits. The composition of visitors to particular countries within these regions may, of course, vary significantly from the regional average. Where possible, differences in the spatial behaviour of particular types of visitors should be taken into account.

Geographic analyses in particular are often complicated or handicapped by the combination of markets in published statistics. The degree of aggregation usually depends on the markets' importance at a given destination. In most European countries, other countries from within Europe are listed separately; in more distant destinations, such as much of the Pacific, they are commonly listed together under 'Europe'. Conversely, New Zealanders and Australians, who constitute major markets in the Pacific, appear separately in Pacific statistics but are frequently lumped under 'the rest of the world' as far as many European statistics are concerned. This clearly limits wide-ranging and detailed international analyses. The varying use of 'country of residence' and 'nationality' further complicates geographical and marketing analyses.

Figures on outbound travel are subject to many of the same limitations as the arrivals statistics but pose particular problems when attempts are made to disaggregate the destinations involved. Most countries routinely collect information on only one destination, usually the main one, the one in which the most time was spent or the last country visited. Where multi-destination travel is involved significant underestimates in country to country travel may result with a consequent lack of correspondence between the figures reported by the origin and destination countries. These and other technical considerations are usefully reviewed in greater length by Edwards (1991) and Dann (1993).

Consideration must also be given to what it is that is being measured. Absolute number of travellers, even if they can be classified by purpose of visit, do not tell the whole story. Length of stay and expenditure are also decisive factors in determining the impact of markets on particular destinations. When demand is measured in terms of person nights and total expenditure rather than arrivals, the Australian share of international tourism to New Zealand in 1989 falls from just under one-third to around one-quarter. Conversely, the high daily expenditure of the Japanese (NZ$384 per day compared to the overall average of NZ$95) means that their contribution to total expenditure is much greater than their share of arrivals, while their percentage share is much less due to their shorter visits to New Zealand. Variations on these three measures are less pronounced for the American market, while the British are notable for their increased share of total person nights resulting from a much longer stay (Pearce 1990a).

Care must therefore be exercised in the analysis and interpretation of international visitor statistics, particularly when different sources or data from different years are being used. In many cases the resultant patterns will be indicative rather than definitive but these too can provide important insights into global patterns of international tourism.

Patterns

The major generating and receiving countries, provide a useful starting-point for trying to order international tourist flows throughout the world.

Given the limitations in recording outbound flows noted above, the World Tourist Organization now depicts major markets in terms of expenditure on international tourism rather than departures. Over half of all international tourism expenditure in 1992 was generated by just five countries, in order: the USA, Germany, Japan, the United

Kingdom and Italy. Japan's third ranking is in large part a function of heavy expenditure per tourist rather than the absolute number of departures (11 million in 1990). The leading fifteen world spenders accounted for 80 per cent of expenditure worldwide; all but two of these countries (Japan and Taiwan) are located in Europe or North America.

In terms of destinations, international tourism, whether measured by arrivals or receipts, exhibits a slightly more dispersed pattern, but one which remains nevertheless highly concentrated. That the fifteen leading destinations accounted for 69 per cent of arrivals and 74.3 per cent of expenditure worldwide. The top eight countries received over 50 per cent of arrivals; the first six accounted for over half of the receipts. The relative rankings of the leaders may change depending on the measure used: France and the USA alternate for first and second places and lower down the table, destinations come and go. Some, such as Hungary and former Czechoslovakia, receive large numbers of visitors who appear to spend relatively small amounts, others, such as Hong Kong and Singapore, attract smaller volumes of large spenders. Overall, the table reinforces the broader regional patterns namely the prominence of Europe and North America and the emergence of certain Asian destinations, while also highlighting the concentration in particular countries within these regions.

While the leading fifteen destinations' share of all tourist arrivals remained unchanged over the period 1985-92 (around 89 per cent), increased concentration occurred in terms of the leaders' share of worldwide receipt (relates to the income received by the receiving countries) (66.2 per cent in 1985; 74.3 percent in 1992) and expenditure (relates to the spending by the generating countries) (75.4 per cent to 79.9 per cent).

International tourist flows

The major international tourist markets and destinations throughout the world. A next step is to establish global patterns of flows between generating and receiving countries. This can be attempted using several different approaches.

The ten largest individual flows throughout the world using comparable, available WTO figures. That the single largest exchanges in the world occur across the Canadian-United States border, the flow from north to south being by far the greatest. With the exception of the Mexican flow into the United States, the other largest flows are between neighbouring countries in Europe, with Italy and France being the major recipients. The difficulties of recording accurately large volumes of traffic in these should be noted, nevertheless to provide a good indication of where the major flows do occur.

A more comprehensive global picture might be established by identifying dominant flows, that is first- and second-order flows, towards each destination throughout the world. These flows for each of the 134 destinations in 1990 for which appropriate data arc available from the WTO (some destinations had to be excluded as their major markets were not disaggregated to a country level).

On this basis, United States visitors are clearly the most dominant group, constituting the major market and generating first-order flows for 38 destinations, or one-quarter of those portrayed, while ranking second at a further 20 destinations. Three-quarters of the destinations where the United

States constitutes the leading market are found in the Americas, the inclusion of a number of small Caribbean states clearly affecting the overall importance of the country on this increase. At the same time, United States visitors generate first-order flows to a range of other destinations including the United Kingdom, Germany and Israel. In addition to generating the single largest flow—to the USA—Canada takes second place to its larger neighbour in half a dozen Caribbean destinations and is the dominant market for Cuba, from which Americans are excluded by their foreign policy.

Germany (12 first-order flows, 12 second-order flows), France (14,9) and the United Kingdom (5,12) constitute an important set of major European markets. Many of these flows are intra-European but longer-haul traffic is also evident, particularly to former colonies and overseas territories in the cases of France and the United Kingdom. Japan (7, 6), Australia (5, 4) and South Africa (4,1) and Argentina (4, 0), are the only other countries to constitute the dominant market for four or more destinations. Each of these constitutes a secondary regional source in Asia, the South Pacific and southern Africa and South America respectively, regions which are more remote from and thus less influenced by the major markets of the United States and Europe. Virtually all the other first-order flows are between pairs of neighbouring countries, for example Spain and Portugal, India and Bangladesh.

The overall impression to emerge from this brief examination of first- and second-order flows is thus one of comparatively short movement between countries in the same region of the globe. Distance clearly plays a major role in shaping international tourist flows. On top of this general pattern are superimposed some more selective longer-haul flows, particularly from the United States with its large and relatively affluent population. Africa stands out as a continent less frequented by American visitors but one where flows are influenced by former colonial ties and selective charter tourism from Western Europe.

Concentration ratios

Clearly an analysis of first- and second-order flows dues not bring out all the complexities of global patterns of tourist travel. It is important to note, however, that market-wise international tourist flows are more often highly concentrated than dispersed. A straightforward measure of concentration applied in the manufacturing industry, the concentration ratio, might usefully be employed here. In manufacturing, the concentration ratio simply expresses the share of any sector controlled by the largest few enterprises in that sector, for example by the top three (Ellis 1976), and is commonly measured in terms of gross output or employment. In the case of tourism, the concentration ratio might be used to express the percentage of a region's market, as measured by the number of visitors coming from say the three largest markets, or the percentage of the total number of visitors from one country who go to the three most favoured destinations. Calculation of such ratios is limited in some countries where the published data aggregate individual national markets into, for example, 'Europe' or 'Africa'.

The concen-tration ratios of 129 WTO destinations, the majority of which are based on tourist arrivals at frontiers for 1990, together with comparable data for 1979 where available. The general pattern is one of dependence on a small number of markets. In 1990 two-thirds of all the destinations derived half or more of their traffic from only three markets, while 45 per cent received 60 per cent or more of their visitors from just three countries. Some deconcentration occurred over the period shown; for the 102 destinations for which data were available in 1979 as well as 1990, three-quarters had a concentration ratio of 50 or more and 47 per cent of 60 or greater. However, little systematic variation could be found in these changes and only a weak relationship with absolute growth over the period existed.

In 1990, 11 destinations had a concentration ratio in excess of 90, most of which were Caribbean destinations heavily dependent on the United States markets. Other high-ranking destinations such as San Marino and Lesotho are small enclaves surrounded by their major markets. Top-ranked Mongolia is scarcely a major tourist destination (124,000 arrivals) but one which is located between two of the world's largest countries, China and Russia. At the other end of the scale, the 20 destinations having a concentration ratio of 40 or less, with the notable exception of Germany, are all developing countries, many of which have a small total volume of visitors. Overall, however, there is no correlation between the concentration ratio and the size of the tourist traffic.

Circuit Tourism

International tourism is not simply limited to travel between pairs of origins and markets. As shown in Thurot's model travel to one destination may be combined with visits to other destinations in what is variously known as circuit tourism or multi-destination travel. The essence of the concept was clearly outlined by Cullinan *et al.* (1977) in their Central American study, namely 'A circuit tour is a pleasure trip which includes two or more countries by a resident of a third country'. This basic concept has been expressed and measured in a variety of ways throughout the world, but in most of these instances the analysis involves all travellers not just those on a pleasure trip (Pearce 1994). Many countries, however, continue to record arrivals in isolation, taking account only of the part of any trip spent within their frontiers.

In French Polynesia a distinction is made between destination and circuit travel. Classification of visitors into these two categories is based on cross-tabulating ports of embarkation and disembarkation from arrival/departure (A/D) cards. Where the two are the same, then French Polynesia is considered to be a visitor's sole destination; where they differ, the territory is deemed to be visited as part of a larger circuit. This logic is not infallible but for most travellers the matching of ports of embarkation and disembarkation provides a reasonably reliable measure of circuit travel.

Tourist organizations in other countries, for example Hong Kong (Hong Kong Tourist Association 1993a) and Vanuatu (Tourism Council of the South Pacific 1989), use the term 'multi-destination travel'. In both cases the data are drawn from sample surveys of departing visitors. In the case of the annual Hong Kong survey, reference is to 'overnight destinations during current trip away from home'. In one of the few examples of this information being collected for outbound travellers the large (n = 40,000) inflight survey of United States travellers to overseas countries (Canada and Mexico excluded) seeks information on the number of countries visited (USTTA 1991).

Elsewhere the concept of stopovers is employed. In its international visitor survey the Australian Bureau of Tourism Research (1990) defines a stopover 'as a stay of one night or more on the way to or from Australia in any country including stopovers made in the visitor's country of residence'. By extension, when a stopover is made, circuit tourism or multi-destination travel would normally occur, though the inclusion of the possibility of stopping over in one's home country blurs the definition which Cullinan et al. presented. The term stopover is also used in Singapore but in absolute rather than relative terms as there 'A maximum length of stay of four days has been used as the cut-off point, to determine "stopover" traffic' (Singapore Tourist Promotion Board 1992). As such a definition fails to distinguish adequately between those visitors staying less than four days but on a single destination trip or five days or more when Singapore is still part of a longer itinerary, Singaporean stopovers cannot accurately reflect the extent of circuit tourism experienced by the state.

Leiper (1989) adopts a different approach, deriving a Main Destination Ratio. This he defines as 'the percentage of arrivals by tourists in a given place for whom that place is the main or sole destination in the current trip, to the total arrivals in that place'. The approach combines the use of several sets of official statistics, not only those on arrivals in the selected destinations but also departures from the markets. The latter are usually expressed in terms of the outgoing residents' 'main destination'. These figures are then expressed as a percentage of all arrivals from these markets recorded at the destination(s) analysed to give the Main Destination Ratio. This approach has the advantage of drawing on more commonly available data, thereby enhancing the scope for comparative studies—Leiper uses the examples of outbound travel from Australia, New Zealand and Japan. However, the, clear distinction between mono- and multi-destination travel is lost as 'main destinations' include both sole destinations and those which constitute the main but not exclusive object of a trip.

Crcuit tourism is not particularly pronounced in the world's largest outbound market. In 1990 three-quarters of United States travellers visited only one country on each trip overseas, only a small percentage of travellers visited three or more countries and the overall mean was just 1.4 countries per trip. Little variation occurred by type of traveller but the propensity to make multi-destination trips did differ by destination. Virtually all United States travellers to the Caribbean confined their visit to a single island. In contrast, the opening up of Central Europe appears to have occasioned more itinerant visits there, with a mean of 3.2 countries visited. Africa and the Middle East also generate higher than average multi-destination trips. The mean reported for Western Europe was 1.6 countries in 1990, compared to 1.9 in 1977 and 3.9 in 1967 (O'Hagan 1979).

Similar low values are recorded in Hong Kong, one of the few destinations which appears to collect such information. In 1992 visitors to Hong Kong stayed overnight in only two different international destinations, that is, on average they were visiting Hong Kong plus one other country. Visitors from the long-haul markets of North America, Europe and Austasia tended to combine a visit to Hong Kong with about two other countries, while Asians, particularly Japanese, averaged only one and a half countries per trip, including Hong Kong.

A basic measure of the extent of circuit tourism in four Asia Pacific destinations for which relatively comparable data were obtained (Pearce 1994). The overall proportion of circuit visitors ranged from about one-third in Vanuatu to just under two-thirds in Hong Kong. Part of the explanation for this variation appears to lie in the function of these four destinations. Hong Kong, as both a well-connected regional hub and a physically small destination with a limited range of attractions, relies primarily on circuit visitors. In contrast, the small South Pacific destinations of French Polynesia and Vanuatu are more isolated and have a 'sun-sand-sea' image that is perhaps more conducive to stay-put holidays. Between these lies Australia, a large destination with a diverse range of attractions which encourages single destination travel, but also a well-developed air network which facilitates circuit tourism. Distance and accessibility (the presence or absence of direct routes) also appear to play a role in influencing the proportion of circuit tourism at each destination generated from the different markets, though the number of destinations limits the generalizations which can be made. A tendency for higher levels of circuit tourism to be associated with long-haul travel (e.g. the North American and European ratios in the region) and destination tourism with short-haul direct travel (e.g. New Zealanders to Australia and French Polynesia, Australians to Vanuatu). Several interrelated factors may affect this pattern. Greater lengths of travel will increase not only the need for technical stopovers but also a desire to break one's journey and perhaps derive a better return on transport costs by combining visits to two or more destinations on the one trip. Japanese circuit tourism exhibits the opposite trend to that just outlined, a function perhaps of the generally shorter holidays taken by this market. That is, the more time spent travelling, the less desire there is to visit more than one destination. Given these variations, the market mix of any one destination will be a major determinant of the overall level of circuit travel experienced there—the large share of short-haul Australians, for example, depresses the total proportion of circuit tourism in Vanuatu.

By way of comparison, in 1992, 42 per cent of visitors to Great Britain from outside Western Europe reported their intent to combine a visit to Britain with at least one other European country (BTA/ETB 1992). The propensity to make a combined visit was highest among those from English-speaking countries outside North America, making relatively short stays (less than a week) on their first trip to Britain.

An indication of the relative importance of any destination on a circuit can be obtained by deriving the proportion of any trip spent there. This requires details not only on the length of stay in each destination but also the length of the total trip. While the former figures are readily available, not only from surveys but also A/D cards, the latter are recorded less often. The sort of results that can be obtained and the variations which may occur from segment to segment. Visitors to Hong Kong, for instance, were on average spending only one-fifth of their trip in that destination compared with around 70 per cent of those visiting the USA and Australia. Unfortunately the published tables do not enable separate values for circuit tourists alone to be established but such values do contribute to the identification of different countries' tourism functions, in particular the hub and staging post role of Hong Kong, and raise questions about the role of size and resources.

Other data from the Hong Kong survey enable aggregate patterns of the circuits incorporating the territory to be established. For the total vacation traffic passing through Hong Kong, China, Thailand and Singapore stand out as the three most important other nodes on the visitor circuit. However, significant variations occur from market to market, particularly between the long-haul markets. Hong Kong is clearly part of a broader Asian circuit for North American and European travellers, but Japan and Taiwan are linked more closely into the circuits of Americans than Europeans. Regional links, particularly with Singapore, are also part of Australasian travel through Hong Kong but the prominence of European destinations also points to its role as a midway stopover for through traffic between Australasian and Europe. This also occurs to a lesser extent with the European market, for whom some travel to or from Australia and New Zealand is recorded. For most Asian travellers, Hong Kong is part of a more restricted intra-regional circuit, incorporating in particular trips to China.

Route plan data from Fiji also highlight differences between short-haul intra-regional circuits and midpoint stopovers on longer end-to-end routes. These data, it should be noted, relate only to sectors directly linked to Fiji, that is the immediate flights into and out of Fiji, and thus do not provide coverage of the full circuits involved. The majority of New Zealand visits to Fiji consist of destination travel or circuits involving other Pacific destinations. Australia also follows this pattern. In contrast, less than one-fifth of American visits to Fiji involve mono-destination trips with the most popular circuits incorporating travel to and from the United States and either New Zealand or, to a lesser extent, Australia. European circuits show a broadly similar pattern to that of the Americans but visiting Fiji en route to or from Australia and New Zealand is also complemented by a greater amount of travel along circuits involving linkages elsewhere in the South Pacific.

The examples here tend to dispel the notion of globetrotting tourists 'collecting' countries as they flit from one destination to the next. This may be true of a small segment of the market but the overall pattern to emerge from this limited sample is one in which international tourist travel is characterized by a large proportion of single destination trips or of circuits limited to two or three countries. Little remains known about the motivations and preferences of circuit tourists and what distinguishes them from those who visit only one country. More work is required on these aspects along with extending the analyses discussed above to a wider range of markets and destinations.

Tourist Flows

The evolutionary models suggest that the volume of traffic to more distant destinations will increase over time and that the character of the tourists visiting given destinations will also change. Few attempts have been made, however, to verify these trends through empirical analysis. The studies that do exist generally focus on one country, with the evolution in outbound travel being but one component of the markets reviewed (e.g. Schnell 1988; Cook 1989). A more systematic approach is attempted here in which the spatial evolution of the world's four largest outbound markets is analysed with the aim of deriving some general observations. Data on the four markets - the United States, Germany, the United Kingdom and Japan—are not strictly comparable as they are drawn from different sources, they are based on different definitions and they are presented in varying degrees of geographical detail. Nevertheless, using a common approach - spatial variations in market share - it is possible to draw out some common trends.

Good longitudinal 'data on the leading European markets—Germany and the United Kingdom—are provided by two longstanding surveys, respectively the Reiseanalyse of German households undertaken by the Studienkreis fur Tourismus (Dundler 1988; Gilbrich 1991) and the British International Passenger Survey (BTA 1989). The results of the German surveys refer to main holidays abroad (five nights or more) while the British findings are more comprehensive, being based on a survey of all overseas trips.

Considerable growth occurred in German outbound travel over this period as the propensity for holiday-taking in general and international travel in particular grew. Important changes in the relative composition of German travellers also occurred. Neighbouring Austria saw its share of the German market for main holidays decrease from 28 per cent to 10 per cent in two decades. Italy also experienced a marked drop in market share from 22.6 per cent to 14.5 per cent. In contrast, Spain's share doubled to over 18 per cent, with similar rates of growth being experienced by France and Yugoslavia but from a smaller base. While most of the German traffic is still intra-regional, steady increases were recorded in the traffic beyond Europe, with the rest of the world's share growing from just on 2 per cent in 1970 to almost 14 per cent in 1990. Turkey and the USA/Canada were the most significant of these destinations.

From 1965 to 1990 the number of British visits abroad increased from 6.5 million to 31.2 million. In relative terms, a major redistribution of the British traffic occurred as Ireland's share dropped from one-quarter to under 7 per cent. Italy's share also decreased steadily from 10.9 per cent to 3.8 per cent and smaller declines were registered by the Alpine destinations of Austria and Switzerland. The major beneficiaries of these changing patterns were France (12.8 per cent in 1965 to 22 per cent in 1990) and Spain although the latter experienced fluctuating fortunes in the latter part of the period. Steady increases were also being recorded by Greece, Portugal and former Yugoslavia. Other important European destinations such as Germany and the Netherlands experienced stable market shares throughout this period. The 'Beyond Europe' share doubled in the period from 1970 (7.5 per cent) to 1980 (16.2 per cent; of which North America, 7.9 per cent) and retained this level in 1990 after falling away in the mid-1980s due to some decline in the transatlantic traffic.

The evolution of the Japanese outbound traffic for the years 1965-90, a period which begins with the market at a much more immature phase than either the British or German markets. Japanese Ministry of Justice figures record only 163,000 departures in 1965 compared to almost 11 million in 1990. More than half of all this growth occurred between 1985 and 1990, when outbound travel was boosted by a strong yen and the Japanese Ministry of Transport's Ten Million Programme which aimed at doubling the number of Japanese going abroad over five years as a means of reducing Japan's trade surplus. The Ministry of Justice figures record departures by main destination only but given the relatively low propensity for multiple destination visits noted in the preceding section and the tendency for these to involve nearby countries, these figures should still be reasonably representative of the overall geographical pattern of Japanese travel, especially at the regional scale.

Throughout the period 1965-90, Asia has accounted for about half of the Japanese departures, peaking at 59 per cent in 1978, but over time some redistribution of flows within the region has occurred. Hong Kong's share has steadily declined and been replaced by Korea as the single largest Asian destination. In relative terms Taiwan rose rapidly in the late 1960s before declining, the decrease in the late 1980s being particularly pronounced. Similarly, but at a lower level, the Philippines' share increased gradually then dropped back. In contrast, smaller and more distant Singapore has experienced consistent increases from a smaller base.

The largest destination for Japanese travellers to be the United States which by the late 1970s accounted for about one-third of the total traffic. More detailed arrival figures show that in 1980 Hawaii recorded about half of Japanese travellers to the United States and Guam, about 20 per cent (Bailey 1986). Europe has registered about 10 per cent of Japanese outbound travel since 1980, with France (2.7 per cent in 1990), the United Kingdom (2.6 per cent) and Germany (1.6 per cent) being the three leading destinations there. In the latter part of the period Australia started to show some growth, accounting for almost 4 per cent of Japanese departures in 1990.

United States citizens' departures for the period 1980-8. The data set is based on the National Travel Survey and arrivals figures for Canada and Mexico, the latter being complicated by a change of definition from 1984 (Cook 1989). At the end of the period Canada, Mexico and overseas destinations combined each held about one-third of the US market. The major redistribution involves the number and share of the visitors going to the United States' northern and southern neighbours, the analysis of market share clearly being skewed by the definitional change noted. However, in absolute terms Cook reports that United States travel to Canada weakened significantly during the 1970s, and although it recovered somewhat in the mid-1980s the 1988 figure was still below the 1973 peak of 14.3 million departures. Conversely, United States travel to Mexico grew steadily in the 1970s, dropped in 1980 but picked up again throughout the rest of the period. In absolute terms United States travel to most overseas regions grew reasonably steadily throughout the period shown, growth in travel to Europe, the largest destination, being temporarily checked in 1986 by terrorist attacks against Americans. Other world regions attract only a minor and relatively stable share of US travellers.

Comparison of the patterns and trends among the evolution of the four largest markets draws attention to several major points.

This further highlight the importance of the intra-regional flows noted earlier, particularly for the two British and German markets for whom Europe holds a much more dominant place than does Asia for Japan or North America

(Canada and Mexico) for the United States. The proportion of Germans travelling 'beyond Europe' is increasing rapidly but from a much smaller base than extra-regional travel from either Japan or the United States. The British 'beyond Europe' share in 1990 was similar to what it had been a decade earlier (16 per cent). The Japanese extra-regional traffic was reasonably constant throughout the period as was the American (definitional problems noted) in the 1980s. Some notable exceptions such as the increase in Japanese departures to Australia aside, what this means in most cases is that the growth in the longer-haul traffic from each of these four markets is primarily a function in the overall growth in demand rather than a relative redistribution to more distant desti-nations outside each region.

The changes in market share that do occur are essentially recorded within each respective region. The most fundamental is a decline in departures to traditional neighbouring 'non-sun' countries and a corresponding growth in the traffic to 'sun-sand-sea' destinations, most of which are characterized by lower living costs. Thus the German traffic to Austria declines as holidaymakers head towards cheaper Mediterranean destinations, as do British vacationers forsaking Ireland. Mexico gains in popularity for United States travellers as Canada's appeal is weakened. The Japanese pattern is less straightforward, there being few readily accessible sunlust destinations. Hong Kong declines in importance, much of the 'sun-sand-sea' traffic is oriented to Guam, Hawaii and later to Queensland in Australia, but part of Korea's growth can be attributed to developments on the semi-tropical Cheju Island (Bailey 1986). In the cases of the United Kingdom and Germany this near-neighbour decline extends the drop in domestic demand noted earlier. Italy also loses market share in both these markets, a function perhaps of lack of price competivity in comparison with other Mediterranean destinations.

Overall it appears that the growth in demand in outbound tourism from the world's four major markets in the 1970s and 1980s was largely associated with a boom in departures to sunlust destinations. This may reflect a fundamental underlying change in holiday preferences, the basic tastes in the new groups acceding to international travel and generating mass tourism, and changing price structures reflecting the relative strength of the markets' currencies, technological developments and the emergence of lower cost destinations. Particularly important in this latter respect have been the development of inclusive charter tours and aggressive tourist development programmes in Spain, Mexico and to a lesser extent other Mediterranean destinations (Pearce 1983b, 1987a, 1987b). Similarly, the upsurge in Japanese travel to Hawaii followed the introduction of contract inclusive tour fares in 1970 (Bailey 1986).

Destinations will be effected by these and other market trends in different ways and to varying degrees depending on their location and individual market mix for, each is likely to be subject to overlapping spheres of influence. For example, shows the effect of the expanding Japanese market on the growth and composition of visitor arrivals in Australia. By 1990 the number of Japanese arrivals had eclipsed those from neighbouring New Zealand, traditionally Australia's largest market but in absolute terms a small one and one which was experiencing irregular increases in its outbound traffic during the 1980s. Strong growth is also shown from other parts of Asia and, to a lesser extent, Europe. An earlier study of demand in the South Pacific showed how the larger destinations of Australia and New Zealand drew proportionately more of their visitors from markets outside the region while the small destinations (in terms of visitor arrivals) depended heavily on intra-regional travellers. Given the low generating potential of the South Pacific, growth was seen to lie in the destinations' ability to attract longer-haul visitors (Pearce 1983a). By 1990 the Japanese had also become the leading market for New Caledonia, Japanese visits remaining relatively stable during the mid-1980s while Australian numbers never fully recovered from their 1984 peak after the civil unrest of 1985 and subsequent years.

The evolutionary models also suggested that over time the character of the tourists will change. However, beyond the evolution in the geographic attributes noted here and one-off studies of profile characteristics (Cockerell 1989; Cook 1989; Oum and Lemire 1991) it is generally difficult to assess more systematically long-term changes in demand due to a basic lack of appropriate time-series data, for example of psychographics. These two examples of how the Japanese market has evolved which might serve as examples for studies in other locations where similar information is available.

This depicts the regional breakdown of purpose of visit for the period 1965-91 and provides some evidence of the evolution of tourist travel in the total travel picture. In this case, tourist travellers have been defined as those giving 'sightseeing' as their prime reason for travelling. Other travel purposes include business, both private and official, study and research, immigration, accompanying spouse or parents. Over the period examined, tourists increased from 19 per cent of all travellers in 1964 to 83.9 per cent in 1989 before dropping back slightly. The overall increases in the Japanese outbound traffic noted earlier thus seem to be largely a function of bigger tourist flows. It also appears, however, that an increase in the tourist traffic is related initially to existing exchanges between Japan and any given region as evidenced by the volume of other traffic. In the cases of South America and Africa where the total volume of traffic is small, the proportion of tourists has increased much more slowly and still remains the lowest overall. As well as distance and cost involved, lack of information appears to have played a role here (Tokuhisa 1980). On the other hand, in Asia, North America and Europe where the total traffic was much greater at the beginning of the period, the proportion of tourists has evolved more rapidly. In Asia and America the proportion of tourists has stabilized at over 80 per cent whereas in Europe the figre falls below 70 per cent in 1991—whether this reflects the Gulf crisis or some other trend is not yet clear. A steady growth in travellers to Oceania throughout this period has been accompanied by a constant increase in the proportion of Japanese tourists visiting the region, with the highest levels of all regions being recorded (in excess of 90 per cent since 1987).

Changes in the demographic structure of Japanese arrivals in one Oceania destination, New Zealand. In 1974/75 Japanese tourists in New Zealand were overwhelmingly male (66 per cent) and predominantly middle-aged to elderly. By 1986/87 the genders were evenly balanced and the 20-34 age group constituted half of all Japanese tourists (34 per cent in 1974/75). Much of this change can be attributed to the growth in the honeymoon market, together with the emergence of other segments, notably the 'office ladies'. While package tours remain dominant, there has also been a significant increase in independent travel. The changes evident in New Zealand appear to reflect more general changes in the Japanese market which has matured to include a wider range of segments than in its early phases.

These demographic segments tend to favour different destinations, with the Japan Travel Bureau (1992) reporting that a disproportionate number of middle aged and elderly people go to Asian destinations, single working women to beach resorts in places such as Hawaii and Guam, a higher proportion of newly weds to Australia, and of mature married couples and middle-aged people to Europe. The same report also notes that while 'nature' destinations (mountains, lakes, etc.) remain the most popular, from 1987 to 1991 preferences for urban cultural elements or easy-to-reach destinations have strengthened relative to nature.

Many of the general patterns identified in this chapter conform with the ideas proposed in the models particularly that of Miossec. Throughout, a broad distance decay effect in international tourist flows can be observed, with intra-regional traffic predominating in many parts of the globe and reciprocal flows developing between countries, particularly neighbouring ones. The size and affluence of the major West European countries along with the United States also give rise to long-haul international flows which are superimposed on more general regional patterns. While some dispersion in outbound travel from these markets and that of Japan has been apparent since the 1970s, these markets remain dominated by intra-regional travel with most of the growth in longer-haul flows being a function of an overall increase in the volume of travellers rather than a marked redistribution of the destinations favoured by them.

Globally, international tourist travel remains very concentrated, both in terms of the shares of the major markets and destinations and the selectivity evidenced by the concentration ratios. The analysis of circuit travel also highlighted the limited amount of interaction which occurs between origins and multiple destinations at a country-to-country level-mono-rather than multi-destination travel was the norm in the countries examined.

Tourism Development

In formulating the tourism policy and plan, it is important to understand the different forms of tourism development and types of tourism related to specific travel motivations that can be considered for the country or region. The forms of tourism described in the following sections are mostly those which represent the planned develop-ment approach. Some of them have also developed spontaneously, but often with problems resulting from lack of planning and development controls, and they require planned rejuvenation.

Resorts

One of the most common forms of modern holiday tourism is some type of resort-based development. A tourist resort can be defined as a destination area that is relatively self-contained. It typically provides a wide range of tourist facilities and services including those designed for recreation and relaxation. Because of the present trend of more tourist wanting to participate in recreation, sports, cultural and other activities, resorts are now emphasizing the provision of a wide variety of facilities and services. These often include major commercial and conference/meeting facilities.

Some resorts, located where there are seasonal differences in climate (summer and winter or dry and rainy), have traditionally experienced wide seasonal variations in guest arrivals. The current trend is for these resorts to offer facilities and services for year-round use, often catering to different types of guests during the different seasons. In addition to containing their own facilities for tourist use, many resorts also serve as a base for tourists to take sightseeing trips to points of interest in the nearby area.

Resorts have their primary orientation to several types of attractions and activities—beach, relaxation and recreation; marine sports in both lake and ocean coastal areas; water recreation and sports on rivers; mountain winter skiing and summer hiking and horse riding; golf and tennis sports; health facilities related to mineral springs (spas) or dry sunny climate; important archaeological and historic sites and national parks; or a combination of features. Some resorts are very large with a variety of types of accommodation, including self-catering units, and many recreation and commercial facilities. Other resorts may be composed of only one hotel but still offer a range of facilities, services and activities. 'Retreat' type resorts may be small and isolated, but they provide a high quality level of facilities and services. They cater to guests who want a quiet remote environment. Holiday villages are a type of resort.

Integrated resorts are ones which have been carefully planned as single entities, even though larger integrated resorts are usually constructed in phases over a long period of time. Most new resort areas are carefully planned to function efficiently and provide an interesting environment for tourists while not generating any serious environmental and social problems. Many unplanned resorts also exist in various parts of the world, but some of these are experiencing environmental and social problems and require redevelopment.

Town resorts combine the usual land uses and activities of a town community, but are economically focused on resort activities. They include hotels, other types of accommodation and a variety of tourist facilities and services. They contain or are located near major attraction features, such as beaches or ski facilities. Town resorts were often not initially planned as integrated developments. Many of these places are now undergoing redevelop-ment and applying controls in order to improve their environmental quality and economic viability. Some recently developed planned resorts include new towns where the resort support population lives. These then function as viable resort towns.

Urban Tourism

Tourism in towns and cities is very widespread. These urban places often offer a broad range of historic and cultural attractions, shopping, restaurants and the appeal of urban vitality. Many urban attractions and amenities are primarily developed to serve residents, but their use by tourists can greatly help to support them. Additionally, urban areas may function as points of arrival and departure of tourists to the country or region, and serve as a base for tourists to take excursions to nearby areas. Hotels and other tourist facilities are an integral part of the urban fabric and serve both business and holiday travellers.

Urban tourism must also be carefully planned. Determination must be made of the location of hotels and other tourist facilities, location and development of attraction features, the additional infrastructure required for them, and perhaps institutional improve-ments. It is now common practice to develop or redevelop certain urban areas - such as historic districts and waterfront sites - which are oriented particularly to tourism and residents' leisure use. Major convention and sports facilities are often developed to attract more tourists.

Adventure Tourism

One of the rapidly expanding types of tourism is special interest and adventure tourism. This type of tourism reflects the increasing fragmentation of tourist markets. Special interest tourism refers to tourists, usually in small groups, who are travelling to learn about and experience particular features of an area. These special interest themes are often associated with the tourists' long-term avocational or professional-vocational interests.

Special interest tourism can focus on a wide range of features. Cultural themes include dance, music, drama, fine arts, handicrafts, architecture, archaeology, history and historic routes, traditional life styles, and unusual economic activities. Nature themes relate to flora, fauna, geology, scenic beauty, national parks and marine environ-ments. Professional interests involve visits to meet people of similar professions and exchange ideas. Educational tours are a type of special interest tourism. Participatory activities are common, such as tourists working under supervision at an archaeological site excavation.

Adventure tourism involves the tourists engaging in physically and personally challenging and sometimes dangerous activities. These include safaris and trekking in remote areas, hiking, mountain climbing, river rafting and white water boating through river rapids. Hunting and fishing may be considered as an aspect of special interest and adventure tourism.

Related to special interest tourism is a form that has been variously termed alternative, responsible, appropriate and even sustainable tourism. (However, the tourism development approach used in this publication is that all forms of tourism should be planned to be responsible, appropriate and sus-tainable.) This form of tourism refers to small-scale, non-conventional types of development, including the following:

- Village tourism—small groups of tourists staying in or near traditional, often remote, villages, and learning about village life and the local environment. Facilities are owned and managed by the villagers.
- Rural, farm or agro tourism—tourists staying with farm families and learning about farming activities, or staying on tropical plantations and learning about plantation life and activities, or staying in fishing villages with fishermen's families and going on fishing trips.
- Walking and cycling tours—tourists travelling by walking or bicycling and staying in inns, hostels, private homes or bed and breakfast houses, meeting local people and learning about the culture and environment.
- Ecotourism (a controlled form of nature tourism)—tourists hiking or boating in natural areas, with local guides to explain about the flora, fauna and ecology. Ecotourism may also include visits to local villages

and farms. This type of tourism is currently receiving much attention because of its emphasis on environmental conservation and learning about nature.

- Community assistance programmes—small groups of tourists, often community organizations in their home countries, visiting an area and assisting local people with a particular development project such as building low-cost housing or constructing a village water supply.

Other Forms

There are several other forms of tourism that are suitable in many places. These include:

- Water transport tourism—cruise ship travel, boating on rivers and canals and yachting, all of which are very popular in certain regions of the world. Shore-based facilities of piers, docks and marinas and related facilities and services are required for this type of tourism.

- Residential tourism—development of various types of housing, and related community facilities and services, for use as vacation or retirement homes. This is a very common form of tourism.

- Camping and caravan tourism—development of camping facilities, usually near an important attraction or recreation feature, and caravan or parks for recreational vehicles located along highways or near attractions.

- Transportation-oriented tourism—hotels and other tourist facilities and services located near major transportation centres, especially airports for transit passengers. Airport-related tourism development is now providing meeting facilities for business travellers. Associated with road travel is the development of motels along major highways, especially in the peripheral areas of towns and cities and at major highway intersections.

- Youth tourism—travel by young people and students for education, sports and recreation has long been an established form of tourism and is currently being encouraged in many countries. Youth tourism requires development of inexpensive accommodation, often hostels or dormitories. 'Elderhostel' programmes for older people undertaking educational travel and staying in hostel-type accommodation are also popular.

Not related to any particular form of tourism, but based on specialized travel motivations, are the following types of tourism:

- Religious tourism—travel by pilgrims to places of religious significance, such as the Hajj to Mecca and visits to the Vatican in Rome and Varanasi in India, is very important in some countries. Religious pilgrims often require tourist-type facilities and services.

- Ethnic tourism—as used here, refers to persons who are visiting their own original homelands or places of their ancestral origin. Some countries are encouraging persons who have migrated overseas to visit their homelands as an important type of tourist market.

- Nostalgic tourism—persons visiting places where they previously had been involved in some activity. Visits by Americans and Japanese to places where they were assigned and fought in World War II is an example of nostalgic tourism. Nostalgic tourism may be important in an area for only a limited period of time.

As can be seen, many of these forms of tourism, especially those related to special interest and sightseeing activities, demand heavily on the natural and cultural resources of a tourism area. Consequently, environmental and cultural heritage conservation and interpretation is one of the major themes of contemporary tourism development. Many of the techniques that have been developed for interpretation of heritage sites are quite imaginative in educating visitors in an interesting and entertaining manner.

There has been increased awareness of the economic importance of tourism in the 1980s and this stems from a number of sources, including appreciation of how long-term structural changes in demand are leading to expansion of the service economy. With increasing real incomes and leisure time there is growing demand for recreation and holidays, and this benefits tourism. Not surprisingly, therefore tourism is often considered to be one of the economic sectors which has realistic potential for growth beyond the short term. The importance of this trend for employment is strengthened because of the relatively labour-intensive nature of tourism and the limited substitution—up to the present, at least—of capital in the production of tourism services. Given the growth of large-scale and long-term unemployment throughout Western Europe in the 1980s, it is hardly surprising that policy-makers have seized upon tourism as a source of employment creation. At the same time, the increasing share of services in international trade has focused attention on tourism as a major contribution—either positively or negatively—to the balance of payments. In short, tourism—along with some other select activities such as financial services and tele-communications—has become a major component of economic strategies in many parts of Western Europe.

As tourism emerges from the shadows of economic policy to a centre-stage position, it has become imperative to evaluate its role in economic development. The industry is shrouded with myths and stereotypes, and there is a need to examine critically recent trends in tourism, its economic organisation and its contribution to economic development. There have been previous attempts to question whether tourism is 'a passport to development' or is 'a blessing or blight' as well as more broadly based assessments of the economic, social and environmental impacts of tourism. However, this volume seeks to make a distinctive contribution to the growing literature in this field by focusing in depth on recent trends in Western Europe.

Western Europe is a coherent unit for analysis for many reasons. Although, of course, there are international flows out of and into the region, Western Europe actually accounted for 68 per cent of all international tourists in 1984. Compared to all other macro regions, there is a very intense level of international tourist flows within Western Europe, so that the fortunes of the tourist industry in particular countries are heavily depen-dent on movements from—and events in—other countries within the continent. The major exception to this is the quantitatively important (and econo-mically even more significant) inflow of tourists from the United States. The event's of 1986 testify to the importance of North American tourists because the sudden reduction in arrivals following the Chernobye incident and the US bombing of Libya had a notable effect on the tourist economies of several European countries. To some extent, emphasis on international tourism tends to overstate the importance of Western Europe because the geographical scale of the United States and Canada means that, in comparison, similar-length tourist journeys are recorded as domestic tourist flows in these two countries. Nevertheless, it is also important to study Western Europe as a unit because there is a communality of policy interests. Most obviously, the European Community (EC) constitutes a single market for tourism and, while EC policy initiatives in this field have been limited, the very existence of the Community affects the industry. At the level of demand, it facilitates international tourist movements while, at the level of industrial organisation, the free movement of international capital and labour is eased. There are also some instances of EC-wide policy measures for tourism, notably in Social Fund assistance for training and European Regional Development Fund (ERDF) grants for infrastructure. However, most tourism policy is formulated at the national rather than the EC level. Even so, the countries of Western Europe are interdependent in respect of state interventionism. Policy measures in one country—whether to stimulate new forms of tourism, to influence the holiday destinations of nationals or the attract more foreigners—impinge upon competing tourist industries in other countries. This is underlined by the fact that, while the income elasticity of demand for tourism may be strongly positive in the long term, in the short term total demand is (almost) fixed.

Having considered the geographical parameters of this volume, we now turn to a consideration of tourism itself. The definition of tourism is a particularly arid pursuit. It is sufficient to note that in this volume tourism is understood to constitute travelling away from home for periods of more than 24 hours; the principal purposes are recreation or business activities, but may also include visiting family, educational motives or health reasons. Excursionism involves visits of less than 24 hours. Although the major focus of this volume is on tourism, its development and, indeed, its economic impact are linked with excursionism, and so the latter cannot entirely be excluded. While the definition of tourism may be an arid exercise, the definition of the tourist industry is crucially important. In most countries tourism is 'statistically invisible' and usually, only the most obvious sectors or those exclusively devoted to tourists are enumerated in official tourism data. Inevitably, this tends to be the accommodation sector and, perhaps, cafes and restaurants. Yet the tourist industry is far larger than this. Tourists also spend money directly on recreational facilities, tourist attractions, shops and local services. In turn, these have indirect effects on agriculture, wholesaling and manu-facturing, while secondary rounds of spending of tourism income create induced linkages in the economy. This, indeed, is the basis for the research which has been undertaken on tourism multipliers. In this volume, we have sought to encompass as broad a definition as possible of tourism but the constraints of space and of data inevitably mean that much of the discussion is centred on the accommodation sector.

This volume seeks to analyse the major changes which have occurred in Western European tourism in recent years. This is justified by the emphasis we wish to place on domestic versus foreign tourism, and by the concentration of policy-making powers at this level. While space precluded the inclusion of chapters on all seventeen major Western European countries, the ten which have been selected represent the major types of tourism economies. While each chapter has been written so as to take into account the particular character-istics of tourism in each country, certain themes recur throughout. The most important of these are changes in the demand for tourism (international and domestic, by region, by season, etc.), the organisation of the tourist industry and its responses to demand changes, and the contribution of tourism to economic development.

The case studies concentrate on two levels of analysis—the national and the regional—and on the relationship between these. Any analysis which ignores either level is likely to be incomplete. National developments affect regional develo-pments and vice versa. For example, the effectiveness of national marketing programmes, of national investment schemes and of international currency fluctuations influence the ability of regional tourist industries to attract tourists and to restructure in the face of changing market conditions. However, these interrelationships are not unidirectional for the attractiveness or effectiveness of the national tourist industry is in large part a sum of its regional components. Furthermore, the national and regional levels are also linked by capital and labour movements, both interregionally and internationally. This is illustrated in a case such as Austria for the national performance of the industry is usually an aggregate of decline in some regions and of rapid expansion in others. These and other relationships are addressed in the country studies which follow in however, the remainder of this chapter outlines some of the essential elements in the relationship between tourism and development.

National perspectives

The importance of tourism to national economic development can be measured in a number of ways, the most important of which are its contribution to the balance of payments, income/GDP, employment and other sectors of the economy (via indirect effects). The balance-of-payments contribution has received most attention. The importance of tourism in the 'invisibles' account in international trade has long been obvious in countries such as Spain where, indeed, it was promoted as part of a long-term economic strategy. It helps to pay for imports (whether of food, technology, capital or consumer goods) and this can be important both in economies in development (Greece, Spain, Portugal, etc.) and mature economies (such as the United Kingdom), which have a negative balance on merchandise trade. In this respect, the importance of tourism is usually greatest in small open economies, such as Cyprus or Malta, but it is also a source of vulnerability in such countries, especially when—as in the latter case—its is heavily dependent on a single foreign market.

Estimates of the contribution of tourism to the balance of payments are usually based on direct tourist expenditure. However, this is a rather narrow (if relatively easily measured) indicator, for it excludes the indirect transactions.

Which follow from tourism. Baretje (1982) therefore recommends the use of the broader concept of 'tourism's external account', which includes a variety of economic linkages but, it must be emphasised, there are practical difficulties in seeking to operationalise this. The breadth of the definition makes it equally difficult to estimate the contribution of tourism to national income or GDP. In addition to the linkages suggested by Baretje, calculations of income or GDP also have to include the effects of domestic tourism which, in Northern Europe at least, sometimes exceed those of foreign tourism. There is also the even more intangible consideration of how tourism impinges on general lifestyles and expenditure patterns. International tourism can have a demonstration effect leading to increased indigenous demand for new types of goods or services, and these may be produced by domestic or by foreign companies.

While there has long been an interest in the contribution of tourism to the balance of payments, this has been surpassed in the 1980s by a concern for its potential employment creation. Again, there are practical difficulties involved in any evaluation of this role: some jobs in shops, recreation centres, etc., are only partly dependent on tourism, while there are considerable difficulties involved in tracing secondary linkages. Furthermore, jobs are not a homogeneous category to be measured in simple units—as with income or net foreign exchange earnings. Instead, there are a variety of job types and these can be classified as seasonal/all-year, part-time/full-time, family-labour/waged-labour, voluntary/waged-labour, manual/non-manual, skilled/unskilled, etc. According to some stereotypes, tourism employment tends to be low-waged, seasonal, non-unionised, part-time and the preserve of family and/or female workers. This may hold true in some cases but, in most instances, it is at best a partial description. Jobs in tourism may be jobs in hotels, shops, government administration, air transport or factories, amongst others. The need to be critical of the quality of jobs generated by tourism, and to resist the political 'hype' surrounding its potential for job creation. The variety of experiences outlined in these chapters also emphasises the need to avoid stereotypes and excessive abstraction. Consideration of the tourism-related demand for manufactured goods underlines this point, for the impact depends on where the goods are produced, whether it is by craftmen or factory workers, on the alternative work opportunities available locally, and on the evaluation of these jobs by the individuals and by the community.

While the previous discussion has stressed the need to examine individual cases in detail, it does not preclude identification of the key elements which condition the relationship between tourism and development. Amongst the most important of these are the type of tourism, the structure of the national economy, and relationships with capital and labour movements.

Types of Tourism

There are many different types of tourists but, in terms of their contribution to economic development, the critical considerations are per-capita spending power and the forms of tourism in which they par-ticipate. The most important distinction is probably between domestic and foreign tourists, although there are also important differences within both categories. For instance, American tourists tend to have a high spending capacity so that, in most countries their economic contribution is far greater than their absolute numbers might suggest. In addition, there are also other differences between national groups and, indeed, amongst domestic tourists, depending on their incomes, duration of stay, mode of travel, range of activities and type of accommodation. Much of the debate on whether to pursue strategies of mass-tourism or quality tourism is based on these differences. This is a debate which is common in such diverse locations as Venice, the Algarve and South-West England.

National Economic Context

It is also important to see tourism in context of the national economy for, as de Kadt (1979) stresses, 'tourism is not a unique devil'. Instead, the ability of the national economy to benefit from tourism depends on the availability of investment to develop the necessary infrastructure (hotels, golf courses, etc.) and on its ability to supply the needs of tourists, whether for food, souvenirs or hotel beds. While the types of demand are conditioned by the types of tourism, there are also important differences in the capacity of particular economies to respond to these demands. In general, small economies are more likely to be dependent on imports, and the same is also true of economies where tourism is not very well developed and where, therefore, there are poor economies of scale for suppliers.

There is also an important relationship between development and tourism in that the former conditions the level of domestic demand. Increasing real incomes result in growing demand for tourism but this is distributed between domestic and foreign destinations. One hypothetical scenario whereby domestic tourism is overtaken in relative importance by a considerable expansion of foreign tourism. This shift can lead to a stagnation in domestic tourism. However, with further increases in income and leisure time, there may be a growth of second and third holidays—including short breaks—and there may be sufficient demand for domestic resorts, to renew growth in this sector. If, having reached saturation point, the growth of foreign tourism also slows down, the gap between this and domestic tourism may close. Elements of this relationship can be found in the experiences of several northern European countries, including the United Kingdom.

The organisation of capital: domestic versus foreign sources

The role of tourism in national development also depends partly on the organisation of capital and, in particular, on the penetration of international capital. This assumes a number of forms and, although foreign investment initially may assist the development of tourism, it also leads to leakage of income abroad through payment of royalties, profits and dividends. International capital can be involved in tourism development in a number of ways, including direct ownership of facilities by large companies, individual ownership of second homes, and ownership of the means of transport (especially airlines). In terms of the ownership of foreign facilities, hotels have been the most obvious recipient of direct foreign investment. The largest hotel groups are enormous and in 1986, for example, Holiday Inn owned 1,907 hotels worldwide, followed by Quality Inns with 801 hotels. The largest European groups were the United Kingdom's Trust House Forte (793) and France's Accord (534). Many of the major tour companies also have interests in hotel chains. While direct ownership of hotels and of other facilities is important, of even greater significance is the bargeining power of a large foreign tour companies such as Thomson, Tjaereborg or Schaernow- Reisen. For example, Thomson had 3.75 million overseas holidays on offer in 1987 and its sheer size allows it—and other major groups—to secure very low pieces from sub-contracting to nationally-owned hotel chains. Given the oligopolistic position of the tour companies in the delivery of tourists, especially when faced with large numbers of relatively undifferentiated hotels, their bargaining power is considerable. International migration also plays a role in the tourist industry and, in this, the experience of tourism is not dissimilar to that of other economic sectors, including manufacturing. The dominant international migration flows in Europe are from the South to the North (King 1984), and from less developed countries to Northern Europe (Castles et al. 1984). Countries such as the United Kingdom, France, Switzerland, the Federal Republic of Germany, the Netherlands, and Sweden rely on the labour of an estimated 6 million immigrants. They occupy a variety of jobs including less well-paid posts in such services sectors as hotels and restaurants. Their role is twofold: the supply of a flexible labour force contributes to depressing wages in the tourist industry, while their remittances to their home countries contribute to the balance of payments and to the levels of consumption in those countries (King 1986). There is also an important link between tourism and the generation of emigration. Tourism contri-butes to familiarisation with foreign culture and lifestyles (Lanfant 1980) and this may encourage emigration. There are some instances where tourists—or at least foreign settlers—have found jobs for locals abroad. Moore (1976) reports such a link in the Canaries where immigrant Swedes found jobs in Sweden for some of the local people.

Regional perspectives

The distribution of tourism is inherently uneven; not only is this polarised but, traditionally, it is concentrated in less urbanised area. Therefore, as Peters (1969, p. 11) states, 'tourism, by it nature, tends to distribute development away from the industrial centres towards those regions in a country which have not been developed'. There are many studies which have illustrated the extent of such regional polarisation and the rapidity of the process. Quite apart from every single case study in this volume, previous studies of the United Kingdom (Duffield 1977), Greece (Buckley and Papadopoulos 1986) and Yugoslavia (Allcock 1983) reinforce this argument. What is surprising is not that tourism has featured in regional policy and regional development strategies (see Chapter 3), but that it has featured so little in these. Belatedly, however, local authorities are awakening to the possibilities of using tourism as a basis for regional development, as is evident, for example, in urban tourism projects in the United Kingdom and France.

The contribution of tourism to regional economies is measured in similar fashion to that for national economies. Its share of regional income or output can be estimated either in terms of direct effects or, via multiplier studies, or direct and indirect effects. The levels of interlinkages and dependency identified depend on the spatial scale of the analysis (Henderson 1976). Smaller tourist region are more likely to be dependent on tourism than are larger regions, which are more likely to have more diversified economies. As tourism can be developed in a short time-span, and with only moderate levels of investment, its impact on a regional economy can be very rapid as, for example, Diem (1980) reports in the Val d' Anniviers in Switzerland. Here, a number of investments linked to a Club Mediterranee project resulted in a dramatic turn-around in the local economy in little more than a decade.

Tourism is also a major source of employment at the regional level. However, as Pearce and Grimmeau (1985) have shown for Spain, the numbers and types of jobs vary considerably between regions in relation to the structure of the tourist industry, especially its seasonality. The year-round tourism of the Costa del Sol provides more permanent jobs than does the summer tourism of the Costa Dorada. Seasonality is but one aspect of employment in tourism, and there is also a need—as at the national level—to consider whether jobs are full-time or part-time, and whether they provide professional or manual work. There is also a need to consider how jobs in tourism interact with other household employment: whether tourism wages are supplementary to or the principal source of income, and whether they are used to support another enterprise such as a farm or a small workshop. Alternatively the employment effects can be negative, and tourism may destroy the basis of other activities as, for example, Greenwood (1976) describes for an agricultural community in the Basque region. There is also the very real problem for many communities of the generational gap, so vividly described by Fraser (1974) in his study in southern Spain, but also evident in may Alpine communities (Kariel and Kariel 1982). Younger members of the family, lured by the easier wages and more glamorous lifestyles of tourist areas, may turn their backs on the traditional economy and, sometimes, society.

At the local level tourism can also have a very considerable impact on land markets. Tourism is highly polarised spatially, along the coastline, in a few cities or in some of the more picturesque inland areas. This is particularly evident along the Mediterranean coast where there is near-continuous urban sprawl largely as a result of tourism (Gonen 1981). The demands of tourism may force up land prices, providing a windfall for local landowners and farmers, as, for example, in the Alps (Vincent 1980). However, rising land values can also cause difficulties for those locals who are not in the tourist industry but who need to build homes or establish businesses in these areas (see Andronicou 1979 on Cyprus, and Boissevain and Inglott 1979 on Malta). The highly polarised nature of develop-ment also generates intense environ-mental problems such as water and air pollution, water shortages, traffic congestion and destruction of traditional landscapes. This reduces the quality of life for locals as well as for tourists and, ultimately, may threaten the viability of the tourist industry itself. This is vividly illustrated in the Alps where the scars left by winter sports reduce the attraction of the landscape for summer visitors.

Types of tourist

As with national development, care must be taken not to overgeneralise about the role of tourism in regional development. This role is conditioned by a number of considerations. One important element is the number of tourists and whether they exceed the 'tourist carrying capacity' (de Kadt 1979) of a region. There are usually critical numbers of tourists which can be integrated into regional economic and social structures and, beyond this, any increase will result in a transformation of these structures. The regional economic effects are also dependent on the types of tourist attracted and, for example, Middleton (1977) shows the uneven regional distribution of (high-spending) foreign tourists compared to domestic tourists in the United Kindgom. Only a few cities and small regions benefit substantially from foreign visitors while other regions—such as the far South-West—suffer from their inability to attract foreign visitors. Similar trends can be observed in the Mediterranean countries where foreign tourist are usually much higher spenders, per capita, than are domestic tourists, although there may also be differences in consumption behaviour between groups of foreign nationals (see Chapter 6). For example, Weatherley (1982) has shown how the economic impact of domestic second home ownership—as opposed to foreign tourism—in the Sierra Morena, Spain, is weakened by a strong tendency for self-building and for buying food and other goods outside the region.

Regional Economic Context

The structure of the regional economy is also important in condi-tioning the economic impact of tourism, and two elements are important in this. First, there is the question of whether the tourist development is integrated into an existing settlement or is on a greenfield site and, also whether the scale of the development is such that it can be absorbed by or overwhelms the existing economy. In the Alps, for instance, there is a major difference between high-level ski villages, built beyond the traditional settlement line, and low-level centres where tourism is better integrated with existing villages (Barker 1982). Each of these types makes different forms of demands on local labour, capital and suppliers and, in extremis, a large specialist, high-level ski centre may be developed almost entirely by capital and labour from outside the local region.

This leads to the second question, which is whether the tourist industry is able to utilise local resources. For example, farm tourism by its nature—mostly utilises local resources, in terms of capital, labour and food supplies (see Beteille 1976 on rural France). However, with the rapid expansion of farm tourism in Europe (Dernoi 1983), there is a tendency for the marketing and, therefore, some of the control of farm tourism to pass into the hands of tour companies. The critical importance of regional economic structures in the utilisation of local resources is highlighted by Loukissas's (1982) comparative study of Greek islands. The economic impact of tourism is most beneficial in the larger islands because these have more diversified economic structures, leakage effects are limited, and the pressures on the local population are reduced because tourism tends to be concentrated in specialised villages. In contrast, tourism tends to dominate the economies of the smaller islands, but may lead to unstable, short-term and dualistic development.

Sources of Capital

Capital in tourism development tends to be highly polarised between a few large groups and a mass of small, family-owned enterprises. The former will have access to the capital resources of large groups (for example, Thomas Cook to it parent, Midland Bank) or to banking or institutional capital (for example, Accor financed its 1987 expansion programme through a share issue to French banks). However, venture capital has been notoriously loath to invest in smaller tourist businesses which—

sometimes wrongly—have been considered higher-risk activities than manufacturing firms. Instead, small tourist businesses may have to rely on public sector grants or loans or, more commonly, on personal or family sources of capital (see Shaw, Williams and Greenwood 1987 on a Cornish case study); this can be a major constraint on business expansion. The polarisation of capital can also be a potential source of conflict between the different interests of small-scale and (often externally owned) large-scale segments of the industry and their labour forces, as Werff (1980) reports in the case of Pescara in Italy.

The sources of personal or family capital can be diverse but usually involve a transfer of resources from another economic activity, such as a small farm, fishing or transport business. One particularly important source of such capital—at least in southern Europe—has been the savings and remittances of emigrants and turned migrants, as King et al. (1984) and Mendonsa (1983a) report for southern Italy and central Portugal, respectively. One final point to be emphasised with respect to capital is that most studies have concentrated on the accumulation of capital and new rounds of investment in tourism, while there has been little research on the restructuring of capital in existing tourist areas (with a few exceptions such as Weg 1982 on Scheveningen in the Netherlands).

Regional labour markets

The type of local economy and of tourist development also condition the impact of tourism on regional labour markets. It may be possible—if the development is small enough—to rely entirely on local labour but, failing this a system of labour migration will develop. This can involve daily movements (from surrounding towns and villages), seasonal migration, or permanent in-migration. These have very different impacts on the local economy depending on whether extra housing and services are required and, also on how the migrant labour force distributes its expenditure between the locality and its home area (see Bernal et al. 1979 on the marked variations which exist between regional labour markets in Andalusia). Given that tourist regions often attract labour from less developed rural regions (see Cavaco 1980 on Portugal), the remittances they send back to these areas can ameliorate some of the features of uneven regional development.

This chapter has only provided a brief introduction to some of the relationships between tourism and economic development. Nevertheless, it has highlighted the complexity of the issues and relationships involved and the need to look in detail at particular cases, taking account of their regional structures and how these have evolved. In this respect, the case studies in this volume do indicate some of the major international and interregional differences which exist in the tourist industry of Western Europe. However, the way in which these and other relationships can be examined and compared depends on the availability of data, and this chapter concludes with a brief review of this topic.

Tourism Data

The unreliability of tourism data a notorious and, although there are usually quite good time series for individual countries or regions, international comparisons are fraught with difficulties (Chib 1977). Many commentators have argued for the need to develop reliable and internationally acceptable methods of data collection and presentation (for example, Baron 1983) and international organisations such as the OECD and the World Tourism Organisation have been active towards this end. However, there still remain considerable difficulties. Several of the authors in this volume provide commentaries on the statistical coverage for particular countries, while some general features are summarised below:

1. There are many sociological (for example, Cohen 1974) and economic considerations of what constitutes tourism (see Peters 1969). Tourism is usually considered to involve visits of more than 24 hours (but less than one year) for business or recreational purposes and has to be differentiated from shorter visits, known as *excursionism*, whether these involve national or inter-national journeys.

2. In many countries, the data on international tourism may be more reliable than those on domestic tourism,. The former may be enumerated at international frontiers and are probably more likely to be accommodated in officially registered premises.

3. Tourists may stay in any one of a number of forms of accommodation. Even discounting friends and relatives and the informal sector, this ranges from hotels, through boarding houses, holiday camps and camping sites, to rooms let in private dwellings. Data tend to be most reliable for hotels and large camping sites, and least reliable for the myriad of privately let rooms and small camping sites which are found in most countries.

4. Each national tourist organisation may record different types of information. For example, duration of stay, mode of travel, expenditure, age, socio-economic group and number of accompanying persons are all important aspects of tourism but these are not recorded in all tourist enumerations.

5. There are different ways of enumerating tourists: the census points can be international frontiers or the place of accommodation, while some countries also undertake special sample surveys. While international borders may seem the most reliable sources (for foreign tourists), relaxation of passport controls within Scandinavia and the EC have seriously undermined the value of these data.

6. Data on the economic aspects of tourism are even more problematic. Tourist expenditure can be estimated from social surveys or from bank returns, but both methods are incomplete and under-record prepaid transport, etc. (White and Walker 1982). There is also poor availability of data on most tourism-related sectors other than accommo-dation and catering in most countries. Therefore, unless special firm-level surveys are undertaken (see Shaw, Williams and Greenwood 1987). Estimates of the real importance of tourism to a national or regional economy can only be crude approximations. This applies equally well to expenditure as to employment data.

5. Elements, Trends and Scope of Tourism Management

TOURISM HAS grown from the pursuits of a privileged few to a mass movement of people, with the "urge to discover the unknown, to explore new and strange places, to seek changes in environment and to undergo new experiences" (Robinson 1976, xxi). During the post-war period tourism grew into a mass tourist industry. The number of international tourist arrivals rose from 25 million in 1950 to 183 million in 1970, an average growth rate of more than 10 per cent (IUOTO 1970). Since 1973 the effect of fuel price increases has merely moderated the rate of expansion. According to estimates by the World Tourist Organization (WTO) international tourist arrivals in 1982 reached 280 million; but even more remarkable is the fact that these members reflect only the minor, and more easily measured, aspects of the tourism picture. Domestic tourism, which involves travel within one's own country, is more difficult to quantify but generally accounts for 75-80 per cent of all tourism activity (Lundberg 1976, 9). According to the WTO there were over 2 billion domestic trips in 1981, representing a 240 per cent increase over 1975 figures.

Such mass movements of people have been described as contemporary migration patterns. Migration can be seen as a response to stress, and Wolfe (1966) identifies three migration patterns in our society. The first, migration to the city, is a continuation of the nineteenth-century phenomenon, and in the opinion of some, may have run its course in the developed world. The second, the journey to and from work, is a result of our large-scale urbanization and spatial separation of workplace and home. The third, recreational travel, is the newest migration and a function of the other two. It has been stimulated by the stress and uniformity of urban life and been accommodated by the standard of living and mobility provided by the same urban-economic system. Being the newest migration, recreational travel has experienced phenomenal growth rates—rates which cannot be maintained but which led to a major change in our lifestyles. Like the other migrations before it, tourism will peak and probably decline, but it will remain a part of our lives and probably change in form and emphasis in the process.

The multifaceted nature of tourism, its various links with the manufacturing and retail sectors, and its numerous seasonal or unofficial businesses make it extermely difficult to assess its market size. One estimate, however, suggests that worldwide travel spending reached $488 billion in 1978 (Waters 1978, 5). This represented 6 per cent of the world's 1978 Gross National Product (GNP), which in turn was the equivalent of West

Germany's GNP at that time. A more recent WTO estimate places the 1981 expenditure on world travel at $919 billion. The growth in tourism revenues has been substantial since the Second World War, but as in the case of visitor volumes the rate of growth has slowed since the oil crisis and inflation of the 1970s. When calculated in real terms the revenue increases have declined from the post-war region of 10 per cent a year to 3 per cent, but it is still growth nevertheless (OECD 1980).

Despite the short-term setbacks of the energy crises and recessions of the late 1970s and early 1980s, tourism is seen as a growth industry of the future. Toffler's Future Shock (1971) described the modern businessman and vacation traveller as the "new nomads" and foresaw:

> a revolutionary expansion of certain industries where sole output consists not of manufactured goods, nor even of ordinary services, but of pre-programmed "experiences" The experience industry could turn out to be one of the pillars of super-industrialism. The very foundation, in fact, of the post-service economy. (Toffler 1971, 208).

His more recent work, The Third Wave (1981), predicted the breakup of industrial society, as we know it, through a process of "demassi-fication," breaking up large units of government and industry into more individual and flexible lifestyles. Among the changes which will relate to tourism he foresaw:

> Large numbers of workers already do paid work for what averages out to only three or four days a week, or they take six months or a year off to pursue educational or recreational goals. This pattern may well grow as two-paycheck households multiply. (Toffler 1981, 277)

The appeal of this industry for the transitory period from an industrial society to whatever future awaits us is not limited to futurologists. Nations, such as Spain and Austria, have based much of their post-war development on growth in their tourism sectors. Earnings from the international tourist account contributed a significant portion of their export earnings in 1977, 22.5 per cent for Spain and 21.7 per cent for Austria. This compared with a European Community average of 4.7 per cent (British Tourist Authority 1981, 13), and created a major source of "hard" currency for other development projects. Furthermore, in a time of growing automation and rising unemployment, tourism as a labour-intensive industry has proved to be both economically and politically appealing. As the then Prime Minister of England, James Callaghan, once described the situation:

> Now new plants in manufacturing and new investment and new methods bring greater efficiency but it does not necessarily mean more jobs, and for this reason, we need to look at the service industries of which tourism is a notable example as an additional and important source of income and work. (English Tourist Board 1977, 5)

The development of mass tourism has created a powerful and influential recreational travel industry. For example, in England it is estimated that "some 1 1/2 million jobs were generated either directly or indirectly by tourism in 1978, equivalent to about 6 per cent of total employment" (English Tourist Board 1978a, 4). In Canada tourism is promoted as big business which is important to all Canadians, because it employs one out of ten workers and is the seventh largest earner of foreign exchange (CGOT 1982). In the United States the tourism industry grosses an estimated $105 billion annually and employs over 5 million workers (Pizam and Pokela 1983). With such impressive statistics and employment opportunities it is little wonder that this industry has become a powerful political lobby. In Britain and Canada the industry has received generous development grants, and in Canada a private sector task force is cooperating with the government to produce the first national tourism plan (Powell 1978).

At the international level the United Nations has noted the economic and social significance of this growth industry. A 1979 report stated that tourism was bigger business than iron and steel or armaments, and that about 500 million workers and their families throughout the world were entitled to paid vacations. While recognizing the beneficial economic effects tourism can bring to national economies and world trade, the United Nations Manila Conference on World Tourism noted that its potential goes beyond just economic considerations. The first declaration of that Conference read:

> Tourism is considered an activity essential to the life of nations because of its direct effects on the social, cultural, educational and economic sectors of national societies and their international relations (UN 1981, 5)

Since tourism is now an integral part of modern societies, its study and analysis becomes imperative if its potential economic and social benefits are to be maximized and developed in a manner consistent with society's goals. The growth of tourism has converted many communities into destination areas, either as major resorts or as temporary stop-overs for travellers. The impact of the industry and its local issues will vary according to its magnitude and relative importance, but in every case politicians, businessmen, and residents are recognizing they cannot ignore tourism if they wish to benefit from it.

The raison d'etre of the industry is the tourist, so all development and planning must be predicated on the understanding of who this person is, if it is to succeed. The term "tourist" is derived from the work "tour," meaning, according to Webster's Dictionary, "a journey at which one returns to the starting point; a circular trip usually for business, pleasure or education during which various places are visited and for which an intinerary is usually planned." As this definition indicates, there are several motives for travel, each requiring its own facilities and having a different impact. Thus, government agencies in search of a comprehensive definition of tourist, and one which will facilitate the measurement of this activity, have resorted to the more general term of "visitor." The definition most widely recognized and used is that produced by the 1963 United Nations Conference on Travel and Tourism in Rome. Which was adopted by the International Union of Official Travel Organizations (IUOTO) in 1968. It states that a visitor is:

> any person visiting a country other than that in which he has his usual place of residence, for any reason other than following an occupation remunerated from within the country visited.

Thus, tourism is concerned with all travellers visiting foreign parts, whether it be for pleasure, business, or a combination of the two. The only exception is someone who is setting up a new residence in a foreign country and will be earning a salary and paying taxes in this new country. The IUOTO definition was intended for international travel but it can accommodate domestic tourism by substituting region for country.

Visitors have been subdivided further into two categories to assist the measurement of tourist traffic and the assessment of its economic impact.

(1) Tourists—who are visitors making at least one overnight stop in a country or region and staying for at least 24 hours.
(2) Excursionists—who are visitors that do not make an overnight stop, but pass through the country or region. An excursionist stays for less than 24 hours, and includes day-trippers and people on cruises.

This division has the practical value of using overnight accommodation records (registrations) as the basic source of tourist information, which can be used in conjunction with border crossing records if international move-ment is involved. By focusing on the accommodation sector of the industry, however, it also produces conservative estimates of the travel picture. There is no way to count overnight visits with relatives and friends and it is often impossible to obtain accurate records from small or temporary establishments like guest houses and farms.

The excursionist, or day-tripper, can be viewed as a special tourist. Such a person visits a destination for a day or spends some time there while passing through as part of a tour. In either case, he or she is a visitor, spending time and money while utilizing space and facilities in the destination area.

Types of tourist

There are as many types of tourist as there are motives for travel. Each type makes different demands of a desti-nation, and has its own particular impacts. Business travel can range from convention and trade fair meetings to vacations that include self-advancement courses or permit the traveller to update certain areas of his profession. Leisure travel can incorporate activity packages where the tourist learns a new sports skill or craft, as well as developing a tan. The impact of tourists' demands will vary according to the demands they place on destination's physical and human resources.

Tourist typologies can be grouped into two general categories. Interactional types emphasize the manner of interaction between visitors and destination areas, whereas the cognitive-normative models stress the motivations behind travel. Both app-roaches indicate the strong links between visitor expectations-motivations and the structure of destination areas. Thus it can be seen immediately that no destination appeals to all tourists and each can develop its own segment of the tourism market.

Among the interaction models are those of Cohen (1972) and Smith (1977b). Cohen classified tourists according to the degree they seek familiar or strange settings and whether or not they were willing to be institu-tionalized (organized) in their travel. Smith's mode detailed breakdown incorporates recent market develop-ments such as the unorganized "hippie treks" to Nepal and the social implications of a highly structured charter business. Smith, like Cohen, views explorers and elite travellers as having little impact upon indigenous cultures. Their small number requires little in the way of special accommo-dation, and their desire to gain insight into local customs is aided by a sympathetic attitude to the local way of life. In constrast, the charter tourists travel in their own environmental bubble, viewing everything from the security of their pre-paid and price-guaranteed package tour. To accommo-date the large numbers and organi-zational structure of charters a community must become commercial in its dealings with tourists, and often needs to import foreign capital and expertise.

In contrast to the interaction models which focus on the market characteristics and symptoms of travel, the cognitive-normative models attempt to reveal the causes of travel. Plog (1972) and Cohen (1979a) both look at the sociological concept of "centre," which considers that every society possesses a centre representing the charismatic nexus of its supreme, ultimate moral values. Plog develops a polar continuum consisting of those who differ from the normal (centric) values of society and follow their independent vacation desires (allocentrics), and those who conform to society's norms and values and thus become part of the mass market of tourism (psychocentrics).

Plog suggests that tourist destinations are attractive to different types of visitors as they evolve from untouched discoveries to popular resorts. A community can enter the tourism business with the arrival of a small number of adventurous allocentrics, but their impact would be small because no special facilities would be desired or required for this type of traveller. As the areas becomes more accessible, better serviced and more widely known an increasing number of mid-centric would visit. They in turn give way to large number of psychocentrics as the destination becomes a popular resort dependent on foreign investment and labour. The new visitors are made to feel at home, with a full range of facilities and attractions that may now be divorced from the natural geographic and social attractions which first attracted the allocentrics.

Cohen elaborates on this theme making further reference to people's "spiritual centre, whether religious or cultural—the centre which for the individual symbolizes ultimate meanings" (Cohen 1979b, 181). Those travelling on vacation believe there is some experience available elsewhere which cannot be found at home and which makes the travel worthwhile. The spiritual centre of this quest may be purely hedonistic, such as in the case of diversionary and recreational travel, or it may be a new type of pilgrimage, with travellers seeking answers through experiential, experimental, or existential forms of travel. Cohen notes that these three levels of tourism represent different depths of meaning for the individual, but unlike traditional pilgrimages they involve movement away from the center of the tourist's culture toward an "elective center," which he has chosen or converted to.

Destination areas.

To satisfy the variety of motives outlined above and to accommodate overnight or passing-through visitors, a physical setting is required. "tourism as an industry occurs at 'destination areas'—areas with different natural and/or man-made features, which attract non-local visitors (or tourists) for [a variety of] activities" (Georgulas 1970, 442). This definition by Georgulas possesses two key aspects which distinguish a destination area; it must contain 'features that will attract and it must appeal to "non-local visitors."

Tourism is a voluntary activity, therefore a destination area must have attractions which appeal to at least one type of tourist. These attractions can be as varied as the tourist types, but they are generally divided into two categories, natural or man-made. Natural attractions include such features as sunshine or scenic landscapes, while man-made features can be primary attractions like

Disneyland and the Edinburgh Festival, or support facilities like hotels and restaurants. A third category, which is now receiving more attention, would be a destination area's hospitality record. The manner in which visitors are received, and the quality of service provided, forms a major component of a destination's tourist image.

To be a destination an area must attract non-local visitors, people who have travelled some distance from their home town to see the attractions or use the facilities. This is an important feature because it differentiates recreational travel, where travel is an important and possibly the most important component of the experience, from outdoor recreation, where the activity is the prime objective and travel to a recreational site is of secondary importance or even an inconvenience. Furthermore, the emphasis on non-local visitors is a major economic consi-deration. Money spent by non-local visitors to an area becomes basic income, or earned income, for that community. If the money was spent by local people it would be redistributed income and thus not so beneficial to the destination area.

To determine whether an area can be classified as a tourist destination has traditionally required criteria to distinguish whether recreational traffic is local and not touristic, or non-local and therefore touristic. Burton (1971) identified five periods of recreational time which may help to distinguish local from non-local recreational travel. The five were (i) very short (up to one hour), (ii) short (a few hours), (iii) a full day, (iv) several days (usually a weekend), and (v) a week or more (usually the annual vacation). Using this classification, those periods extending beyond a single full day would produce a full-fledged tourist because of the need for overnight stops, and it would provide sufficient opportunities for travel on a regional or national basis. Thanks to our increased mobility, however, it is possible to move beyond the physical limits of a home town in a matter of hours, thus making travel on a regional or non-local basis feasible in time periods (ii) and (iii).

Attempts to operationalize such a classification system have produced a rough guide by which to differentiate between local and non-local recreational travel. Wall (1972) in a study of recreational car trips in England classified a traveller as a "pleasure tripper" if he travelled 5 miles or more from his point of origin. Therefore, any village, stately home, or country park beyond this range can be considered a tourist destination if it was included in a day's outing or afternoon drive. Likewise, Clawson and Knetsch (1966, 38) in their classification of North American recreation areas have indentified "intermediate areas" which they described as being "used for all-day outings and on weekends." Such areas include state parks, reservoirs and lakes which can be reached within two hours or so of driving. They possess no, or limited, accommodation yet they are definite destination areas for nearby urban centres. Such empirical classi-fications indicate that any community or area outside of a local recreational and economic hinterland can be considered a destination area.

In North America where freeways and emptier roads allow greater mobility, Wall's 5-mile radius to delimit destination areas needs to be extended considerably. Statistics Canada (1981, 30) uses 80 kilometres (50 miles) as its break point between local and non-local recreational travel. British Columbia (1970, 1) defines domestic tourism as "the travel, activities and services used by any British

Columbia resident beyond a 40 kilometre (25 miles) radius from home for the purpose of personal enjoyment and travel."

In addition to concerns over the non-resident tourist and his generation of basic income, there is a growing awareness of the importance of resident tourists. Those who are making new uses of there local settings. In economic terms it can be just as vital to keep more residents vacationing at home, rather than see them and their money disappear on external trips. Concern over the travel budget account is most frequently expressed at the national level, but since this is the sum of individual community accounts some areas have become anxious about their own deficits. Interest in attracting residents to vacation in their own town or area goes beyond economic considerations, however, to include a growing sense of pride in local heritage and amenities. The growing emphasis on a community's quality of life has encouraged many areas to invest in conservation and facilities that can create a viable, if occasional, tourist destination for residents.

Travel

A common theme in all definitions of tourism is travel, and Peters (1969, 2) went so far as to declare "the tourist industry is an industry concerned with movement." As we have seen, the journey must take a traveller beyond his home turf and because of this unfa-miliarity it becomes an important part of the travel experience. "Getting there is half the fun" when people travel through different areas on their way to a destination. This fact has been recognized by tourism agencies in their attempts to develop scenic and circular routes that will stimulate the senses and curiosity of the traveller.

Travel and time are interwoven and it is necessary to be aware of both in order to appreciate their signi-ficance to tourism. Hartmann (1981), in a paper entitle "Tourism, travel, and timing," notes:

> Whether we decide to travel by package tours where we trust in a fixed route and a pre-arranged time frame, or if we time our stay and change of place completely [by] ourselves, we need to know the principles of timing or at least to appreciate them.

Since tourism involves travel it requires greater blocks of discreationary time than much recreational activity. Thus, Burton's first recreational time period which accounts for much of our urban-oriented recreation has been discounted in the tourism context. The major blocks of discretionary time are the weekends and annual vacations, which account for the peaking of tourist travel in these periods and the problems of seasonality in the industry. Time also affects the demands for travel and structure of the industry. As people grow older their travel demands change. Young adults and elderly couples are considered a prime travel market because they have relatively large amounts of discretionary time and income. Between these two states the cost of buying a home and raising a family tends to reduce the discreationary aspects of a family budget. Likewise, the tourist industry can age and get out of step with technological innovations and consumer tastes. Lundgren (1983) illustrates this travel-time link in his temporal analysis of the Laurentians, north or Montreal, one of Canada's oldest tourist destinations.

Tourism

Tourism is a sum of the above elements, resulting from the *travel* of non-residents (tourists, including excursionists) to destination areas, as long as their sojourn does not become a permanent residence. It is a combination of recreation and business. Mieczkowski (1981) notes that while most tourism is recreational in nature, some tourism, such as business, professional and personal travel is not associated with recreation (Figure 1). Recreation falls entirely within leisure since it is an experience during free or discretionary time which leads to some form of revitalization of the body and mind. Part of this recreational activity takes place outside of the local community and as a result travel becomes an important, component leading this form of recreation to be classified as tourism. Tourism's orb extends beyond recreation to become associated with business trips and family reunions; and beyond leisure itself into personal and business motives for travel, such as health and professional development.

To move from the conceptual level to reality requires a system; therefore tourism is frequently referred to as a business or industry (Wahab 1975, 8; Lundberg 1976, 1; McIntosh 1977, 3). The tourism process combines a demand (tourist), suppliers (tourist industry), and a product (attractions), which Chau (1977) has summarized as the subject, means and object of tourism.

Most economists and compilers of industrial classifications argue that a tourism industry does not exist because it does not produce a distinct product (Chadwic 1981). One problem is that certain industries which sell a large proportion of their output to tourists, such as transport, accommo-dation, and entertainment, are not exclusively tourism industries, for they sell these services to local residents as well. Kaiser and Helber (1978, 3) maintain that it is not "properly" an industry, but more a cross-section of a regional or national economy. This does not however prevent them using the "industry" nomenclature throughout their book. Opposing this view, Maw-hinney and Bagnall (1976, 383) take the position that tourism is an industry, similar to other industries like agriculture and mining in that it is dependent on the continued availability of those resources upon which it is based. In other words, it is a resource industry, on which sells to local and non-local markets but one whose success and future depend on careful management.

Whether one classifies tourism as an industry or not, one cannot ignore the resource base which is its *raison d'etre*, or the delivery system which permits people to utilize those resources, if tourism is to be understood and managed for the benefit of society. Modern tourism must develop and protect its attractions, whether they be natural or man-made, and become a hospitality industry to make visitor experiences as enjoyable as possible. The tourism industry is highly frag-mented with many types of businesses and many levels of industrialization, but they all have a common purpose and that is to help a visitor enjoy his trip. The travel experience is this industry's product, but unlike other industries it is the consumer who travels and not the product. Figure 2 demonstrates the supply and demand characteristics of tourism and how the industry attempts to bring these market forces together.

The Tourism Industry

Demand factors

Some understanding of basic demand motivations is necessary if the industry and planner are to fulfill tourists desires. Four basic travel motivators have been indentified by the industry (Figure 2). *Physical or physiological* motivators, such as relaxation and medical treatment are major reasons for a vacation, and the quality of food, drink, and comfort frequently represents an important criterion in assessing the travel experience. Cultural motivators have long been associated with the desire to learn about foreign countries and customs. Social motivators include visits with relatives and friends, meeting business associates at conferences, and pursuing activities associated with status and prestige. Combinations of cultural and social motives could be seen in the early tours of China, where influential people vied not only to see this previously closed society but also for the prestige of being one of the first to report on this great unknown. Fantasy motivators form an important element of travel demand and illustrate its individualistic nature. Dann (1976, 19) notes "holidays are essentially experiences in fantasy."

A good deal of this fantasy takes place before the trip itself:

> a certain picture is built up of a world that marks an escape from present reality, and environment for acting out psychic needs, and the playing of certain roles which cannot be fulfilled at home, and it is this which forms part and parcel of tourist motivation. (Dann 1976, 22)

He goes on to identify two types of fantasy, the "Anomic" where the average city dweller desires to transcend the monotony of everyday life, and "ego-enhancement" which provides psychological boosts through such activities as gambling holidays or sexual adventures—real or imagined.

To convert such motivation into a trip requires knowledge about the conditions and opportunities that exist within our reach. Unfortunately, as consumers and geographers we are flawed, we have fragmentary information and distorted images (mental maps) of the real world (Gould and White 1974). these images are our perceptions. Studies have shown that some regions have very favourable images while others have relatively negative ones, and the differentiation is fairly consistent (Mayo 1973). The dominant attributes people use to sort out these mental images are often related to cost, climate, scenery, personal safety, and sanitation, and thus can have an important bearing on their choice of destination (Anderson and Colberg 1973; Crompton 1979).

Perception of holiday options and various destination areas is conditioned by three important elements. Individual preferences, reflecting an individual's personality, will direct the search for specific forms of gratification. They will dictate whether a person wishes to indulge in the gastronomic delights of a cruise or pit his skill and stamina against some mountain. Perceptions will be coloured by past vacation experiences, with a satisfactory experience tempting repetition and possibly encouraging more adventurous pursuits. These two elements reflect the two schools of thought concerning image causation (Kotler 1975). One school suggests that images are largely person-determined whereas the other approach suggests that people's mental image is largely destination-determined.

The third element in image creation is hearsay, information from friends and relatives, the media, or travel agents. A study by Henderson and Voiland (1975, 91) revealed "communication or second-hand sources seem to play the strongest role when a person assesses an area's recreational utility." This conclusion supports the general communication and marketing models regarding a two step flow of communication. According to this theory, ideas flow from radio and print to opinion leaders and from them to the more conservative sections of the population (Lazarsfeld et al. 1944; Cox 1964). Within the opinion leadership are two groups, the innovators and influentials. Much of the promotion for new destinations or experiences is directed at the adventurous and innovative market, and word of their pioneering experiences is channeled to the influential opinion leaders with the hope that they will adopt this new vacation and spread the concept by example to the masses. As we will see later this two-step theory of communication fits in very well with the general evolutionary pattern of resorts.

Motivation and perceived options build an *image* of each tourist destination. This image may be defined as the sum of beliefs, ideas, and impressions that a person has regarding a destination. It is a personal composite view of a destination's tourism potential, and where prices are comparable it is often the decisive factor in a tourist's selection process. The images are not necessarily the same for each visitor and this makes it difficult to allocate resources and plan for future land use in destination areas. To overcome this problem many areas attempt to appeal to a specific group through extensive and expensive promotion, presenting themselves as a family-oriented resort, a place for rugged outdoor enthusiasts, or a swinging locale for night people.

One problem which emerges with this system of image building is the time-let between initial purchase, based on a projected image, and the actual experience. Tourism is unique, for as Metelka points out:

> the would-be customer must decide to expend his valued resources of time and money BEFORE he actually consumes the product or service. Blatantly stated, a person decides to visit Tahiti and purchases the transport seat, the hotel and many other items long before he arrives in Tahiti. This dichotomy between time of decision/purchase and time of use has permitted if not encouraged promotional practices which some regard as dishonest. (Metelka 1977, 4)

Thus the time-lag makes misrepresentation easier, and the creation of a false image can spoil a vacation not only for the visitor but also for those around him, as they try to accommodate and humours a person who feels he has been sold "a pig in a poke."

The potential for diverse perception can create a critical situation if it extends to differences between the residents and the industry. Metelka notes.

> A second functional dichotomy exists between the residents of tourism destination areas and the would-be customers in the market place. Past and present marketing practices reflect the fact that destination area residents are overwhelmingly unaware of how their homeland is described in promotional material. (Metelka 1977, 4)

The image builders are often marketing or advertising experts who select and arrange "facts" about the destination that will entice would-be visitors. These promotional messages are beamed to other states and countries, and therefore the resident is in no position to correct mistakes or misrepresentations because he is not the intended viewer or purchaser. This lack of inherent control for the industry' marketing can lead to advertisments of questionable taste and of a self-destructive nature. Metelka gives some examples:

> the Seychelles have been dubbed "The Promiscuous Isles."

In Honolulu, an aerial sightseeing firm prints brochures in English and Japanese asking tourists to imagine: "Ifs December 7th and you are there Fly over Pearl Harbor, follow the same flight plan as the attacking Japanese planes."

Elegant, erotic, exotic! This is how the brochure describes a new jungle resort for the jet set, Habitation Le Clere, a spread of luxurious villas surrounded by areas of poverty.

"Ibiza: The invaded paradise." Living here is cheap...and was, until recently at least blissfully tranquil. But lately, Ibiza's slumberous calm has been jarred by the shockwaves of notoriety. (Metelka 1977).

As Metelka asks when he presents these and other examples, as a destination area resident, how would your opinions regarding local tourism be affected by these words?

Supply Factors

Such a question is pertinent to an industry which regards itself as a host industry and is dependent on local goodwill, but it also needs to develop the resources and product which will substantiate the image. With such diversity of tourist demands and interests destinations need to focus on a particular market subset, one they can satisfy in terms of resources and faci-lities. When the supply side of the tourism market is considered the twin foundations of the industry are its destination area attractions and hospitality.

Tourism is a resource industry, one which is dependent on nature's endowment and society's heritage. Visitors are attracted to areas of outstanding beauty and this beauty can take many forms. In some areas it is the climate which is the major attraction, as can be seen with the sunbelt and Mediterranean resorts. In others it is landforms such as the Grand Canyon, the Rockies, or Alps, or specific terrain within these areas which may facilitate certain activities like the skiing in Vail, Colorado, or mountaineering around the Matterhorn. Water has always appealed as a source of relaxation whether it be associated with a seaside beach, a waterfall, or lake and river fishing. Flora and fauna provide idyllic setting and as such enchance a visit, such as the host of daffodils in the English Lake District at Easter, or provide a specific purpose to the visit, as with walks through alpine meadows or observing game in national parks and game reserves. Wherever an accessible area processes several of these natural attributes it becomes a major attraction and in many cases has been designated a national park, so as to conserve these resources for future generations.

In addition to nature's resources, people are attracted by the cultural attributes of society and its heritage Centres of learning (Oxford, Heidelberg), of culture (Stratfor-upon-Avon, Athens), and of entertainment (London, New York) have long been magnets for travellers. Likewise, the splendor and history attached to various buildings and locations have created major attractions. Numerous castles (Windsor, Caernarvor), palaces (Versailles, Blenheim), stately homes (Woburn Abbey, Mount Vernon), ruins (Colosseum, Parthenon), and battlefields (Gettysburg, Pearl Harbor) feature prominently in the tourist literature. As the significance of heritage and its conservation has spread, whole city districts have been preserved because of their architectural merit, historical significance, and potential tourist value. "Venice is an extreme example of a tourist-dominated city," where the original city on the islands has become a tourist Mecca and the scene of an international restoration rescue, while its mainland twins of Marghera and Mestre provide the bulk of the region's industry and housing, and local life (Appleyard 1979, 15).

As important as the natural and cultural resources, which combine to form the major attractions, is the welcome which is accorded to a visitor. Public goodwill is an essential ingredient of any trip, for if the host community is antagonistic to visitors, no amount of attractions will compensate for the rudeness or hostility. It is for this reason that various governments feel obligated to remind residents of the value of tourism to local economies and encourage local people to be hospitable and friendly toward the visitor.

There are three facets to note about tourism's' resource base. First, it is a combination of physical and human resources which form the basis of the industry. Nowhere is this more important than in the case where the major attraction is a public amenity, either publicly owned or subsidized by the public purse. Under these circumstances the industry's foundation is a public good (a beach, a plaza, a park, or museum), and as such the industry should be cognizant of its special relationship with local community. It has a responsibility to foster what is in fact a community resource, and has no right to enclose or destroy it for its own purposes. Second, the physical resources often possess a seasonal element that encourages variations in visitation patterns. The most obvious is the climatic variation experienced in northern latitudes which encourages most people to consider vacations during the sunny summer weather. This climatic variation also affects the flora and fauna and attractiveness of various locations, providing each with a periodic climax.

Thus, many of its attractions ensure that tourism will remain a seasonal activity, and any attempt to extend the seasonal life of a destination will need to consider supplementary activities. Finally, tourism has frequently been described as a search for the four S's—surf, sand, sun, and sex. If this sarcastic description of the industry has any truth in it, it is that prime attractions can be found in many areas of the world. This makes the industry very competitive and flexible, for it can often find substitute resources and locations if an original destination turns sour because of growing residential hostility or changing fashions and economic circumstances. As Peters (1969) has noted, the optimum situation for a destination is to offer "an asset so outstanding and unique that the tourist industry can largely depend on, and be prompted by, this feature." Since this situation occurs rarely the industry and communities often attempt to supplement the natural tourist resources of an area with other facilities and man-made attractions.

To develop the tourist resources, making them more accessible and comfortable to experience, requires considerable *capital investment,* in some cases so considerable it is beyond the capability of the individual businessman and private sector. A major expense, and prime area of government support, is in the provision of water supplies, public utilities, sewage systems, and highways. These are the pre-requisites for extensive development and are known as "infrastructure." These facilities are usually available in urban areas but must be created specifically for the industry in rural or isolated areas. Examples of government assis-tance in providing such basic services are very clear in new isolated resorts, such as federal-provincial support for the

Whistler Mountain ski resort north of Vancouver, or in mega-projects such as the French government's support of the Languedoc recreation-tourism complex. But such assistance also occurs within the city, for its existing infrastructure frequently requires adjustment to accommodate new tourism facilities. For example, the building of a major hotel can necessitate changes to local water and sewer lines, the building of a convention or trade centre usually requires direct financial aid and complementary adjustments to local traffic flows and parking. In most cases government assistance appears inevitable if extensive development of tourism resources is to occur, and such assistance is offered in the hope that future employment and taxes will justify the public expense.

To make a destination area more appealing and diversified in the competitive tourism market the industry often creates support facilities and artificial attractions. The objective is to create a more enjoyable and comfortable visit and thereby earn more revenue by inducing visitors to stay longer. An old maxim in tourism is "the longer they stay the more they spend," thus the industry continues to pursue the objective of enticing visitors to stay.

Ideally, the support facilities and attractions will supplement and complement the natural resources of the area. Hotels and motels should blend with the local architecture and landscape. Stores should emphasize local customs and handicrafts and, where possible, visitors should have access to local markets where informality and daily bustle add an air of authen-ticity and local flavor. Likewise, attractions are hopefully in keeping with the natural resources and customs of the area, providing complementary educational and entertainment themes. For example, coastal cities are developing marine exhibits to show sea-life, historic centers develop museums and tours, industrial centres are stressing industrial heritage as in the case of Stoke-on-Trent's renovated Potteries and Dayton, Ohio's National Air Museum. Unfortunately, as we will see, such ideals are not always met and uncoordinated development can result in montonous homogeneity and garish low-quality tourist traps, which clash with the destination's ambience.

In some cases the quality of the facilities and created attractions has been high enough, however, to rival to the original tourist resources as a major destination attraction. Famous examples of this are Disneyland, California, and Disney World, Florida. They attract millions of visitors to what were previously agricultural areas, with Disneyland recording nearly 11 million visitors in 1978 and Disney World attracting over 14 million visitors in 1978-only 6 year after being opened. In the process, these Disney parks have set the standards by which all other thematic parks are judged.

Artificial attractions take many forms. A decommissioned battleship, the USS Massachusetts, was introduced to the non-tourist area of Fall River, Massachusetts, to help boost and diversify the local economy (Figure 3). It has more than fulfilled those expectations, for the ship has over 200,000 visitors a year and generates over $2 million into the local economy annually (Lundberg 1976, 40). Such success has encouraged similar ventures in Long Beach, California (Queen Marry), and London (HMS Belfast), and now competition for retiring famous vessels has become intense. Newsweek (1980) reported a battle between the US Naval Academy in Annapolis, Maryland, and the submarine base in Groton, Connecticut, over who would have the honour of putting the world's first nuclear submarine, the USS Nautilus, on display.

Facilities designed to improve accessibility are a key capital investment for destination areas since the industry is based on travel. Investment in various forms of transport is considered desirable in order to remain competitive and flexible with ever-changing transport technology. Each new form of transport changes the accessibility equation for tourist destinations, especially those in peripheral regions. For example, Rudney considers:

Like most other tourist regions, the Cote d'Azure attained its "take-off" point when a means of fast comfortable transportation was introduced. In this case it was the railroad...By 1889, the train trip from Paris to Nice took a mere 18 hours, where once it had taken 13 days by coach (Rudney 1980, 215).

Similarly, development of the freeway system has brought certain scenic peripheral areas closer to urban-industrial centres, in term of time, with dramatic increases in visitor volumes being the result. In the United States, Interstates 75 and 81 bring people from the Midwest and Atlantic states within a few hours of Gatlinburg and the Great Smoky Mountains National Park. As a result, this park receives over 8 million visits a year, more than three times the number of any other national park in the United States (Coppock and Rogers 1975).

Although transport links are seldom built solely for tourism purposes, the tourism market potential plays a major role in upgrading existing facilities and creating new ones. Competition for international tourists has encouraged various governments to build new airports or operate national airlines. Development of Hawaii's airport enabled it to take advantage of new generations of jet aircraft and their associated economies (Farrell 1982, 23). In some cases the importance of a tourist link becomes so important that governments will protect it with special legislation. British Columbia's government, for example, has promised to incorporated the ferry connection between Vancouver Island and the main-land into an Essential Services Act, to ensure it is not disrupted by labour disputes. A major factor in bringing this about is the importance of tourism to the Island in general and to Victoria, the Island's provincial capital, in particular.

The resources and created facilities of a destination combine to produce an amalgam of activities and functions called a *tourist product*. Due to the interrelated nature of the industry and its dependence on public facilities and goodwill, destination areas attempt to create a package or basket of goods for the visitor to perceive and experience. Naturally, the more co-ordinated the individual items, the more noticeable and effective the package. Thus, destinations attempt to present a theme that will attract attention and appeal to tourist images. Prominent successes in product formation include Las Vegas and Monte Carlo, which have become associated with gambling, enter-tainment, and luxury, or Disneyland which is synonymous with quality family entertainment.

The creation of a product that is noticeable and marketable in a competitive business world appear to be a simple task for most industries, but for one made up of numerous individual businesses and entrepreneurial spirits, it is a major challenge. In a free enterprise system there is little control over market entry or quality. As Disneyland in Anaheim experienced, there is no way of influencing the quality and type of neighbouring facility, there a carefully planned and developed attraction is surrounded by a jungle of neon lights, garish architecture, and snarled traffic. Not only is it difficult to develop a harmonious product within a destination, but it is even more difficult, with the competition for visitors, to get various destinations to combine their development and promotion into an effective regional product. Yet regional cooperation is required as the public become more mobile and is no longer content to spend its entire vacation in one place. Therefore, the need for government coordination and promotion has become more essential in drawing businessmen and destinations together in order to form regional product units, where the whole has more appeal than the sum of individual parts. This approach can be seen at the national level in England where the English Tourist Board has divided the country up into 12 regions, and, at the state/provincial level, with British Columbia's strategy of developing and promoting nine geophysical-tourism regions.

Market Place

To be successful, an industry must sell its product in the market place. Since tourism's product is immobile and its potential customers need to build and compare destination images before they travel, some form of intermediary is required. This is the function of the travel agent, who must successfully match a tourist image and tourist product if the travel experience is to have any chance of success. Four phases in this process have been identified. First, the development of a tourist product and promotion of an image is the role of tour wholesalers. Three of the biggest companies are Thomas Cook, Amex, and Intertourist, and they send out representatives to find new destinations or combinations that can be put together as a saleable package. Second, the actual selling of individual vacations is the responsibility of the store front travel agent. These people act as advisors and consultants, and a sense of geography is vital if they are to match their customer's wishes with suitable customs and climate. Third, the travel agent either arranges accommodation directly or leaves it to the destination area to provide such services and supplementary information concerning local attraction and events. In this way it is hoped that most tastes and budgets can be satisfied. The final objective is to have a satisfied customer, who is likely to make a return trip and act as a goodwill ambassador, for this is the most effective way of nurturing the industry and fulfilling the goals of tourism.

Community Approach

The product and image that intermediaries package and sell is a destination experience, and as such creates an industry that is highly dependent on the goodwill and cooperation of host communities. Many destination area attractions are public property or public goods, and the hospitality needed for a memorable visit must come from members of the public as well as employees of the industry. Increasingly, development of new facilities requires public investment in infrastructure and shared facilities; and many festivals or events that evolved to fill local needs are being commercialized and promoted as tourist events. It is the citizen who must live with the cumulative outcome of such developments

Elements, Trends and Scope of Tourism Management

and needs to have greater input into how his community is packaged and sold as a tourist product on the world market.

The vacation decision is influenced, if not shaped, by various "forces" external to the individual. This chapter examines these forces.

The culture of which we are a part serves as a barometer of general trends within a country, and it exerts social pressure to conform to the broad cultural values represented by the majority of individuals making up that culture.

The amount and type of time available also helps determine if and where we can vacation.

Marketers have long segmented the travel market along the socioeconomic criteria of age, income, sex, and education. It is therefore appropriate to determine whether tourism demand differs on these criteria.

The characteristic patterns of demand at various stages in the family life cycle are examined, with particular reference to the effect of children on the family's demand, the demand pattern of the empty nester, and the various barriers to leisure enjoyment at different life-cycle stages.

Finally, the role of personality in shaping demand is explored. It has been felt that a link between personality and vacation behavioural exists. Do certain types of people take certain kinds of vacations because of their personality characteristics? From a marketing viewpoint the segmentation of a target market by life-style provides a better picture of the characteristics, likes and dislikes of the potential tourist.

Many factors external to the individual act as inhibiting factors on travel-purchase behaviour. In this chapter the effect of these variables will be examined. Although these factors will be explored separately, it should be noted that their effect is often a compound one.

Effects of Culture

While an individual acts to satisfy certain internal needs and wants, the way in which these wants are satisfied is heavily influenced by forces external to the individual. As individuals we are part of larger social groups by which we are influenced. These groups themselves are part of and influenced by the surrounding culture. A knowledge of the culture of a country or submit within that country is important to an understanding of how individuals within that country or subunit will behave.

Culture can be defined as a "set of beliefs, values, attitudes, habits and forms of behaviour that are shared by a society and are transmitted from generation to generation."

Culture and Society

Culture affects society in four ways. First, the overall values of the culture determine which goals and behaviour will gain social approval or disapproval. To the extent that people are concerned about how others think of them, they will be influenced to seek gratification of their needs and wants in ways acceptable to society. This means that in order to induce those individuals to buy various products and services, it will be necessary to state the appeals and benefits of those products and services in terms acceptable to society. The many advertisements that advertise the hedonistic vacation life-style can only work because society is increasingly condoning this value. Several decades ago, such an appeal would not have worked because it was not socially acceptable to be self-indulgent, even on vacation.

The many social institutions of a society are also reflective of its culture. In the United States, for example, the ideas of individual initiative and equal opportunity for all (part of the culture) influence the way in which the educational system is organized to provide for mass education with a somewhat liberal child-rearing philosophy. Yet this expresses itself in different ways throughout society. Although lower-middle-class parents in the United States tend to be child dominated and concerned with satisfying their children, upper-class parents are more interested in seeking ways to help their children seek status achievement. This suggests that upper-class parents can more readily be sold a travel vacation if that vacation is perceived by them as being something that will advance their child's progress in society.

The third way in which culture affects the social backdrop is in the established conventions and practices of society. Society adopts various practices relative to such things as which foods can be eaten, how to entertain, and which gifts are or are not appropriate. It is acceptable, for example, for horsemeat to be eaten in France but not in the United States; it is appropriate for a U.S. dinner guest to bring the host a bottle of wine, but in France this would be an insult. When traction or servicing a market from a culture different from our own, it is necessary to know the established practices to avoid inadvertent behaviour.

Last, culture's effect on society is felt in the language people use to communicate with one another. It is important to consider not only words but also gestures, expressions, and other body movements. A smile in Western culture is a warm signal to further a relationship, but in Oriental culture it may be used to cover embarrassment and shame.

Culture and Social Groups

Social groups have roles or standards of behaviour peculiar to each group. These group norms differ from one culture to another. Groups can be classified either as primary (family or friends) or secondary (unions, fraternities, church, and so on). An individual will belong to more than one group, and consequently he or she will adopt a role for each social group. These roles may overlap. The surrounding culture will help define for each group the appropriate objects people use to show their membership in the group as well as the relevant status symbols.

Is there a distinct "vacation role"? One of the attractive features of taking a vacation is that it allows the freedom to be someone other than who we are in everyday life. Travelling to places where we are not known, meeting people who do not know us allows us to choose how we will behave.

The social role that an individual takes is learned through socialization—the process of social learning by which cultural role expectations are handed down from one generation to another. The link between participation in recreational activities as a child and subsequent participation as an adult has been repeatedly demonstrated. If we also accept that travel is a learned experience, the importance of encoura-ging travel participation at an early age can be demonstrated. The norms of behaviour for a group change by virtue of both internal and external sources. Within a group there are those people (innovators) who are more willing than others to try new things. Usually these group members are better educated, have high income, and are more achievement-oriented than other. The innovators also tend to be opinion leaders and, as such, highly sought-after by marketers. A common saying in explaining destination development in "Mass follows class." This phrase suggests that a destination first attracts a relatively small number of high-status individuals whose actions are eventually copied by a larger number of less-innovative others.

Culture patterns also change by virtue of external forces. As a result of contact with other environments, previous attitudes and behaviours may change. A visit to a foreign country may result in a change in attitude towards the people of that country as well as a stimulation of a desire for cuisine from that country. Travel may also stimulate the sale of other products from the destination visited. A vacation in Germany might improve the chance of purchasing a German car upon one's return home.

Culture and the Individual

The effect of culture is felt by the individual in three ways. First, culture affects the daily life patterns of individuals in society. An afternoon siesta is common in certain countries in Southern Europe to cope with high mid-day temperatures. In the United States, the physical separation of work and residence leads to an uninterrupted workday and consequently a smaller lunch compared to those in Southern Europe. Concepts of time vary from culture to culture. In the United States, time is money; in other cultures time is of less consequence. Second, culture affects the way emotions are expressed. In the Latin culture there is much touching—people feel comfor-table at distances from one other that would make an American or Briton uncom-fortable—and emotions are expressed in a spontaneous and enthusiastic manner. Last, there is every indication that certain cultures have a predominance of certain personality types. The German national character exhibits a predominance of authoritarian personality traits. In this culture, we would expect that a decision as important as an annual vacation would be made primarily by the male in a family.

It can readily be seen that in order to truly understand a consumer it is necessary to understand the surrounding culture of that consumer. A knowledge of how the culture affects the individual, the social groups to which that individual belongs, and society as a whole will better enable the marketer to sell a travel product. Insight will be gained as to what to say, to whom to say it, and how the message should be phrased. As hosts, we will be better able to understand why visitors act the way they do and be in a better position to anticipate and satisfy their need and wants.

Analysing a Culture

Louden has developed a checklist of factors to be considered in analysing a culture. The analysis would be particularly appropriate before developing a marketing approach to people from different cultures.

1. *Determine relevant motivations in the culture:* Which needs do people seek to fulfil?
2. *Determine characteristic behaviour patterns*: How often are vacations purchased?
3. *Determine what broad cultural values are relevant to this product*: Are vacations, leisure, and recreation thought of in positive terms?
4. *Determine Characteristic froms of*

decision making: Who makes the vacation purchase decision? When is it made? What information sources and criteria are used in making the decision?

5. *Evaluate promotion methods appropriate to the culture*: What kinds of promotional techniques. Words, and pictures are acceptable or not acceptable to the people of this culture?

6. *Determine appropriate institutions for this product in the minds of consumers*: Do people tend to purchase vacations directly from suppliers, or are retail travel agents used? What alternative, acceptable to the consumer, are available for distributing the product?

The U.S. Culture

Within the culture of a country various subcultures can be found. Nevertheless the following characteristics are those that are generally found in the dominant culture of the United States.

Evaluative and moralistic. The dominant culture in the United States is one that is evaluative and moralistic in its judgement of objects, people, and behaviour. The judgements that people make are usually quite simple and concise, that is, something or someone is either right or wrong, good or bad, or moral or immoral.

Humanistic and egalitarian. Americans as a whole believe in equal rights for all and that people are created equal. If possible, these people are generous to charitable casuses.

Human mastery over nature and human perfectability. This attribute is protrayed by corporations and individuals continuously devising new technology and ideas that will be of benefit to their economic goals and to the goals of people to become knowledgeable and well-educated.

Materialism and progress. People place values on the amount of possessions one has and the necessity to be progressive both materially and educationally.

Individualism and achievement. The U.S. dominant culture places a great deal of emphasis on a high level of achievement motivation, which distinguishes it tremendously from certain subcultures and cultures of other countries. We achieve goals and become individualistic through intense competition.

Time orientation. Time is important to many because it is equated with money. Many things are organized and run by the clock.

Youthfulness. Many people turn to youth activities and procedures for renewed inspiration. Advertising, promotion, and products are all geared toward youthfulness.

Activity. Americans value hard work and also hard play. This stems form the Puritan ethic that idleness is evil.

Efficiency and practicality. People in the United States are continually searching for better ways of doing things, whether it is with a new product, service, or procedure. A product or service that is not quite "in" will be set aside and the new product or service will be implemented, even if the old product or service had not become obsolete.

Religious and moral orientation. A large per centage of Americans are religious. Many in the culture believe that the U.S. culture and way of life is the best and feel that it is their duty to bring others around to this country's way of thinking and acting.

Social interaction and conformity. Even though many in the United States value individualism, marketers promote products of all kinds that incorporate the theme of how beneficial these products are in achieving pleasureable social interaction.

Subcultures

The point was made earlier that, not only do countries have unique cultures, but within a country subcultures exist. Within the United States there are, to name a few, Spanish, black, and Jewish subcultures. Each subculture is different in several ways to the national culture. In the Spainish subculture, family ties are very strong, with the husband having strong authority over buying decisions. The upper-class Spanish-American has been almost totally assimilated into American culture. Because Spanish-Americans are respected for this, they are regarded as opinion leaders and are a useful group to reach to penetrate the market.

In the black subculture, women have a great influence on the attitudes and behaviour of black children and on purchase behaviour in general. It is dangerous to generalize even when talking about the characteristics of a subculture. It appears, however, that blacks tend to spend their income on personal consumption items with which they feel they get value. Although some blacks base their purchase behaviour on the whites they may seek to match, others go in the opposite direction.

The Jewish subculture is strongly family oriented, with joint decision making more common than in the subcultures of the previous examples. A strong emphasis is placed on education, and there is a willingness to buy new items, try new places.

Regional differences are also apparent. Southerner are regarded as being more conservative, westerners as being more liberal and tolerant of others, and easterners as being more self-reliant than those in the rest of the country. Thus, it can be seen that it is necessary to understand not only the national culture but the regional, racial, and religious subcultures in order to effectively understand and market to the travel consumer.

Cultural Changes

The culture within which the travel consumer exists does change. It is difficult to determine when a movement becomes a trend and when a trend becomes part of the culture. Yankelovich, Shelley and White is a very successful marketing and social research organization that specializes in identifying and tracking social trends. Many trends or tendencies in the United States have been developed, all of which have significance for the marketer of travel and tourism.

Psychology of Affluence

Trend toward physical self-enhancement: Spending more time, effort, and money on improving one's physical appearance; the things people do to enhance their looks.

Trend toward personalization: Expressing one's individuality through products, possessions, and new lifestyles; the need to be "a little bit different" from other people.

Trend toward physical health and wellbeing: The level of concern with one's health diet, and things to do to take better care of oneself.

Trend toward new forms of materialism: The new status symbols and the extent of deemphasis on money and material possessions.

Trend toward social and cultural self-expression: The cultural explosion and what it means to various segments of the population.

Trend toward personal creativity: The growing conviction that being "creative" is not confined to the artist. Everyone can be creative in her or his own way, as expressed through a wide variety of activities, hobbies, and new uses of leisure time.

Trend toward meaningful work: The spread of the demand for work that is challenging and meaningful more than just being well paying.

Implications: Greater demand for spa vacations; physically and mentally active vacations; allowing tourists more options on packages to let them personalize their trip; themes that say "This one's for you."

Antifunctional Trends

Trend toward the "new romanticism": The desire to restore romance, mystery, and adventure to modern life.

Trend toward novelty and change: The search for constant change, novelty, new experience, reaction against sameness, and habit.

Trend toward adding beauty to one's daily surroundings: The stress on beauty in the home and the things people do and buy to achieve it.

Trend toward sensuousness: Placing greater emphasis on a total sensory experience—touching, feeling, smelling, and psychedelic phenomena; a moving away from the purely liner, logical, and visual.

Trend toward mysticism: The search for new modes of spiritual experience and beliefs, as typified by the growing interest in astrology.

Trend toward introspection: An enhanced need for self-understanding and life experiences in contrast to automatic conformity to external pressures and expectations.

Implications: Greater demand for packages (that simplify vacations planning); "get away from it all" appeals; finding one's roots; deemphasizing large size of airline, destination, and so on; selling personal attention; regions rather than countries.

Reaction Against Complexity Trends

Trend toward life simplification: The turning away from complicated products, services, and ways of life.

Trend toward return to nature: Rejection of the artificial, the "chemical," the man-made improvements on nature; the adoption of more "natural" ways of dressing, eating, and living.

Trend toward increased ethnicity: Finding new satisfactions and identifications in foods, dress, customs, and lifestyles of various ethnic groups such as black, Italian, Irish, Polish, or German.

Trend toward increased community involvement: Increased affiliation with local, community, and neighbourhood activities; greater involvement in local groups.

Trend away from bigness: The departure from the belief that "big" necessarily means "good," beginning to manifest itself with respect to "big" brands, "big" stores.

Implications: Greater demand for

packages (that simplify vacation planning); "get away from it all" appeals; finding one's roots; deemphasizing of large size of airline, destination, and so on: selling of personal attention; regions rather than countries.

Trends That Move Away From Puritan Values

Trend toward pleasure for its own sake: Putting pleasure before duty; focus on self.

Trend toward blurring of the sexes: Moving away from traditional distinctions between men and women and the role each should play in marriage, work, and other walks of life.

Trend toward living in the present: Straying from traditional beliefs in planning, saving, and living for the future.

Trend toward more liberal sexual attitudes: The relaxation of sexual prohibitions and the devaluation of "virtue" in the traditional sense among women.

Trend toward acceptance of stimulants and drugs: Greater acceptance of artificial agents (legal and illegal) for mood change, stimulation, and relaxation as opposed to the view that these should be accomplished by strength of character alone.

Trend toward relaxation of self-improvement standards: The inclination to stop working as hard at self improvement, letting yourself be whatever you are.

Trend toward individual religions: Rejection of institutionalized religions and the substitution of more personalized forms of religious sects and cults.

Implications: Greater demand for "do it now," you deserve to have fun" type of appeals; greater acceptance of sexual innuendo in advertising.

Trends Related to Child Centredness

Trend toward greater tolerance of chaos and disorder: Less need for schedules, routines, plans, regular shopping, and purchasing; tolerance of less order and cleanliness in the home, less regular eating and entertaining patterns.

Trend toward challenge to authority: Less automatic acceptance of the authority and "correctness" of public figures, institutions, and established brands.

Trend toward the rejection of hypocrisy: Less acceptance of sham, exaggeration, indirection, and misleading language.

Trend toward female careerism: Belief that homemaking is not sufficient as the sole source of fulfillment and that more challenging and productive work for the woman is needed.

Trend toward familism: Renewed faith in the belief that the essential life satisfactions stem from activities centring on the immediate family unit rather than on "outside" sources such as work or community affairs. Restructuring of the way the family operates, from self-sacrifice on behalf of other family members to wanting a family setup in which each member can focus on self without guilt.

Implications: Greater demand for vacations off-peak and of shorter duration to fit into "two career" schedules; increased consumerism, including questioning of advertising claims; accent on "you deserve to have fun."

Effect of Time

Time, or rather the availability of time, acts as a major inhibiting factor to tourist travel. The amount of available time and the form in which it is available is, in fact, a major shaper of the destinations that can be visited, the modes of travel that can be used, and the activities that can be engaged in at the destination or enroute. The desire to travel and the financial ability to travel are insufficient if one does not have the time to travel. All three factors must be present for travel and tourism to take place.

Spending Time

Time is spent in many maintenance activities. Maintenance activities can be thought of as activities that involve a certain degree of obligation and that are necessary to sustain and maintain life. Included in this definition are such activities as eating, sleeping, maintaining the house, and caring for the lawn. Time can also be spent at work. For most of us this involves a degree of obligation greater than that spent in maintenance activities. Leisure can be defined, although some people may feel it is a rather simplified definition, as the time remaining after work and maintenance activities have been completed. By its very definition leisure implies that the individual has a level of discretion over how to spend time that is not present in the other two categories. Leisure is often contrasted with the economic activity of work, and it is connected with pleasure and a feeling of freedom with a minimum of obligation. Leisure is also seen as inner directed rather than other directed. It is the time for one's self. Although leisure time offers oppor-tunities for creativity and personal growth, the accent must be on freedom of choice. Traditionally, researchers have talked about leisure as time spent in productive pursuits. Yet this imposes a value system upon the individual's discretionary time. "Productive" is a term defined by the researcher. The crucial point is that leisure-time activities are those that are undertaken freely by individuals within their discretionary time.

By seeing time broken down into these three categories, it is easy to demonstrate a relationship between all three. Because time is absolute—there are twenty-four hours in a day, seven days in a week, fifty-two weeks in a year—any change in one of the three parts will automatically affect the others. As the workweek declines, more time is freed for maintenance and/or leisure activities. This is important because in the study of tourism we are concerned with the use of leisure time, and a recognition that leisure time is bound to the other two concepts will help us to be concerned with changes in those concepts as they might affect leisure time.

How is time actually spent? In a "typical" week most time is spent on maintenance activities. This is true for both females and males. The significant differences between the sexes is that females spend more time on housework, necessary home maintenance. Lawn care, and playing with or helping the children than do males. Leisure-time activities take up between 20 to 25 per cent of the average workweek. This amounts to approximately thirty-nine hours per week. There are no major differences between the sexes as to how leisure time is spent. Most leisure time is spent watching television.

We might expect that the above distribution would change relative to changes in the family life cycle. In the young and single phase, people are characterized by great physical capacity, disposable time, and few demands on their income. In the family phase, discretionary income and time decrease, and the physical capacity of the family is limited by that of its weakeast member. The third phase is characterized by an excess of discretionary time and a decrease in physical capacity.

Historical Development of Leisure Time

The distribution of time between the three categories mentioned has changed over the year. In 1850 the average work week was close to seventy hours; today it is approximately for several reasons for the long workweek in the nineteenth century have been traced to the industrial revolution. Prior to the industrial revolution in Britain, most people were connected with the farm. Hours of work and leisure were dictated by the farming seasons. People worked long hours when the harvest had to be brought in, but in winter, because of the lesser number of daylight hours, hours of work were less. The industrial revolution brought a movement of a rural population which had work hours conditioned by nature to an increasingly urban population which had work hours increased by employers who sought to have output on a continuous basis year round. In addition, many of the leisure-time pursuits of the working class were rough and violent. In order to better control their workers, owners adopted various strategies. Wages were kept low so that saving money was difficult and people had to continue working rather than take time off in order to live. In addition, the Sabbath was strictly enforced. As a complement to this, the idea of work was made the most important part of life. The idea of spending time at work was praised almost to the point of sanctification, but the idea of spending time at leisure was derided. Religious movements developed this thought into an ethic—the Protestant ethic. Leisure time was first given to celebrate various religious festivals. These holy days were the forerunner of our holidays, as the idea of associating a break from work with religion has gradually diminished.

Although the workweek has undoubtedly decreased, other factors have prevented more people from seeing an increase in their leisure time. As affluence has increased the incidence of material possessions, much of the reduced work time has manifested itself in increased maintenance time to take care of the new possessions, such as the car and the house. In addition, as cities have grown as a result of the country becoming more urbanized, commuting time to work has increased. A related factor is that, for many, the stress of big-city living means that more time is required before individuals are mentally ready for leisure pursuits. A third factor is that, as the economy moves from primary and manufacturing industries to a service economy, the distinction between work and nonwork becomes increasingly blurred. It is easier for the steel worker to punch out at the end of a shift and forget about work problems than it is for the manager of a business. In addition, the growing number of part-time workers has hidden the fact that over the past twenty-five years the average non-student workweek has remained steady at about forty-three hours.

Attempts have been made to show a relationship between the type of work and the type of leisure activities engaged in. Leisure has been seen as a compensation for work in that leisure activity is quite different from work activity. A passive job, for example, may result in active leisure-time activities. A second view is that the development of certain skills and life-styles learned at work will spill over into a demand for similar kinds of leisure-time activities. The problem, of course, is that any leisure-time behaviour can be explained by reference to whichever theory is more appropriate to one's purpose. The link between type of work and leisure activities has not been demonstrated. In fact, several studies have demonstrated that there are no significant differences in leisure activity between workers who are doing what they consider boring jobs and those who are doing more interesting and enjoyable jobs. It does seem clear, however, that the place of leisure in a person's life is becoming more important relative to that of work.

More important than the absolute amount of leisure time available, however, is the way in which it is spent. An individual who finishes dinner at seven o'clock and plans to go to bed at midnight has five hours of leisure time. The amount of time available limits what activities can be done and where they can be pursued. Leisure time may be thought of as being divided into three categories.

Leisure occurs on weekdays, weekends; and on vacations. The importance of this distinction can be illustrated by means of an example. If the workweek were to be reduced by 20 per cent, the opportunities for tourism activities would be affected by the way in which the reduction was taken: the workday could be shortened to six-and-a-half hours from eight; the workweek from five to four days; one week's paid vacation could be granted in each of three quarters of the year, with one month's vacation in the fourth quarter, with six months vacation every five years. All three alternatives represent a cut of 20 per cent in the workweek, yet the form in which it is taken affects the opportunities to participate in various activities and to visit various desti-nations.

It is clear that, although the absolute amount of leisure time may have increased little over the past several decades, the form in which it is being taken is changing. Although most of the gains in leisure in the past century have been taken in the form of a shorter workweek, since 1950 added leisure time has increasingly been taken in blocks of extended periods away from work. Yet the vast majority of full-time U.S. workers still are engaged in a five-day workweek.

The concepts of work, leisure, and money are intertwined as far as tourism is concerned. Individuals need both leisure and money to travel. Usually this money is earned by working. Thus, it is necessary to work in order to earn money to engage in leisure-time pursuits. The more one works, the more money is earned (and, therefore, available for leisure activities), but the less time one has to spend and enjoy it. consumers can thus be thought of as having both a time budget and a money budget, and some make rational decisions in allocating one over the other. The auto worker who takes Friday off to lengthen the weekend for a fishing trip chooses time over money; the college professor who chooses not to teach during the summer, but to travel cross-country chooses time over money. This idea has been expressed as the *principle of resource value inversion*. As consumers incomes rise, time becomes increasingly precious to them compared to money. Money, after all, can be saved; time cannot. Combined with this is a perception on the part of many that "time is now." To what extent are people increasingly unwilling to put off gratification? Are people choosing more time over more money? Several generalizations can be made. First, although Americans desire both more income and free time, it appears that three units of income are preferred for every unit of free time worth one unit of income. Second, this preference gap seems to be closing as free time gradually is increasing in importance relative to more income. In times of economic slowdown, this statement does not hold true. Third, the income-free time choice is made within the context of other factors and values associated with an individual's perception of the quality of life. Fourth, the choice between income and free time may be affected by the way in which the free-time options are offered. Some options were demonstrated above with the example of the 20 per cent workweek reduction. It appears that most workers prefer free time in the form of extended time away from work.

Much has been made of the effect of a four-day workweek on pleasure travel. People representing a nationwide sample were asked to indicate what activities would be undertaken if every week included a three-day weekend. The activities chosen by more than half of either male or female respondents.

The major response given indicated that a significant proportion of both male and female respondents would take weekend trips. However, studies of workers engaged in a four-day, forty-hour workweek have indicated that, because of fatigue from the workweek, most people tended to be more favorably inclined to home-centred relaxation. Another study compared the leisure participation of four-day-a-week and five-day-a-week workers. It found that both sets of workers devoted approxi-mately equal amounts of time to partici-pation in leisure activities. The only difference was that those who worked only four days a week pursued, on average, a greater number of different activities than the five-day-a-week worker. It may be that the extra day offers an opportunity to experiment with new activities, spending less time on each of more activities. This is rather interesting because, if this can be generalized, an extra day of nonwork actually places more time pressure on leisure activities.

What will be the effect of these time trends on travel products? We can conclude the following:

1. A growing importance for goods and services that economize on the consumers' use of time.
2. A growing importance of goods and services that require spending leisure time in blocks.
3. A decline in the effectiveness of monetary incentives relative to leisure-time incentives.

These trends can already be seen in the development of shorter cruises, thus capitalizing on those who can afford the trip but not the traditional three weeks, which was a previously common cruise time. As these trends continue, we would expect an increasing demand for time-intensive activities such as golf, water skiing, and eating out, as well as for two-and three-day holiday weekends.

Socioeconomic Variables

Age

The amount of available time is, by itself, insufficient to explain age as a factor in tourism behaviour. It is safe to conclude that the rates of participation in the overwhelming majority of leisure activities declines with age. The decline in participation varies relative to the type of activity. There is a greater decline for active recreational activities than for the more passive forms of recreation. Preferred activities among the elderly are the more passive ones such as visiting friends and relatives, sightseeing, fishing, and playing golf. Yet for many retires, although the number of activities participated in may drop upon retirement, the amount of time spent on each remaining one in terms of participation often increases.

There appears to be several differences between patterns of travel based on age. Older people tend to have a smaller share of tourists in proportion to their number than do younger people. This may also be influenced by other socioeconomic factors, such as income. Although younger people tend to select more adventurous destinations than do older people, older tourists tend to travel to farther destinations. The older tourists tend to dominate ship travel, spend less than middle-age tourists but more than younger tourists, and, while preferring to travel in the summer (in common with younger travellers), tend to travel more in the spring than do younger tourists.

In summary, leisure time decreases with age until children leave the nest; then the amount of leisure time increases. This increase continues with retirement. Though participation in physical activities declines with age (together with a corresponding rise in participation in the gentler forms of recreation) interest levels in activities previously participated in remains high. Opportunities may exist for tapping these interests by developing non-participatory means of expressing that interest. A skier, for example, may be unable to ski for reasons of age, but may be interested in other related activities such as watching skiers or sharing experiences.

Income

Income is obviously an important inhibiting factor in shaping the demand for travel. Not only does travel itself entail a certain cost, but the traveller must pay for services rendered at the destination as well as have money to engage in various activities during the trip. In addition, expenditures may be required in the form of specialized equipment to engage in various recreational activities while at the destination or enroute. It is difficult, however, to determine the relative importance of income per se, because this variable is interrelated with outer socioeconomic variables. Generally speaking, higher income is associated with higher education, with certain jobs, and with certain age groups. Total family would has risen steadily as more wives have entered the labour force. The fact that family income has risen will have an effect upon tourism demand. Yet the fact that more families have two spouses in the labour force will also affect the shape of tourism demand. Different types of vacations and recreational activities may be demanded because of the time pressures involved in having two working spouses. The difficulty arises in determining the effect of these two interrelated variables on the demand for new tourism and recreation products.

It is important to see that the income spent on travel is spent at the expense of something else. Travel expenditures are in compe-tition with other expenditures, some of which are discretionary.

An individual's personal is dispossible income is the amount of income left after taxes have been paid. After various necessary personal outlays to maintain basic living needs have been spent, an individual has discretion to do with the remainder whatever is desired. A mink coat may be purchased, money may be saved, or a trip taken to Hawaii.

It is important to look at income in this way to realize that the trip to Hawaii is in competition not only with a trip to the Bahamas, but also with various other recreational activities and other uses of that discretionary income. As the level of personal income increases, so does the amount of discretionary income.

Many studies have attempted to determine the per centage of income spent on recreation as a whole. It appears that at the lower levels of income and education approximately 2 per cent of income is spent on recreation. As income increases the proportion spent on recreation increases to between 5 and 6 per cent for all education levels. The highest recrea-tional expenditures, 7 per cent, are reported by respondents who are heads of households, under forty years of age, and without children. Other studies have indicated a positive correlation between income and recreation expenditures. In fact, it appears that increases in income result in a proportionately greater increase in recreation expenditures. As might be expected, higher-income tourists stay longer and spend more per day than do those with lower incomes. The type of recreational activities participated in differs based upon income. Higher-income people tend to participate in activities such as reading, bridge, fencing, squash, and chess; and middle-income people tend to engage in bowling, golf, and dancing. Lower-income families are identified with television viewing, dominoes, and bingo. The implication of these activities is clear to companies who wish to put together travel packages with specific activities involved aimed at particular market segments. A package, for example, aimed at a high-income segment of the market might be built around a recreational activity in which that segment tends to participate.

In addition to the relationship between income and recreation expenditure, some work has been done on the amount of participation in recreation and income. It has been shown that participation in most recreational activities increases as income increases up to a certain point (dollars 10,000 in 1972), but declines slightly at incomes higher than this.

The only significant demographic difference between U.S. domestic and foreign travellers is that of income. A greater per centage of foreign travellers had incomes of dollars 25,000 or more, and a smaller per centage had income of dollars 10,000 to dollars 20,000.

Sex

There are more similarities than differences between the sexes in terms of leisure participation rates. Overall, participation rates in leisure activities do not differ between men and women, although many engage in slightly fewer activities than do men. As might be expected, nonworking women have slightly higher participation rates than do employed women, except for such things as going out to dinner and either taking part in active sports or watching sports. There is a clear difference between the sexes in terms of preferred activities. Women are more involved in cultural activities, and men lead in outdoor recreation and playing and watching sports.

Education

The strong correlation between education, as it relates to income has been well-established. Independent of income, however, the level of education that an individual has tends to influence the type of leisure and travel pursuits chosen. The amount of education obtained most likely will determine the nature of both work and leisure-time activities. By widening one's horizons of interest and enjoyment, education influences the type of activities undertaken. Education itself can serve as the primary reason for travel.

Researchers have found that participation in outdoor recreation tends to increase as the amount of education increases. There is also some evidence to suggest that the more educated prefer those activities that require the development of interpretive and expressive skills. Such activities include attending plays, concerts, and art museums, playing tennis and golf, skiing, reading books, attending adult education classes, and undergoing a wilderness experience.

In summary, it appears that the more education people have the broader their horizons and the more options they can consider. The more-educated travellers also tend to be more sophisticated in their tastes. They may not, however, be bigger spenders. A study of visitors to Hawaii found that visitors with less education spent more per day while on vacation in Hawaii. The authors suggested that the less-educated visitor may equate having fun with spending money.

Life-Cycle Stages

Families evolve through a certain life cycle. The characteristics of the family at the various stages of its life cycle offer certain opportunities or exert various pressures that affect purchase behaviour.

Single-people take part in a much wider variety of activities outside the home than do married people. Married life brings about certain changes in leisure habits. Activities that were previously done alone or with friends are participated in less for reasons intrinsic to the activity itself.

Presence of Children

The narrowing of the types of activities participated in is intensified by the presence of children. When a married couple has children, there is a shift from activities engaged in primarily for intrinsic satisfaction to activities that are role-related, such as "family" activities. Before children come on the scene, the spouse was the chief leisure companion. This companionship is diluted by the presence of children. The presence of children seems to be crucial. Travel is curtailed, more leisure time is spent at home, and few new leisure interests are acquired. In at least one case, that of camping, the onset of parenthood has varied effects. Although the addition of young children in a camping family may produce a curtailment of camping activity, the shift to the empty-nest stage produces either an increase or a decrease in the activity. For those couples who enjoy camping, the situation of children leaving the nest may actually increase their participation. For others, who saw camping primarily as a family activity, the departure of children from the home may result in less camping.

Basic attitudes and behaviour patterns of family life established in the early years of the family life cycle affect the future activities of both husbands and wives throughout the marriage. For the young child, leisure pursuits are restricted by the dictates of parents and the limitations of money. As children enter school, leisure activities outside the home increase. As children grow older their leisure habits and attitudes are more heavily influenced by their peers. Because of the high rate of social interaction among young people, leisure fads are easily spread. There is also at this stage an attempt to duplicate the behaviour and attitudes of older age groups. Particularly important in this respect are college students, who tend to be leaders, often being the first to try new products and services.

Empty Nesters

As children leave the home, more time and money tend to be available for leisure. The empty nesters left behind have been the subject of a focus group study conducted by Plog Research. A focus group consists of a small group of people, usually ten to twelve, getting together for a two-hour discussion. The groups are made up of individuals, who have already been screened through questionnaires and interviews to arrive at a group that has members similar to one another in background. The discussion is led by a psychologist who attempts to develop a picture of the needs, interests, and personal psychologies of the group. The findings of the study are quite revealing. The typical empty nester doesn't think of extended trips by air, especially to foreign destinations. Their thinking is geared to the kinds of trips taken with their children, trips which have typically involved travel by car and visits to friends and relatives. There appears to be a strong desire for travel experiences as a means of self-actualization. Several barriers present themselves. The surface barriers of lack of time and money are true up to a point. For couples who work, scheduling may be a problem, and there is a reluctance towards using all of one's vacation time at once. Financially, although more discretionary income may be available, many empty nesters feel uncomfortable in spending their money on an intangible, such as travel. In addition, they tend to believe that the cost of a trip is more expensive than it really is, estimating the cost at twice the actual one. More than anything however, key express fear as a barrier to travelling. They are afraid of not knowing how to act in a new environment, of being taken advantage of. In a more subtle way, they feel that travel may be a way for them to learn how to be a couple again. Combined with this, however, is the fear that they may discover that they really do not like each other.

It is necessary to understand the particular inhibiting factors felt by each of these market segments at each stage of the family life cycle in order to be able to offer a pro-duct or service that will overcome the barriers and induce purchase behaviour. For the empty nesters, for example, a tour would be very appropriate. A package tour relieves the participants of making decisions they may well feel inadequate to make. The regular tour may have a negative connotation for them, however. Empty nesters usually want to spend more time in fewer places than many tours offer. Popular kinds of destinations are those that help the empty nesters find their roots. This appeals to the need to find some meaning to their lives. The tour also helps alleviate some of the fears of being a couple again with no children around. The fact that there are other people around means that the empty nesters do not have to totally rely upon each other for companionship and support during the trip.

Barriers to leisure Enjoyment

The barriers to leisure enjoyment have been the subject of a study by Witt and Goodale. They identified the rela-tionship between various barriers to the enjoyment of leisure and stages in the family life cycle. Understanding these barriers is a crucial step towards knowing what to say, do, and offer to lower those barriers. It was found that different patterns of change developed over the family life cycle relative to the barriers under discussion. The fact that various barriers showed an approximately U-shaped pattern, with the barriers having the least effect when the youngest child was between six and eighteen years of age. These barriers refer to difficulties in knowing with which activities to get involved and with whom to share participation. This suggests that as children reach school age, parents have more knowledge of what is available and how to utilize those opportunities. It may also be, as mentioned earlier, that their leisure activities are more closely defined for them by the expectation of their role as parents of school age children. The time when the youngest child leaves home appears to be a critical passage relative to these barriers, a point made in the earlier discussion of the empty nesters.

A second group of barriers exhibit an inverted U-shaped pattern when expressed over the life cycle of the family. During the child-rearing period, family obligations increase significantly for women and, to a similar but lesser degree, for men. This fact and the fact that neither parent feels there is enough free time represent the barriers felt; they increase until children leave the home, and then their effect drops off sharply.

The effect of various barriers has been found to increase as the family goes through various life-cycle stages. The expectations of family and friends increase for women, but for men they are more constant and less of a limitation over the family life cycle. The feelings of daily stress increase for both sexes as time goes on, while often the feeling of not doing anything stays somewhat constant during the child-rearing stage and increases dramatically when children leave the home. Two other barriers have been analyzed for males only. It has been found that there is an increased effect by males who don't feel fit enough or don't have the physical skills for certain activities. This is reflected in the effect of a falling off in physical skill and fitness levels with age.

Certain points are worthy of note. First, it appears that stages in the family life cycle can help explain and help predict leisure-time behaviour. Care must be taken, however, in the use of correlation or regression techniques for projecting or forecasting leisure activities because of the non-linear pattern of many of these barriers. Second, it is noted that the family life-cycle stage can only very partially explain leisure behaviour. Third, it is determined that noting which barriers are predominant at various life-cycle stages will enable product, packages, and messages to be targeted to reflect an understanding of these barriers and potential objections of the many market segments.

Personality

An individual's personality has an effect on the purchase behaviour described in Chapter One. It has been suggested that most people view their vacation as an extension of their personality. Howard and Sheth have postulated that the effect of personality is felt on two areas—nonspecific motives and the alternatives considered for purchase. They have proposed that the more authoritarian a person is, for example, the fewer alternatives that will have to be considered in arriving at a purchase decision. The relationship between personality and nonspecific motives has been explored by various researchers in an attempt to better understand existing behaviour and better predict future behaviour.

The personality of an individual can be described as "the summation of the characteristics that make the person what he or she is and [that] distinguish each individual from every other individual." It is logical that there is a link between the type of person one is and the type of purchases one makes. A "conservative" person will tend to make "conservative" purchases. But which influences which? Is a person called conservative because conservative purchases have been made, or is the fact that many conservative purchases have been made a sufficient reason to label someone "conservative"?

Personality Traits

Personality can be thought of as consisting of a variety of traits. Individuals who participate in recreational and tourist activities can be typed in terms of their personality traits in an attempt to determine whether such participants exhibit markedly different personality traits than do non-participants. The purpose of such analysis is to determine whether or not personality can be used as a variable for segmenting the market. If it is found that certain personality traits are dominant in winter vacations, marketers will know better the kind of tourist to appeal to and will gain valuable information as to what to say to appeal to this potential vacationer. To date, the research evidence is inconclusive as to whether or not personality is a significant variable in explaining purchase behaviour. Although several studies indicate a strong relationship between personality and consumer behaviour and a few indicate no relationship, the great majority indicate that existing correlations are weak.

The relationship between personality and participation in recreational activities is also of interest. As we have seen, recreational activities can serve as a major reason or motivation for vacation travel. If a relationship between certain activities and certain personality traits can be established an appropriate marketing strategy can be developed.

Hikers, river tourers, and women golfers are all seen as leaders and people who talk about their personal achievements. Hikers see themselves as people who are able to come and go as they desire, and both they and river tourers have scored high on the traits of doing new and different things and doing one's best or accomplishing something. River tourers are also viewed as people who have attacked contrary points of view or who have gotten revenge. Hikers and women golfers both are seen as people who have analyzed their motives and feelings.

The desire for social contact within an outdoor setting seems to be the primary motivating factor for individuals who participate in nature/pleasure activities, social sports, and water-oriented activities. Lack of structure and competitiveness characterizes both nature/pleasure activities and uses. Although competitions more of a factor in social sports, socializing is still important. Participants in predator sports are more dominant and aggre-ssive. The relationship between persona-lity traits and those who participate in the conquering nature/riding horses and bike riding/concert-going is less evident, but is suggested, as expressed in the above figure.

Personality Types

Often a person is described as having a certain type of personality. Personality types consist of character-istics that, when taken together, form a certain kind of person. One way of typing people is to the extent that they are perceived as being introverted or extroverted. Introverts look into themselves and tend to be shy and reserved. Extroverts are other-oriented, looking outside the self, and tending to be objective rather than subjective in outlook. Participants in vigorous physical activity in general tend to be extroverts. In fact, outdoor recreational activities in general are not participated in by introverted personality types. The following relationships between recreational participants and personality types have been made:

Psychographics and Life-Style

The application of studies of personality to the business world has been hampered because the terminology of personality has come from clinical sources. Psychographics has developed as a way of describing consumer behaviour in terms of a distinctive way of living in order to determine whether or not people with distinctive life-styles have distinctive travel behaviours. Psychographics is the development of psychological profiles of consumers and psychologically based measures of types of distinctive modes of living or life-styles. There are three recognized dimensions of life-style—attitudes, interests, and opinions. These three categories can be described as follows:

Is It, in fact, possible to identify different segments of the market based upon life-style? It appears that an individual's life-style is influenced by participation in various social groups and is a social rather than a unique behaviour. Further, a person's life-style spills over to other aspects of behaviour. These life-style differences are patterned rather than random. Knowing how an individual behaves in one aspect of his or her life may enable us to predict how the individual will act in others. Some feel, however, that one of the problems in using life-style variables is that often general variables are used rather than those that are product specific. They argue that to understand vacation intentions it is necessary to determine attitudes and opinions about and interest in vacations and vacation destinations rather than information about general life-style. This division of the market into psychographic segments would be of no practical value unless these segments could be identified and reached. It has been shown that life-styles vary according to different socioeconomic variables. Although it may be beneficial to initially segment a market on the basis of life-style dimensions for marketing purposes, it is necessary to identify the socio-economic characteristics of these segments in order to effectively reach the target markets.

Tourism for Public Good

Although this macro-view of tourism is becoming increasingly accepted, we have failed to appreciate the significance of this trend on tourism policies, and on the structural changes needed to turn policy into action. The object of this paper is:

(a) to analyse the trend towards growing public involvement in tourism;

(b) to explain what this means in terms of public interest;

(c) to discuss what needs to be done to ensure that tourism is full responsive to the public interest;

(d) and finally, to emphasise the key role of the State in creating the conditions needed to satisfy public interest.

Public Involvement

At the actual point of contact, there has always been an appreciation of the importance of tourism, as a force which is both positive and negative. This appreciation has invariably been confused, with some people having a clear understanding of the positive aspects—and others seeing only the negative features. At the actual contact point—in the hotel, at the airport, on the beach, in the shop—both parties to tourism, the visitors and their hosts, are well aware of the direct personal effects of tourism on *themselves*. But they are not necessarily aware of the indirect, impersonal effects on themselves, or of the effects on other people.

As a result of this confusion, the history of tourism is littered with examples of cases where people acted not only against the public interest but against their own selfish interest. People allow a beach to become so dirty that visitors are driven elsewhere, thus depriving them of their livelihood. Property developers erect hotels which are so ugly as to reduce the attractiveness not only of the locality but of their own hotel. Taxi drivers and waiters and shopkeepers who are so unpleasant as to drive away visitors-thus reducing the business of taxi drivers and waiters and shop keepers. It is indeed difficult to think of any other activity which is so characterised by self-inflicted damage.

The reasons for this absurdity are extraordinary complex and lie outside the scope of this paper, but they reflect an inherently delicate relationship between members of the host community and their visitors. As perceived by the hosts, the visitors are aliens in almost every respect: they are possibly more relaxed; they possibly have different social class; they possibly have different social class; they possibly have different social customs; and they often speak a foreign language. It is no exaggeration to say that people in host countries who deal with tourists are invariably dealing with a completely different sort of people to those they deal with in normal everyday life. It is no surprising that a big communication problem exists, and that ignorance and prejudice abounds.

This problem has long been recognised at a local level. Most Chambers of Commerce and local tourist offices have for many years considered it as a primary duty to "educate" those who have contact with visitors into adopting constructive and sympathetic attitudes. There is today hardly a single desti-nation which does not project itself, not only to its visitors, but also to its natives, as being "friendly". And it has gradually become accepted that this "education" must extend beyond the minority who have direct personal relations with visitors, to the majority who have no personal contact whatever. Many members of this majority actually feel damaged by the flow of arriving visitors. To use an orthodox economist's expression, they are 'competing for scarce resources'. Hence the effects of visitors are perceived in some quarters as being entirely negative: of mono-polising a restricted amount of the best beach space.....of creating uncomfortable congestion... of driving up food prices... of introducing unwel-come life styles. It is from the ranks of people holding such views that the stone-throwers and pick-pockets are readily recruited.

Rightly, local authorities are increasingly coming to recognise that this is posing a double problem. On the one hand, there is the problem of education: of persuading those people who are annoyed by tourists that it is in their interest to conceal their annoyance; on the other hand there is the problem of mitigation: of identifying those genuine instances where people are actually suffering from the inflow of tourism and then, having identified the specific injury, of either eliminating the damage or compensating the victim.

The process of identification itself can be extraordinarily difficult. It too several months patient research to discover that disturbing instances of violence towards American tourist visiting a small Caribbean Island, which were at first attributed to poor race relations, in fact reflected a spontaneous revolt against the rise in price of local fish following an increase in demand from newly opened resort complex on the island. The irony was that the hotel management had been persuaded by well meaning government officials into buying fresh local fish rather than frozen imports, in order to boost the foreign exchange benefit of tourism. In this case the answer to inflation—and to stone throwing—was to allow the hotel to import fish until adequate steps had been taken to boost supply to the point where the hotel demand could be met without causing a shortage in the market place.

This problem was recently illustrated on a large scale when the London Tourist Board interviewed several Londoners on their attitude to tourism. Although a clear majority recognised that tourism as a whole is beneficial to Britain, only a small minority conceded that they derived any personal benefit. And a significant minority in the areas most effected by tourism were attracted by the idea of negative future growth in tourism. It is no exaggeration to say that the survey showed among the relatively sophisticated citizens of the affluent London suburbs, and extraordinary failure to comprehend the benefits of tourism. It is therefore not surprising to find similar misunderstandings in unprivileged segments of society in underdeveloped communities.

As long as tourism was a small scale activity, these problems could be delegated to local authorities. They were not even considered in many quarters to be a proper topic for national tourist offices—which were still seen to be in existence to "sell" tourism.

But as tourism has grown in size, so its effects have become all-pervading. And its successful development has become a matter of interest not only to the travel industry but to an ever increasing segment of the entire community. In more and more countries tourism has become like a stone thrown into a pond whose ripples now reach every corner of the shore. As has been well said, *"tourist has become too important to be left to tourism experts."*

Public Interest

There is no need here to list the many sectors of the economy and of society which are affected by the growth of tourism. On the economic side the primary aspects are the provision of employment and the provision of foreign exchange. On the social side the primary aspects are the recognition that people expect to have more time for leisure— and expect to utilise their leisure time more pleasantly—and also recognition that the growth of leisure, in particular, foreign travel, is bringing about fundamental changes in the pattern of society. While tourism was a still a "fringe" activity, i.e. on an unimportant scale, then there was little public interest in it. It was not a matter deserving the attention of senior civil servants, of politicians, of academics, of the influential media. But the sheer growth of tourism has made community leaders aware that it is a force which already has a major impact on the welfare of the general public—even though the general public does not yet clearly recognise this. Take a few examples. In developed countries, most of which lie in temperate climatic zones, the demand for foreign holidays in warm countries has become a major debit item on the foreign exchange account. It has become evident that this problem is exacerbated by failure to organise the domestic tourism product to be more competitive with holidays abroad. As a result, in developed countries, almost everywhere a considerable effort is being injected into the improvement of the domestic holiday product. Another example from the field of foreign exchange: it is becoming increasingly obvious in most developing countries that an undue proportion of foreign exchange expen-diture by incoming tourists is wastefully repatriated abroad. This is not a problem which can be left to the industry to solve. Only by carefully coordinated State action can this be minimised.

Take an example in the employment field. Throughout Europe there are regions which are relatively backward. They are usually remote rural areas which cannot compete in the market place, even for agriculture, so they are decaying. Yet these regions afford considerable tourism potential. The very backwardness, the very isolation, is now becoming a major attraction to a society which is increasingly offended by being over-urbanised. So it strikes the national economic planners that tourism is a valuable tool in the aid programme for regional development. A similar situation exists in many developing countries. The magnetic attraction of city life, coupled with rapidly rising mechanisation of agriculture and a tendency to see farming as a relatively unattractive life style, is meaning that people are being sucked from the country side into the towns at an alarming rate. In many cities this mass migration cannot be supported by public services and as a result we see the collapse of public utilities—water supplies, sanitation, power, communications—and even law and order. The true social, economic and political cost of dealing with this alarming problem is almost beyond measure. This is why bodies like the World Bank are now placing more emphasis on rural development. Yet the rural places where the economic problem is most urgent are very often the very places which offer untapped tourism potential. So the State starts to think about encouraging the development of tourism not only in cities, where the employment benefit of tourism is insignificant, but in the villages, where the effect can be extraordinary.

Take another, more subtle, example in the field of employment. In many developing countries the authorities are alarmed at the erosion of traditional culture—the arts, handicrafts, cottage industries—by what has aptly been called the process of colonisation. At a certain stage of social development, society as a whole seems to lose faith in traditional values. Tourism is a contributing factor here—and as a result some receiving countries have sought to discourage inward tourism, or segregate it carefully, so as to limit the infection. This is a policy which deserves sympathetic understanding, even when the fear is exaggerated, for it represents a rational effort to optimise tourism by minimising its bad effects. However, the main factor in colonisation is not tourism but the media—and not just T.V., radio and news-papers, but all media of communication, of which the most significant is probably the text book and the teacher. Because of the international nature of communi-cation, all people, but especially young people, are being daily bombarded with the intriguing nature of foreign culture. And as a result, traditional ideas and products are being put on one side. Returning now to tourism, it is the traditional ideas and products which the foreign tourist is searching for. He is not wanting to see abroad a replication of what he sees every normal working day. Thus we find that the demand of the tourism industry can become a positive factor in the protection and preservation of indigeneous culture. The island of Bali provides a striking example of this. In Morocco and Tunisia the traditional textile industry owes its survival largely to the tourism industry. In many parts of Africa traditional woodcarving would be an obsolete art had it not been for tourism. Until now this has normally happened by accident. But it has now happened so often by accident that State authorities recognise it deserves to become a matter of State intervention. India is probably the best example of successful promotion by the State of a nation's cultural heritage, not merely to boost tourism, but to boost the basic quality of life in India.

The point of all these examples is that they all have one element in common: none can be left to the working of the market economy, none can be solved by even the most enlightened capitalism unless it has the backing of the State, and certainly none can be solved by the so called tourism industry in isolation. This inevitably means that the growth of tourism demands a more than corresponding growth in State inter-vention, regardless of the political flavour of the local economy.

It is possible to identify four main streams of tourism activity in which this public interest is becoming significant:

(a) first, the general need to ensure that tourism develops along planned, prepared, premeditated lines and not in a haphazard manner;

(b) second, the more specific need to ensure that the product not merely the accommodation but the entire range of facilities and attractions is developed in step with the target demand;

(c) third, the even more specific need to ensure that the product is efficiently marketed, both domestically and abroad;

(d) and finally to ensure, by a mixture of training, management, supervision and level protection-that the system works as intended, for both hosts and visitors.

Organisational Structure

The basic theme of this paper is that few States have evolved; -let alone even considered, the most appropriate organisational structure to meet the public interest. In most countries a piece-meal, fragmented approach has been adopted. Let me describe what could fairly be presented as the typical actual arrangement.

At the top there is possibly a Minister, usually of junior rank, who has a vague responsibility for tourism, probably linked with a separate portfolio such as civil aviation, or antiquities, or information. He will be supported by a small group of officials who will be preoccupied with day-to-day problems, often of a political nature. Under his supervision will also come a director of tourism whose attention is concentrated on somehow mounting an international marketing operation with quite inadequate budgetary and human resources. Somewhere in the government machine there will be a State owned organization responsible for providing hotel finance.

Elsewhere there will be another State owned organisation responsible for managing certain major hotels. Similarly there will be a State owned, airline, quite possibly under the close influence of the airforce.

Alongside these and other State agencies there will be several hundred—in larger countries, several thousand—hotel, owners, restaurant owners and travel agents. Not to mention the many individuals who serve the tourist in countless small ways. Some of these have trade associations but many do not and in some cases these exist only on paper. Efforts are occasionally made to establish some form of liaison with the State. But these arrangements are seldom successful if only because the State itself is seldom organised to conduct a meaningful dialogue.

This essential feature of this situation is that it is unsystematic. The left hand not only cannot influence the right hand, it does not even know what the right hand doing. This has come about imperceptibly. When tourism was too small is this lack of system did not matter. But tourism has gradually grown, not only in size, but in terms of its social, economic and political impact. Today we have generally failed to evolve systems appropriate to today's scale. As a result the tourism industry is too often failing to satisfy the public interest.

A Systematic System

It would be nice to conclude by describing simply how the tourism effort should be organised in order to satisfy the public interest. Alas, there is no simple answer. And there is no single answer. No two countries are the same, or have the same problem. It is therefore inevitable that each country must evolve its own solution to the problem. Although I happen to believe that we in Britain have evolved a particularly effective system. I would not pretended that our system is suitable for export to other countries. However there are several ideas which can be gained from British experience which provide some useful guidance to others who wish to improve their effort:

(a) The most important element is participation at all levels, by all sectors in the planning process—plans and policies must not be imposed from above, evolve at the level at which they are implemented—and as a general rule, the lower the better.

(b) A distinction must be drawn between State intervention and State control—in many cases the State role is best limited to that of a catalyst, a catalyst which is necessary if others are to act in the right way.

(c) At the highest level there should be a permanent body whose members span the entire tourism spectrum in all its many aspects, which meets regularly, say once a quarter, and—ideally—whose prior appro-val is needed for any major investment or decision effecting tourism.

(d) There should be a carefully interlocking network of directors and executives on the boards of government departments, governments run bodies (such as airlines), major private companies, appropriate trade associations and training/education organisation, the idea being to ensure communication between the key sectors of the industry.

(e) The affairs of the industry should be deliberately subjected to public scrutiny and debate—in particular, all major policy proposals should be thoroughly ventilated in public before becoming officially adopted as policy.

(f) Last but not least, regardless of the function of the national tourist office, the director (or director general) of tourism must exercise positive leader-ship in persuading all sectors of the tourism industry to recognise the need to colla-borate in order to serve the public interest.

6. Tourism Planning, Marketing and Management

TOURISM IS a rather complicated activity that overlaps several different sectors of the society and economy. Without planning, it may create unexpected and unwanted impacts. Tourism is also still a relatively new type of activity in many countries. Some governments and often the private sector have little or no experience in how to develop tourism properly. For countries that do not yet have much tourism, planning can provide the necessary guidance for its development. For those places that already have some tourism, planning is often needed to revitalize this sector and maintain its future viability.

First tourism should be planned at the national and regional levels. At these levels, planning is concerned with tourism development policies, structure plans, facility standards, institutional factors and all the other elements necessary to develop and manage tourism. Then, within the framework of national and regional planning, more detailed plans for tourist attractions, resorts, urban, rural and other forms of tourism development can be prepared.

There are several important specific benefits of undertaking national and regional tourism planning. These advantages include:

- Establishing the overall tourism development objectives and policies—what is tourism aiming to accomplish and how can these aims be achieved.

- Developing tourism so that its natural and cultural resources are indefinitely maintained and conserved for future, as well as present, use.

- Integrating tourism into the overall development policies and patterns of the country or region, and establishing close linkages between tourism and other economic sectors.

- Providing a rational basis for decision-making by both the public and private sectors on tourism development.

- Making possible the coordinated development of all the many elements of the tourism sector. This includes inter-relating the tourist attractions, activities, facilities and services and the various and increasingly fragmented tourist markets.

- Optimizing and balancing the economic, environmental and social benefits of tourism, with equitable distribution of these benefits to the society, while minimizing possible problems of tourism.

- Providing a physical structure which guides the location, types and extent of tourism development of attractions, facilities, services and infrastructure.

- Establishing the guidelines and standards for preparing detailed plans of specific tourism development areas that are consistent with, and reinforce, one another, and for the appropriate design of tourist facilities.
- Laying the foundation for effective implementation of the tourism development policy and plan and continuous management of the tourism sector, by providing the necessary organizational and other institutional framework.
- Providing the framework for effective coordination of the public and private sector efforts and investment in developing tourism.
- Offering a baseline for the continuous monitoring of the progress of tourism development and keeping it on track.

The planned approach to developing tourism at the national and regional levels is now widely adopted as a principle, although implementation of the policies and plans is still weak in some places. Many countries and regions of countries have had tourism plans prepared. Other places do not yet have plans, but should consider undertaking planning in the near future. In some countries, plans had previously been prepared but these are now outdated. They need to be revised based on present day circumstances and likely future trends. Founded on accumulated experience, the approaches and techniques of tourism planning are now reasonably well understood. There is considerable assurance that, if implemented, planning will bring substantial benefits to an area.

Approaches

An underlying concept in planning tourism is that tourism should be viewed as an inter-related system of demand and supply factors. The demand factors are international and domestic tourist markets and local residents who use the tourist attractions, facilities and services. The supply factors comprise tourist attractions and activities, accommodation and other tourist facilities and services. Attractions include natural, cultural and special types of features—such as theme parks, zoos, botanic gardens and aquariums—and the activities related to these attractions. Accommodation includes hotels, motels guest houses and other types of places where tourists stay overnight. The category of other tourist facilities and services includes tour and travel operations, restaurants, shopping, banking and money exchange, and medical and postal facilities and services. These supply factors are called the tourism product.

Other elements also relate to supply factors. In order to make the facilities and services usable, infrastructure is required. Tourism infrastructure particularly includes transportation (air, road, rail, water, etc.), water supply, electric power, sewage and solid waste disposal, and telecommunications.

Provision of adequate infrastructure is also important to protect the environment. It helps maintain a high level of environmental quality that is so necessary for successful tourism and desirable for residents.

The effective development, operation and management of tourism requires certain institutional elements. These elements include:

- Organizational structures, especially government tourism offices and

private sector tourism associations such as hotel associations.
- Tourism-related legislation and regulations, such as standards and licensing requirements for hotels and tour and travel agencies.
- Education and training programmes, and training institutions to prepare persons to work effectively in tourism.
- Availability of financial capital to develop tourist attractions, facilities, services and infrastructure, and mechanisms to attract capital investment.
- Marketing strategies and promotion programmes to inform tourist about the country or region, and induce them to visit it, and tourist information facilities and services in the destination areas.
- Travel facilitation of immigration (including visa arrangements), customs and other facilities and services at the entry and exit points of tourists.

The Institutional elements also include consideration of how to enhance and distribute the economic benefits of tourism, environmental protection measures, reducing adverse social impacts, and conservation of the cultural heritage of people living in the tourism areas.

As an inter-related system, it is important that tourism planning aim for integrated development of all these parts of the system, both the demand and supply factors and the physical and institutional elements. The system will function much more effectively and bring the desired benefits if it is planned in an integrated manner, with coordinated development of all the components of the system. Sometimes, this integrated system approach is also called the comprehensive approach to tourism planning because all the elements of tourism are considered in the planning and development process.

Just as important as planning for integration within the tourism system is planning for integration of tourism into the overall development policies, plans and patterns of a country or region. Planning for this overall integration will, for example, resolve any potential conflicts over use of certain resources or locations for various types of development. It also provides for the multiuse of expensive infrastructure to serve general community needs as well as tourism.

Emphasis is given to formulating and adopting tourism development policies and plans for an area in order to guide decision-making on development actions. The planning of tourism, however, should also be recognized as continues and flexible process. Within the framework of the policy and plan recommendations, there must be flexibility to allow for adapting to changing circumstances. Planning that is too rigid may not allow development to be responsive to changes. There may be advancements in transportation technology, evolution of new forms of tourism and changes in market trends. Even though allowed to be flexible, the basic objectives of the plan should not be abrogated although the specific development patterns may be changed. Sustainable development must still be maintained.

Planning for tourism development should make recommendations that are imaginative and innovative, but they must also be feasible to implement. The various techniques of implementation should be considered throughout the planning process. This approach ensures that the recommendations can be accomplished, and provides the basis for specifying the implementation techniques that should be applied. Implementation techniques can also be imaginative and not only rely on established approaches. It is common practice for a tourism plan to include specification of implementation techniques, and sometimes a separate manual on how to achieve the plan recommendations.

Tourism Planning For Sustainable Development

The underlying approach now applied to tourism planning, as well as to other types of development, is that of achieving sustainable development. The sustainable development approach implies that the natural, cultural and other resources of tourism are conserved for continuous use in the future, while still bringing benefits to the present society. The concept of sustainable development has received much emphasis internationally since the early 1980s, although tourism plans prepared even before that period often were concerned with conservation of tourism resources.

The sustainable development approach to planning tourism is acutely important because most tourism development depends on attractions and activities related to the natural environment, historic heritage and cultural patterns of areas. If these resources are degraded or destroyed, then the tourism areas cannot attract tourists and tourism will not be successful. More generally, most tourists seek destinations that have a high level of environmental quality—they like to visit places that are attractive, clean and neither polluted nor congested. It is also essential that residents of the tourism area should not have to suffer from a deteriorated environment and social problems.

One of the important benefits of tourism is that, if it is properly developed based on the concept of sustainability, tourism can greatly help justify and pay for conservation of an area's natural and cultural resources. Thus, tourism can be an important means of achieving conservation in areas that otherwise have limited ·capability to accomplish environmental protection and conservation objectives.

A basic technique in achieving sustainable development is the environmental planning approach. Environmental planning requires that all elements of the environment be carefully surveyed, analyzed and considered in determining the most appropriate type and location of development. This approach would not allow, for example, intensive development in flood plain and steep hillside areas.

An important aspect of sustainable development is emphasizing community-based tourism. This approach to tourism focuses on community involvements in the planning and development process, and developing the types of tourism which generate benefits to local communities. It applies techniques to ensure that most of the benefits of tourism development accrue to local residents and not to outsiders. Maximizing benefits to local residents typically results in tourism being better accepted by them and their actively supporting conservation of local tourism resources. The community based tourism approach is applied at the local or more detailed levels of planning, but it can be set forth as a policy approach at the national and regional levels. The benefits accruing to local communities are also beneficial to the country, through the income and foreign exchange earned, employed generated and support that local communities give to national tourism development and conservation policies.

Also related to sustainable development is the concept of quality tourism. This approach is being increasingly adopted for two fundamental reasons—it can achieve successful tourism from the marketing standpoint and it brings benefits to local residents and their environment. Quality tourism does not necessarily mean expensive tourism. Rather, it refers to tourist reactions, facilities and services that offer 'good value for money', protect tourism resources, and attract the kinds of tourists who will respect the local environment and society. Quality tourism development can compete more effectively in attracting discriminating tourists. It is also more environmentally and socially self-sustaining. Achieving quality tourism is the responsibility of both the public and private sectors. This concept should be built into the tourism planning, development and management process.

Long-Range and Strategic Planning

Long-range comprehensive planning is concerned with specifying goals and objectives and determining preferred furture development patterns. Tourism development policies and plans should be prepared for relatively long-term periods—usually for 10 to 15 and sometimes 20 years—depending on the predictability of future events in the country or region. These may seem to be long planning periods, but it commonly requires this length of time to implement basic policy and structure plans. Even development of specific projects, such as major resorts or national park-based tourism, can require a long time.

A planning approach which has received considerable attention in recent years, and is applicable to some tourism areas, is strategic planning. While the outcomes of strategic and long-range comprehensive planning may be very similar, strategic, planning is somewhat different. It focuses more on identification and resolution of immediate issues. Strategic planning typically is more oriented to rapidly changing future situations and how to cope with changes organizationally. It is more action oriented and concerned with handling unexpected events.

Applied only by itself, strategic planning can be less comprehensive in its approach. By focusing on immediate issues, it may deviate from achieving such long-term objectives as sustainable development. But if used within the framework of integrated long-range policy and planning, the strategic planning approach can be very appropriate.

Public Involvement in Planning

Planning is for the benefit of people, and they should be involved in the planning and development of tourism in their areas. Through this involvement, tourism development will reflect a consensus of what the people want. Also, if residents are involved in planning and development decisions—and if they understand the benefits the tourism can bring—they will more likely support it. At the national and regional levels of preparing tourism plans, the common approach to obtaining public involvement is to appoint a steering committee. This committee offers guidance to the planning team and reviews its work, especially the draft reports and policy and planning recommendations that are made. A planning study steering committee is typically composed of representatives of the relevant government agencies involved in tourism, the private sector, and community, religious and other relevant organization.

Also, open public hearings can be held on the plan. These hearings provide the opportunity for anybody to learn about the plan and express their opinions. Another common approach, when the plan is completed, is to organize a national or regional tourism seminar. This meeting informs participants and the general public about the importance of controlled tourism development and the recommendations of the plan. Such seminars often receive wide publicity in the communications media.

In a large country or region, the usual procedure is for the tourism plan to be prepared by the central authority with public involvement as described above. This can be termed the 'top-down' approach. Another procedure sometimes used is the 'bottom-up' approach. This involves holding meetings with local districts or communities to determine what type of development they would like to have. These local objectives and ideas are then fitted together into a national or regional plan. This approach achieves greater local public involvement in the planning process. But it is more time consuming and may lead to conflicting objectives, policies and development recommendations among the local areas. These conflicts need to be reconciled at the national and regional levels in order to form a consistent plan. It is important that the development patterns of the local areas complement and reinforce one another, but also reflect the needs and desires of local communities. Often a combination of the 'top-down' and 'bottom-up' approaches achieves the best results.

Processes

The process for preparing tourism plans at the national and regional levels—based on the sustainable, integrated and implementable approaches can be described as a step-by-step procedure.

The first step in the planning process is careful preparation of the study so that it provides the type of development guidance that is needed. Study preparation involves formulating the project terms of reference, selecting the technical team to carry out the study, appointing a steering committee, and organizing the study activities.

The terms of reference (TOR) for the planning study should be carefully formulated so that the study achieves its desired results and outputs. The TOR for a national or regional plan indicates the outputs and activities that are necessary to prepare the development policy and plan. The special considerations to be made in planning—such as economic, environmental or social issues and the critical institutional elements-should be specified in the TOR. Identification of implementation techniques are also specified. The TOR format typically follows the planning process explained here, but it is tailored to the specific characteristics and needs of the planning area.

Many places already have some limited tourism development, and these existing patterns must be considered in formulating the TOR. Other countries or regions will have considerable existing tourism development, but it may be declining or not be in a form that generates optimum benefits. The TOR will therefore emphasize how to rejuvenate and improve existing development, along with how to provide guidance on the future expansion of tourism.

It is common for a single study to include various levels of tourism planning, such as national and regional plans along with detailed planning for priority development areas and projects. The planning for all these levels will need to be specified in the TOR. An advantage of including various levels of planning in one study is that there is greater continuity and consistency of the recommended development patterns. However, for detailed planning, only those areas and projects to be developed in the near future should be included in the overall study. The longer-term development areas and projects should be planned in detailed in detail later, based on circumstances prevailing at that time.

The TOR should indicate a horizon year when the plan and its target and recommendations are to be realized. Planning horizon years are typically for 10,15 to 20 years. Development phasing or staging—usually for five-year periods—should be specified. Estab-lishing a horizon year and staging periods provides a time framework for making projecting, setting targets and phasing development. This also explains other aspects of preparation and organization that are essential to carry out a successful planning study.

Determination of Objectives

Early in the planning process, the objectives of developing tourism should be determined. Deciding on objectives is very important because they state the desired results of developing tourism in the country or region. Objectives usually relate to various types of socio-economic benefits. They also specify the special considerations that must be made in tourism development, such as minimising negative environmental and socio-cultural impacts. Objectives should be determined in close consultation with the government (or steering committee) because they are basic determinants of the tourism development policies and plan.

Objectives are first established in a preliminary manner. They are later refined based on the results of the surveys and analysis and the plan formulation. Certain preliminary objectives may be found to be in conflict with one another, and they cannot all realistically be achieved. For example, one objective may state that the economic benefits of tourism should be maximized, and another objective may stipulate that environmental and socio-cultural impacts must be minimized and sustainable development maintained. It may not be possible to prepare a policy and plan that simultaneously achieves both of these objectives, at least over the long-term period. The objective must balance economic, environmental and socio-cultural considerations.

Tourism development objectives should also reflect and reinforce any general development objectives already adopted for the country or region. This is important so that tourism is well integrated into overall development patterns. In some cases, however, it may be decided to modify the general objectives in order to achieve those tourism objectives that seem to be reasonable, and contribute to overall national and regional development.

Survey of All Elements

The survey stage of the planning process involves collecting data, both quantitative and qualitative, on all relevant aspects of tourism. These include the components of the tourism system and other factors as follows:

- Global and regional tourism patterns

and trends. Regional here refers to several geographically related countries such as Africa, East and South Asia, Pacific Islands, North and South America, Western Europe, etc. This information can be obtained for the World Tourism Organization.

- Characteristics of existing or potential competing tourist destinations that offer similar tourism products and attract much the same tourist markets.
- Tourist arrival trends in the planning study country or region. These include the number and characteristics of tourist arrivals.
- Existing and potential tourist attraction and activities.
- Existing and already planned tourist accommodation and other tourist facilities and services.
- Existing and already planned transportation facilities and services, including both access to the country or region and the internal transportation system.
- Other types of infrastructure which are existing or already planned.
- Existing natural resource, land use and land tenure patterns. Land tenure refers to land ownership or leasing patterns.
- Existing economic and employment patterns, including employment in tourism, and economic and manpower development plans.
- Physical and social development plans—these are sometimes combined with the economic and manpower development plans listed above.
- Environmental characterisitics and environmental quality. Environmental characteristics include such factors as climate patterns and topography. Environmental quality includes the extent of air, water, noise and visual pollution, congestion, architectural interest and other factors.
- Socio-cultural patterns, especially as they relate to the effects of tourism development on the local societies and cultural patterns.
- Existing and already planned education and training programmes and trained institutions designed to prepare persons to work in tourism.
- Existing government and private sector organizations in tourism, and their organizational structures and staffing.
- Present investment policies and availability of capital for investment in tourist facilities, serviced and infrastructure.
- Present tourism legislation and regulations.

One of the most important elements of the survey is that of tourist attractions and activities. These are what induce tourists to visit the country or region. Tourist attractions and related activities are categorized by type, and evaluated with respect to accessibility to development, market trends of what tourists want to see and do, and other factors. They are also identified as primary attractions—those which basically attract tourists to visit the place (if the attractions are properly conserved and developed with facilities), or as secondary ones—those attractions which are less important but comple-ment the primary attractions and increase touristic interest and length of stay.

For many of these elements—such as tourist attractions and activities, accommodations, other tourist facilities and services and some types of infrastructure—field surveys are required. These surveys should include evaluation of the elements along with noting their characteristics. Evaluation of tourist attractions was described above. Tourist facilities and services must also be evaluated as to their suitability, quality and efficiency to serve tourists properly. Infrastructure must be assessed as to how adequately it serves tourism development. Often market surveys are conducted, with visits made to interview tour operators in the market source countries.

Other types of surveys require document research and discussion meetings with local persons. Some of the types of surveys—such as for infrastructure, natural resources, land use and land tenure patterns and environmental characteristics—are carried out generally at the national and regional levels. They are conducted more specifically in the detailed planning for tourism development areas such as resorts.

Analysis and Synthesis

Both quantitative and qualitative analysis and synthesis of the survey information must be carefully carried out. Synthesis refers to combining and integrating the various components of the analysis, in order to obtain a more comprehensive understanding of the situation. Major aspects of the analysis and synthesis are described as follows:

- The market analysis is derived from several sources. They survey of global, national and regional tourism patterns and market trends is essential input. The survey and evaluation of the tourist attractions, facilities and services in the study area is also very important. The tourism development objectives must be considered. Accessibility to the country or region from the major tourist markets areas, including cost, distance and convenience of travel, is a very important factor too. However, accessibility can often be improved if it is presently a problem. The market analysis includes establishing market targets of the number and types of tourist that potentially can be attracted, but only if the development and marketing recommendations are implemented. Market targets are usually established by five-year periods, up to the horizon year of the plan.

- Several calculations can be made from the market analysis. The number and types of accommodation required are projected, and other tourist facilities and services needed are identified. Analysis of the economic impact of tourism is derived from the market targets and tourist characteristics. This includes the projection of the number and type of employee needed to work in tourism.

This is explains how accommodation needs are projected.

- Based on the projection of tourist facilities and services needed and the movement patterns of tourists, the transportation and other infrastructure facilities and services required can be determined.

- From several of the surveyed elements, the integrated analysis or synthesis or physical, economic and social factors is prepared. This synthesis provides much of the basis for formulating the structure plan. It includes establishing carrying capacities, an essential consideration in achieving sus-tainable tourism development. The carrying capacity of an area is the maximum level of development or use that the area can absorb without resulting in serious environmental damage, socio-economic problems, or decline in the quality of visitor experience.

This explains how carrying capacity is calculated.

- All the institutional elements are evaluated and analysed as a basis for formulating policy and recommendations about each of them.

An important type of synthesis in identification of major opportunities and problems or constraints for developing tourism. This provides a focus for formulating recommendations, and how to take advantage of opportunities and overcome constraints, all leading to better development of tourism.

The offerings of possible competing destinations that have similar tourism products and markets should be evaluated. There may be sufficient growth in the tourist markets to satisfy the needs for tourists in both the country or region being planned and competing destinations. But there may not be that much market growth. If the planning study area can offer some comparative advantages over competing destinations in its development of attractions, facilities and services, it will be better positioned to attract the desired numbers and types of tourists.

Policy and Plan Formulation

This step in the planning process involves formulating policy on tourism development and preparing the physical structure plan. The best approach to policy and plan formulation is first to prepare and evaluate alternative development scenarios. There is seldom a single ideal set of policies and plans, but rather optimum ones that balance costs and benefits. Alternative policies and plan are evaluated according to several factors- meeting the development objectives; optimizing economic benefits; reinforcing positive and minimizing negative environmental and socio-cultural impacts; and effectively competing with other tourist destinations. Based on this evaluation, the final policies and plans are selected and refined.

Policy and plan formulation should be carried out in close consultation with the steering committee and other interested parties, in order to ensure that they reflect a consensus about the most appropriate future tourism development patterns.

Institutional Recommendations

Based on the survey, analysis and evaluation of the institutional elements, conclusions and recommendations can be made. For many types of recommendations, alternatives must be evaluated before the most suitable ones can be determined. There may be no need for changes in some of these elements, but this fact should be stated. In certain cases, alternative recommendations, all of which are acceptable, can be made. The government or private sector can later decide on which course of action to pursue, depending on furture circumstances. It is also essential to involve the steering committee and other interested parties in formulating the institutional recommendations.

Implementation and Monitoring

The final step in the planning process is specifying implementation technique. The means of implementation should be considered throughout the planning process, and especially during the formulation of the policy, plan and other recommendations. This is important so that the final plan and recommendations are realistic to achieve and implementable. During and after imple-mentation, tourism development must be monitored to ensure that it is accomplishing the objectives and achieving the recommended policies. Monitoring will detect any problems that arise to that remedial measures can be taken before the problems become serious.

Elements of A Comprehensive Tourism Plan

An integrated and comprehensive national or regional tourism plan contains many different elements. Appendix 4 present a checklist of the elements that should be included in a typical tourism plan. This can serve as a guide for ensuring that all the necessary elements are considered in preparing the plan.

Achieving successful integrated tourism development and management depends as much as effective institutional factors as it does on development policy, physical planning and impact controls. This chapter examines the major institutional elements of tourism—organizational structures, manpower planning and training, tourism legislation and regulations, and attracting investment in tourism development.

Organizational Structures for Tourism

The most appropriate types of public and private organizational structures for tourism must be adapted to the particular circumstances in each country or region. The types of structures may also be changed through time as situations change. Before deciding on organizational structures, a basic decision to be made is determining the respective roles of government and the private sector in the development and management of tourism.

The government or a statutory board typically has several responsibilities— policy, planning and development coordination; statistics and research; industry standards and regulations; investment incentives; some marketing services, tourism manpower planning and training, including establishing education and training standards; and provision of basic infrastructure and major public-type attractions. The private sector is responsible for the commercial development and operation of accommodation and most other tourist facilities and services, along with marketing of these. In newly developing tourism areas, however, the government may need to be initially involved in some commercial development in order to get tourism started.

In order to handle its functions, the national government must establish a National Tourism Administration (NTA)— a Department or Ministry of Tourism. This ministry may be single portfolio only for tourism, if this sector is currently or expected to become a major activity in the country. Or the ministry may be a mixed portfolio, combining tourism with some other related functions. If the ministry is single portfolio, this gives tourism more priority and importance in the government structure. Regional governments also often establish their own tourism organizations.

The NTA is organized into various divisions and sections, often similar to that. Separate sections are typically organized for planning and development, statistics and research, education and training and marketing services.

Many countries have established a separate autonomous entity for marketing services, and sometimes other management functions. Assigning marketing to an autonomous body, such as a national promotion board, offers the advantage of its being able to apply flexible internal management that is more responsive to changes in market trends. Also, it allows for the possibility of coordinating with the private sector (if that is relatively well developed in the country) on joint promotion activities. However, close liaison must be maintained between the board and the NTA in order to ensure that a consistent development policy is carried out. The board must be held accoutable for effective use of its funds, usually through an annual review of its programmeme and expenditures by the NTA.

Because tourism is a multi-sectoral activity, it is essential that maximum coordination be maintained between the NTA and other relevant government agencies and between the public and private sectors. This can best be achieved by establishing a Tourism Advisory Committee to the NTA, with representation from government agencies, the private sector and other relevant organizations.

Adequate funding and staffing are essential for effective operation of the NTA. Funding is from the government, although there may be joint public and private sector funding of some marketing activities. If there is some type of tourism tax, such as a hotel or tourist expenditure tax in the country, that can be a logical source of funding for part or all of the NTA budget. In this manner, tourism can help support its own management.

If the government needs to become involved in development of resorts or other types of tourist attractions or facilities, a commonly used approach is to organize a public development corporation. This entity is funded by the government, but functions as an independent company subject to government review. When the private sector becomes more mature in the area, the public corporation may sell its assets to private investors.

Tourism private sector organizations serve several important functions: providing a forum for discussing and resolving common problems of tourism enterprises, making coordinated recommendations to the NTA for improvements in the tourism sector; providing representation on tourism boards and committees; conducting research and training for their member enterprises; establishing and maintaining adequate facility and service standards of their members; and sponsoring special events. The private sector can be organized in various ways. There can be separate hotel, restaurant, tour and travel, and other special purpose associations, some combination of these or, in a small tourism area, perhaps a single tourism enterprises' association. Private sector associations are funded by membership dues.

Tourism Manpower Planning

Manpower planning is applying a systematic approach to ensure that the right people are in the right place at the right time. This is especially important in tourism, which is a service activity depending in large part for its success on the quality of personal working in tourism. Manpower planning involves the four steps of:

- Surveying and evaluating the present utilization of manpower in tourism and identifying any existing problems and needs.

- Projecting the future manpower needed. Projections are made for the number of personnel required in each category of employment. Then the qualification for each category of job are determined.
- Evaluating the total human resources that will be available in the future.
- Determining training needs and formulating the education and training programmeme required to provide the qualified manpower.

All types of tourism employees must be considered in manpower planning. These include both public sector employees in the NTA and employees needed in private sector—hotel, catering and tour and travel operations including tour guides. Also, some training of tourism-related personnel may be required. Immigration and customs officials often need to be sensitized in how to handle tourists properly. There may be need for specialized training of persons working in tourism-oriented retail shops, handicraft producers, entertainers, and others. It is important that the need for upgrading the knowledge and skills of present employees be identified. Often these persons have been properly trained. Satisfying this need for upgrading must be incorporated into the training programmeme.

Evaluation of human resources refers to review of the total manpower which will be available in the country or region, and allocation of this manpower to the different economic activities including tourism. Future tourism manpower needs are projected based on application of formulas to the types and amount of expected future tourism development.

Many kinds of education and training programmes are applicable to tourism—on-the-job training; correspondence (distant learning) courses; short upgrading and specialized courses; study tours; and one, two-, three or four-programmes at the vocational school and university levels. In countries where tourism is being developed into a substantial sector, tourism education institutes are established. The manpower planning programme needs to be periodically reviewed and updated to meet current and projected future needs.

Tourism-Related Legislation

Tourism legislation includes the basic tourism law. This law typically sets forth the policy for developing tourism and establishes the functions, structure and sources of funding of the NTA (or regional tourism office). Various specific regulations are necessary. These relate to the standards, licensing requirements and inspection procedures for hotels, tourist restaurants, tour and travel agencies, tour guides and other tourism enterprises. In some countries, a hotel classification system has been established and requires administration. These regulations are carefully prepared based on understanding the needs of the country or region. The necessary mechanisms and staff capabilities must be available to apply the regulations on a continuing basis. Procedures for administering the industry standards should be set forth in the regulations.

Certain related laws and regulations are also important for the development and management of tourism. There is need for zoning regulations to designate the regional tourism zones, and control land uses and apply development standards in specific tourism development areas. If zoning regulations already exist, it may be necessary to modify them to include tourism-type land uses such as hotel zones. Environmental protection legislation, including the EIA requirements, will be necessary if these do not already exist. Public health, sanitation, safety and fire codes, building codes, facility operating regulations, liability laws relating to guests and their belongings, labour and taxation legislation are all important for the development and operation of tourist facilities. Regulations on transportations facilities and services —control of fares, licencing of carriers, safety requirements and travel routes—also affect tourism operations.

In many countries, tourism development is based on scenic areas, nature parks and archaeological and historic places. Legislation on parks and conservation is very important to protect these resources. Conservation areas need to be legally designated and planned, with land and visitor uses carefully controlled.

Tourist consumer protection legislation is being adopted in many countries. This legislation is designed to protect tourist from being taken advantage of by unscrupulous or mismanaged tourism enterprises.

Tourism Investment Policies And Incentives

As indicated previously, the government typically must finance major infrastructure projects and public-type tourist attractions. Some or all of this investment—such for electric power, water supply, sewage and solid waste disposal, and even attraction features—can eventually be recovered through payment of user fees. Financing of on-site infrastructure such as for hotel or resort sites is typically the responsibility of the private developer, or a public corporation if one is involved.

For private investment in hotels and other commercial facilities and services, the investment policy will depend on the local situation. If sufficient private capital resources are available, there is no problem. If capital is limited and tourism must compete with other sectors for its use, then international capital must be sought. International capital can be allowed for total financing, or there can be joint ventures organized between international and local companies. Joint ventures are obviously preferable, in order for the country to receive some of the investment profits.

Often investment incentives offered by the government are needed to attract sector investment. Some of the common types of incentives, which can be offered singly or in combination, are as follows:

- Provision of development land, and assembly of the required amount of land, at moderate or no cost at suitable sites.

- Provision of off-site infrastructure (which is usually provided in any case), or provision of on-site infrastructure at no cost to the investor.

- Complete or partial exemption from customs duties on imported items used in the development and operation of tourist facilities and services. These may include building materials, machinery, equipment and supplies, and transportation vehicles such as tour buses.

- Complete or partial exemption from company income or property taxes for a specified number of years, and offering favourable depreciation allowances which reduce taxes.

- Provision of financial assistance—loans at regular or low interest rates; extended periods of repayments of

loans; subsidies for payments made on interest of private loans; or guarantee by the government of private loans made. Outright grants of money can also be provided.
- Unrestricted repatriation of all or part of foreign capital, profits, dividends and interest, after taxes have been paid.
- Guarantees against nationalization or appropriation of the investment.

It is important that the incentives be provided only for approved projects that conform to the development plan and programme and are suitably designed. Incentives may also be restricted to certain types of development that the government wants to encourage, for example, certain quality levels of hotels, certain types of services such as tour operations, and tourism development in remote areas. The types of incentives offered should be reviewed periodically and adjusted to current investment needs. Incentives offered during the initial stages of development may no longer be needed at a later time or should be modified to suit current needs.

In many places investment incentives are not required and the profitability of tourism development is assured. In such areas, the government may require that developers make payments, perhaps through an association, for their proportionate share of the costs of infrastructure development. Even other costs, such as for any environmental or social problems resulting from the development, can be required to be paid by the developer. These costs, for example, may include buying land and planting forest cover elsewhere to replace that which was removed from the development site, and resettlement costs of families dislocated from the site.

Implementation and Monitoring

Specifying how to carry out the plan's policy and recommendations is an essential aspect of the planning process. As has already been emphasized, techniques of implementation should be considered throughout formulation of the plan. This gives greater assurance that recommendations are implemen-table. Specific techniques of implemen-tation should be set forth. An increasingly common practice is to prepare an implementation manual which the government can use as a guide on implementation techniques and procedures. The major elements of implementation are explained in the following sections.

Plan Adoption and Allocation of Responsibilities

After careful review and agreement, the tourism plan should be adopted by the government as its official guide for developing tourism. Through adoption of the plan, the legal basis for its implementation is established. It then becomes more difficult to deviate greatly from the policy and plan, although some adjustments will inevitably need to be made. Also essential for effective implementation is political commitment to development tourism on a planned basis, and strong leadership exercised in both the public and private sectors of tourism.

In the implementation approach, the first step is to decide on the respective roles of government, the private sector and special bodies such as public corporations. Whichever respective roles are decided on, close cooperation and coordination between the government and private sectors on implementation must be maintained.

Staging and Programmeming Development

To achieve the physical development recommendation systematically, the first step is to determine the general staging of development. Staging is usually indicated as part of the structure plan.

Within the framework of the recommended staging, specific projects are identified for development, and then organized into an integrated development programme. This programme should include all types of development—government infrastruc-ture, attractions and facilities, and private sector development of commer-cial facilities and services. It is preferable also to specify other actions that are needed for implementation—establishing certain tourism organi-zations; adopting tourism laws and regulations; or carrying out socio-cultural and environmental programmes. A model tourism action programme demonstrates the approach used to prepare such a programme.

The projects and actions are shown by year, usually for a five-year period. For long-term projects, continuation of the projects over two or more years in indicated. Pre-development activities, such as detailed planning, design and feasibility analysis for future projects, should be include in the programme. General cost estimates of development projects are shown, and the responsible parties for carrying out the projects or actions a re specified. The responsible parties involved may include, for example, the relevant government agency, the private sector or a public corporation.

The tourism programme should be carefully coordinated with the programmes of related agencies, such as the transportation, parks and cultural departments. In order to give greater assurance of programme coordination, the tourism programme may even include a listing of projects that are the responsibility of those agencies, such as national park or museum projects. The programme must also be carefully coordinated with the overall development programme of the country or region. In fact, tourism is typically incorporated into the overall development programme.

The first stage action programme is often prepared as part of the initial tourism planning study so that it is well integrated with the planning recommendations. Alternateively, it can be prepared later after the plan has been adopted. Action programmes for the subsequent stages of development are prepared at a later time near the completion of the previous stage programme. These later stage pro-grammes can incorporate any minor adjustments made to plan, as well as actions and projects which could not be accomplished in the previous programme. Thus these programmes become 'rolling plans' that are always relatively up-to-date.

A common technique for achieving efficient development programmeming, especially at the project development level, is critical path analysis. This involves preparing a special type of chart—a network—consisting to arrows and circles. These depict the entire development process, with an event, such as developing a hotel in a resort, being represented by a circle, and an activity, such as constructing the hotel foundation, by an arrow. The circies are connected by the arrows. Logically, an event cannot take place until all activities leading up to it have been completed. Estimated 'time to completion' values are then placed on each activity. The critical path of the network is determined by considering each event in turn, and calculating the earliest possible time in which it can occur. If an event is dependent on two or more activities, the earliest time for completion is determined by the longest activity.

The critical path is the resultant sequence of inter-concerned events and activities which will require the longest time to accomplish. Adding together all the times on the critical path will give the shortest time for the project to be completed. Critical path analysis for major programmes or projects can be complicated. However, computer technology can be used to simplify preparation of the chart and for evaluating different development implementation scenarios to arrive at the most effective one.

Applying Aoning and Other Regulations

At the national and regional planning levels, zoning should be applied to designate tourism development regions or areas—the tourism zones. These zones may include other types of land uses but their zoning for tourism indicates that they are places where tourism is to be developed. The appropriate types of tourism development are also often shown for each of the tourism zones. Within the designated zones, the government can develop infrastructure suitable for tourism-tourist attractions and other public-type tourist facilities and services. Designation of the tourism zones also informs the private sector where and what type of tourism is desired, and will more likely be approved. If necessary, the government can offer incentives for private sector development in the tourism zones.

At the local level of planning, tourism zoning regulations demarcate specific area for different types of land uses, and the standards to be applied within each of the land uses. In a resort area, for example, the zoning will designate the accommodation, commercial, recreation and conservation zones.

Other tourism related laws and regulations were described in Chapter 13. These need to be adopted as soon as possible, in order to provide the basis for managing tourism and applying facility standards.

As a tourism area develops, it is often desirable to apply a hotel classification system, usually based on star classification levels. The advantages of a hotel classification system are that they inform tour operators, travel agents and tourists about the general quality level of the facilities so that they can better select the ones they want to use. The application of a classification system also gives incentives to the private hotel enterprises to upgrade hotels to a higher star level, where that is desirable, and provides a guide for development of new hotels. For the same reasons, classification systems can also be applied to restaurants. If needed, other types of regulations, such as those on hygiene, sanitation and building construction, should be adopted. In areas prone to earthquakes and high winds, special construction standards should be incorporated into the building code.

The government procedures for reviewing and taking action on tourism development project proposals—such as hotels, and their licensing and inspection procedures—should be clearly set forth. These procedures should be efficient and fair to enterprises making the proposals but also ensure that proper standards are met.

Applying Development Standards

Application of suitable development standards and design guidelines for tourist facilities helps ensure that tourism development is environmentally appropriate, and meets tourists' and residents' expectations. These may be applied at the national, regional or local levels of government, depending on the particular governmental situation. However, it is the central or regional government's responsibility to make certain that appropriate standards are applied at the local level. Therefore, development standards and design guidelines are usually included in national and regional plans, and are adopted as part of the plan. The types of development standards to be considered are as follows:

- *Density of development*—usually expressed in terms of number of accommodation units such as hotel rooms per acre or hectare. The density of development greatly determines its overall character.
- *Heights of building*—also very important in setting the character of development and environmentally integrating it. For example, in many rural resorts, buildings are not allowed to exceed the heights of trees so that they blend well into the natural environment.
- *Setbacks of buildings*—from amenity features, shorelines, roads, site boundaries and other buildings. Setbacks are important for various reasons. For example, adequate setbacks from beaches and shorelines prevent damage to building resulting from possible shoreline erosion, preserve the natural appearance of the shoreline, and allow sufficient space for landscaping, recreation and public access to the shoreline.
- *Floor area ratio (FAR)*—the ratio, expressed in percentage, of the total area of all the floors of the building to the total site area. FARs also help determine the development character and sense of openness.
- *Coverage of the site by buildings and other structures*—expressed as a percentage of the site covered by buildings and structures. Establishing maximum site coverage ratios particularly determines the amount of open space and landscaping in the development.
- *Vehicular parking spaces and other requirements*—the amount of landscaping and open space, public access to amenity features, sign controls and under-grounding of utility lines, all of which are important in making a development more attractive and functional.

These development standards are usually set forth in zoning regulations, or may be adopted separately for particular tourism development areas. The actual standards applied will, of course, vary among different types of tourism areas, depending on the desired type and character of development. It is also very important to adopt suitable engineering standards to be applied in the development of infrastructure.

Guidelines for site planning and architectual and landscaping design should be adopted. They also affect how well the development is integrated into the natural and cultural environment. These are usually prepared as guidelines, and not regulated standards, because they need to be flexible and allow for the creative imagination of the designer. Site planning refers to the exact location of buildings on the development site. Site planning guidelines should consider several factors—preventing environmental hazards of erosion, landslides and flooding; achieving proper relationships among buildings; and maintaining views from buildings and vista points. Architectural guidelines should be related to use of local traditional building styles and materials, as well as overall design attractiveness. Landscaping guidelines should consider various factors—use of local indigenous plants; appropriately designed outdoor furniture; suitable night lighting; low-cost landscape maintenance; and conservation of water in dry areas.

Site planning, architectural and landscaping guidelines are typically administered by a design review committee composed of professional persons. The committee reviews all development proposals and makes any recommendations for improvements needed to their design. The guidelines should be made available to the designers before they do their work, so that they will know what the design parameters are.

Implementing Other Programmes

Other programmes recommended by the tourism plan need to be implemented. These may include, for example, the training programme for employees in tourism, public awareness programme on tourism, and an economic programme to produce more local food items used in tourism. The promotion programme will require implementation. Environmental awareness and protection programmes often must be pursued. Park, historic conservation and cultural programmes must be carried out.

Certain critical aspects of tourism may need to be resolved. The government and private sector should be conscious of maintaining tourist health. Any special health problems, such as endemic malaria on AIDS, should be addressed and tourists informed. Travel facilitation require-ments and procedures, especially immigration and customs, should be made as efficient and 'user-friendly' as possible, while still enforcing the regulations.

Monitoring and Management

Monitoring should be considered an integral part of plan implementation and management. Monitoring will detect problems in their early stages, so that remedial measures can be taken. The progress of implementation, especially of action programme, should be continuously monitored. The number and characteristics of tourist arrivals should be monitored to see if the market targets are being maintained. Determining tourist satisfaction levels through special surveys of them is especially important. Monitoring the economic, environmental and socio-cultural impacts of tourism generally, and for specific projects, is essential. A checklist of factors that should be monitored to determine if the plan and programme are being implemented properly and on schedule.

Even though time-based targets are established, they should be considered flexible based on changing circumstances. There are many unpredictable influences on meeting targets. The overall recommendations are not necessarily invalid just because certain targets are not met exactly on schedule. During the shorter term, it is more important to maintain a balance between the development of tourist facilities, services and infrastructure and actual market demand. By maintaining a balance, resources are not wasted. Over the long term, efforts can be made to catch up on and achieve the various market and development targets.

One of the necessary tools for research, monitoring and the overall management of tourism is establishment of a tourism information system. This needs to be an integrated system, using computer technology. Various data are placed into the system—tourists' arrivals and their characteristics; accommodation and other tourist facilities and services; economic, environmental and social data; the results of special surveys; comparisons can be made over a period of time. Any significant problems and trends can be determined, and actions taken accordingly. It is essential that data fed into the information system be reliable and accurate, or the research results will not be usable.

Review should be made periodically of whether the overall tourism development policy, plan and programme are the most effective ones to achieve the development objectives. Each country or region is unique and development approaches must be adapted to each specific place. If, through experience in applying them, certain approaches and recommen-dations are seen to be deficient, then different ones should be considered. Through experimentation, the most effective approaches can be determined.

Emphasis must be given to the continuous management of tourism. Tourism management relates to many considerations—adapting to changing market and product trends; maintaining and improving the quality of facilities and services; continuously expanding the benefits of tourism socially and geographically, solving problems as they arise; and other matters. Both effective implementation of the plan and efficient management are required for the long-term success of tourism and its sustainable development.

TOURISM MARKETING

The problems of marketing in tourism are somewhat different from the problems of traditional product marketing. The differences are the result of the characteristics of tourism supply and demand. Tourism, first of all, is a service. An intangible experience is being sold, not a physical good that can be inspected prior to purchase. Because it is a service, production and consumption take place at the same time. In manufacturing, goods are produced, stored, and sold. The inventory process serves as a way of linking these stages of production and consumption. Tourism supply cannot be stored. Unlike a can of food which, if it is not sold one day can be sold the next, airline seats, hotel rooms, or restaurant seats not sold today lose that particular sale forever. Although the inventory cannot be stored and adjusted to changes in demand, the capacity to produce these tourism services must be developed ahead of time. This puts a great deal of pressure on producers to effectively plan the proper amounts of facilities and, having developed those facilities, to keep them as fully used as possible. This in itself creates another kind of problem, for tourism supply is relatively fixed. The resources and infrastructure of a destination cannot change as quickly as can tourist demand.

A second important factor that makes tourism different from other industries is that the service provided—a vacation—is in fact an amalgam of several products and services. A vacation has a transportation component, a lodging component, a food and beverage component, an attractions component, an activities component, and so on. These components are usually offered by different firms, and they may be marketed directly to the tourist or combined into a package in which they are offered as one vacation but the services are supplied by different firms. This lack of control over the entire vacation means that a great deal of interdependence results. A satisfied tourist results from many independent businesses, each providing a satisfying part of the total vacation. The marketing efforts of each of the parts are thus affected by the efforts of the others providing a part of the vacation. The satisfaction provided is also a function of the human element providing the service. This also is very difficult to control in terms of the consistent quality of service provided.

A third factor that makes tourism different from other industries concerns the role of travel intermediaries. Because most tourist services are located at distances far from their potential customers, specialised intermediaries—organisations that operate between the producer and the tourist—are often necessary to bridge the gap. Also, the fact that many tourism producers are relatively small means that they cannot afford to set up their own retail outlets. Thus, while in most industries, the producer exerts much control over every stage in the development and delivery of the product, in tourism the travel intermediaries can influence if not determine which services should be offered, to whom, when, and at what price.

The last factor that makes tourism different from other industries relates to demand. Tourism demand is highly elastic, seasonal in nature, and subject to subjective factors such as taste and fashion as well as the more objective factors of demand such as price. In many cases, the "product" sought can be satisfied by any number of destinations, with particular emphasis on no one in particular.

"Marketing is a management philosophy which, in light of tourist demand, makes it possible through research, forecasting and selection to place tourism products on the market most in line with the organisation's purpose for the greatest benefit." This definition suggests several things. First, it indicates that marketing is a way of thinking about a situation that balances the needs of the tourist (as indicated through tourist demand) with the needs of the organisation or destination. This can be explained by an examination of the development of an appropriate orientation. Second, the definition stresses tourist research that culminates in the selection of tourist demand. The concept of market segmentation is useful here. Third, the concepts of the product life cycle and positioning are useful to underscore the proper placement of tourism products on the market and to suggest the appropriate marketing policy and strategies resulting from that decision.

Orientation

Before embarking on a programmes to market tourism in general or a specific tourism product or service in particular, it is necessary to develop a philosophy or orientation that will guide one's marketing efforts. Such a philosophy will set the tone for every subsequent decision made as part of the overall marketing effort. Although several different orientations are possible, experience has shown that they are not all equally effective.

Some destination areas have marketing efforts that are guided by a product orientation. A product orientation suggests that the emphasis be placed upon the products or services available. A destination area has many physical, historical, and cultural resources, for example. The extent to which "our" resources are better than those of the competition will determine how many tourists visit our destination. This orientation has been used by the local authorities of a town on the south coast of England who decided in the late 1960s to print brochures only in English. When it was pointed out that a major potential market was the French residents across the English Channel, the reply was given that if the French wanted to visit, then they would be interested enough to learn to read English in order to understand what was available. Although it cannot be denied that the quality of resources is important, a total emphasis on tourism supply fails to take the wishes of the potential tourist into account. A product orientation may, in fact, be successful if there is a surplus of demand over supply. In this case, the destination or company that offers the best product will get the tourist. The old adage that reflected this said "build a better mousetrap, and the world will beat a path to your door."

When there is more supply than demand, however, the problems becomes "How can I sell all these mousetraps?" The number of destinations actively seeking tourism has increased as has the number of places throughout the world with easy accessibility. The entry into the market-place of more professional tour packagers has increased competition for the tourist dollar and has meant that destination areas can no longer sit back and wait for tourists to come to them. It has become increasingly necessary to sell tourists on the benefits of visiting a particular destination or of purchasing a particular product or service. The orientation for many has moved from one of emphasising product to one of emphasising selling. The accent has been placed on promotion of what is available for sale. Yet, this selling orientation focusses on the needs of the seller—to sell the product—rather than the needs of the buyer—What will satisfy me? The attempt here is to convince the potential tourist that what is available will please.

A further development in orientation is one in which the needs and wants of the tourist are placed foremost in the mind of the marketer. This is a marketing orientation philosophy that begins with the needs and wants of the tourist and seeks to provide a product or service that will satisfy those needs and wants. It involves being open when the tourist wants us to be; serving breakfast when the tourist wants it rather than when it is convenient for management; providing the kind of experiences that tourists want rather than what we feel they "should" want. It is realising that, from the example used above, an individual does not want to buy a mousetrap; rather she wants to kill mice. If and when a better way is developed of *satisfying a need*, people will use it. This philosophy is evident at the beginning of this book when an emphasis was placed on the satisfaction of needs and wants.

The uniqueness of tourism suggests that a philosophy that concentrates solely on the needs of the market is not the best orientation, even for the market itself. Tourism supply is oriented toward the resources of a community. To become totally marketing oriented, all aspects of the community would have to be oriented toward satisfying the needs and wants of the tourist. The risk for the community as well as for the tourist ultimately would have to be oriented toward satisfying the needs and wants of the tourist. The risk for the community as well as for the tourist ultimately is that by orienting strictly and totally for the tourist's needs, the needs and integrity of the community may be abused. Consider the situations explored in earlier chapters of tourist destination areas that have adapted to the needs of the tourist and have, in the process, lost their uniqueness, their heritage, and their natural resources while getting a relatively poor economic return on their natural resources while getting a relatively poor economic return on their investment. Destination areas that have attempted to adapt their resources to satisfy tourist needs may have lost the very thing that has made them attractive and unique in the first place. The tourist is the ultimate loser, as more and more destinations take on an increasingly similar and familiar appearance.

A solution to the problem is to develop a marketing approach that focusses on the satisfaction of tourist needs and wants while respecting the long-term interests of the community. This orientation is often referred to as a societal marketing approach. Such a philosophy will provide for planning, development, and marketing activities that will focus on the needs of the tourist, but it will also enable one to equally consider the effects of such action on the long-term interest of the community before the action is taken.

All marketing activities will be guided by the philosophy of those responsible for the marketing campaign. It is essential that any marketing effort have an agreed-upon philosophy to guide the further development and marketing efforts of any property, company, or destination.

Segmentation

The second aspect of our definition of marketing refers to selection of tourism demand. Market segmentation is a recognised and universally accepted way of analysing demand. Market segmentation refers to the process by which people with similar needs and wants are grouped together for the purpose of better focussing on and serving the market.

Segmentation is based on four assumptions. First, the market for a product or service, for example a vacation, is made up of particular segments the members of which have distinctive needs and preferences relative to the product or service being marketed. Second, these potential tourists can be grouped into segments the members of which each have similar and identifiable characteristics. Third, a single product offering, such as a Caribbean cruise, will appeal to some segments of the market more than others. Fourth, firms and organisations can improve their overall marketing effort by developing specific product offerings to reach specific segments of the market. A cruise package will be suitable for one part of the market, but an historical tour may be more suitable for another.

The process of segmenting a market can lead to many strategic management decisions. Market segmentation can be more than a statistical technique used to analyse demand. It can be utilised as a management tool that leads to specific marketing decisions. The development of such a strategy begins with the identification of profiles of segments of the market. At one extreme, a firm or destination may maximise its marketing orientation by developing a unique product offering for every potential tourist. Limitations of time and money prevent this. At the other extreme, the firm or destination may save time and money by offering one basic option to everyone. Although that one option will undoubtedly appeal to some potential tourists, it will not to others. The compromise is to assemble potential tourists into segments, each segment having similar preference characteristics, and produce offerings geared to the needs of these segments.

To determine the compromise point between developing a product for everyone and offering one product for all, it is necessary to examine the criteria a segment must meet to determine its viability. A segment must be:

1. *Measurable.* Can we determine how many potential tourists are in this segment?
2. *Accessible.* Can these tourists be reached through promotion and through existing or potential methods of distribution? How easy will this be?
3. *Substantial.* Are there sufficient numbers of tourists in this segments to support a marketing effort aimed specifically at them?
4. *Defensible.* Are the tourist characteristics unique enough to justify a separate programme targeted at them? Is such a programme immune to the mass marketing approach of competitors?
5. *Durable.* As the market develops, will this segment maintain its differences, or will these differences disappear?
6. *Competitive.* Do we have a relative advantage over the competition in our attempts to serve this market segment?

Many criteria have been developed by which a market segment can be constructed. Four general categories have been developed: (1) socio-economic, (2) product-related, (3) psychographic, and (4) geographic.

Social

Early segmentation studies used socio-economic criteria as the basis for forming market segments. These criteria remain the most commonly used today. This is probably due to the relative ease of collecting data, the comparability of such information through census as well as media data, and the fact that such data is easy to understand and apply. Age and income have, in fact, been very successful predictors of recreation participation. However, the use of only socio-economic criteria to segment markets has come under attack. It has been argued that the rapidly changing nature of society makes it impossible to rely solely on demographic data as a means of plotting marketing strategy. Just because a segment of people are within a particular age or income group does not necessarily mean they will have similar vacation preferences. Also, socio-economic information does not give the marketer sufficient information about likes and dislikes to properly position the product in the marketplace. Positioning refers to the decision to serve a particular segment of the market with a product offering that is specifically aimed at satisfying its needs and wants.

Greater success has been found in using demographic criteria that are multivariate. Status, for example, includes dimensions of income, education, and occupation, and family life cycle is a composite of marital status, age, and the numbers and ages of children at home. Life-cycle segmentation has proven to be an effective way of segmenting in a number of tourism and recreation cases.

It is unlikely that segmentation on the basis of socio-economic criteria will cease to be used. Although other segmentation methods provide substantial information useful for strategic decisions on what to offer, it is still necessary to reach the market segment so described. For all its shortcomings, demographic segmentation offers the best way to determine the accessibility of the market.

Product Related

A major advantage of segmenting by means of product-related criteria is that the information gained is directly related to the particular product in question. Indeed, a major flaw in some studies is that information is sought from the potential tourist that deals with general benefits sought or, in the case of psychographic segmentation, general attitudes about types of products/services rather than with specific products and services. Some attempts have been made in recreation and tourism to use heavy-half segmentation. Heavy-half segmentation refers to the idea of segmenting a market on the basis of quantity purchased or consumed. As with other types of products, however, heavy-half segmentation has been found lacking. A major problem is that, in many cases, the characteristics of the heavy half (the major purchasers) have been found to be similar to those of the light half. In a study of down hill skiers, it has been found that preferences and use patterns of both heavy and light skiers are similar except for such volume-related characteristics as level of skill, incidence of ski vacations, ownership of equipment, and quality of slopes. Similar difficulties have been found when one tries to segment on the basis of brand loyalty.

Benefit or attribute segmentation is fast becoming a very popular segmentation method to use in recreation and tourism. This method involves segmenting a market according to the relative importance assigned to benefits that consumers expect to realise after purchasing the product. The method entails determining the relative importance of specific product benefits to prospective consumers. Clusters are then formed of people who attache similar degree of importance to the same product benefits. Although results can have important ramifications for the development of new products and the determination of advertising messages, it is necessary to develop demographic profiles of those identified in the clusters in order to reach the market segments.

Psychographic

Much has been made of this relatively new tool. This technique of segmentation, although expensive to use and difficult to carry out, has been useful for describing segments. It can probably be best used in highly specialised and extensively developed markets to supplement the information gained from simpler analyses. Demographic data may be likened to the bones of a skeleton, and psychographic data may be likened to the flesh. The bones form the basis of the structure, but it is only by covering the form with flesh that the features become recognisable. Information about an individual's attitudes, interests, and opinions give a much closer picture of the segment being described.

Geographic

Geographic considerations are very important to tourism. Much of the attractiveness of a tourist destination is based on contrast—contrasting cultures, climates, or scenery, for example. This implies there being a certain distance between origin and destination. Also, we have already seen the crucial role that accessibility of tourists to a destination plays in tourism. To date, destinations have used geographically based studies solely to identify primary, secondary, and in some cases, tertiary markets. State and national tourist offices tend to use geographic segmentation for the purposes of determining the extent of their promotional efforts.

Once market segments have been identified and profiles drawn up, it is necessary to select which segment(s) the firm or destination will seek to attract and serve. This decision can be made only in light of an analysis of which market segments will bring most benefit to the firm or destination. Such an analysis involves four concerns:

Sales potential: What is the current, and future potential for revenue from this segment? Revenue is a combination of the number of current and potential tourists and their current and potential per-person spending.

Competition: To what extent does competition exist for the segment(s) in question? How strong is our advantage compared to the competitors?

Cost: How much investment is required to develop products to attract this segment?

Serviceability: Do we have the financial and managerial capability to design, promote, and distribute the appropriate products and satisfactorily serve the market segments attracted by the products produced?

The segments chosen become the target market. The process of selection and the corresponding decisions to develop a marketing programme suitable to meet the needs of those segments is known as "positioning."

The concept of the product life p 1 cycle is useful to the marketer at this stage as an additional guide to appropriate strategies to use in choosing, attracting, and serving target markets.

Product Life Cycle

The concept of the product life cycle suggests that a product, service, or destination moves through distinct stages. In Chapter Twelve the various stages were described from a planning perspective.

The stage of development in which a product or destination finds itself has profound marketing implications.

Thus, within the context of the earlier definition of marketing, it is necessary for the benefit of the organisation or destination to adopt a marketing outlook, to segment the market by appropriate means, and, taking the stage in the product life cycle into account, to position effectively the product or destination within the marketplace. This decision is operationalised by developing specific marketing strategies on price, product, promotion, and distribution within the context of a market planning approach.

MARKET PLANNING

Market planning implies a future orientation. It involves identifying suitable marketing objectives as well as determining appropriate marketing strategies to achieve those objectives.

External Forces

Marketing objectives can be set only after an analysis of the interaction of five factors-product, market, competition, overall development of objectives of the firm or destination, and the external forces within which the destination or firm in question must act.

Planning must be accomplished within the framework of the external environment over which the marketing manager may have little or no control. The first of these factors concerns the legal environment. Certain countries in the past have placed legal restrictions on their residents that have hampered the flow of tourism. Residents may be restricted from travelling, or they may be unable to take more than a certain sum of money out of the country. Political factors must also be considered. Tensions or hostilities between country of origin and a country of destination will affect the marketing function. On the cultural level, it is important to consider the educational background of the countries being considered for tourism purposes. More international travel is generated from countries exhibiting higher educational standards, from societies regarded as more cultured, and from countries having a higher degree of industrialisation. An important factor is the technical consideration. The destination must be accessible to tourists from the generating countries being considered. A final factor is economic. It is obviously important that there exist in a country of origin sufficient numbers of people that can afford to travel.

The marketing plan should be part of the overall business goal of the firm or the development plan of the destination. Tourism is one, and only one, strategy for development. As it was noted in previous chapters, tourism can be used as a political, social, and economic force. Yet, other alternatives are available. The overall plan for tourism must be consistent with the overall plan for the destination area.

Market/Product/Competitor Analysis

The overall objective of the market/product/competitor analysis is to determine where our product presently stands compared to the competition in the eyes of the market. Competition is defined as any firm or destination seeking to serve the same market as ourselves. This objective is accomplished by analysing product, market, and competition. The product and competitor analysis consists of a comparative evaluation of the following factors:

1. *Natural tourist resources*
   such as climate and topography
2. *Cultural and historical resources*
   such as historical monuments, museum, traditional events, ways of life
3. *Infrastructure*
   such as fresh water supply, road network, and communications
4. *Means of access and internal transportation facilities*
   such as airports, railroads, and bus companies
5. *Attractions and facilities*
   such as sporting events, hotels, and restaurants

The culmination of such a comparison between a product and its major competitors is a determination of comparative strengths and weaknesses. What do we have that is better than our competition? This information is important by itself, but in keeping with the marketing orientation stated above, it is necessary to place such intelligence in the context of the existing and potential market. Although marketing is not a science and has no scientific laws to guide its actions, there are several useful principles that guide its actions. For a firm or destination developing a marketing plan for the first time, one such principle may be: Attract people similar to those you already serve. This implies defining our existing market and seeking to develop more people with characteristics similar to those already attracted. An analysis of people in the market seeks to answer:

Who are they? How many of them are there? What are their socio-economic and psychographic characteristics?

Where do they come from and travel to?

How do they make plans, travel to and within the destination?

When do they vacation and for how long? When is the decision made?

Why do they vacation? What are their important motivations?

The crucial task is to determine a picture of the actual tourist, then project that picture into the future by considering trends in the country of origin. A second task is to discover potential markets by compiling a picture of the present tourist and seeking to find other markets that meet that profile. For example, if most people in the existing market come from within a 500-mile radius, potential markets may be discovered from areas within 500 miles from which visitors do not yet come.

From a consideration of the above five elements, a picture will emerge of problem areas and areas of opportunity. This will enable planners to set marketing objectives, to determine where they are, where they want to be. If one recognises the guidelines of overall business or development objectives, is aware of the constraints of the external environment, and is cognizant of the strengths and weaknesses of product compared to competition in light of market demand, objectives can be set. Objectives may relate to:

Type of image—elite or main market

Type of tourist—low spending — — spending, repeat or new business, historical buff. and so———

Type of spending—foreign exchange generation or domestic

Type of product—high class hotel or small, locally owned facilities or foreign owned ones

Remember that objectives can only come from an analysis of the elements discussed previously. The next step in the planning process, target market selection, can only come after objectives have been defined.

Target Market Selection

The concepts, discussed earlier, of product life cycle and market segmentation are extremely useful when selecting target markets. The tourism producer can, in fact, select a target segment. Once the target segment is selected, a marketing mix is developed that will meet the needs of the target. Yet, the very provision of the marketing mix will help ensure that the segment selected is attracted. For example, if a high-income, high-status target segment is selected, products will be developed to appeal to high-income, high-status tourists. Prices will be set high, and promotional messages may show pictures of tourists in tuxedos at dinner or older couples dancing cheek to cheek. Thus, the provision of the elements of the marketing mix means that only high-income, high-status tourist can afford to visit. The elements of the marketing mix are the way we "tell" the market what kinds of tourists we want.

Target segments will be defined in demographic, product-related, psychographic, or geographic terms. Which of these segments are actually chosen depends upon the size of the market and its position. The size of the market can be measured in terms of the number of tourists, the number of tourist nights, or the amount of tourist expenditures. Market segments that are large offer less of a risk than ones that are relatively small. The position of the destination relative to the market refers to the extent to which the market has been penetrated. If a destination area has managed to obtain a significant share of the market of a particular segment, efforts should be made to break into a new, unexplored market.

MARKET POTENTIAL INDEX

The following example of how the United States Travel and Tourism Administration selects market segments also shows how one destination area combines the analysis elements discussed above. The selection of target markets is done through a market potential index. The index consists of three parts. The first part shows the number of individuals in each country that have the financial means for a visit to the United States. It can be seen that on the sole basis of income, Canada is ranked number one. The first six countries listed account for 57 percent of the market potential. The second part of the index shows some qualitative market factors that are used to modify the first set of figures. The regulatory factors as a whole are equally as important as marketing factors. The regulatory factors are essentially cost oriented and refer to restrictions placed on potential tourists in the country of origin as well as on the costs of travelling to and spending within the United States. The relative weights of these factors should also be noted. These weightings, as with the others, are subjective and based upon the experience of those making the selection of the segments.

In the marketing factors, competition refers to the amount of competition the United States would face from other countries in attempting to attract visitors from a particular country. The greater the competition, the more difficult the marketing task and the less attractive that segment. The attitude of potential tourists to the United States as a tourist destination and to the American people as a whole is regarded as an important item, being weighed at 25 percent of the total marketing factors. Trade structure refers to the role of wholesalers and travel agents in selling travel as well as in shaping and influencing tourist decisions. It is easier to reach the tourist in Japan, where a few wholesalers control a great deal of international travel. Closely related to trade structure is the factor of buying habits, which is an indication of whether tourists tend to buy travel on their own, as they do in France and Mexico, or whether they buy packages developed by wholesalers. The latter will obviously receive higher ratings in the matrix. Being able to communicate in English is given a surprisingly low rating of 5 percent. Product awareness is a measure of the extent to which potential tourists are aware of the United States as a travel destination.

The effect of applying these factors to the previous figures is to reduce the number of potential tourists. An estimate is developed that reflects the unique marketing situation of each potential market relative to the United States. The top six countries now account for almost three-quarters of the potential market numbers. Australia and Venezuela have moved up in rank (due to concentrated trade structures, favourable attitudes toward the United States, and relatively good product awareness). Brazil, on the other hand, has moved down sharply from eight to seventeenth place, because of government-imposed restrictions on travel.

The third part of the index involves applying per capita spending figures to the second part. Because Australian and Latin American tourists spend more than other tourists in the United States, their relative rank increases. In the year that these figures were developed, actual arrivals from the six primary geographic markets accounted for 86 percent of all arrivals. This type of occurrence is not uncommon. In many cases a large percentage of the business comes from a relatively small number of sources. Obviously, the figures presented in this example will change from year to year. Over several years rankings will also change. The important consideration is the method used—one resulting from product, market, competitive, and external forces in line with the overall objective of using tourism to improve the balance of payments situation.

Marketing Mix

Once the target markets of a property or destination have been determined, an appropriate marketing mix can be developed. The marketing mix is comprised of four elements—product, price, promotion, and distribution. All four elements are provided in accordance with the needs of the target markets.

PRODUCT

It has already been noted that a action consists of a number of different parts or products—from transportation and lodging to sightseeing and souvenirs. It is clear that a variety of providers will offer one or more of these products or services. Each provider is thus interdependent with the others to offer an attractive and satisfying overall vacation experience. The philosophy of a marketing orientation suggests that products be developed to satisfy the needs and wants of those in the market. Also market segmentation indicates that properties or destination areas cannot possibly provide products that will satisfy everyone. It is necessary to select a target market and then provide a variety of products and services that will satisfy its needs. The balance between providing narrow customised products to appeal to a particular market segment and providing sufficient variety to appeal to a wide diversity of tastes is a difficult one for management.

Crissy has suggested several important criteria that should be met in the decision to provide a product or service. First, there should be a relatively heavy demand for the product or service from at least one important market segment, with the possibility of additional business from other segments of the market. It may be that the product can expect to break even on the basis of business from the major market segment and produce profit from business from the rest of the market. There may, of course, be a period of time before sales for a new attraction or service reach the break-even point.

Second, new products and services should fit in with the general image of the property or destination area and complement existing offerings. This does not mean that a destination area must appeal to only one segment of the market and that all products must meet the needs of that market segment. A great deal obviously depends upon the size of the destination area. One part of a destination area may appeal to the jet-set, while another part may be appealing to senior citizens. Within each of these parts, however, it is important that separate products and services be oriented around the one theme and market segment.

Third, any new offerings should be proposed in keeping with the available supply of manpower, money, and natural resources. Although new products and services should exploit an advantage that a property or destination area has, it is important that new offerings be within the ability of the destination area or the management to satisfactorily provide them. A destination area may have magnificent mountain terrain suitable for skiing but may lack management knowledge in ski-area operations. Experienced management may have to be hired on a permanent or temporary basis before a ski area can be proposed.

Finally, it is necessary that any product or service added contribute to the profit and/or growth of the entire property or destination. In some cases the new offering may bring in no profit itself, but its provision may contribute to growth. The hotel pool, for example, may cost the operation money while bringing in no direct revenue from admission for swimming. However, the provision of a pool may bring in additional room business, and its elimination may drive existing room business elsewhere. Similarly, a destination may institute its own airline, not as a revenue-producing venture but as a necessary means to bring visitors in to spend money.

PRICE

Several factors influence the pricing policy set as part of the marketing mix. The price charged in any situation is unique to that situation and is affected by the combination of the factors to be discussed. Nevertheless, some guidelines can be suggested to assist in the pricing decision.

In purely economic terms, price is a result of supply and demand. When supply exceeds demand, price will tend to decrease. The reverse is true also. Of greater importance is the extent to which demand changes (as measured by the amount purchased) as price changes. This refers to the elasticity involved. A 5 percent reduction in price may result in a corresponding 10 percent increase in the number of buyers and a subsequent increase in total sales revenue. Demand in this case is elastic. General products aimed at the luxury end of the customer scale are less susceptible to changes in price and consequently tend to be price inelastic. For destinations or properties that are open only part of the year, supply is limited and prices will have to be correspondingly higher (everything else being equal) than destinations open year round. Because demand is not often uniform throughout the year, it is common to charge higher prices during the peak season and lower prices when demand slackens. The expected length of an the product's place in the previously discussed product life cycle is also relevant here. A "fad" item with an expected short life cycle will have to charge sufficiently high prices to recoup the investment in a relatively short period of time. A product that expects a long life can be priced lower.

The price charged is influenced by the competition. If our offerings are essentially the same as those of our competitors, our prices must be similar to theirs. The extent to which we are unique reflects the extent to which we can charge more than the competition. Related to the influence of competition is the management policy regarding market share. If a decision is made to increase market share, prices will probably be lower than if a decision to skim a small number of tourists from several market segments is made.

Pricing policy is obviously related to the needs of the market segment that is served. If a destination or property is seen as serving the needs and wants of the market and if those needs and wants are perceived as being important to the members of the market segment, those members will be willing to pay a higher price for the destination or property. The price charged must also be perceived by the market as less than or at least equal to the value received. In certain situations the influence of the market seems to go against economic principles. With certain luxury items, demand may increase as price increases. This phenomenon reflects a certain amount of snobbishness on the part of the market. The feeling may be that the higher the price the greater the perceived value and the greater the demand. But the actual value in the minds of the buyers must still equal or exceed the price paid.

The effect of each of these variables cannot be determined exactly in quantitative terms. The effect of their interaction is more difficult to determine. However, the general guidelines stated above can give guidance on pricing decisions for particular destinations or properties.

Planning and Marketing Destination

Even though the end products of regional tourism planning should include stimulation of tourism awareness, new interagency governmental cooperation, greater public-private collaboration, and identification of zones of greatest potential, seldom does this process immediately results in new brick-and-mortar tourism development. This can only take place at the destination and site scales and as follow-up to regional planning. It is in and around communities that tourism development can and will succeed. The vision, the policies, and the integration at the regional scale provide the blueprint for a systems planning approach, essential to the elimination of many obstacles and the determination of desirable directions. But, eventually, commitment and land use decisions at the destination and site scales are necessary in order to translate these guidelines into reality. It is at these levels that economies may be strengthened and visitors may be enriched.

The concept of designation-community, attractions, and traveller access—is used here for several reasons. It regionalizes the significant role of community in traveller flow, providing the majority of service needs. Communities also contain many of the attractions sought by travellers. All transportation modes lead to communities contains. But, in addition to these factors, the area around communities contains a great many resources and outlaying attractions upon which the community travel services also depend. Using the concept of destination allows these important rural areas to be included in planning framework and principles.

It is no coincidence that this destination zone concept agrees with contemporary views of urban development. At one time, apparently in response to urban congestion, the principle of dispersion was put forward. Many conservation proponents still adhere to this principle. But, dispersion can reduce the indigenous value of both community and hinterland whereas combining a central city with its periphery into a single unit allows each to function in a symbiotic relationship. The regiopolis combined the advantage of social, human, and economic development within and around communities. Likewise, the tourism destination concept allows retention of community identity but also recognizes the important interde-pendency of the surrounding area.

It is the intent of this chapter to put forward the fundamental of place for planning at the destination scale and offer models, concepts, and processes for planning tourism at this level.

THE IMPERATIVE OF PLACE

The greatest imperative for all of tourism is *place*. Throughout history, place has played a dominant role in society. Sovereignty of place continues to foster strong land protection, and even, to stimulate wars. For many peoples of the earth, the qualities of place mean survival or death. In spite of man's gargantuan efforts to reshape the earth possesses its own peculiar characteristics, both as result of natural physical forces and acts of man.

As the topic of tourism planning shifts from the macro (the region) to the micro (destinations and sites), the importance of place dominates every concern. As tourism developers and promoters tend toward homogenizing the world with sameness, the opportunities for extracting the unique qualities of place so important to the traveller are being missed.

Characteristics of Place

Place, as defined by Motloch (1991, 279), "is the mental construct of the temporal-spatial experience that occurs as the individual ascribes meaning to settings, through environmental perception and congestion. "Explicit in this definition are important meanings for tourism. All travellers must have a place to go. Simple as this may be, it is not well understood. Place qualities are absolute for all developers of services, facilities, transportation, information, and promotion—the components of supply.

Temporal aspects of place are critical to tourism planning. Visitor impressions and experiences very greatly with time a place is visited. When visitors report they have already visited a location and see no point in visiting it again, they may miss an entirely different experience at a different time. Weather conditions—brilliant midday sun, cloudy sunset time, snowclad winter, cold, heat, stillness, or wind—can give places quite different meanings. Places seen at night may be in absolute contrast when viewed in daylight. Not only will the landscape differ but also will the patterns and colours of activities and users be quite different. For example, a dramatically different experience results from visiting the French Quarter of New Orleans in the day as compared to night. Places of a singular year-round climate have different appeals to travellers as compared to places with seasonal-change—spring flowers, summer green, autumn foliage colours, and a white landscape of winter. The new market surge of nature tourism selects places as much on the time of viewing wildlife as on their habitat location. Animal migrations are critical to viewing wildlife.

An equally important dimension of place is its *age*—ancient to new. Generally the older the place, the greater its amenities. An author of the southern region of the United States has stated. "Older places have accumulated more meaning, but they also very often are more tied to a specific setting or are simply more humane in scale or character—and thereby more engaging—than new places". Viewing the ruins of Delphi on the wooded slopes of Mount Parnassus cannot help but evoke dramatically different images for the visitor than visiting the more recently planned cities of Canberra or Brazilia. Even within a lifetime, "the special places of childhood are not sacred but the memory of them is necessary for attaching sacredness to place". An enlarging travel segment seeks the experiences of visiting historic sites and places of prehistory. Planning for visitor use of these sites creates challenges never before faced by designers' and managers—maintaining the integrity and patina of age at the same time providing for mass visitor use. For example, the removal of ancient skeletons from grave sites for display in museums is opposed by many native populations.

Spatial distribution of places around the earth has deep meaning for tourism and its planning. Each place has its own unique relationship to all other places, far or near. Analysis of geographic content described in the last chapter for regional planning are attempts to identify spatial characteristics of importance. In modern context with changing air fares and access, spatial distribution of destinations takes on new meaning. What once was *far* may now be *near* in terms of ease of access, changing dramatically the competitive position of places.

Another important characteristic of a place is its name. " Landscapes without place names are disorienting; without categorical forms, awful". Place names call up fantasy and imagery. The names of places from northern Michigan to the Arkansas River in the United States—Wisconsin, Peoria, Des Moines, Missouri, Osage, Omaha, Kansas, Iowa, Wabash, and Arkansas—stimulate recollection of French Jesuit explorers, Louis Joliet and Jacques Marquett's trip through this land in 1673. For settlers of Taxas, religious themes dominated place names; San Antonio, San Jacinto, San Saba, Corpus Christi, and the Brazos River. Deeper analysis of market characteristics would probably prove that few travellers seek out places with unfamiliar or no names.

In spite of today's great mobility and migration of peoples, certain landscapes retain *people-place qualities*. A travel writer stated, "I believe you could exterminate the French at a blow and resettle the country with Tartars, and within two generations discover, to your astonishment, that the national characteristics were back at norm". Thus is the dominance of the landscape as place. Landscapes have special values, even when some cultural labels are the same. Durrell points out that the spirit of place has modified Catholicism to the extent that it is different in Ireland, Italy, Spain, and Argentina. The theology and practices result from modification due to place. Although these subtleties are not always readily available to travellers, with some time and introspection they become real. Visits to the Scottish landscape evoke the adventurous landscapes of Stevenson.

Of course, place can be described by *technical and scientific facts*, For example, Mount Everest is five-and-one-half miles (8.9 kilometres) above sea level, is located in the Himalaya range, and was named for a British Surveyor-General of India, Sir George Everest. Madrid is located at latitude 40^0 20' 30" North and longitude 0^0 14'45" West and occupies about 550 square kilometres. In resource analysis, as has been cited in the discussion of regional planning, the quantities of natural and cultural resource facts are listed: arrest of forest land, sizes of lakes, lengths of streams, numbers and species of wildlife, and so on. Often, this is called *inventory*.

Human Attribution of Place

Although such inventorying is necessary in describing place, it is of little value unless interpreted and given meaning. *Human attribution of* resource facts is essential. "Neither the environment as such nor parts or features of the environment *per se* are resources; they become resources only if, when, and insofar as they are, or considered to be capable of serving man's needs. In other words, the word 'resource' is an expression of appraisal and, hence a purely subjective concept". Resources are not; they become. For tourism and travellers. "The environment is encountered in a way in which self and place are related". Statistics of resources are of value to the planner only as anticipated visitor contact can be assessed. This intimate amalgam of place and human experience is again expressed by Shepard as

The desert is the environment of revelation, genetically and physiologically alien, sensorially austere, aesthetically abstract, historically inimical. It is always described as boundless and empty, but the human experience there is never merely existential. Its solitude is not an empty void, a not-quite silence. Its forms are bold and suggestive. The mind is beset by light and space, the kinesthetic novelty of aridity, high temperature and wind. The desert sky is encircling, majestic, terrible... The moon, sun and stars are perceptually exaggerated lower in the sky. Apparent motion in the horizontal plane is always greater.

An excellent example of place attribution is the concept of *scenery*. No such thing existed until after the Middle Ages. Forests were filled with demons and were of no value until felled for agriculture. Not until the painters and writers of the nineteenth century romanticized nature did vistas of landscapes become scenery." The terrible away of God was made into an aesthetic—or, if you prefer, the forests and mountains of the earth came to be revered with religious intensity. The enjoyment of primeval wilderness had not been possible before".

Another aspect of human relationship to place is *social*. Cheek and Burch's early work emphasized the many social dimensions of leisure and place relations. There may be activities, such as picnicking, where the social group has higher priority than the location of place, as long as the needed amenities are present. Wilderness buffs often subscribe to Thoreau's tenet of seeking such places to find one's self. Certainly, the social context-solitude, friend, family, and lover—can evoke different visitor meanings even from the same place.

Perhaps the greates lesson from this brief examination of place is the understanding of its powerful and almost inexplicable necessity for tourism. And, if its power and necessity are accepted, planning and design action must follow-*placemaking*. Areas that seek to become destinations for tourism have no choice but to become involved in placemaking. But, this process is not to be interpreted as artificially contrived. Quite the opposite. The challenge before the designer is to have sufficient understanding of both physical and human dimensions of place in order to design. Again, from Motloch, "placemaking should include the effective management of order and spontaneity for understanding and exploration." Throughout the discussion of planning destinations and sites for tourism, the importance of place is a continuing theme.

DESTINATION PLANNING ISSUES

Opportunities

Although much marketing of tourism is done at the regional (national, state, and provincial) scale, for most travellers this is too generalized. That size of geography is often too large to comprehend as being able to satisfy travel objective. It may be open to question as to whether travellers really seek their rewards in the United States, Canada, and Australia, or in destinations such as in and around New York, Montreal, or Sydney. Communities and their environs—destinations—more frequently carry with them images of appeal for both business and pleasure travel.

At this period in the history of tourism, it would appear that so many destinations have already been developed that there are few opportunities left. This is a half-truth because of the dynamics of both the market and supply sides of tourism. Changes in markets—

demographics, economics, lifestyles, fads, and interests—are constantly opening up new areas for development. Change in transportation, attractions, information, services, and promotion are introducing new areas as having potential.

The destination discovery process demonstrated how one can identify potential destination zones. In most instances, when current market trends are examined, communities will discover much greater opportunity than popularly considered.

The geographic model, dramatizes a basic fundamental of all destination zones. They function for tourism only because of a *symbiotic relationship between focal cities and the surrounding area*. A destination function does not stop at the jurisdictional city limits. The surrounding rural area and small towns are an integral part of a destination zones. This symbiosis derives from tourist use which involves visiting attractions both inside cities and in surrounding areas and using tourist services-such as lodging, food services, and car service—primarily in the cities.

On the other hand, when travellers have participated in these activities, they seek lodging, food service, and other amenities and services of a focal city. Furthermore, feasibility of these service businesses favours city locations because they serve both resident and traveller markets.

Issues and Constraints

If opportunities for destination development are so abundant, why haven't more destinations occurred? One might glibly answer that this is due to lack of planning, but that is too simple because destination tourism planning is complicated. Because communities are the focal points for tourism destination, it appears that there are several constraints for community action toward tourism development.

Blank (1989) outlines several salient limitations.

- Lack of comparative advantage (location, quality of potential).
- Carrying capacity limitations.
- Lack of community's acceptance of change—preference for status quo.
- Power structure's preference for other development.
- Myopic view of tourism.
- Fear of tourism—erosive characteristics.
- Environmentalist resistance to any development.
- Narrow and inflexible policies on public lands.

Canada has experimented with much planning for tourism, most of which has stimulated valuable development. Yet, in working with destination planning, a few researchers have observed some important constraints at the local level. Go et al. (1992) analyzed imlementation of tourism strategies there and derived the following resistances:

- Tourism involves such a diversity of actors that clear mandates for development are lacking.
- Lack of local guidance and will.
- Mandates are unclear or in conflict.
- Local jurisdictions seek a quick fix and fail to provide financial and human resources to do the job.
- Lack of monitoring system to measure success.

A consequence of the geographic reality of a destination zone is that it *transcends political jurisdictional boundaries.* This fact complicates planning and development. Tourism leadership and political decisionmaking, such as for promotion, taxation, and development of amenities also usually stops at such boundaries. Within the several small towns, rural areas, and focal cities there may be different population characteristics and different traditional, attitudes, customs, and even conflict or animosity.

If tourism is to be developed, these barriers against cooperation must be removed or at least ameliorated. Tourism leaders and constituencies of all jurisdictions within a zone must be equally committed to tourism development or it will not take place. Conversely, *tourism may be the catalyst to bring peoples of these separate parts of the zone together* for a common cause.

Misunderstandings

The concept of destination, even as defined here, is plagued by several misunderstanding in field applications. They are related here only so that those involved in planning may avoid these problems.

1. *Destination zones are singularly defined.* Some writings refer to nations or continents as destinations. Certainly, this is a half-truth because images of these areas are often so defined in the minds of travellers. For example, Africa may have a stronger image than Krueger National Park. Destination zones are not uniformly defined. Some governments have divided regions into destination zones on the basis of administration. Such zones are suited to governance but have no relation to marketable or potential development areas. Sometimes marketing zones have been delineated but these lack consideration of resources yet to be developed. Zones based only on existing developing and travel trends have been identified by Ferrario (1979). Ruest (1979) and others prefer to base destination zones on geographical resource factors, and this is the emphasis given in this book.

2. *Destination zone boundaries are fixed.* This fallacy needs special emphasis. As markets change and as developed grows or decays, destination zones can take on new size and shape or even disappear. It is an error to publish maps of zones with the implication that the edges are well defined. Zones are generalized areas that have broad and soft edges. Even though some resource characteristics appear to be fixed, new interpretations may cause change in the future, such as today's new emphasis on ecotourism.

3. *Destination zones are of one type.* When one kind of development becomes popular and successful, there is tendency to copy this development at other locations. There is room for repetition but within a different market range; witness the Disney attraction in Paris. However, there is usually a stronger competitive edge when each destination builds upon its unique characteristics of place creating a tourism theme of its own. Although the elements and principles of tourism development may be the same, they can be expressed differently, depending on the special resources of each place.

4. *The best zones are developed by the private sector.* Those who support a tourism industry philosophy are inclined to believe that private investment is the only solution to destination development. Although no one can deny the very important role of private investment and development, it represent only part of the formula for successful tourism destination zones. Even in capitalistic and industrialized nations, governments

and nonprofit organization continue to play important roles by providing may historic and natural resource attractions. Most isolated restarts, for example, fail not necessarily because of poor management but because they do not benefit for nearby attractions and government input in the from of roads, water supply, waste disposal, police, fire protection, and a governed community nearby. The best destination plan is created jointly by nonprofit organizations, government, and the private sector.

5. *Zones succeed the best where tourism is the only economic provider.* Experience has clearly demonstrated the fallacy of this statement. Areas dependent only on tourism are plentiful and many continue to survive. But, they are very vulnerable, Fads, fashions, politics, wars, competition, and economic changes can be devastating for tourism. Industrial developers for many years have promoted the principle of economic diversity. Such diversity provides a buffer against exigencies of change. A tourism destination can remain much more stable if the area includes a diversity of industry and services.

6. *Zone identification assures success.* Because basic factors are geographically clustered in a destination zone, all three developer sectors have better chances of success. However, it should not be construed that individual project feasibility is assured. If, for example, it is indicated that a historic site might be developed into a major attraction, the question of developer feasibility remains. If development fits the policies and abilities of government park and historic agencies, one may see that it is feasible. Or, it may be more feasible for a nonprofit organization or commercial enterprise to be the developer. Mere zone identification does not assure success. Many investment and management factors remain to be resolved.

DESTINATION PLANNING GUIDE

In recent years, governments and other organizations have prepared guideline manuals for public use at the local level. Often these are titled community planning manuals but in the context of definitions used in this book, they generally include an entire destination zone. The guides offer step-by-step processes that can be of great value to leaders and local population constituencies in their search for better tourism development.

Alberta Manual

An excellent example is the Community Tourism Action Plan Manual (Alberta Tourism 1988) developed by the provincial tourism agency of Alberta, Canada. It was prepared over several years of study by staff, outside consultants, and representatives of the private sector. It was prepared over several years of study by staff, outside consultants, and representatives of the private sector. It contains five main sections.

Book 1. Introduction. This section begins by defining tourism to include attractions, promotion, infrastructure, hospitality, and services. It emphasizes that deficiencies in any of these components can limits tourism. The content includes answers to questions such as, Where do we fit in? Who benefits? Who doesn't benefit? And Is it for us?

Book 2. Organization. This chapter opens with emphasizing the need for organization but only after full commitment to tourism. There must be first a strong desire for tourism by residents, business, and the municipal council. The first step following expression of commitment is to create a tourism policy and Tourism Action Committee. A sample policy would be stated as follows:

> Tourism will be encouraged within a zone and its surrounding area in ways that will attract more tourists, increase their length of stay, increase the amounts of money they spend here, and ensure that any adverse social, economic and/or environmental effects are minimized as a result of activities to improve tourism. (Alberta Tourism 1988, 2/6)

According to the manual, the Tourism Action Committee should be mandated by local government with support from organizations such as the chamber of commerce and local tourism zone association (if one is in place). Members should include representatives of the following:

Chamber of commerce	Economic Development Board
Hotel/Motel operators	Service station operators
Restaurant operators	Historical society
Service clubs	Youth groups
Tourist zone representatives	Municipal administration
Recreation board	Tourist attraction operators Tourist event organizers

Members should meet the following criteria: knowledge of the community, commitment to tourism, ability to work in group, ability to invest sufficient time in the committee and reliability.

Book 3. Process. The suggested flow of twenty four action steps to develop a tourism plan at the local level. Step 1 is market analysis. Step 2 is gaining input from organizations and agencies. Steps 3-7 involve study of the area to determine assets and concerns. Step 8-10 include identification of goals, objectives, and strategies for reaching objectives. Steps 11-18 involve completion of the plan, obtaining input from several public, and gaining official approval. The final steps 19-24 consist of action implementation and reporting to the city council.

Book 4. Appendices. This book contains sources of assistance, such as private and governmental sources of grants as well as individuals and agencies that can offer technical and educational assistance.

Book 5. Workbook. The manual includes outlines for use in detailing the results of the several steps in the planning process.

As of September 1, 1990, approximately 250 of 429 eligible Alberta communities had developed tourism action plans. Based on the Alberta experience, Go *et al.* (1992) have identified five conditions for destination tourism development:

- A clustering of communities, each supporting the other.
- Avoiding duplication.
- Key players who are ready, willing, and able to cooperate.
- Resident cooperation.
- Finance for start-up is available.

Wight (1992), as a member of the provincial tourism agency, further emphasizes the need for local stakeholders to integrate their ideas with governmental agency initiatives. When communities waver in their involvement, progress bogs down. In recent years, developers have seen the new regulations of the Alberta Environmental Protection and Enhancement Act (AEPEA) and the Natural Resources Conservation Board (NRCB) as red-tape hurdles that are costly in both time and money.

A plan for the Calgary-Canmore destination zone (Pannell Kerr Forster 1985) identified many opportunities for tourism. Table 7.14 lists these together with potential impacts and funding support. Wight (1992) expands on the analysis and information required for public and private tourism development decisions, summarized as

- Tourism projects inventory
- Muncipal financial impacts
- Transportation analysis
- Service and utility needs
- Private sectors EIAs and NRCB
- Tourism market demand study
- Visual impact assessment
- Assessment of natural areas
- Needs of expanded public services
- Water quality evaluation of Bow River
- Analysis of environmental issues
- Environmentally significant areas
- Quality of tourism/recreation experience
- Baseline information summary
- Municipal operative workshops
- Annexation proposals
- Employee housing issues
- Rock industry study
- Recreation trails study
- Updates of general muncipal plans
- Rock Mt. utilization study
- Sustainable wildlife study

Rural Tourism Guide

Based upon general decline in the U.S. rural economy, Congress in 1988 directed the Travel and Tourism Administration to sponsor a study of tourism potential in rural areas (Edgell 1990,32). Their report, *The National Policy Study on Rural Tourism and Small Business Development* (Economic Research Associates) was issued in 1989. Another product was the preparation of a planning and development guide. *Rural Tourism Development Training Guide* (Koth *et al.* 1991), in cooperation with the Tourism Centre of the University of Minnesota. It is a destination planning and development guide for rural areas and small towns and contains thirteen parts, including description of five cases of self-help. Although the manual covers other aspects, a planning process is outlined:

1. Getting organized.
2. Identifying community values.
3. Attraction inventory.
4. Attraction assessment.
5. Attraction packaging.
6. Organizational funding strategies.
7. Bussiness inventory.
8. Marketing situational analysis.
9. Identifying a community tourism product.
10. Identifying target markets.
11. Setting market objective.
12. Selecting promotional strategies.
13. (Optional) Tourism business retention and expansion.
14. (Optional) Community appearance.
15. Evaluation.

The educational materials within the manual are directed toward a five step model, paraphrased as follows.

1. Values. Community groups must first explore the importance of their values, such as their geography, history, culture, and lifestyle. This is necessary to make sure tourism is not approached as an overlay or merely as a cosmetic treatment. Tourism should play an important role in enhancing and preserving basic community values.

2. *Attractions.* It is essential to identify the activities, cultural, arts, and historic resources, and developments that have the power to attract visitors. Both surrounding as well as internal community attractions attractions are important. Attraction quality, drawing power, grouping, and management must be assessed.

3. *Service.* Both public and private services need to be evaluated. Water supply, sewage disposal, drainage, snow removal, fire protection, health control, police, and other public services by government need to be checked. Service business-lodging, food, transportation, entertainment, and retail trade—need to be offered in high quality. Entrepreneurship and business retention factors are important. New business should reflect the character of the community as well as fulfil tourism needs.

4. *Marketing.* Marketing is driven by traveller needs. Claims must be honest, accurate, and constant with product delivery. Analysis of current programmes should reveal officiencies and need for change. Identification of market segments and use of most effective marketing strategies should be made.

5. *Organization.* Because tourism involves so many facets and political jurisdictions, it requires special organization and leadership. The tourism organization need to

- Create a vision.
- Have a clear understanding of goals.
- Develop consistent leadership.
- Be adequately founded.
- Conduct periodic evaluation.

Cooperation with all other public and private groups is essential.

U.S. Community Guide

Sensing a need for guidelines for communities and areas to develop their tourism, the US Department of Commerce, US Travel and Tourism Administration, and the U.S. Economic Development Administration requested the University of Missouri to gather information and produce a manual. The first edition was published in 1978, and the second in 1986, and revised and updated third edition in 1991. The following discussion summarizes the contents of this guide.

Appraising Tourism Potential

This section of the guide provides information on how tourism can benefit communities with incomes, jobs, and tax revenues, especially as an aid to a diversified economic base. It also identifies costs of development: transportation, roads, parking, signs, water, sewage, restrooms, safety, health, and welfare. Included is the relationship of the community to attractions, services, and markets.

Planning for Tourism

Included here is the recommendation for leadership and organization. The need to coordinate the many components of tourism is addressed. The following planning steps are suggested:

1. Inventory and describe the social, political, physical, and economic development.
2. Forecast or project trends for future development.
3. Set goals and objectives.
4. Study alternative plans of action to reach goals and objectives.

5. Select preferred alternative(s) to serve as a guide for recommending action strategies.
6. Develop an implementation strategy.
7. Implement the plan.
8. Evaluate the plan.

It is recommended that all segments of the community participate in all steps.

Assessing Product and Market

This chapter of the guide offers methods of market analysis—characteristics of visitors, expenditures, and activity preferences. Ways of inventorying and evaluating the match between market preference and attractions are presented. Forms for inventorying other elements of the supply side are included.

Marketing Tourism

Development of a promotional plan, target market advertising, local advertising and promotion, public and community relations, cooperative promotion, and souvenirs and promotional mementos are the main topics of discussion in this chapter of the guide.

Visitor Services

Visitor services are defined as all the normal city services together with those needed for hospitality. Recommendations on anticipating and planning service needs, coordination of visitor services, training for visitor services, hospitality training, public awareness, establishing tourist information centres, and evaluating visitor services are offered.

Source of Assistance

Suggested help sources from federal, state, and local agencies as well as private consultant aid are recommended in this section. Examples of tourist organizational structures and tax legislation are included in the Appendix of the guide.

Community Tourism Guide

Another helpful guide for planning tourism development at the destination scale is *The Community Tourism Industry Imperative: The Necessity, the Opportunities, Its Potential* authored by Uel Blank (1989). This book is organized into twelve chapters and is directed to local individuals and organizations interested in development of tourism. Although all chapters provide basic guidance, of special value in planning are the following final three chapters of the book.

Getting It Together—The Matrix of Decision Making, includes important topics, such as the process of decisionmaking, how to assess opportunities, the importance of long-term planning, and how to move from knowledge to action.

Getting it Together—Tourism Development Policy, empha-sizes and relationship to state and federal tourism policy. The section on planning cities the need for several agencies, organizations, and individuals to exercise planning roles. Planning guidance must include:

- Attraction development
- Hospitality services
- Activities
- Promotion/advertising
- Transportation Systems
- Community ambience and aesthetics
- Local information, direction, and interpretive system
- Community ambience and aesthetics
- Local information, direction, and

interpretive system
- Community infrastructures
- Financing of development
- Resource quality and management
- Agency responsibility and co-ordination
- Special market thrusts
- Seasonality
- Residents' living quality

Getting it Together—From Policies to Plans to Actions, provides guidance on preconditoning for action, brining out the genius of the community, and the following action steps:

1. Initiative—recognition of need.
2. Set goals and objectives.
3. Collect needed information
4. Analyze information.
5. Develop concepts for future development
6. Develop specific strategies.
7. Carry out the plan.
8. Monitor and evalutate on regular basic.

Local Government Tourism Policy

As an aid to destination zone planning and development for tourism, the Western Australian Tourism Commission has created a model policy statement to be implemented by the city council. Because of its value, it is quoted here in its entirety (Western Australian Tourism n.d.)

Objectives

In establishing a tourism policy, the council has as its major objectives:

1. To recognize tourism as a social and economic force and as a major or potential major employer within the Council area.
2. To foster and create a community awareness of the benefits of tourism within Council's area.
3. To ensure that Council will guide and influence the development of tourism in the Council area.
4. To provide the basic facilities and infrastructure sufficient to encourage development.
5. To ensure that facilities within the area are adequate to cater for visitors and residents.

Policy Document Guidelines

The following policy guidelines provide a basis for consideration and adoption by council to guide and direct the development of tourism throughout the Council area, and to ensure a consistent approach to this development.

1. Council will liaise with the Western Australian Tourism Commission and other relevant Tourism and Government Departments and members of the public in all aspects of tourist development.
2. Council will establish an Advisory Committee which will address Tourism issues.
3. Council will endeavour to provide an adequate budget allocation for tourism expenditure.
4. Council will endeavour to assist (financially and by other means) tourist organizations or events which have the potential to develop tourism in the region.
5. Council will seek representation on Local tourist associations.
6. In the formulation of its planning regulations and preparation of by-laws and other regulations. Council will have regard to the requirements of tourism development.

7. Council, in its review of planning instruments, i.e. Strategic Plans. Town Plans and Development Control Plans, will take into consideration policies on tourism and other leisure related issues.

8. In the preparation of by-laws and regulations, Council will have regard to their impact on tourism and the balanced development of the Council's area.

9. Council will encourage tourism product development and investment through out the area and will facilitate the development application process.

10. Council will encourage a high standard of design and aesthetics in all forms of tourist development.

11. Council will ensure the welfare of the whole community when supporting tourism development and the provision of facilities.

12. When considering tourism developments, Council will consider the social, cultural, economic, and environmental impact of the proposal within the area.

13. Council will ensure that where sensitive environmental, historic or cultural areas exist, these areas will be adequately protected in relation to development or usage.

14. Council will initiate the provision of facilities sufficient to cater for destination and day trip visitors to appropriate areas within its boundaries.

15. Council will seek financial involvement form other sources wherever possible in the provision of tourist facilities.

16. Council will encourage the landscaping of residential and commercial centres within Council's area.

17. Council will, where practicable, support the establishment of National Parks, enhancement of specific natural features, conservation areas of outstanding beauty, and recognize items of heritage significance.

DESTINATION PLANNING MODEL

Reference again to the destination model illustrated in Figure 13.1 will help in identifying the key components that make up a tourism destination.

The engine that powers the destination for travellers is composed of the *attraction complexes*. These are geographic places, rooted in resources that have been developed to provide for visitor activities. These attractions serve two functions—drawing people to the places and fulfilling their expectation from a visits. The term *complex* is used to imply that there is value in clustering compatible attractions together, either physically or by tour. Attraction complexes may be within the focal city, nearby, or reasonably remote, such as a national park. (A national park is usually a complex unto itself because of the great number of compatible attractions it contains.)

Several other components of a destination zone function as facilitators. The *linkage* corridors between the key city and attraction complexes are important planning elements, requiring careful design consideration in order to provide a visual prelude to the attraction objective. For rural and remote attractions, self-guided and guided tours should provide the visitor with interesting explorations of the background and characteristics of the landscape being traversed. Key to planning these corridors are elements such as signage, maps, and other wayfinding information. Long linkages may require travel stops for rest rooms and food services, and interpretation of the travel corridor. Often, these are located along designated scenic highways. Again, the principle of adapting to the land resources and development as well as visitor desires and needs is paramount.

For all destination zones, one or more *cities* (communities) are essential. They provide several critical functions. All travel modes lead to terminals at cities. Terminals—train depots, airports, bus terminals, and highway exits-perform an entering function important to travellers. The quality of physical planning, development, and management can set the psychological setting for further visitor activities. Cities offer the preferred location for most travel services-hotels, restaurants, car services, travel agencies, tour companies, shops, and ancillary services such as post office, drug stores, health services, and communications. Cities are preferred settings because they offer greatest financial feasibility, catering to both resident and traveller markets. Cities contain a basic infrastructure that would be costly to develop at remote locations—water supply, waste disposal, police protection, fire protection, and power. Cities have an organized management structure providing public services and amenities important to tourism. Cities often contain existing and potential attraction complexes—entertainment, parks, exhibits, festivals, historic sites, sports arenas, convention centres, trade centres, industries, institutions (midical, religious, and organizational), and homes of friends and relatives.

Many destination zones will be served by a major city surrounded by several small towns in rural areas. Many advantages to both small and larger cities can be derived through cooperation- tour efficiency, increased mass of attractions, and greater promotional impact.

Another important component of a destination zone is *access* from markets. Too often, communities internalize their tourism planning to the extent that cooperation and assistance are not provided to developers and managers of transportation systems. Many transportation agencies focus policies primarily on resident or nearly markets, thereby developing routes and signage not easily mastered by outside visitors. For example, the main places of transport route penetration of a destination zone and city deserve special planning attention for visitors. It is at these sites that directional information is critical. A major information centre at the *gateway* that provides maps, brochures, and personal guidance is essential.

Although the actual configuration of destination zones will vary around the world, these same components and relationships will require planning and integration for best service to the traveller. All components must function in concert, each depending on the successful rendition by the other.

Destination Planning

A project should include the follow basic steps:

1. Identify sponsorship and leadership.
2. Set goals.
3. Investigate strengths and weaknesses.
4. Develop recommendations.
5. Identify objectives and strategies.
6. Assign priorities and responsibilities.

7. Monitor feedback.

1. Identify sponsorship and leadership. Because the focus of the destination zone will be on the principal community, it may provide the best organization and leadership. Although a chamber of commerce, convention and visitor bureau, or industrial development agency or organization may initiate destination tourism planning, a new ad hoc or permanent council or commission may be needed. The organization and leader should be drawn from a wide cross-section of the 'community and surrounding region. Again, it is important to have representation from the greatest diversity of constituencies possible, not only the primary tourism business. Commitment to tourism and the desire to collaborate on planning are more important than expertise in tourism.

2. Set goals. The same goals as were stated for regions apply to destination planning—enhanced visitor satisfactions, protected natural and cultural resources, improved economy, and integration into the life and economy of the entire destination area.

3. Investigate strengths and weaknesses. Local people, with perhaps input from a tourism specialist or consultant, should gain a good understanding of the area's strengths and weaknesses. Each destination will pose different problems but an objective study of the following in the entire zone would be useful:

- Natural resources: location, kind, quantities, qualities, problems, issues, viability for attractions.
- Cultural resources: location, kinds, quantities, qualities, problems, issues, viability for attractions.
- Potential environmental impact
- Transportation and access: capacities, access, quality, deficiencies
- Service business: quality, suitability to all markets, problems, issues
- Information about area for tourists: quality of maps, guidebooks, descriptions, hospitality.
- Promotion: effectiveness of advertising, publicity, public relations, incentives
- Organizations: sectors, organizations, agencies best suited to take leadership and implement development
- Present commitment of public and private sectors—resident attitude toward tourism growth

4. Develop recommendations. From the above investigation, those performing it will be able to conceive of how the positive factors can be enhanced and the negative issues can be ameliorated or corrected. Specific recommendations should be expressed on the same list of topic included in the investigation:

- Natural and cultural resource potential
- Transportation improvement
- Service business improvement
- Information improvement
- Promotion improvement
- Key organizations to take action
- How to improve commitment

5. Identify objectives and strategies. The step is a refinement and expansion of the last step. It should identify specific objectives and how to reach them for each of the recommendation above.

6. Assign priorities and responsibilities. The entire list of objectives and strategies should be reviewed for assignment of priorities. Short-range objectives are critical and deserve highest priority. They should be of small enough size and cost to demonstrate immediate improvement. But, long range objective need to be kept in mind so that each increment of shorter range accomplishment will build toward a well-planned overall destination zone. At this stage, it is important to assign responsibilities for action—who and what organizations are most logically the ones to get the job done?

7. Stimulate and guide development. With the identification of specific project development needed derived from steps 1 through 6, these opportunities should be publicized for action by business, nonprofit organizations, and governments. It is their responsibility to develop feasibilities, plan and design, build, and manage the needed development within the destination zone.

8. Monitor feedback. Regularly, all implementation of action should be monitored. Enthusiasm and commitment may wane if it appears that no one is concerned about whether the objectives and strategies are working. Each increment of development, whether it be a newly built project or a new programme, will change overall relationships and demonstrate new market-supply experience. Part of this feedback is to check on the relationship between this and other destinations and regional plans. Especially for touring circuit markets who visit the destination en route, it is important to know about planning and action in the zones that come ahead and after in the touring sequence. Also, the relationship between zone and regional promotion should be understood. Related to this feed back step may be the need for new research and education—seminars, workshops, conferences, and hospitality training.

Organic/Rational Planning Process

The process outlined above for a Destination Planning Project, can be classified as a rationalist approach. It focuses on problemsolving, using a process that promises to implement specific objectives. However, this approach has its critics who claim that at a scale such as tourism destination, the problems are too complex to resolve in such a direct manner. Within such an area there are too many factors—decisionmakers, influences, resource conditons, and trends in public opinion—to deal with in a strictly rational manner. Called for is a more organic approach.

Steiner (1991, 520) proposed a process that "reflects a middle ground approach to physical planning, somewhere between a purely organic and a truly rational one." Its basic premise is a flexible, iterative method that has the merits of a project as well as a continuing process that allows for contingencies. Again, it represents an integrated and interactive planning approach. The model sequence of steps is illustrated in Figure 13.4. The following summary paraphrases this process for a tourism destination zone.

Step 1. Problem and Opportunity Identification. By means of workshops and other public participation, concerns, opportunities, and issues within the destination area can be identified. For example, issues of growth, tax potential accompanying growth, quality of new development, and ability of governments to respond with services may be major concerns in a destination zone.

Step 2. Goal Establishment. Local people and governments as well as outside investors develop a consensus on the kind of area they seem in the future. Based on the issues and concern, goals are identified. These goals are long range and, for tourism, would involve a balance growth and resource protection.

Step 3. Area Analysis. For a destination zone, analysis of factors is needed for the focal communities, surrounding area, and sites within. Key bio-physical factors are examined. Such as geology, physiography, climate, hydrology, soils, vegetation, and wildlife. Cultured factors, including historic settlement, economic development, land use patterns, demographics, and services, are identified. Documentation in narratives and maps represent this analysis step performed jointly by consultants and local people.

Step 4. Local Land Analysis. More detailed documentation is obtained for this step. Change taking place and their environmental impacts are assessed. Population trends, relationship to physiographic features, and wildlife management issues are parts of this more specific descriptive analysis.

Step 5. Detailed Studies. These studies focus primarily on suitability analysis—how suitable portions of the destination are for projected development. Policies of public and private landholders are an important part of such studies. Although the focus may be on tourism, this step allows equal consideration of overall future growth such as housing, recreation, business and industrial expansion, and transportation.

Step 6. Planning Concepts and Options. Based on the foregoing steps, consultants can begin to conceive of planning concepts and options that these studies suggest could lead toward the desired goals. This step is based on logic and imaginative processes and suggests allocation of potential land uses. These concepts could include ideas for future tourism development projects, natural resource and cultural interpretation, transportation, and settlement appropriate to the interests of the public and resource base. included could be appropriate themes for subareas.

Step 7. Guidelines. This step produces what may be described best as guidelines, rather than a plan, because they contain much flexibility. Local officials, property owners, investors, and consultants jointly identify options for growth and development. In some areas, such guidelines must be formalized into a master plan or comprehensive plan in order to meet legal mandates for planning.

Step 8. Education and Citizen Involvement. Although public input has characterized the entire process, this step assures that the plan concepts and guidelines are disseminated widely. Interaction between consultant planners and the many constituencies affected is essential. Use of the press and public meetings can stimulate open discussion on how well the concepts are directed toward all percieved goals.

Step 9. Detailed Designs. In some instances, the timing is appropriate for initiating project designs. Such design plans will require owner-developer initiative. Often, these are not possible until some later date until there are sufficient owner-developer interests and support for actually building these projects. These projects carry the destination planning guidelines to actual case development.

Step 10. Implementation. This step includes all policy and management implementation measures as well as specific projects. By means of close collaboration among local representatives, tourism business, and government agencies, initiation of land easements, zoning, and initiatives for purchase of private and public lands for development can be made.

Step 11. Administration and Evaluation. Public and private organizations and agencies that initiated the Planning process now monitor progress of implementation. As projects are selected and begun, feedback may indicate changes needed in the overall plan. In cases where the city, country, or grouping of several legalized the plan, official administration and monitoring will take place.

Steiner concludes that such a design and planning process at this scale must be dynamic and reflect newly gained incremental experience. Any land planning process must begin with understanding landscapes, and then making changes only in ways that protect and conserve these important foundations.

Destination Continuous Planning

Although a destination planning project for tourism development can stimulate specific action, accomplishment is likely to lag if a continuing planning function is not in place. The destination zone planning document can provide guidelines for development, but every change needs to be monitored for its impact. For example, the destination plan may have called for first creating new parks and historic sites but, because sponsorship for an interesting outdoor recreation parks became available first, it was established first. In the recreation park's first year of operation, it demonstrated that there was a strong travel market interested in natural resource-based activities. Thus the potential was suggested for expanding existing parks, developing adventure travel, nature trails, camping, and natural resource interpretation.

However, unless there is a permanent body charged with tourism leadership and continuous planning, new opportunities may be missed. Such a body would represent a diversity of interests within the destination zone and also be capable of carrying out specific functions on a regular basis.

As was done in Alberta, a Tourism Action Committee may be the best organization for continuous planning at the destination level. This committee should have representation from all governing bodies within the destination area: major city, satellite towns, countries, and regional government. Committee members should also represent important constituencies, such as developer, businesses, nonprofit organizations, and residents.

Among the duties of such a committee would be the following:

- Foster the renewal of a Destination Zone Planning Project every five years.
- Monitor each increment of supply development to determine how well it is succeeding, resolve issues that impede its success, and examine its integration with other tourism development.
- Promote new and expanded attraction development based on the special natural and cultural resources of the area.
- Promote the establishment of needed service business to meet needs of travellers.
- Encourage resource protection, not only by tourism supply development, but other threats to the environment.
- Integrate tourism planning with city, county, and regional plans.

- Integrate all plans for information services and promotion.
- Monitor changes in market trends in order to determine new supply needs.
- Gain cooperation and integration of tourism development by all three sectors—governments, nonprofit organizations, commercial enterprise.
- Cooperate with regional tourism planners, managers, and policy makers to assure a continuing viable role for the destination.

Evaluation

Planning action at the destination level need regular evaluation. Communities and their surrounding regions are involved daily in a great many public and private actions other than tourism—services, education, sanitation, land use, and policing. Whatever is done to plan tourism will need to be evaluated frequently in context with all other planning and development. If the destination area has a tourism plan in place, it will need monitoring and frequent assessment. Go et al. (1992, 33) have developed a taxonomy for implementation of a community tourism action plan.

Integration with Community Planning

Because communities play such a critical tourism role in destinations, all plans and planning processes at this level need to be integrated.

Official community plans traditionally focus on physical public needs, especially for updating and enlarging public structures and systems. These needs are often for resident transportation, water supply (potable and industrial), sewage disposal (solid and liquid waste), electrical and gas,) fire protection, and policies and public safety. Regulations for land use and structures, such as zoning ordinances and building codes, are included in most city plans. Also included are concerns over housing, education, trade, amenities (zone, parks, and recreation areas), and industry.

Unfortunately, in most communities, these traditional plans do not include issues of tourism and visitors even though their decisions affect tourism and vice versa. Too often, planning for the five components of the supply side of tourism—attractions, services, transportation, information, and promotion—are not seen as responsibilities of city officials and city plans.

Dredge and Moore examined this issue as found in Queensland, Australia. They cited several inhibitors to the integration of tourism planning into traditional community plans. Much of tourism involves private sector facilities and services, often outside the perceived role of local planning. Local understanding of the complicated multi-owner supply side of tourism is not helped much by their perception of industry involving only a few physical plants. The overlap between the needs of visitors and residents, as well as their differences, is not well understood. The dynamics and interdependence of the components of the tourism functional system are foreign to their day-to-day decisions relating to residents. Finally, the training and education of planners and designers have not encompassed tourism as a curriculum topic.

The conclusion of Dredge and Moore equally applicable elsewhere in the world, is that town planners have not only great opportunities but responsibilities to incorporate vision, guidelines, and specific plans for tourism into their traditional local roles.

SPECIAL DESTINATION NEEDS

Scenic Highways

Driving for pleasure, implying the use of scenic roadways, continues to be one of the top travel market activities. Although some scenic highways are major regional access routes, most lie within the context of a destination zone.

Many areas have designated scenic highway segments of travel routes. But, in creating such roads, their planners have discovered that what appeared to be a simple task became very complicated. Their dual function—transportation and scenic appreciation—poses a great challenge to policy makers and designers.

A report of the U.S. Department of Transportation (Federal Highway Administration 1991) pertaining to "scenic byways" identifies some of the key issues of design and designation for these special places:

Ambiguity of Definition. Although there may be common public opinion of what a scenic road is, the issue of defining it in order to plan, build, and protect its assets becomes very difficult. Generally accepted is the principle that it embraces both the visual countryside as well as the roadway. But there is no accepted definition of design standards—visual depth beyond the roadway, roadside maintenance, vertical and horizontal curvature, and vehicle speed and capacity. Each case needs its own definition and standards.

Corridor Protection. Because the entire highway corridor is involved, the protection of the natural and cultural resources that caused it to be identified becomes an issue. Owners of adjacent lands have property rights that sometimes conflict with the scenic highway concept. Special land use planning that is acceptable to adjacent owners must be employed.

Traffic Issues. When high-speed commuters and truckers are mexed with slower-speed, roadside-viewing tourists there may be increased conflict and accidents. Roadway design standards for these two types of users may need to be different, even requiring entirely new roadways.

Signing and Classifying. At present, there is considerable proliferation and diversity of policies on how scenic highways are to be classified and signed. Travellers are confused over the policy rules and identification of attractions and driving hazards. These need to be integrated and clarified.

Community Acceptance. Because many scenic highway designations have been put forward by others, local people may not agree that the rewards (tourist revenues) are worth the added traffic and land use restrictions.

Bicycle Conflict. Because both bicyclists and automobile tourist may enjoy the same qualities of scenic highways, their use is often in conflict. More automobile traffic creates hazards for the safety of slower bicylclists.

Funding and Management. Because scenic highways traverse many political jurisdictions and a multicity of properties with different owners, questions of who will fund and manage these special routes are not easily answered.

Even though the issues just described are widespread, the movement toward establishing more scenic road designation continues. For example, by 1990 there were 51,518 miles of designated and potential scenic byways in the United States, Virgin Islands, and Puerto Rico (Federal Highway Administration 1991, 8). All but seven states have some kind of scenic highway programme. Germany has more than 70 scenic highway, including the Castle Route, Fairy Tale Route, and Route of Emperors and Kings. (Federal Highway Administration 1991, 36).

Although the criteria for designating scenic routes vary, most are similar to those adopted by the North Carolina Board of Transportation in 1990 (Federal Highway Administration 1991, 13):

They should be at least a mile long.

The development along the byway should not detract from the scenic character and visual quality.

There should be significant visible natural or cultural features along its borders. These include agricultural lands, historic sites, vistas of marshes, shoreline, forests with mature trees or other areas of significant vegetation, or notable geologic or other natural features.

There should be preference for roads that are protected by land use controls.

There should be provisions for de-designation should the character of the road change over time.

Smardon (1987) describes a survey process used in analysis of scenic highway potential for the 450-mile Seaway Trail, located along the Lake Ontario and St. Lawrence River waterfront in northern New York. Investigative panels of 50 college students and 45 area residents, guided by professional planners, documented and evaluated the entire corridor. Positive and negative attributes, listed by priority, included the following:

In order to provide guidance for the designation and maintenance of scenic roads, the state of New York has developed a manual *Preserving New York State Scenic Roads* (n.d.). The manual recommended a five step process.

1. From a Nominating Group. A community nominates at least three members who then notify the Department of Environmental Conservation (DEC) of their intent. They are then given forms and further guidance.

2. Select Candidate Roads. The nominating committee tours roads for visual inspection needed to nominate potential scenic reads. The search should encompass the landscape characteristics that typify the scenery.

3. Prepare Narrative Description. Each candidate road is to be described in terms of topography, water, vegetation, sky, human or animal activities, structures, and patterns or rhythms. Cultural as well as natural resource features should be included in this description .

4. Evaluate Candidate Roads. The nominating committee, accompanied by special interests if needed, travel the roads again but with more detailed examination. This step usually climates some candidates and the team must describe its reasoning for the selections, noting the components that contribute most to its scenic quality. This form serves two purposes—a checklist of uniform criteria and an organized cataloging for future reference. Both negative and positive characteristics must be identified. Designating team member roles will assist in the process. The driver identifies odometer readings as a front seat passenger appraises the scenery. Visual scanning should cover both sides of the highway. A recorder checks the characteristics as they are identified by the team. In order to expedite the process, a team of volunteers may be assigned to evaluate each candidate road.

5. **Nominate Roads.** The recommendations are then refined by team consensus. Further evaluation before nomination may include the length of the highway segment; relationship of road to other development, and implications for protection and future maintenance. The team's recommendations are submitted to the local government for approval. The evaluation forms and resolution of government support are then submitted to the DEC staff.

Historic Scenic Roads Advisory Committee (PHSRAC) for final apprival import by the Arizona Department of Transportation (ADOT). This advisory committee is made up of eleven members, including six citizen appointees by the governor, and each from ADOT, Arizona State Parks Board, Arizona Historical Society, Arizona Office of Tourism, and Tourism Advisory Council.

The PHSRAC reviews, prioritizes, and evaluates the requests from individuals and organizations for designation.

Documentation of an inventory process is included in each request and application for approval. Historic road application emphasize cultural resources, and scenic road applications emphasize natural and visual resources. A list of the features for which information is to be determined and described follows.

Natural Resources

Geology	Biota
Hydrology	Topographic
Climate	

Cultural Resources

| Architectural | Archeological |
| Historical | Cultural |

Visual Resources

Visual Quality Assessment Procedures
- Landscape Classification Process

　Identify on map proposed highway segments.

　Identify biotic community.

　Identify transition zones.

　Describe vegetative cover.

- Landscape Inventory (a Visual Assessment Inventory and a Viewpoint Rating).

Criteria used by the PHSRAC for evaluating parkways and historic and scenic roads include the following:

Parkways

One mile distance between access roads.

Meet criteria for historic or scenic roads.

Interpretive area space is available.

Controlled access and property rights obtained.

Historic Roads

Impact of route- importance within national, state, or local framework.

The Arizona Parkway, Historic and scenic roads designation process

Impact of area—contribution to exploration, settlement, or development.

Proximity—physical and/or visual access to historical place.

Uniqueness—relative scarcity or abundance.

Scenic Raods

Vividness—memorability of visual impression.

Intactness—integrity, freedom from encroachment.

Unity—harmonious composite.

Important criteria and standards of operation include protection of vegetation, freedom from negative impacts, and compatible development (if any) along all designated routes. Recommended are local and county protective zoning and design review overlay along all designated highways in order to protect, maintain, and enhance the quality of the highway corridor environment. Special emphasis is placed on the establishment of pull-outs for interpretation. Normal highway standards of design and construction may be amended in order to protect and enhance special features or unique resources important to such designated highways. Final approval lies with the Arizona Transportation Board.

This examination of scenic highways, their importance, and planning issues, demonstrates the need for close collaboration among decision-makers, local people, and designers/planners. It seems that the answer to better planning lies within each situation rather than a set of rigid standards and policies.

Historic Resource Inventory

Pollock-Ellwand (1991) developed a computer-aided technique for identifying and analyzing historic landscapes. Increased tourism development and use of historic areas requires several planning steps, the first of which is to know where they are and their characteristics. This technique has been tested in southwestern Ontario. It is unique in its approach, inventorying three modes of information: textual, audio, and images.

The first step is a generic scan of a study area by likely local sources—historical societies, garden clubs, environmental activists, and others. These individuals follow a questionnaire that asks for the historic event, historical activity, native and famous people, exemplary design, plants associated with history, and human and aesthetic impressions.

The next step is performed by historic specialists and local representatives to narrow and deepen the analysis. All data is submitted to the Inventory Centre located at the University of Guelph where it is facsimilied directly into the computer system. Visual images, such as historic and contemporary photographs, context mapping, and original planning documents are scanned and stored directly with typed or handwritten descriptive data. Audio clips also can be received.

The final output can be assessed in several ways. Direct computer linkage and facsimile transmissions can be converted to hard copy printouts. Thousands of institutions are now on an Interned system that allows access to the process. However, the designer recommends an intervening step of clarifying relative significance. The Ne XT computer and software package, Media Station, was used for this Southwest Ontario Cultural Heritage Landscape Inventory. Many others may be equally suitable.

Historic Cities

As travel market interest in historic background continues to increase, cities face special planning and design issues to cope with great volumes of visitors. Because historic sites and district function as attractions for tourism, planning for their development may be aided by applying the spatial model. The diagram focuses planning/design issues on three zones.

Considering historic sites, buildings, or districts as the *nuclear* of the attraction, their planning requires more than restoration and protection. Too often, masses of visitors stimulate tasteless and inappropriate services within this zone. Adaptive use is more acceptable, whereby appropriate shops, restaurants, and other services are contained within structures that retain their architectural integrity. As visitor volumes increase, the zone may have to be closed to automobile traffic.

Of great planning importance is what could be called an *inviolate belt*-the area surrounding the historic district. This area serves as the psychological setting for introducing the visitor to history. Incompatible land uses, such as modern high-rise office buildings, encroach upon the nucleus and offer poor visual entrance to the main feature. Business and residential uses may be acceptable if designed in manner that is in harmony with the historic district.

It is in the surrounding area, the *zone of closure*, that new structures and land uses including modern travel services would be most appropriate. Rather than locating them in the nucleus or inviolate belt where their design could clash with the historic theme, it is here that new hotels, restaurants, and other travel services should be located. Planning and managing these zones may require special legislation.

In the United States, the Main Street Programme is a major planning aid to tourism development in destinations, particularly at the community level. It is function of the National Trust for Historic Preservation, created in 1980, and by 1991 it was working in 630 communities and 38 states. Although some public moneys are used, for every $1.00 of public funding over $11.00 of investment is generated because the emphasis is on local initiative and economic enhancement. Its focus is primarily on smaller communities; the present average is 16,000 residents.

The programme is directed toward economic revitalization by means of local protection and restoration of existing assets. Emphasis is on business retention, preservation, and investment in the built environment rather than new shopping centres, "Main Street is a management approach, a structure, and a process for a community to use to discover its resources, take advantage of them, and build the kind of leadership capacity and vision needed".

A study of four successful historic cities in the United States (Said 1987)— St. Augustine, Savannah, Charleston, and Williamsburg-showed that even with distinctively different characteristics, several common contributing factors were identified. First, local citizen participation and commitment to historic protection was found to be critical. The community's financial support, efforts of volunteers, and donations, of properties greatly fostered historic redevelopment. Second, the general economic viability of the city and surrounding area appeared to be an important factor. Private and public funding assisted these efforts greatly. Third, accessibility from travel market sources was found to contribute to success, even location within the city was important. Finally, a strong commitment by the local government was consistently essential. Planning of historic redevelopment requires processes that include inputs of professional planners and designers, governments, developers, and local citizens.

The Destination Zone Planners

Who plan tourism destinations? Increasingly, this is seen as a public private cooperative venture. But, there are more guidelines and proposals than demonstrations of how destinations should be planned and by whom.

There is little question that this

process must involve at least the following groups: tourism developers, public officials, resident groups, existing tourism businesses, organizations, and planners. They are all needed if decisions on a planned future are to be meaningful and have a good chance of being implemented. Such a process requires a great amount of leadership and coordination. Of the many planning groups, the following are cited for the promise they hold for effective destination zone planning.

Consultants

Increasingly, the design and planning professionals are taking on tourism planning assignments. Because of tourism's complexities, a team approach is often taken. Overall planning and integration with official planning is often assumed by professional planners, individuals with education and experience in urban and regional planning. Land use planning and site design, as well as detailed construction plans, are usually performed by professional landscape architects. They are individuals with training and experience in site planning. Specific structural design is usually handled by professional engineers with training and experience in structural design and specifications. For the design and specific planning of buildings, architects are engaged because they have the training and experience for this speciality.

Some firms have all or most of these specialities represented by staff members. Such firms are best capable of the larger scale planning projects for tourism—regional and destination. For tourism, often additional specialists are needed—golf course architect, museum design specialist, zoo designer, historical restoration specialist, archaeologist, interpretive visitor centre designer, and market researcher. The advantage of these firms is that they can perform a wide range of services, from general studies of tourism potential to complete working drawings and specifications for project construction.

Increasingly, other types of consultant firms are doing tourism planning work. Firms traditionally focused on accounting, finance, and feasibilities. Such as Price Waterhouse and Pannel Kerr Foster, have now performed tourism planning projects. These firms usually are directed more toward policy and marketing than to physical planning. Sometimes marketing firms, such as Davidson-Peterson Associates and KPMG Peat Marwick become involved in tourism planning. Professors at universities are some times called upon to engage in tourism planning projects.

Task Forces

Task forces for tourism planning vary greatly in their makeup but provide an effective mechanism for a variety of needs. Some are made up entirely of planning professionals whereas others are composed of public and private representatives of groups interested in tourism.

For several years, the Pacific Asia Travel Association (PATA) has been co-sponsor of many tourism task force studies including planning. Generally, the request for outside overview assistance comes from the nation or city within the Pacific basin. Their needs are detailed and submitted to PATA. In response, PATA contracts four or five tourism specialists who have the competence and experience to address the issues of concern and requests their services. PATA then provides a leader. A rapporteur maintains close contact with the team and is responsible for the final manuscript of a written report. Travel expenses (but no professional fees) are provided by the host area. What ensues is an intensive on-site evaluation with a tightly scheduled agenda. The process includes site inspection, rapid review of documents, and interviews with individuals and representatives of public and private organizations. By the end of the week, consensus on recommendations is reached. Report to the sponsor include an on-site oral report and a written report after the site visit. Compared to a major project by consultants, this technique is much less costly and provided immediate input. It is particularly effective in resolving a smaller number of issues and those requiring no long-term in-depth research.

The task force concept is also used in initial stages of planning to crystallize interest and organization. As an example, after several studies by the U.S. National Park Service and Pennsylvania state agencies, the state created a task force to develop coordination and guidelines for the industrial heritage corridor in the south western part of the state. It was called the Sate Heritage Interagency Task Force and was made up of 70 representatives of culture and heritage groups, businesses, and public agencies having jurisdiction in the area. These agencies included state departments of Community Affairs, Commerce, Environmental Resources, Education, and Transportation, and the Pennsylvania Historical and Museum Commission, the Pennsylvania Heritage Affairs Commission, and the Pennsylvania Council on the Arts. This task force studies reports, evaluated the resource base, reviewed several alternatives, and selected a preferred approach. Allied with the task force was a consulting team of planners. Together, they held meetings, open houses, and workshops as planning concepts were developed. After two years, a general conceptual plan emerged. The use of a task force demonstrates an effective approach to integrate the ideas and policies of the many constituencies that often are involved in destination and regional tourism development.

Extension Tourism Planning

An effective method of public education about tourism and guidance for planning has been adult educational programmes sponsored by govern-ments and universities. In the United States, the Cooperative Extension Service (CES) was created by Congress in 1914 (Smith-Lever Act) to carry educational information directly to farmers of the nation. An adaptation of this first took place in Michigan in 1945 with the Tourist and Resort Service Programmeme, based at Michigan State University. The programme was designed to assist tourist and resort businesses with their technical problems. The programme had three themes: business management, building and grounds planning, and food service. The methods used were preparation of technical bulletins, workshops, conferences, news release, and personal onsite consultation. Through this programme, carried out by three Extension Specialists (Robert W. McIntosh, Clare A. Gunn, and Cladys Knight), thousands of motels, hotels, restaurants, campgrounds, marinas, and parks benefited from better location, site, and building design, operational management, accounting, financing, food production, and management for over two decades.

Many states patterns new programme after this pioneering effort. Several states, such as Minnesota, have established university research and extension centres to develop new information and disseminate it to those in need. Approximately 15 of these centres are located across the United States. Their main functions are: to foster multidisciplinary efforts, to provide on- and off-campus educational programmes, and conduct applied research. In addition, adult education specialists in many states are providing tourism technical assistance, supported primarily by governments (federal, state, and local) with additional input from private organizations and businesses. Some 38 presentations have been published as *Usage Tourism & Travel as a Community and Rural Revitalization Strategy*, proceedings of the national workshop of May 10-12, 1989. The USDA-CES now publishes *Update Tourism and Commercial Recreation*, as a newsletter of activity by CES in tourism.

Reviewing files of accomplishments by CES specialists also reveals much activity in tourism planning. The following illustrate some of these projects.

Boundary Water Canoe Area

In the United States, wilderness areas are designated by Congress through the Wilderness Act of 1964 and managed by the U.S. Forest Service. Several regulations of use apply in order to fulfil the criteria demanded by the wilderness designation. Because of controversy over this change in one area, the Agricultural Extension Service, University of Minnesota, was requested to investigate the impact of these new administrative controls in the Boundary Waters Canoe Area, an area in northeastern Minnesota along the Canadian border. The economy, supporting 13,000 residents, was based on timber production, iron mining, and tourism. In the Extension tradition, action to resolve issues is as important as identifying them. Following the federal legislation that designated the area as wilderness, there was much negative local reaction on two issues. Private holdings were to be eliminated and motorized vehicle access was to be prohibited. Over a period between September 1,1979 to September 30, 1982, the Extension Service fulfilled a leadership and catalytic role to resolve issues and stimulate planning in the area. This effort included the following subprojects:

A Need Assessment—determining needs of firms impacted by the area.

Educational and Technical Assistance to Tourism Related Firms—152 occurrences: physical plant, business management.

Educational and Technical Assistance in the Management of Community Grants—catalytic function.

Educational and Technical Assistance in Marketing Programmes— improved materials, strategies, and delivery.

Educational and Technical Assistance in Special Project Management—Canadian custom station closings, licensing outfitters, etc.

Applied Research Efforts—fostering data collection, management.

Building Communication Flows— integrating many agency and firm plans and actions.

The Extension role has resulted in new understanding of public and private roles, new cooperation, new investment in facilities and services, much greater visitor use, greatly increased tourist business, and a significant increase in resource protection. One example was the marketing assistance for the Lake Vermillion area, generating $360,000 in new business. Another was the case of catalytic action between the U.S. Forest Service and U.S. National Park Service for establishing the Cook Visitor Centre (Simonson 1992). The Extension programme in Minnesota has greatly enhanced tourism there for several decades.

Southern Kentucky

An example of constructive extension education was offered by Allan Worms (1992), a recreation and tourism Extension specialist at the University of Kentucky. In 1986, a steering committee of representatives from a 27-county area including members of a newly formed Southern Kentucky Tourism Development Association was formed. Midwest Research Institute prepared a market study that included information on unfulfilled potential, relationship to the I-75 highway corridor, natural and cultural resources, and suggested project development. These results were then disseminated by means of several extension techniques: meetings of key leaders, presentations to civic clubs, press releases, and workshops. Study tours were held to expose local participants to development opportunities.

In a region of economic decline, these activities changed public attitudes, encouraged entrepreneurism, initiated new programmes, and stimulated new interest in developing local resources into viable attractions. New cooperation between communities was begun, resulting in awareness of opportunities overlooked before. In addition to sociocultural improvements, following are some of the tangible results totalling over $72 million from local and outside effort, coordinated by the Extension specialist as a leader-catalyst.

A major first project: $14.5 million Jamestown Resort and Marina on Lake Cumberland.

Renfro Valley Music Park & Museum ($7.5 million).

Five new motels in London, one each in Carbin, Somerset, Jamestown, and Russell Springs.

Sycamore Island boat slaes business and several dry storage businesses. Several new resort and/or retirement complexes.

In addition, an estimated $46.7 million in marins and a great many other projects are in the planning stages—houseboat construction, new restaurants, and new festivals and events.

As a result of Extension guidance and technical information, the volume of visitors has increased greatly (one festival drew 200,000 in 1991) and is stimulating the local economy with jobs, incomes, and taxes paid.

Delaware Bays

Similar in function to CES but focused on coastal areas is the Sea Crant College Marine Advisory Service that include tourism and recreation among its objectives. The service carried out a project in cooperation with the Delaware Department of Natural Resources and Environmental Control to determine carrying capacity issues and recommendations for management of the state's inland bays.

The study included on-site interviews of recreational users, a mail questionnaire survey of shoreline residents, and reconnaissance of boating activity on Little Assawoman, Rehoboth and Indian River Bays.

Results indicated that:
- High boating density was creating safety hazards.
- Marine debris and litter were becoming a problem.
- Environmental degradation was taking place.

From the findings of the study several planning and management options were put forward and reviewed by the constituency groups. Main conclusions reached were:
- Discharges of pollutants into the bays should be stopped.

- Boat speed and jet ski use should be controlled for safety.
- Number of marinas should be limited.
- Fishing management should be improved.
- Water use should be zoned.
- Boat users should accept funding support for bay improvement.
- Monitoring and enforcement need improvement.
- Boat use-and safety education programmes are needed.

In many coastal locations throughout the United Stated, the Sea Grant Programme has provided educational and technical guidance for better planning of tourism.

Several very important conclusions regarding destination tourism planning can be drawn from past approaches and examples of development. As communities look toward the field of tourism for greater economic support, they need to be aware of the issues that accompany the opportunities. Following are some of the key conclusions that may be of assistance to communities and their surrounding areas as they plan for destination tourism development.

Integration into Regional Plans

Communities and their surrounding areas must plan their tourism expansion within the context of regional plans. If regional tourism planning is not in place, lobbying for such planning may be the first item on the community's agenda. Destinations are dependent upon regional (federal, state, and provincial) policies and action on such matters as transportation network, national parks and protected resource areas, incentives for community tourism development, and cooperative marketing and promotion.

Placeness as a Fundamental

In today's competitive travel market, excessive replication of the same theme of tourism development dampens rather than fosters economic success. Travellers seek destinations becuase of the special qualities of place. Otherwise, why travel? Every destination has a different set of geographical factors, traditions, relationship to markets, and host characteristics. Analysis of these factors can lay the foundation for building upon the uniqueness of place.

Community-Area Potential

Because a destination includes cities and their surrounding areas, the planning for future tourism must include the entire geographic area—not just the city. Tourism's attraction potential lies within nearby rural area, as well as the cities, within a destination zone. It is likely that the abundance of cultural resources will be found within communities, whereas most natural resource assets are located in the surrounding area. The logical location for most travel service businesses is within communities where they can benefit from public services and both the residential as well as the travel market. However, the reason travellers will come to the destination will depend on the quantity and quality of attractions in the surrounding area as well as within the city.

Public-Private Cooperation

At issue in many potential destinations is the lack of cooperation between the public and private sectors. City and county governments are preoccupied with public services, such as water supply, waste disposal, police, education, and related functions. Essential as these are for the residents, they are of equal concern in tourism planning and development. Too often city councils believe tourism is the prerogative of business only. Even though the business sector does play an important role in tourism development, a successful destination is one in which policies and actions of both public and private sectors are complementary, rather than competitive or divisive. In addition to the need for government—business cooperation on tourism planning is the equal need for them to cooperate with nonprofit organizations as they plan and make decisions on historic restoration, parks and preserves, and festivals and events.

Destination Leadership/Organization

It is becoming clear that for effective tourism planning at the destination scale the traditional functions of a chamber of commerce or tourism department may be too narrow. These organizations usually restricted to within the city limits. They also lack representation from needed constituency groups.

Instead, a special tourism council is usually required. Such a council needs the official support from the jurisdictions encompassed within the zone-cities and countries. Its member-ship must include representatives of government, tourist business, civic groups, nonprofit organizations, planners, and environmentalists. Planning guidelines have a much greater chance of implementation if these influencers and decisionmakers are represented.

Destination Planning

Destination area will be less successful, less fulfiling to visitors, and less sensitive to environmental stress if not planned in an orderly step-by-step sequence. A combination of both approaches—planning project and continuous planning—is likely to produce the best results.

Although planning processes vary, all have similar basic elements: setting goals and objective; analyzing the present situation: identifying issues, constraints, and opportunities; creating alternative concepts for development; and identifying action strategies. Destination planning can identify project ideas and recommend action in order to stimulate development by those best able to create and manage a new supply side.

Environmental Degradation

Because most pollution of air and water and erosion of land resources occurs within and around cities, the challange for tourism planners is to foster environmental improvement and continued protection.

This responsibility at the destination scale must address all sources of environmental degradation, not only from tourism. Municipal sewage and industrial waste must be brought under control if tourism is to thrive. Land use regulations are necessary to avoid overdevelopment, excessive congestion, and incompatible development. They are necessary to protect the environmental resources that are so critical to tourism's success.

Special Cultural and Natural Resources

Because of geographic differences, opportunities exist for destination areas to capitalize on their unique cultural and natural resources. Two major categories of potential should be considered in planning processes. First, within the surrounding areas of cities, and even connecting corridors between destinations, there may be great opportunities for designating, planning, and maintaining scenic and historic routes. Second, because most history was developed at cities, most have the potential for identification, restoration, protection, and interpretation of historic sites within communities.

7. Tourist Travel Management

TRANSPORT IS an integral part of tourism which facilitates the movement of holidaymakers, business travellers, those people visiting friends and rela-tives and undertaking educational and health tourism. Transport is also a key element of the 'tourist experience' (Pearce 1982) and some commentators (e.g. Middleton 1988; Tourism Society 1990) view it as an integral part of the tourism industry. Despite the contro-versy over the extent to which tourism can be defined as both an industry and a service activity, it is widely recognised that tourism combines a broad range of economic activities and services designed to meet the needs of tourists.

Transport provides the essential link between tourism origin and destination areas. Transport can also form the focal point for tourist activity in the case of cruising and holidays which contain a significant component of travel (e.g. coach holidays and scenic rail journeys). Here the mode of transport forms a context and controlled environment for tourist' movement between destinations and attractions, often through the medium of a 'tour'. The mode of transport tourists choose can often form an integral part of their journeys and experience, a feature often neglected in the existing research on tourism. So how has transport been viewed in existing textbooks on tourism?

Tourism Studies and Tourist Transportation

The majority of influential tourism textbooks are a product of the 1980s and early 1990s, despite some notable expections. The rapid expansion in the number of tourism textbooks published is one indication of the emergence of the subject as a serious area of study at vocational, degree and postgraduate level throughout the world. As many national governments recognise the contribution can make to GDP and national economic development, the expansion of their tourism industries has led to a consideration of the imme-diate and long-term human resource and training requirements. New courses have developed to fill a niche in the educational marketplace and these have generated a demand for course materials to meet the international expansion of tourism education (Goodenough and Page 1993). The range of available textbooks for tourism studies has generally been written from a North American (e.g. Lundburg 1980; Mathieson and Wall 1982; Mill and Morrison 1985; Murphy 1985; Gunn 1988; McIntosh and Goeldner 1990), European (e.g. Foster 1985; Lavery 1989; Laws 1991; Ryan 1991; Witt et al. 1991) or Australasian perspective (e.g. Pearce 1987, 1992; Collier 1989; Leiper 1990; Bull 1991; Hall 1991; Perikans and

Cushman 1993), with few widely available student texts written from an Asian or Less Developed World perspective. An examination of these textbooks indicates that travel and transport is a topic frequently cited in relation to its role as a facilitator of the expansion of tourism, as new technology (e.g. the railway and jet engine) and novel forms of marketing and product developments (e.g. package holidays) have contributed to the development of tourism as a mass consumer product. For example, Hall (1991: 22) argues that the evolution of tourism in Australia is inseparable from the development of new forms of transport and a clear relationship exists between transport development and tourism growth (Hall 1991: 80). The development and expansion of tourist destinations are, in part, based on the need for adequate access to resort areas., their attractions and resources. Hence the relationship between transport and tourism is usually conceptualised in terms of accessibility within most tourism textbooks.

A number of other textbooks (e.g Holloway 1989; Mill 1992) have sought to develop this relationship one stage further, by discussing the historical development of tourist travel and accessibility, and the principles governing tourism's expansion within the context of different forms of tourist transport (e.g. air, road, rail and sea travel). Yet tourism studies do not have a monopoly on the analysis of transportation for tourists. Textbooks on transport studies indirectly discuss the movement of tourists. Many transport studies texts are written from a disciplinary pers-pective such as economics (e.g Stubbs *et al.* 1980; Glaister 1981; Bell *et al.* 1983; Banister and Button 1991) while other texts focus on the operational, organisational and management issues associated with different forms of transport (e.g. Button 1982, 1991: Faulks 1990). However, the tourist is rarely mentioned in these books as the term 'passenger' fails to distinguish between the reasons for tourist movement, inferring an impersonal contractual relationship where operators move people between areas on transport systems, systems which are only concerned with the throughout of passengers. In reality, a different situation exists, with transport operators in the 1990s equally concerned with many of the issues facing the tourism industry, particularly customer care and the tourist's experience while travelling. Owing to the choice of transport available and the competitive environ-ment for tourist travel in free market economics, transport operators recognise the importance of ensuring that the travel experience is both pleasurable and fulfils consumer's expectations. In state-planned economies, both the demand and supply for tourist transport is regulated by the state and a different political and ideological agenda affects the availability of tourist transport compared with free market economies.

Halsall (1992) identifies the overlap between transport, tourism and recreation arguing that in reality it is often difficult to distinguish between tourist and non-tourist use of different forms of transport; the exceptions are dedicated forms of tourist transport such as charter flights and cruises. Even so, operators such as British Railways (hereafter BR) do not use the term 'tourist', preferring to distinguish between 'business and leisure' travellers when identifying their potential passenger market. Therefore, the tourist is not explicitly recognised by such, but as a passenger. In contrast, some tourism researchers recognise the tourist trip as an important feature to examine in its own right (Pearce 1987; S.L.J. Smith 1989). Although it receives only scant attention due to the simplistic notions of the tourism-transport relationship. Consequently, the relationship between tourism and transport is only discussed in the context of the 'tourist experience'.

Both transport and tourism studies fail to provide an explicit and holistic framework in which to assess the transportation of tourists. For this reason, it is possible to build on the complementarity of these two areas of study to identify the concept of the 'tourist transportation system' which highlights the integral role of transport in the 'tourist experience'. This also has the potential to accommodate different approaches to the analysis of tourist travel and transportation. What is a 'tourist transport system'?

The Tourist Transport System

To understand the complexity and relationships which co-exist between tourism and transport. One needs to build a framework which can synthesise the different factors and processes affecting the organisation, operation and management of activity associated with tourist travel. The objective of such a framework is to provide a means of understanding how tourists interact with transport, the processes and factors involved and their effects on the travel component of the overall 'tourist experience'. Any such framework for analysing tourist transport needs to incorporate the tourist's use of transport services from the pre-travel booking stage through to the complextion of the journey and which recognises the significance of the service component. It also needs to incorporate the different modes of transport used by tourists (e.g. air travel by scheduled or charter service, sea travel using ferries or cruiseships, and land-based transportation including car, rail, coach, motor carvan, motorbike and bicycle).

One methodology used by researchers to understand the nature of the tourism development is a system approach (Laws 1991). The main purpose of such an approach is to rationalise and simplify the real world complexity of tourism into a number of constructs and components which highlight the inter-related nature of tourism. Since tourism studies are a multi disciplinary area of study (Gilbert 1990), a systems approach can accommodate a variety of different perspectives because it does not assume a predetermined view of tourism. Instead it enables one to understand the broader issues and factors which affect tourism together with the inter-relationships between different components in the system. According to Leiper (1990) , a system can be defined as a set of elements or parts that are connected to each other by at least one distinguishing principle. In this case, tourism is the distinguishing principle which connects the different components in the system around a common theme. Laws (1991: 7) developed this idea a stage further by providing a systems model of the tourism industry in which the key components were: the inputs, outputs and external factors conditioning the system (e.g, the external business environment, consu-mer preferences, political factors and economic issues). As external factors are important influences upon tourism systems, the system can be termed 'open', which means that it can easily be influenced by factors aside from the main 'inputs'. The links within the system can be examined in terms of 'flows' between components and these flows may highlight the existence of certain types of relationships between different components.

For example:

- What effect does an increase in the cost of travel have on the demand for travel?
- How does this have repercussions for other components in the system?
- Will it reduce the number of tourists travelling?

A systems approach has the advantage of allowing the researcher to consider the effect of such changes to the tourism system to assess the likely impact on other components.

Leiper (1990) identified the following elements of a tourism system: a tourist: a traveller-generating region; tourism destination regions; transit routes for tourists travelling between generating destination areas, and the travel and tourism industry (e.g. accommodation, transport, the firms and organisations supplying services and products to tourists). In this analysis, transport forms an integral part of the tourism system, connecting the tourist-generating and destination region, which is represented in terms of the volume of travel. The significance of transport in the tourism system is also apparent in the model developed by Laws (1991), where a series of smaller sub-systems was also identified (e.g. the transport system) which can be analysed as a discrete activity in its own right while also forming an integral part of the wider 'tourism system'. Thus, a 'tourist transport' system is a framework which embodies the entire tourist experience of travelling on a particular form of transport. The analytical value of such an approach is that it enables one to understand the overall process of tourist travel from both the supplier's and the purchaser's perspective while identifying the organisations which influence and regulate tourist transport. How does this book aim to integrate tourist travel more fully into the study of tourism?

It is designed as a framework in which the reader can gain a clearer understanding of the tourist transport system and some of the ways in which we can analyse the provision, operation and factors influen-cing this activity. One objective is to overcome the existing perception of tourist transport as a passive element in the tourist's experience which has to be endured to reach a destination area (cruising and touring excepted). The actual process of travelling is an integral part of the tourist's experience even though it is perceived as less important than the activities and pursuits of tourists in the destination. Offers a number of perspectives of tourist transport which the reader may find as a useful starting point for further research on transport and tourism. One underlying theme emphasised throughout the book is that transport for tourism constitutes a 'service' which is increasingly judged by consumers and providers in relation to the quality, standards and level of satisfaction it engenders. For this reason, both a systems approach and the emphasis on the multidisciplinarity of tourist transport help to transcend the rather fragmented view of this aspect of tourism studies.

Here the multidisciplinarity of tourist transport is examined, drawing upon the concepts and approaches used in economics, geography and marketing. Each area of study provides a useful insight into the specialised nature of research on tourism and transport studies which is rarely discussed in terms of the way each complements our understanding of the tourist transport system. As Leiper and Simmons show, researchers from different disciplines consider various aspects of tourism depending on their background and focus, which inevitably means that they consider specific inputs, outputs and external factors which affect the tourist transport system. For this reason, it is useful to examine some of the common approaches and concepts used by different disciplined in analysing tourist transport. It considers the role of transport policy and planning and its effect on operational and consumer issues, and the progress towards a common transport policy in the EC. A case study of tourist travel by rail in the UK is used to illustrate how national transport policy objectives are implemented and the significance for tourist experiences of rail service provision. It deals with an analysis of the demand aspects of tourist travel and the data sources available to tourism researchers. It looks at the supply of tourist transport, focusing on the supply chain and how companies with transport interests seek to exercise control over the distribution and quality of tourist travel services. The response of the US domestic airline market to deregulation is used to illustrate how concentration in the aviation market has affected the supply of services. The human and environmental conse-quences of tourist travel and the operation of different modes of tourist transport are then discussed concluding with a discussion of the potential for developing sustainable tourist transport. Examines some of the main issues discussed in the book while identifying further directions for research on what is a rapidly changing area of study.

Tourism, like transport studies, is a multidisciplinary field of study which has borrowed and refined concepts and theories from other social science subjects as it establishes itself as a legitimate area of academic-study. This poses a number of problems for researchers when exploring the relationship between transport and tourism in the context of tourist transport systems. For example, what approaches and methods of study should one use to analyse tourist transport systems? In most cases, research is based on those social science disciplines with an interest in tourism and/or transport studies. This has an important bearing on the analysis of tourist transport systems because the type of questions a researcher asks, and the focus of their work, is often determined by their disciplinary background.

Each social science subject has its own range of concepts, research methods and literature and has made distinctive contributions to the study of tourism although no one discipline is all-embracing enough to understand the complexity of the tourist transport system. For example, social science subjects such as social psychology, sociology, and business and management studies have an interest in tourism and transport studies although there is a relative paucity of published research which analyses the tourist transport system.

It must be stressed that because this is an introductory level book, it is only possible to outline some of the main principles which have been developed to analyse tourist transport. This chapter does not attempt to provide a comprehensive review of the literature and main areas of research on transport and tourism. A wide range of books has already been published in economics, geography and marketing which provide an insight into tourism and transport although none have developed a particular focus on transport for tourism. The approach adopted here is which economists, geographers and marketers have made to the analysis of tourist transport, and readers are directed to the specialised studies in the text for a more detailed insight of particular issues.

Economist Tourist Transport

The economist's approach to the analysis of tourist transport is based on two distinct areas of research, transport economics (e.g. Strakie 1976; Beesley 1989) and tourism economics (e.g. Bull 1991; Sinclair 1991) and each area of study uses similar concepts to understand how the tourist transport system functions. For this reason, it is useful to consider what issues are examined by economists as a basis for a more detailed discussion of the concepts they use.

What is Economics?

Like many social science subjects, there is little agreement on how to decline an area of study such as economics. However, according to Craven (1990: 3) 'economics is concerned with the economy or economic system ....[and].... the problem of allocating resources is a central theme of economics, because most resources are scarce'. Therefore Craven (1990: 4) argues that economics is the study of methods of allocating scarce resources and distributing the product of those resources, and the study of the consequences of these methods of allocation and distribution.

What is meant by scarcity and resources? The term scarcity is used to illustrate the fact that most resources in society and finite and decisions have to be made on the best way to use and sustain these resources. Economists define resources in terms of:

- natural resources (e.g. the land)
- labour (e.g. human resources and entrepreneurship)
- capital (e.g. man-made aids to assist in producing goods)

and collectively these resources constitute *the factors of production* which are used to produce commodities. These commodities can be divided into:

- goods (e.g. tangible products such as an aircraft)
- services (e.g. intangible items such as in-flight service

and the total output of all commodities in a country over a period of time, normally a year, is known as the *national product*. The creation of products and services is termed *production* and the use of these goods and services is called *consumption*. Since, in any society, the production of goods and services can only satisfy a small fraction of consumers needs, choices have to be made on the allocation of resources to determine which goods and services to produce (Lipsey 1989). The way in which goods and services are divided among people has been examined by econo-mists in terms of the distribution of income and the degree of equality and efficiency in their distribution. Many of these issues are dealt with under the heading of 'microeconomics' which Craven succinctly defines as:

> ...the study of individual decisions and the interactions of these decisions... [including]... consumers' decisions on what to buy, firms' decisions on what to produce and the interactions of these decisions, which determine whether people can buy what they would like,

whether firms can sell all that they produce and the profits firms make by providing and selling.

(Craven 1990:4)

Therefore, microeconomics is concerned with certain issues, namely:

- the firm
- the consumer
- production and selling
- the demand for goods
- the supply of goods

Economists also examine a broader range of economic issues in terms of microeconomics which is concerned with

> the entire economy and interactions within it, including the population, income, total unemployment. The average rate of price increases (the inflation rate), the extent of companies' capacities to produce goods and the total amount of money in use in the country.

Craven 1990: 5)

Therefore, macroeconomics is mainly concerned with:

- how the national economy operates
- employment and unemployment
- inflation
- national production and consumption
- the money supply in a country

Within micro and macroeconomics, both transport and tourism economists examine different aspects of the tourist transport system which is based on the analysis of the concepts of demand and supply.

Demand

Within economics, the concern with the allocation of resources to satisfy individuals desire to travel means that transport economists examine the *demand* for different modes of travel and the competition between such modes in relation to price, speed, convenience and reliability. Economists attempt to understand what affects people's travel behaviour and the significance of transport as something which is rarely consumed for its own sake: it is usually demanded as a means of consuming some other goods or service (i.e. commuting to work or the travel components of a holiday). The demand for tourist transport is also characterised (Mill 1992: 83-4) by:

- its almost instantaneous and unpredictable nature, which requires operators to build overcapacity in the supply to avoid dissatisfied travellers.
- the variability in demand, ranging from *derived demand* (where tourist transport is a facilitating mechanism to achieve another objective, such as business travel) to *primary demand* which is the pursuit of travel for vacation purposes.
- non-priced items (e.g. service quality, reliability and punctuality).

Transport economists have developed mathematical models to analyse the trip-making behaviour of travellers (Ortuzar and Willumsen 1990), the factors influencing demand and why variations occur in the trip-making behaviour of consumers due to relationships between socio-economic factors (e.g. age, income, profession and family status) and the effect of macroeconomic conditions (e.g. the state of the economy). In contrast tourism econo-mists have examined the demand for travel and tourist products, recognising the significance of demand as a driving force in the economy. This stimulates entrepreneurial activity to produce the goods and services to satisfy the demand (Bull 1991). More specifically, tourism economists examine the *effective demand* for goods or services which is the aggregate or overall demand over a period of time. Since income has an important effect on tourism demand, economists measure the impact using a term known as the *elasticity of demand*. As Bull (1991:37) has shown, it is measured using ratio calculated thus:

Elasticity of demand =

$$\frac{\text{percentage change in tourism demand}}{\text{percentage change in disposale income}}$$

in relation to two equal time periods. The significance of this concept is that the demand for goods to fulfil basic needs (e.g. food, water and shelter) is relatively unchanging or *inelastic* while the demand for luxury items, such as holiday and pleasure travel, is variable or *elastic*, being subject to fluctuations in demand due to factors such as income or price. Thus, elasticity is used to express the extent to which tourists are sensitive to changes in price and service. For example, primary demand is usually more elastic than derived demand. In tourist transportation, researchers recognise the importance of price which is acknowledged as a more complex issue than income, owing to the varying impact of exchange rates, the relative prices of destinations and the high level of competition between destinations for tourists. Furthermore, the different elements which comprise the tourism product (e.g. transport, accommodation and attractions) are complementary and it is difficult to separate out one individual item as exerting a dominant effect on price since each is inter-related in terms of what is purchased and consumed.

To assess the impact of price on the demand for tourism, economists examine the *price elasticity of demand*, where an inverse relationship exists between demand and price (Bull 1991). For example, it is generally accepted that the greater the price, the less demand there will be for a tourism product owing to the limited amount of the population's disposable income which is available to purchase the product which is calculated thus:

Price elasticity of demand =

$$\frac{\text{Price elasticity of demand}}{\text{percentage change in tourism product price}}$$

Other contributory factors which influence the demand for tourism include the impact of tourist taxation, the amount of holiday entitlement available to potential tourists as well as the effects of weather, climate and cultural preferences for holidaymaking which are expressed in terms of seasonality. These factors also need to be viewed in the context of the economics of operating each mode of tourist transport to understand how the demand is met by the operators' supply of a service. However, in view of the variations that exist between different forms of demand for modes of transport, readers should consult more detailed studies on the economics of transport (e.g. Bell *et al.* 1983; Button 1982; Glaister 1981; and Stubbs *et al.* 1980). The significance of tourist demand for transport is examined in case study 1. This considers how tourism demand for a country relatively inaccessible and distant from many of the world's main tourist-generating markets has realised its potential in the late 1970s, 1980s and 1990s as additional capacity for tourist transport was provided. Hence the case study also suggests that the demand for tourist transport cannot be examined in isolation from supply issues, which are introduced in the next section, after the case study.

Travel Management

In the last 5 years increasing interest has been shown in the potential of global travel and tourism as an important contributor to economic development. There is also increasing concern about the effects of tourism on the global environment, in terms of use of energy and water supplies; impact of global warming; and damage to marine environments and the ecosystems of destinations developed as major tourism resorts. Some of the influences on host communities and on the built and natural environment are positive and beneficial (WTTERC: 1992); others are undoubtedly negative and damaging; Marketing is a subject of vital concern in travel and tourism because it is the principal management influence which can be brought to bear on the size and behaviour of this major, global market.

Within the total market there are many submarkets, or segments, card many products designed and provided by a wide range of organisations. Because travel and tourism is defined as a market, it is best understood in terms of demand and supply. Marketing is introduced as a vital part of the linking mechanism between supply and demand focused on *exchange transactions*, in which consumers exercise preferences and choices, and exchange money in return for the supply of particular travel experiences or products. For reasons discussed subsequently, the practice of marketing is also highly relevant to tourism resources for which no market price is charged, such as national tourist offices and other area organizations, most of which are not directly engaged in the sale of products.

Travel and Tourism demand

In defining travel and tourism for the purposes of this book it is useful to follow the basic classification system, which is used in nearly all countries where measurement exists. This system is discussed in detail in most introductory texts; see, for example, Burkart and Medlik (1981/41). It is based on three categories of visitor demand with which any country is concerned; each is a different sector of the total market:

1. International visitors, travelling to a country, who are residents of other countries (inbound tourism).
2. Residents of a country, travelling as visitors to other countries (outbound tourism)
3. Residents visiting destinations within their own country's boundries (domestic tourism)

Defining travel and tourism is a primary responsibility for the World Tourism Organisation (WTO), which undertook a major review of its definitions at an international conference on travel and tourism statistics in Ottawa in 1991. In 1993 revised definitions were put to the UN Statistical Commission. The following are the principal terms:

- *Visitors* to describe all travellers who fall within agreed definitions of tourism.

- *Tourist or staying visitors* to describe visitors who stay overnight at a destination

- *Same-day visitors*, or excursionists, to describe visitors who arrive and depart on the same day. Same day visitors are mostly people who leave home and return there on the same day, but may be tourists who make day visits to other destinations away from the places where they are staying overnight.

Tourist Travel Management

As outlined above, these three categories are easy to understand. In practice the technicalities of achieving statistical precision in measuring visitors are extremely complex and, despite various international guidelines, no uniformity yet exists in the measurement methods used around the world. For example, should visitors who are remunerated from within the countries they visit be countered as tourists? Should national of a country who are resident abroad be treated as foreign visitors for statistical purposes? At what point, measured in distance covered away from home, or time travelled, or activity followed, should a resident or a city be counted as a same-day visitor, as distinguished from a resident pursuing his or her normal daily activities? In cities, for example, some shopping trips are evidently tourist or recreational excursions, but other trips, to make routine purchases, are not.

While the definition of travel and tourism outlined in this chapter will be adequate for the working purposes of those involved in marketing, this book does not set out to be a detailed study of the nature of tourism. Readers seeking further elaboration of concepts and measurement issues are referred to the reading suggestions noted at the end of the chapter. Marketing managers will, of course, require their own definitions of the market segments with which they are involved, and these will be far more precise than the broadly indicative international categories referred to here.

International Tourism

People who travel to and stay in countries other than their country of residence for less than 1 year are normally described as international tourists. They are usually treated as the most important market sector of tourism because, compared with domestic tourists, they spend more, stay longer at the destinations, use more expensive transport and accommodation, and bring in foreign currency, which contributes to a destination country's international balance of payments.

Around the world, measured as *arrivals* or *trips*, the numbers of international tourists and their expenditure have grown strongly since the 1950s, notwithstanding temporary fluctuations caused by the international energy and economic crises of the 1970s and 1980s. The overall growth pattern is revealed in Tables 9.6 and the reasons for it are discussed later in some detail. For the purposes of this introduction it is sufficient to note the recent growth and current size of the international market, and to be aware of consistently confident projections in the early 1990s that international tourism will continue to grow for the rest of the twentieth century. Although annual fluctuations in volume, reflecting economic and political events, are virtually certain, current expectations are for annual growth of the order of some 4 per cent per annum over the period 1992-2005 as a whole.

At present, in Northern Europe, it is common for over half of the adult populations to have made one or more international tourist visits during the previous 5 years, mostly on vacation Experience of international travel is very much less for Americans, reflecting the size of the USA and the distances most of them would have to travel in making international trips. US interstate tourism e.g. between the North East and Florida, should perhaps be viewed as similar, in principle to tourism between European countries over similar distances.

International same-day visits are an important market sector in countries with common land frontiers, such as the USA and Canada, the Netherlands and Germany, and Malaysia and Singapore. Because of the speed and efficiency of cross-Channel ferries and the Channel Tunnel, same-day visits between Britain and France, and Britain and Belgium, are also important.

Domestic Tourism

People who travel and stay overnight within the boundries of their own country are classified as domestic tourists. Estimates of the size of this sector of the market vary because in many countries domestic tourism is not adequately measured at present. In the USA, where good measurement does exist, Americans take only one trip abroad for every 100 domestic trips defined as travel to places more than 100 miles distance from home. Even for longer visits of over 100 nights' duration, international trips were no more than 3 per cent of the total. For the British, where the statistics are also good, and reflecting the shorter distances to travel abroad, there were some four domestic tourism trips (including overnight stays) for every visit abroad in the early 1990s.

Evidence from surveys of the vacation market in Europe and North America in the early 1990s indicates that, in most countries, between a half and three-quarters of the adult population took holidays away from home in any 12 months period. This includes international and domestic holidays, although the latter are the largest category. Increasing numbers of people take more than one vacation trip a year, a factor of great importance to marketing managers, for reasons to be discussed later.

Market research data analysing the complete tourism experience of the same individuals over periods of more than 1 year are rarely available. But excluding the very old, the sick, the severely disabled, and those facing particular financial hardship, recent and frequent experience of some form of staying and same-day tourism now extends to over nine out of ten people in most economically developed countries.

Within the total, domestic same-day visits taking place within a country's frontiers are the most difficult to quantity. In most developed countries the frequency of day visits is already so great that it is not easily measured by traditional survey techniques, because people find it hard or impossible to remember the number of trips they have taken over a period of months or even weeks. In the early 1990s there is, however, a rough but useful estimate for developed countries, that there are at least as many domestic day visits for leisure purposes within a country as there are tourist days or nights spent away from home for all purposes. Thus, for example in the UK in 1989 an estimated 110 million domestic tourism visits for all purposes generated 443 million nights away from home. An additional 630 million same-day visits for leisure purposes were made by the British in the same year with a duration of at least 3 hours from home and a minimum distance of 20 miles. With a population of some 55 million in British, this is equivalent to over ten visitor days per person for leisure purposes over a year. UK estimates of day visits for business and social purposes do not exist, although such visits are obviously a very large market, for transport operators in particular.

The total market for travel and tourism comprises three main elements; international visits in bound to a country' visits made to foreign destinations by a country's residents; and domestic visits including day trips. The total market has grown rapidly in recent years and it is very large indeed, comprising the great majority of the population of economically developed countries. Frequent, repeat purchases of travel and tourism products in any period of 12 months are already a normal experience for many people. Although the statistics are inevitably open to dispute, travel and tourism is already the largest sector of international trade and in developed countries usually contributes 5-10 per cent of Gross Domestic Product. One may safely predict that marketing in travel and tourism will be a subject of growing significance and interest.

Before drawing the discussion of the main markets in travel and tourism into a working definition, we need to clarify one important potential source of confusion. What, if any, are the differences between *tourism*, and *travel*, used on their own as single terms and *travel* and *tourism* used as a combined term? What can a definition of tourism mean if it does not include travel? This book proceeds in the belief that an acceptable definition of tourism necessarily covers all relevant aspects of travel. In normal usage *tourism*, and *travel and tourism*, are terms that relate to exactly the same market and they are used interchangebly.

Travel and tourism tends to be the term used most often by managers, especially in North America, because it is convenient, particle, and widely understood. Accordingly, this usage is adopted generally throughout the book. As the US Travel Data Centre puts it, 'Tourism is synonymous with travel' (USTDC: 1987 Appendix B). Where, for the sake of convenience, *tourism* is used alone, it also means travel and tourism; students should be aware that no conceptual difference is implied between the two expressions in this book.

Although academics have debated conceptual definitions of tourism for several decades, and there are international agreements on statistical definitions, it was not until 1991-2 that the WTO endorsed the following statement. 'Tourism comprises the activities of persons travelling to and staying in places outside their usual environment for not more than one consecutive year for leisure, business and other purposes' (WTO; 1992—subject to ratification by the UN).

In the UK the Tourism Society adopted a definition in 1979 based on the work of Burkart and Medlik (1974), which in turn draws on earlier definitions and is widely accepted. 'Tourism is deemed to include any activity concerned with the temporary short-term movement of people to destinations outside the places where they normally live and work, and their activities during the stay at these destinations' (Tourism Society; 1979, p. 70).

There is nothing particular to the UK about this definitions. It is comprehensive, it holds good for all countries and it encompasses all the elements of visitor categories noted earlier in the chapter. The new WTO definition is similar to it and it serves as the working definitions of the total market that is relevant throughout this book.

The definitions pulls together the three main elements of travel and tourism:

1. Visitor activity is concerned only with aspects of life outside normal routines of work and social commitments, and outside the location of those routines.

2. The activity necessitates travel and,

in nearly every case, some form of transport to the destination.

3. The destination is the focus for a range of activities, and a range of facilities required to support those activities.

Five important points should be noted in relation to the definition.

- There is nothing in it that restricts the total market to overnight stays' it includes sameday visits.

- There is nothing in it that restricts the total market to travel for leisure or pleasure, and it includes travel for business, social, religious, educational, sports, and most other purposes, provides that the destination of travel is outside the usual routines and place of residence or work.

- All tourism includes an element of travel but all travel is not tourism. The definition excludes all routine commuter travel and purely local travel, such as to neighbourhood shops, schools or hospitals.

- Travel and tourism includes large elements of individual leisure time and also many recreational activities, but it is not synonymous with them because the bulk of all leisure and recreation takes place in or around the home.

- All travel and tourism trips are temporary movements; the bulk of the total market comprises trips of no more than a few 'hours or nights' duration.

One of the greatest difficulties in understanding and dealing with travel and tourism as a total market or industry is the extent to which so many of the supplying organizations see tourism as only a part of their total business operations. For example, airlines, trains, buses, restaurants and hotels, all deal with a wide variety of market segments, many of which do not fall within the definition of travel and tourism. Hotels have local trade for bars and meals, transport operators carry commuters. Many visitor attractions, such as museums, and most visitor information bureaux, also provide services to local residents.

This mixture of products designed to serve both tourism and other markets has great significance for marketing decisions; it is discussed in some detail in Part Five of the book which considers marketing applications in the components sectors of the industry.

The component sectors

Travel and tourism was discussed at the beginning of this chapter from the demand side and identified as a total market comprising three main sectors of international tourism, domestic tourism, and same-day visits or excursionism. It is appropriate to complete the introduction by discussing briefly the sectors on the supply side, which are loosely known as the *travel* and *tourism industry*.

It is obvious that the 'industry' comprises the products or outputs not of one but of several different industry sectors, as these are conventionally defined and measured in most countries economic statistics. In practice, convenient though the concept is for all working within it, travel and tourism is not economists. In assessing the performance of industry sectors it is normal for economists and statisticians to measure the outputs of transport, accommodation, and catering separately. But they cannot easily distinguish what proportion of each output is generated by visitor spending. While this is a topic of almost infinite debate for statisticians and economists, and for complicated visitor survey techniques, it is fortunately not a matter of prime concern for marketing managers. Accordingly, the term travel and tourism industry is used throughout this book in the broad sense that it is recognized without difficulty in practice.

The five main component sectors of the industry are reflected in the chapter headings and case studies included in Parts Five and Six of the book. Each of them comprises several sub-sectors, all of which are increasingly concerned with marketing activities, both in the design of their products and the management of demand. Such principles greatly facilitate the understanding of the subject and help to explain the common interests in marketing that practitioners recognize. Students may find it a useful exercise to extend the list in Figure 9.6, using the same five sector headings and aiming to produce up to fifty sub-sectors involved altogether in the *travel and tourism industry.*

It can be seen that some of the sub-sectors are fully commercial, operated for profit; some are operated commercially for objects other than profit; and some are in the public sector and operated mainly on a non-commercial basis. To illustrate, in the first category come most hotels; in the second category many attractions, such as safari parks and heritage sites; and in the third category many state-owned national museums, national parks, and most of the operations undertaken by tourist offices. Internationally, growing recognition of the value of marketing in non-commercial operations in the second and third categories has been a remarkable feature of the 1990s.

Links between demand and supply and the role of marketing

Vital linkages between demand and supply in travel and tourism that are fundamental to an understanding of the role of marketing. The figure shows the relationship between market demand, generated in the places in which visitors normally live (areas of origin), and product supply in areas of destination. In particular, it shows how the five main sectors of the industry combine to manage visitors' demand through marketing influences.

Readers should note that the linkages focus on visitors in the left-hand box. A detailed knowledge of their customers character-istics and buying behaviour is central to the activities of marketing managers in all sectors of the industry. Knowledge of the decisions, is generally known as *consumer orientation;* a concept developed in the next chapter.

It should be noted also, in the lower half of the diagram, that not all visits to a destination are influenced by marketing activity. For example, domestic visitors travelling by private car to stay with their friends and relatives may not be influenced by marketing in any way. On the other hand, first-time buyers of package tours to exotic destinations in the Pacific area may find almost every aspect of their trip is influenced by the marketing decisions of the tour operator they choose. The operator selects the destinations to put into a brochure, the accommodation, the range of excursions, the routes, choice of airline, and prices. In between these two examples a traveller on business selects his own destinations according to business requirements but may be influenced as to which hotel he selects. The range of influences, noted as 'marketing mix', is obviously very wide, and it is varied according to visitors' interests and circumstances.

There are, of course, many other linkages between the live sectors of the travel and tourism industry, e.g. between national tourist organizations and suppliers at the destination. These additional linkages are not drawn to avoid unnecessary confusion in this introduction. The linkages are identified subsequently in all parts of the book.

Chapter Summary

This chapter introduces travel and tourism as a nationally and internationally important market, in which the natural focus of management activity is on exchange transactions between visitors (demand) and producers (supply). The dimensions of the market are set out and key definitions provided in a form suitable for marketing purposes. The travel and tourism industry is outlined as five main sectors, the marketing practices of which subsequently form the subject matter. It emphasizes that there are no conceptual differences intended between the use of the terms *tourism*, and *travel and tourism*, which are used interchangeably. All the definitions are based on principles that are valid for all countries, whether they are economically developed or not, and whether their tourism industry is mature or just emerging.

The five sectors of the industry are brought together in the important diagram which traces the main linkages between supply and demand and, in particular, indicates the areas of marketing influences. This is analysed in depth in later chapters.

Students should be aware of a tendency among some authors of travel and tourism books and articles to state or *assume* that tourism is a sub-set of leisure and recreation. Such texts frequently identify tourism as essentially concerned with one or more forms of holiday. In fact as clearly endorsed by WTO in 1992, tourism encompasses travel for business, social and many other non holiday purposes. For many hotels, airlines and for most travel agents, business travel is the most important sector for marketing purposes. For many visitor attractions, educational markets and same-day visits from home are more important segments than holiday visitors. It is important for marketing managers to keep firmly in mind this broad and internationally endorsed concept of travel and tourism.

Business Travel Agencies Discover Marketing

Until recently the sale of business travel services by travel agencies received scant attention from marketing professionals. It was the travel industry's neglected sector.

This neglect is surprising, bearing in mind that annual, worldwide sales by business travel agents now total almost $150 billion, making travel one of the world's biggest industries. It is even more surprising, given that the market is in an almost textbook state of perfect competition. For, even in the most competitive national marketplace, it is difficult to find a travel company which has more than a ten per cent share of the market.

This sector of the industry was so slow to develop that prior to 1980 only a handful of business travel agents in a country like the UK had a senior manager with the title of marketing director.

The Business Travel Service As A Product

It was probably as recently as 1980

that most travel agencies began to reappraise their need for marketing. As supply began to outstrip demand, agencies came to realise that the business travel service they offered to their customers needed to be marketed as positively and professionally as any consumer durable. As a result, in a dramatically short space of time, competitive activity in the industry has become intense and, as an inevitable consequence, the business travel product has become increasingly complex.

The business travel service is sold as a single entity. But, in reality, it is an activity which comprises a large number of distinct components. These can include relatively tangible items like the air ticket, hotel or car rental voucher. But for the most part they are intangible aspects of service delivery, consisting of features such as the prompt response of the reservation agent to the traveller's phone call; the accuracy of the travel information; the support which is delivered after the sale or the quality and reliability of the accounting arrangements.

Theodore Levitt, Professor of Business Administration at the Harvard Business School and author of some of the classic works on product development, has suggested that, to a potential buyer, a product is 'a complex cluster of value satisfactions'. On detailed investigation, there is probably no better example of this than a travel agency's business travel service. Among the large number of component features which make up a business travel service, customers attach different values according to their own special needs, their perception of the service component's relative value, and the ability of the agency to solve the problems experienced by themselves, their travelling employees and their companies.

Later on in this chapter, we shall explore the way in which the business travel product is adapted to the customer's needs in the selling activity. But first we should deal with the process of product development and show how it has become increasingly important for travel agents to differentiate their own products, which are continuously in danger from either replication by competitors or outright commoditisation.

Effective product development demands that each component of the complex business travel service is disentangled, scrutinised, measured against the competition, systematically improved and then successfully reintegrated into the total product offer. In their product development activities, the most professional business travel agents on both sides of the Atlantic have, wittingly or not, remained very close to Levitt's principles on product differentiation.

Levitt uses a hierarchy of four different levels of product development ranging from the most basic Generic, through the Expected and Augmented, to the Potential product.

Generic Product

This is the 'table stake', the minimum necessary ingredients which are required at the outset if the producer is to enter the 'game'. This level of product has no competition viability on its own.

For a travel agent, it means having a IATA licence to hold and issue airline tickets.

Expected Product

The expected product is just that: it represents the customer's minimal expectations. Competing sellers seek to fulfil their client's expectations by distinguishing their offerings from one another. Delivery, pricing, quantity, format and product content must all be at a level which will ensure market acceptance.

For the travel agent, the premises must look adequate for the job. The staff must have a basic level of competence. Even if the tickets—which the licence in the generic product enables the agent to hold and issue—are handwritten, they must still be totally correct in stated routes, times and prices.

Augmented Product

Nowadays, the progressive marketing of services means more than merely providing the customer with the bare essentials. There must be effective product differentiation. The basic service can augmented to offer the potential client a sophisticated and persuasive product, making the client much more amenable to purchase. An augmented product of this kind is a unique feature of relatively mature markets.

Potential Product

This level consists of everything which is potentially feasible to attract and hold a customer and often occurs with a significant change of market conditions, for example the sudden availability of new technology.

Apart from the features described above, it would be reasonable to expect that the reservation includes a boarding pass for the client's favourite seat selection, e.g. aisle/no smoking/front of cabin, details of which had been previously supplied in response to a travel agent's questionnaire. This information would be stored in the travel agency's own database and used each time the customer made a reservation.

Competition forces suppliers in the marketplace into a constant search for new ways to differentiate themselves and move their products up the hierarchy. As a result, today's potential product could easily become the bare generic offering in five years time.

The long-term survivors in the business travel agency marketplace will be those companies who can demonstrate the inclination and resources to keep investing in the process of differentiation.

Travel Management Services are the ultimate form of business travel product development

The current absolute forms of product differentiation in the business travel marketplace are probably the travel management services (TMS) piloted by companies in the US like Woodside, Gelco and American Express.

In a TMS regime, the customer corporation is looking for total management of the entire business travel activity, a system which covers a large number of distinctly separate, travel-related activities. In articulating its offering to potential customers American Express has termed the process 'The Travel Cycle'.

Each of the stages in the travel cycle involves a subset of processes which the TMS company can develop and refine to improve the service it delivers to the customer.

- The first is Travel Policy Making—defining the rules by which employees travel and how arrangements should be made.

- Next are Travel Arrangements—which includes the logistics of finding the best rates and fares. Increasingly, at this stage, the travel agent monitors adherence to corporate travel policy and creates a management information stream.

- The cycle continues with the Trip itself, when travellers need high quality travel services, a convenient, secure way to pay expenses and the flexibility to change the itinerary and lodging en-route.
- After the Trip comes Expense Reporting, Payment and Reconcillation. During these phases companies are looking for processes which provide either ease of administration or reassurance that the Company's financial assets are being managed properly and efficiently. Some will look for employee adherence to company policy, others to maximise their cash flows by extending their credit situations to the maximum.
- Ideally, the cycle concludes with Review and Analysis and Planning. This phase gives the company the management information necessary to help it maximise corporate rate benefits, plan its t & e budget or modify its travel policy.

There are certain minimum criteria for entry into the Travel Management Service marketplace. For example, a company must have invested or be prepared to invest its capital in producing:

- A highly developed business travel product comprising the benefits.
- State-of-the-art business travel centres
- A networking capability enabling the business travel service to be delivered to customers whose operating units might be dispersed across the country, continent or even the world.
- Global customer servicing through directly owned, representative or franchised offices
- Excellent supplier relations with airlines, hotels and car rental companies
- A charge card system for the payment process and collection of travel data
- Effective data-capture at the point of sale, plus powerful MIS generating software to provide the customer with effecting tracking of purchases and enforcement of company travel policy
- A Travel and Entertainment Consulting Service to assist companies to determine their own internal travel policies, and design and instal the appropriate travel management system for their needs.

In establishing a TMS approach to business travel marketing, American Express did not see itself as operating within the narrow, traditional confines of either the travel agency or the travel and entertainment payment sectors. Rather, it is a provider of a comprehensive range of travel-related or travel management services. In this book 'The Marketing Imagination', Theodore Levitt cited the certain of American Express Travel Management Services in the United States as an outstanding example of marketing innovation, a classic instance of how a company was prepared to modify and develop its product to meet the needs of an important group of purchasing decision-makers.

Consider American Express. Its green credit card ('Don't leave home without it', itself an imaginative positioning with great power), is also sold as a 'Corporate Card'. Corporations have been persuaded to issue it to certain classes of employees instead of giving them cash advances. This helps companies conserve cash and more closely monitor expenses. In 1982 American Express shifted the Corporate Card operations into its Travel Services Division. The Travel Services Division operated, among some other things, travel agencies, making airline and hotel reservations and procuring tickets.

Travel Services concluded that the larger and more geographically dispread a corporation, the greater was the variety of its travel arrangements and the greater its per capita travel cost differences within the corporation. With airline rate deregulation and increased hotel price dealing, the less knowledge about prices the travelling executives, their secretaries, and in-house travel officers became. Financial officers of the corporation had little or no knowledge of the size of their annual travel cost corporate-wide. The numbers were buried under other line items in the various budgets. By helping the corporation establish travel expense rules for each class of its traveller and then offering to handle all of a corporation's travel managements through a single dedicated American Express travel desk, with a seperate 800 telephone number dedicated to each corporation.

American Express was able to help 'control' travel costs corporate-wide. It was able to search and bargain for the lowest possible rates, the lowest-cost routes, and the lowest-cost hotel accommodations within each class of lodging. It sent monthly system wide trade cost analyses to the central financial officers, with flagged indicators of deviations from the travel expense rules. American Express was able to demonstrate that, even after charging its regular fees for Corporate Cards, it could save companies with normal travel budgets over $30 million at least 10 per cent.

American Express looked at the world 'out there' through the eyes of people whose needs it understood totally —the eyes of the corporate controllers of the purse strings. Controllers knew that costs of all kinds have a general tendency to creep up. They were increasingly concerned about the price of money. Knowing a lot about travel and travel-related costs, American Express asked itself simply: 'How can we help the keepers of the corporate purse strings to manage costs that we know a lot about?' The rest wasn't easy but would never have been done had American Express not first done what was uniquely imaginative: combining disparate facts about its corporate customers and itself in ways that yielded new questions and previously inexperienced insights.

The product and the service

An important part of the product-definition activity for business travel is the separation of the product features, the tangible constituent parts, from the delivery process or services. The value which the customer places on the tangible parts of the product will depend, to a large extent, on the quality of the delivery process. A travel agent may develop superior databases, operate state-or-the-art reservations technology or offer the most competitive prices, but these features will have little or no value if a client experiences inefficiency, delay, indifference or even rudeness in the way he is handled by the agency's staff.

The interlinking of product and delivery is commonplace in modern-day service industries. Levitt in 'The Industrialization of Service', a classic Harward Business Review paper, cites three types of industrialised services.

- hard technologies (automatic car washes, automatic toll collectors, etc.) which substitute machinery for

people in the preformance of service work.
- soft technologies (cafeterias, mutual funds and package tours), which are essentially the substitution of organised, preplanned systems for individual service operations and
- hybrid technologies, which combine hard equipment with carefully planned, industrial systems to bring efficiency, order and speed to the process.

The modern business travel centre is clearly a hybrid technology. On-line computer reservations systems; extensive travel and customer databases; high speed document printing and worldwide communications capabilities, are all evidence of how rapidly and extensively the travel retailing process has became industrialised.

It also seems inevitable that business travel centres will become even larger. In the late 1970s, the 'larger' units which Woodside and American Express operated in the US had an average staff of 80. By the mid 1980s, the average was 250 staff and this is being continually expanded by management. This is probably because it is only when travel agencies begin to approach this size that scale productivities start to become available to the travel company. The operating efficiencies tend to show up primarily through the reduction of overhead costs, via:

- better utilisation of central processors and peripheral equipment, e.g. ticket printers
- specialised functions such as centralised hotel reservations, lowest airfare searching, database management
- night time operating: service can be expanded to 24 hours since these staff can also supervise 'through-the-night' running of ticket and documentation printing, management reports, etc.
- more mobility of the labour pool. Staff can be moved to cope with operating bottlenecks
- rent costs should be lower, and the accommodation better equiped to handle the, now industrialised, process of business travel service. If the company is wise, it will move to a location which balances low rents with the availability of a labour pool. Communications networks and satellite delivery arrangements will provide satisfactory local customer servicing from central operating units.

High technology can assist the travel agents (for example sophisticated databases which identify travellers' preferences and habits) but in the hybrid technology environment of the modern business centre, the degree of personal contract, which only human beings can deliver, will inevitably diminish. As a result, travel companies will need to find ways of keeping the service as personal as possible. But, even with continuous training, it is difficult to maintain the personal touch in large, semi-industrialised environments. This will expose the larger operators to competition from smaller, more responsive companies who seek to exploit the advantage gained by offering a personal service. Cleverdon, in his book *Business Travel, a New Mega Market*, does not see a future for the service-orientated, local, small-scale agency, although many will only be fully competitive as members of the larger consortia which are developing. However, the smaller agency, which is able to provide a highly personalised and efficient service, especially at a senior level to the influential, decision-making executives within the chart corporation, will keep the business even when its price is less competitive than that of larger competitors.

Pricing

In a 'worst-case' situation, the services provided by travel agents are free of charge to major corporate customers, being paid for from the commissions granted to travel agents by their industry principals: the airlines, hotel and car rental companies.

We say 'worst case' because, nowadays, the market norm is for most large companies to share this commission with their travel agent suppliers—process known in the industry as 'rebating'. Travel agency commissions vary considerably, but can range from 8 per cent to 30 per cent of the price charged to the customer, depending on the product and prevailing market circumstances. How much of the commission a customer can obtain as a 'rebate' depends on two factors: the size of its annual travel volume and its ability to push the agent to the limit by aggressive negoitiation.

Airline Pricing

The rebate is the consequence of a series of price-wars which occurred after the economic recession in the early 1980s, which left airlines and other travel industry suppliers with an unprecedented surplus capacity. At the same time, travel agents found themselves in a market situation of little or negative growth. Thus, the only means of building sales was to increase market share. Like their industry principals, travel agents decided almost universally that the best way to differentiate themselves from their competitors was by price, rather than by product improvements. In consequences, the corporate consumer found during this period that he could gain in two ways—from falling 'gross' airline commission. As market conditions deteriorated, the airlines decided to make a third inroad into margins which were already reduced, or non-existent, by granting override commissions to the agencies whom they felt could do most to build their market share. As a result, during the early 1980s, travel agencies were able to maintain their margins, while the impact on most airlines was catastrophic.

Only in the summer of 1985 did signs emerge to indicate that the travel industry had been able to regain the ground lost on pricing in the period 1980-82. However, many airlines, particularly those in the US, have never been able to regain the full premium pricing they achieved in the years prior to deregulation. In 1977, the last year before deregulation, only 38.5 per cent of US domestic trunkline revenue passenger miles were flown at discount fares. This proportion has grown year by year until 1983 when 82 per cent of the domestic revenue passenger miles of US airlines were flown at average discounts of 48 per cent of the 'full fare'.

The industry as a whole has been slow to discover all the benefits of the marketing mix, but there are signs now that the pricing of products by airlines has, at last, become a scientific practice at the wholesaler/manufacture level. Airlines deregulation in the US has created such a competitive market environment that experts claim there are as many as 4,000,000 airfares for routes within and originating from the United States, and around 20,000 changes of prices occur during an average day. During periods when airlines are tactically adjusting their prices on some of the highly-trafficked, key-corridor, routes this number can double or treble in a single day.

In their relations with corporate customers, there are, as yet, few very special 'direct deals' from airlines. Those which have emerged are mainly based on specific 'city pairs', often by a carrier that is a new market entrant or new to the route and seeking to establish a market.

In the main, the airlines prefer to keep the corporate customer at arms length, dealing via and agent. This allows them to maintain good relations with travel agents (who abhor direct selling) and maintain integrity in their pricing structure.

Lodging industry

In the hotel industry, the position is now much more complex than it was even a few years ago. In the past it has been practice for rooms to be offered at different prices on different nights and during different seasons, but nowadays an increasingly significant number of hotels are prepared to negotiate the price of rooms with frequent or major customers.

Major corporations who can deliver a substantial number of bednights to a hotel chain or single property are often able to negotiate preferential rates. Negotiating leverage will depend on how much can be delivered. If the hotel, is near a plant which produces 20 per cent or more of the property's occupancy from Monday through Thursday night, plus conferences, meetings, lunches and other functions, a company should nowadays expect to negotiate a very competitive deal for itself.

A major company which buys an extermely large volume of rooms, on a global or national basis, might also be able to strike a corporate deal with a major hotel chain if it is able to direct its employees into their rooms.

Beyond these arrangements, which are clearly exceptional, companies can fall back on the negotiated corporate rates of the principal business travel agents. These provide significant savings on the 'rack rate' and can lead to a worthwhile reduction of costs over the course of a year, thus maximizing price savings. Travelling employees should be encouraged, whenever possible, to book through the appointed travel agent, rather than going direct to favoured properties (where rack rates are generally paid). This will ensure that the lower rates are always obtained and that volume, which is critical to the negotiation process, is both maximised and proven.

Nowadays, all the larger multiple travel agents (American Express, Thomas Cook and Woodside, for example) have negotiated superior corporate rates giving significant savings over regular corporate rates.

A typical range of the hotel prices offered to commercial accounts is illustrated in the above figure. (The figures are illustrative only; there are wide variations from country to country and even from property to property.)

Car Rental

The car rental suppliers operate a similar tariff structure although the distribution of supply points is less complicated than for lodging industry. Corporate-rate deals tend to be related strictly to volume, although they are sometimes offered by companies wishing to achieve prestige or secure exclusively.

Car hire companies will also allow up to 30 per cent discount to the very largest commercial accounts, but most offer only 5-10 per cent commission to the travel agents if they act as the reservation channel for these transactions. At the time of writing there seem to be some initiatives under way to restore car rental pricing to net, rather than discounted, pricing.

Because of the low levels of commission paid to travel agents, many of the multiples are now prepared to sacrifice the revenue from car rental reservations and rebate their commissions to the customer in exchange for the earnings they will receive from airline ticket sales.

Travel agents' commission—the future

It now seems clear that the commission which travel agents receive from their suppliers for distributing their product has a limited future as a pricing revenue mechanism.

A travel agent who receives a fixed commission of 10 per cent for selling an airline ticket will earn a gross revenue of $10 on a $100 shuttle flight, or $250 for a $2,500 Concorde flight from New York to London, for more or less the same input of labour and capital. This seems a very inequitable method of remuneration. All of the parties involved in the travel distribution process—principal, agent, and customer—seem to be approaching the same conclusion: that a method of pricing based on a transaction fee will be the way of the future. Under this regime, pricing would be determined by the wholesale cost plus the agency's operating expenses.

Travel agents, who are generally slow to welcome revolutionary changes of this sort, will only have themselves to blame when a new pricing regime arrives. Over the year, agents have collaborated in a perfectly legitimate regime of competitive market forces to create the rebate as an established factor in the pricing of their products. In consequences, the travel agents' commission is no longer seen by carriers to be an accurate reflection of the costs of distributing airline tickets. The airlines have long since stopped holding agents to either IATA or their own agency agreements and, as a result, will now not be happy to see agents manoeuvre themselves into a position where a net pricing comes into operation. Certainly, this arrangements might appear more attractive to the airlines for, with net pricing, fares should appear cheaper to the end user, without costing the airlines any more.

Robert Cleverdon, in the Economist Intelligence Unit report on 'Business Travel: a new megamarket', suggests 'there seem to be mutual benefits for corporations and agencies in adopting fee-based arrangements' and he considers this arrangement will become increasingly popular:

> The agencies can set specific prices for particular services and transaction, and offer them as a menu to prospective clients. The travel product will be charged at cost and fees added on (from a printed set of charges) for items such as ticketing, cancellations, automated reservations systems and 24 hour emergency telephone lines. Provided the agent fully understands the costs of the transaction, he should be able to generate a better and more controllable return than under the present arrangements.

Most large multiple travel agencies have now concluded their evaluation of net pricing models. Hogg Robinson, the UK Woodside agency, provides net pricing as an alternative costing method when making new business presen-tations. But no breakthrough is envisaged until there is a greater understanding of the principles by all concerned and a trail-blazing customer emerges with sufficient credentials to stimulate the attention of both company travel managers and finance directors.

Another nail in the coffin of the commission rebate may be the advent of the travel management services which are being advanced by companies like American Express, Gelco and Woodside.

Travel management involves looking at each component of the trip to find the lowest cost solution consistent with the maintenance of quality. This means that the agency will select the lowest airfare on each route (irrespective of customer preference), the best value corporate hotel property at the destination and the lowest cost car rental for the transfer. Each of these reservations would be made using data in the agency's computer to calculate the lowest available price, based on a matrix of current market pricing coordinators and negotiated corporate or net pricing arrangements.

The last area to provide a potential cost saving for the customer corporation is that of the travel agent's commission. For airline sales, this ranges from 8 per cent to 20 per cent of the ticket price, depending on route and market circumstances, while for non-airline products it ranges from 8 per cent to 25 per cent

In the exceptional market condition of the last five years, the price of packages (mediated through corporate discounts and rebates given by travel agents) has probably been the single most important factor in deciding which travel agencies secured business. This is because price is the most measurable of all the factors in travel purchasing. It is also the factor which allows company travel managers and purchasing officers to demonstrate to their organisations their skills in securing a favourable deal with suppliers.

The price of the 'product' has also become such a decisive factor in selection because there has been a general feeling that most travel agents offer services of a broadly similar quality. However, in recent years some customers have suffered at the hands of travel agents who priced to win, rather than maintain business. These experiences have shown customers that there is a clear correlation between good service and price. The travel agency which pares down its operating margin finds, sooner or later, that it does not have the resources either to invest in good staff and their development, or to upgrade its technology. The quality of the services offered will inevitably diminish and, as with most things in life, the customer ultimately gets only what he has paid for.

Most of the major agents now run profitability models for new accounts. But agents do not always use a carefully worked out, empirical process to determine the level of rebate they are prepared to offer to prospective customers. Market forces probably still occupy more of the agent's attention than do calculations based on the revenue mix of the business. In the same way, special circumstances (such as a high proportion of aborted or changed transactions; complex itineraries; or the cost of special services like 24-hour service, costly deliveries, visas or management reports) which apply to certain customers' accounts, are not always taken into account.

Market Segmentation

Specialization on Price or Service, or by employee control or Comfort?

In the preceding sections, product development and pricing have been reviewed as the key foundations of business travel marketing. It has also been argued that no prospective customer, however good his negotiation skills, can achieve a final delivery position which provides the maximum product features and highest standard of service at the lowest possible price. The two are mutually exclusive and the customer will be forced into making a compromise between securing the best value and ensuring good service.

It would be wrong to believe that the decision-making process polarises at either end of the price/service axis. Very few companies would want to sacrifice all employee comfort for price, or vice-versa. But there are certainly many signs that most companies tend to give priority to one or other of these objectives.

Those companies which gravitate towards costs savings or employee-control generally have definitive travel policies, a commitment by top management to cost-savings, and a rigorous control and enforcement regime. They strive to obtain the best corporate rates and maximum discounts through a very professional approach to negotiation.

For companies at the other end of the spectrum, travel and entertainment is often seen as a fringe benefit and there is very little concern about achieving the maximum price savings. Such companies will, however, look for a very high level of personal service and expect the travel agency to provide this from its larger gross margin.

Company attitude to travel management provides one dimension of market segmentation for business travel (see fig. 9.19). The other variable is company size. The larger the company's travel activity the more leverage it can apply to gain extra services, benefits and concessions from the travel agent. It will expect a higher degree of product and service customisation, dedicated staff (sometimes, even an inplant travel agency on the company's premises) its own corporate rate programmes and management information reports tailored to its own needs.

These two variables—size and company policy—provide the total market framework.

Within this matrix (see fig. 9.19) business travel companies will decide where they wish to specialise and segment the marketplace according to their own needs.

Certainly, on current trends, it seems likely that we will see a great level of specialisation in the business travel market. It is to be expected that the larger travel organisations will be the only ones which will have the financial resources to invest in the expensive hardware and systems which are required to offer travel management services to major corporations. In the other (bottom left hand) corner of the market, it is likely that many of the smaller agents have the flexibility which is necessary to meet the needs of organisations requiring a high degree of personal service.

Selling Business Travel

When the travel agent has completed a market segmentation analysis and equipped itself with the product appropriate to the sector in which it wishes to specialise, it can move on to the next stage—the selling phase.

This process consists of:

1. Identifying the target company;
2. Locating decision-maker;
3. Probing to reveal needs;
4. Testing product design;
5. Proving ability to deliver;

6. Closing sales;
7. Implementing new account;
8. Adopting account maintenance.

Identifying the Target Company

Different industries have different business travel patterns, and within industries, different sized companies have varying levels of travel activity. Clearly, on a travel-by-employee basis, a firm of multinational management consultants will make a much heavier demand on business travel services than either a coalmining or retailing organisation.

Only a limited amount of research is required to begin to establish the business propensities of particular industries (categorised on the basis of standard industrial classification) and the amount of business travel activity per head of employee population. Client companies and travel agencies should be able to assemble these data with only a limited amount of research into invoices, air tickets, itineraries etc.

Large business travel accounts do bring with them some economies of scale in activities such as ticket delivery or accounting. However, per se they need not be more profitable than any other size of business, because a large company is likely to maximise its perceived purchasing clout and be more aggressive in its negotiation of rebates, so reducing the travel agent's margins.

These are other dangers. An agent with only a small number of large companies within its account portfolio will also find itself in a very vulnerable financial position should it lose, in whole or in parts, a large account which represents a significant proportion of its turnover. Clearly, on winning the business, the agent would have adjusted both its capital and staffing levels to service this customer. In the short term, with the business lost and no sales or commission income to offset the costs of these investments, the travel agent is likely to find its profitability significantly impaired. Nowadays, most small agents are increasingly less prepared to take this risk, preferring to leave the large accounts to the major multiples.

These are other factors which can adversely affect the potential revenue of some business travel accounts. Aside from these organisations within the marketplace which have a reputation for being difficult customers, there are many corporations whose business travel characteristics or whose demands on the agent make them worth avoiding. Some companies insist on the agent issuing all their rail tickets. Others have a high proportion of short-haul airtickets or low-value hotel bookings. In those cases, the value of the transactions (and thus commission income) will make the account considerably less profitable than average.

Most large, multiple business travel agents have developed pricing models which enable them to determine the profitability of an individual account from the information which they gain during the negotiation process. These agents are now much more sanguine about the business they are prepared to pursue and are also increasingly inclined to renegotiate or even re-sign unprofitable accounts.

Locating the decision-maker

Locating the corporate decision-maker is the next step. This process is not to straightforward as there are many people in the organisation who can influence the choice of the appointed travel agent. There is a distinct hierarchy.

At the top of the board the Chief Executive Officer and Chief Financial Officer have the key votes. In addition, there is a large number of other persons who can be involved in influencing the decisions-makers.

One of the principal skills in selling business travel services is to determine who are the key players in the decision-making process and which of the bundle of travel-related products and services which the travel agency can offer best meet the needs of these individuals.

During the negotiation process, which can extend for many months, or even years, the sales person must identify and interpret signals coming from within the organisation from individuals who can advance his or her cause. Of particular concern will be those individuals who have a vested interest in maintaining the status quo or who prefer to favour a particualr competitor.

During the period building up to the conclusion of the negotiations, the successful sales person will have to deal with the following:

- An activity which is often a low-interest area for the company compared with its mainstream business activities.
- Overcoming inertia by finding a reason for the company to change: business travel is only really a visible activity when something goes wrong with service delivery, or a potential supplier presents in extremely appealing proposition.
- The selection of preferred suppliers is made according to a wide range of different criteria. Sometimes these criteria can be in conflict. Different levels in the organisational hierarchy and different functions have varying needs, e.g. sales will look for service or comfort, finance for cost-savings.
- The decision-making process can often be subjective, even biased.
- Probably the best advice which can be given to the sales person entering an environment such as this is:
- Start as high up the organisation as possible: with the decision-maker or a person of very senior influence. Not only will this person provide the best insights into the company's needs, but he or she will also often function as a 'white-knight' within the company, assisting and advancing the cause of the salesperson.
- Try to understand the prevailing corporate culture as quickly as possible. For example, is the company paternalistic or liberal in the way it generally treats its employees; how price sensitive is it in its purchasing of goods and services; does a strong 'class' hierarchy exists; which parts of the company are held in highest esteem—sales, operations, or manufacturing? A proper assessment of these factors will be critical in the final design of the product which the selling company will offer to the buyer.

The latter stages of the sale involve moving through the various levels of customer hierarchy, reassuring all of the decision-makers and people of influence that the travel agent is fully able to meet the specific needs of the individual clients. At the same time, conflicts between differing parts of the hierarchy/organisation have to be managed, and objections overcome.

To become the designated vendor, therefore, requires successful passage through a series of successive gates, managing people as diverse as secretaries, travellers and chief executives. The selling process involves a great deal of customer reassurance. Nowadays selling is a much more sophisticated activity, drawing on a wide range of behavioural skills. The key to the process will be the sales person's skill in persuading the prospective purchaser to reveal his precise needs and then offering the relevant range of benefits to meet them.

As with all intangible products, the sale of the business travel is made more complex because the prospective customer cannot inspect or review the product before buying. For that reason, the customer is forced to make many more decisions on the basis of what is promised or implied, than on the way in which tangible products are produced. While he can be given a guided tour of a typical business travel centre and be shown the kinds of services provided to companies like his own, he can never be absolutely certain of the precise quality of the service he will receive.

This is why the provision of surrogates makes a key contribution towards reassuring the potential customer about the kind of service he will ultimately receive. The customer will be quick to make value judgments about the likely quality of the potential product from the appearance of the sales person, the business proposal, the reservations environment, the computer technology, even packaging, like ticket jackets.

Levitt has described how business proposals submitted to NASA are packaged in binders which match the craftsmanship of Tyrolean leather workers. Most travel agents probably would not go that far but it is important that, in every part of the selling process, the sales people provide reassuring, tangible, and preferably visible surrogates for what is promised in the service. As part of this process, American Express in the UK have now invested in sales presentation tools which include the use of an interactive video disc to enable the client to see how the product can be customised to meet his particular needs.

Implementation and account maintenance are critical to eventual sales success. Even when the client has finally decided 'yes', the account-selling job is far from over. Along imple-mentation phase stretches ahead of the new supplier. Although many business travel sales people will believe that their job has been done, preferring to leave the less glamorous implementation phase to their operations colleagues, they still have a key role to play in determining the ultimate success of the sale. Senior travel agency management must ensure that the sales person does not lose interest. One solution is to appoint the successful salesman to the job of account executive for the next three to six months to supervise the new account implementation process.

A high degree of personalised attention is also vital in ensuring thorough vertical penetration of the account. Despite the incumbent management's edicts to their employees to change to the new vendor, there will be outcrops of resistance, whether from whole departments, certain executive or individual secretaries. The sales person is the key to a successful crossing of this final hurdle. His or her selling skills will constantly be required to ensure that resistance is overcome and the new account is completely penetrated.

Account Maintenance

The next phase of activity is account maintenance. The delivery of intangible products is unique in at least one respect. The customer is, for the most part, unaware that he is being served well and his interests are being protected. While service is being rendered properly and efficiently, the customer remains virtually oblivious to its delivery. Only when things don't go well, or a competitor suggests that they could go better, does the customer really become aware of the product's existence and the identity of the supplier. An important adage in business travel selling is that 'The customer doesn't know what he's getting until he doesn't get it'. As a test, frequent international travellers should be asked to recall business trips which went well. You will find that they will struggle. Yet the last poorly executed or missing reservation, misrouting or instance of overcharging will quickly come to mind.

One characteristic of intangible products is the high number of people involved in their production and delivery: the more 'people-intensive' that a product is, the more room there is for personal discretion, idiosyncrasy, error and delay. The customer can easily be undersold as a result of his expectations being underfulfilled. And that's danger, because the customer's awareness of the supplier will often only be heightened at times of failure or dissatisfaction. This makes the incumbent supplier vulnerable to a competitor who can always use small, visible failures to build a foothold for the introduction of his services. Thus it is vital to remind people regularly at all levels in the client company of the good service they are enjoying, and how well the supplier is looking after their needs. This makes it very important that the promises which initially convinced the customer to buy are regularly re-stated. The techniques which a travel agent can use are:

- follow-up calls;
- newsletter, information updates;
- quality assurance questionnaires;
- 'talks to the managing director'—reviews with senior management;
- recognition of anniversaries with flowers, etc;
- special events for secretaries, e.g. travel seminars, airport and hotel visits, etc;
- vacation offers.

Throughout the life of the account, the agency must never neglect the interests of any sector of the customer triumvirate—the decision-makers, the travellers themselves and the travel organisers—secretaries, personal assistants and company travel managers. If good service is consistently delivered and account maintenance procedures are followed closely, then there is every reason to believe that the account will run for at least its average, natural life—nowadays a period of about seven years.

The Future

In his book 'Business Travel: A new megamarket,' Cleverdon has predicted no significant changes in the distribution of commercial travel products in the next few years. He believes the travel agent will continue to act as the prime intermediary between buyer and seller.

The airlines have remained remarkably consistent in their public assertions about their relations with travel agencies. They intend to maintain the status quo. The Chief Executive Officer of United Airlines, one of the US's largest, recently stated: 'We have no plans to appoint any other form of agents. Travel agents are vitally important to us. They are how United wishes to distribute its services'. For reasons which were explored earlier in this chapter, it seems unlikely that airlines would want at the present time to alternate the agency community, either by attempting to find a lower cost distributor or by contemplating a major, direct-sell push. Nevertheless, it is inevitable that airlines will want to explore further distribution methods which might reduce the cost of agency commissions. These payments are a colossal expense for the airlines. The Eno Foundation for Transportation's Report on Airline Deregulation calculated that the commission paid to airlines in the United States reached $2.4 billion in 1983 and represented 6.9 per cent of total airline operating expense. These figures have changed subs-tantially since airline deregulation. In 1977 commission payments totalled $732 million and represented only 4.5 per cent of airline operating expense.

The cost of commissions paid to travel agents has grown because their share in the reservations market has grown, and the airlines have no one to blame for this but themselves. As a deregulation in the USA created unprecedented pricing options, so the confused flying public turned to the travel agent to perform the role of honest broker. As a result, air bookings via travel agents have grown from around 55 per cent in 1978, the year prior to deregulation, to 75 per cent in 1984.

Many experts like Cleverdon see the trend continuing. There may be a lesson here for those airlines in Europe which are considering embracing deregulation. Freedom of pricing and route selection may offer the chance to increase market share, but what will the effect be on distribution costs?

One alternative distribution opportunity has so far been almost universally declined. This is the option to deal directly with major corporations and offer them a price advantage in return for a guaranteed volume of business. IATA regulations prevent this practice in Europe, and in the USA deals of this kind remain very much the exceptions - despite the oft-cited cases of Delta's deal with General Electric, Eastern's with the Harris Corporation and, more recently, Lockheed's arrangements with several companies. For the present, airlines seem to have reached the conclusion that business travel is not a discretionary purchase, that demand is relatively fixed and, as a result, premium pricing should be maintained for as long as possible.

If long term changes do occur, it is more likely that the airline will turn to combinations of new electronic distribution facilities and their frequent-flyer programmes to encourages direct purchase by the individual employee.

The Frequent-flyer programmes, as practised in the US, have encouraged significant shifts in brand loyalty, particularly in the early years of their operation. American Airlines, who initiated the concept with their American Advantage programme in 1981, were quickly followed by TWA, United, Pan Am and many others. There has also been a significant number of reciprocal arrangements, generally between non-competitive carriers, as well as tie-ins with hotels and car-rental companies. United's purchase of Hertz and their chance to link up with their own Westin Hotel chain subsidiary provide a unique opportunity for a totally integrated, business-travel, crossing-marketing operation.

A similar concept of total management has been created in Scandinavia by SAS. The airline owns travel agents and hotels, as well as the airline. Jan Carlzon, their Chief

Executive, has a vision in which the premium business travel passenger never leaves SAS's hands. He or she would be provided with limousine transfer into as SAS hotel. The practice will be repeated for the return journey except that there is the added benefit of baggage check-in not at the airport kerbside, but with the hotel concierge. It is this kind of initiative (which is totally permissible under IATA regulations) which business travellers who need a prompt and convenient services will relate to, and reward with their custom.

It would be difficult for any chief financial officer or corporate travel department to argue that the traveller has achieved any monetary advantage from the SAS arrangement. However, there has been a good deal of debate in the US about the ethics of the frequent-flyer programmes. Although a great many turn a blind eye, the corporate view held by a number of firms is that employee should not exploit the company for his or her own benefit and that bonuses should accrue to the corporation and not to the individual. Carriers, on the other hand, will continue to prefer to see the bonus travel points accumulated by individuals rather than corporations, thus preserving a trading relationship based on brand loyalty.

To provide an alternative appeal, certain travel agents—primarily Woodside, Gelco and American Express - have developed new travel management proposals. These are designed to provide corporations with travel services at a reduced cost as an alternative to allowing employees the freedom to make their own purchases. In particular, the service would guarantee the lowest logical fare or applicable corporate rate. Because they are based on the application of precisely developed corporate travel policies, make use to software which takes the bias out of the airline systems, and provide and manage information reports which monitor employee aberration or abuse, such travel management systems will enable the corporation (who at the end of the day are underwriting the cost of travel) to regain control of the purchasing decision process.

This discrete tussle between the airline (and other travel principals) which target the employee and the travel agent who gears his support effort to the cooperation, could well be the main focus for business travel marketing over the next few years. However, the changes which take place are likely to be subtle in application, since all parties recognise their interdependence and will be concerned not to create short-term disruption in the distribution process. A key factor in this imminent 'invisible war' will be the ability of the individual protagonists to invest in the technology which will enable them to best meet the needs of their targeted customers. Combinations of the resources described below will be developed and applied to the customer in the appropriate distribution channel.

The long-term competing systems which could result from these developments might look like fig. 19.8

Other travel agents—and particularly those who do not have the resources of the major multiples to invest in independent computer systems —are likely to become even more dependent on the airline for their product and market positioning. In the US, where agents can choose from a variety of different airline systems, there is a possibility that many agents will elect to operate primarily as a dealer for one airline rather than as a broker for many.

As a result, some agencies will achieve 'favoured-nation' status via increased over-ride commission, automation and equipment subsidies, staff training and improvement in providing servicing.

This, in turn, will lead the airlines to consider rationalizing their own distribution networks. As a result, there will probably be a reversal of the growth in the number of travel agency offices which has been increasing unabated for the last twenty-five years. There are probably few justifications for such a proferation of business travel branch offices and, as the transaction process becomes computerised, the number of them is likely to decline substantially.

In the past, customers have felt secure in the knowledge that their travel agent was at hand, to service the company's business travel requirements efficiently. But as distribution is computerised, there is no rational need for the customer to have the agency close by. Business travel customers rarely visit their agency, and nearly all reservations are made over the telephone. It could be argued that a travel agent would improve the efficiency of his business-travel customer service if he were able to concentrate his operations in a central hub, and network arrangements down the spokes to satellite locations whose function would be ticket printing and delivery.

Following Levitt's hybrid-technology theory the business travel agent would establish a national/regional operating centre with perhaps as many as 150-200 reservations agents. These would be equipped with a state-of-the-art reservation system, client and travel information database and a back office accounting and management information system.

The only long-term obstacle to remote servicing is the client's sense of insecurity of starting a business trip without an airline ticket or other documentation. After a period of time this fear could be overcome.

Tickets would be printed via satellite offices at the airport, or even on the client's premises if IATA regulations were to permit it. (Incidentally, one has to consider whether the ticket is really a necessity: certainly its only function appears to be that of a device which facilitates airline interlining.)

If the travel agent were able to achieve this arrangement he would benefit from lower real estate costs, since non-city centre sites and industrial space would be used; better utilisation of management overheads and flexibility of staffing reassures. He would also be able to use more cost-efficient automation, e.g. larger telephone systems, computers etc., rather than operating through smaller multiple units, using telecommunications and data processing systems with no economies of scale.

The ultimate foreseeable development is the installation of a complete networking arrangements whereby all regional centres are linked together to provide even wider distribution of the travel product. This would include national coverage, peak-demand switching and efficient 24 hours servicing. (See fig. 19.10b.) 'Networking is not a theoretical exercise. Already there are a number of multiple travel agents in the US who have sold the concept to large corporations. These corporations have been prepared to offset the apparent loss of local servicing against the benefits of uniform pricing and significant cost control which are gained through the consistent application of travel policy and the consolidation of business with one supplier.

Electronic communications systems now span the world and there is no reason why national borders should restrain travel agents from doing business on a global basis with their multinational customers. Chains like Thomas Cook and American Express have had a worldwide network for decades, and consortia such as Woodside, Hickory and Ask Mr Foster have been putting theirs together for some years. These agents have either built their own corporate data networks or they piggy-back on the airline' own systems. The electronic bridging which is taking place means that London can speak to Boston or New York with Sydney in real time. Thus customers' servicing requirements are passed to the point where they can be most effectively and efficiently dealt with. The travel product offered by the international travel agent thereby becomes sophis-ticated global activity.

8. Tourism Issues and Management Strategies

THE GROWTH and development of tourism has been associated with several idealistic notions concerning its contribution to society, but subsequent experience has shown tourism, like many other human activities, can have both positive and negative impacts. The industry has frequently been promoted as a force for positive contributions to the social, economic, and natural environments of destination communities. Striving for such benefits through the vehicle of tourism development, however, has made tourism a major agent for change in every society and destination it has touched. Change involves a price, and some communities have been unaware of the costs and difficulties associated with extracting the benefits of tourism.

Many people have hoped tourism would help to foster a climate of peace and prosperity by bringing together people of different cultures and nationalities. Two examples of this sentiment are found below:

> There is no better bridge between people, ideas, ideologies, cultures than travel. It can nurture under-standing within a country and between countries (Powell 1978, 3).

> Tourism, in its broadest, generic sense, can do more to develop un-derstanding among people, provide jobs, create foreign exchange, and raise living standards than any other economic force known (Kaiser and Heiber 1978, ix).

However, when the interaction of mankind and development of tourism has been examined in greater detail such worthy aspirations often face a stiff challenge and require some assistance to materialize.

A common theme in much of the tourism literature of the 1970s has concerned latent or actual hostility in destination areas where the indigenous people, "the hosts," are confronted with comparatively wealthy, and culturally different, visitors. Texts such as Turner and Ash (1975), Smith (1977), and de Kadt (1979) paint a generally depressing picture of tourism's impact, citing changed cultural values and the decay of native languages and customs. Turner and Ash equate mass tourism with past barbarian invasions.

> an invasion outwards from the highly developed metropolitan centres into the 'uncivilized' peripheries. It destroys uncom-prehendingly and unintentionally, since one cannot impute malice to millions of people or even to thousands of businessmen and entrepreneurs. (Turner and Ash 1975, 129)

Van den Berghe and Keyes (1984) maintain the problem is particularly serious for the ethnic tourist who is in search of unspoiled natives in their natural surroundings. His very presence, and that of fellow tourists, will destroy the authenticity of the moment and setting because they are intruders.

Similarly, Graburn (1976, 1984) is concerned that the inevitable commercialization of ethnic arts and crafts will lead to the development of shoddy replicas and fakes, as host communities attempt to meet the insatiable tourist demand for souvenirs.

While the majority of these negative social and cultural experiences have occurred in Third World nations, where the contrasts between native hosts and invading tourist hordes have been extreme, growing evidence of similar stress can be found within industrialized nations themselves. Role conflicts and social problems have arisen in areas of Hawaii, Scotland and the French Alps. Women and teenagers, employed by the tourist industry, start to earn greater incomes than the men employed in traditional agriculture, the men lose pride in their new roles as waiters, bellhops, and dishwashers.

Evidence of growing antagonism towards visitors is beginning to emerge in the more popular tourist destinations, where some residents feel overwhelmed by the volume of visitors and change in lifestyle. In some areas local nicknames for tourists may be construed as early warning signs of growing tension. In Cornwall tourists are referred to by some as "emmets" (ants), and in parts of southern England as "grockles" (a commercially worthless shellfish. In Banff, Alberta, the term "gorbies" is used to distinguish the awkward and gawking visitors. A sign of the times in Banff is production of a T-shirt which facetiously records the loss of three tourists to bear attacks one year. In a few regions the hostility is no longer latent with the appearance of anti-tourism graffiti, property destruction, and personal violence. Examples of this include the "Yankee go home" posters in the Europe of the 1960s, the fire-bombing of second homes in North Wales, and reported assaults on Canadian visitors in Hawaii.

The World Council of Churches has examined the issue of tourism-induced social stress and concluded that promotion of human understanding requires more than a simple transfer of people from one region or culture to another. It recommended in its report *Leisure-Tourism: Threat And Promise* (1970) that the industry acknowledge its social responsibilities, by providing more accurate information on the countries to be visited and by arranging informal meetings with local people. It calls for short, pre-trip courses stressing the political, social, and economic issues of destination areas and an extension of "meet the people" programs which have been successful in Sweden and Germany.

The flow of tourists and their revenue to peripheral regions has been viewed by some as a counterbalance to the economic pull of our urban-industrial centers. Christaller, the pioneer of central place theory, states:

> There is also a branch of the economy that avoids central places and than agglomeration of industry. This is tourism. Tourism is drawn to the periphery of settlement districts as it searches for a position on the highest mountains, in the most lonely woods, along the remotest beaches (Christaller 1964, 95).

Studies of national economies in underdeveloped countries have shown a considerable amount of generated tourism revenue has returned directly to the tourist-generating countries. In one study it has been estimated as much as 77 per cent of the tourism money returned to these urban-industrial economies (Perez 1974). This return flow is created by payment of loans and dividends on foreign invest-ment, the importation of goods and services to supply the tourists, and the salaries of senior personnel who are often temporary residents. It has been given the apt name of "leakage," for a community may heel it is building a prosperous industry but when the final bills and bank charges are paid there is often much less left in the community account than expected.

Such a situation is not confined to underdeveloped countries; it can and does occur within advanced economies where small and peripheral communities attempt to transform some local resource into a tourist attraction. The development of mountain resorts or the renovation of heritage usually requires capital and manpower in excess of local supplies, consequently these tourism developments rely on investment and labor from distant urban-industrial centers and face the same leakage situation.

As an agent of transformation, tourism has been friendlier, in general, to the environment than many other activities and past industries. The conservation of beauty and heritage are key factors to the industry's development and survival and there are many examples of its support for the protection of natural and cultural resources. National parks around the world owe a great deal to the encouragement and political pressure of the tourism industry. The development of Yellow-stone National Park in 1872, which was the forerunner of the concept, was intimately connected with the cons-truction of access routes and tourist accommodation.

> When parks such as Yellowstone and Glacier began to emerge in the 1870s, 1880s and 1890s the railroad built lines to them and constructed hotels and other facilities in and near they. Them attempted to attract tourists from all over the world (Nelson 1973, 71).

In central Africa the opening of the Saint-Floris National Park permitted a more effection protection of wildlife, for tourism revenues allowed the proper maintenance of trails and ranger camps, and the presence of tourists helped to keep poachers at bay (UNEP 1979).

The preservation of historic buildings is often supported or financed by tourism-related interests. The renovation of "old town' districts in the older North American cities is frequently founded on a business sector expectation that it will add to the touristic appeal of these cities. Churches which have lost their congregations have at times been saved by changing to a tourist function, such as a museum or "brass-rubbing' center.

The benefits of tourism extend to our cultural environment and daily life because of the diverse nature of its resource base and the intricate way in which it is woven into a community's regular activities. The presence of tourists often adds to the amenities of local areas. Perhaps the most famous example is the live theater of New York and London's West End, which depends on tourist ticket sales to sustain its existence. Of no less importance to other towns and cities are the tourists revenues which support their pageants, sports events, and tradefairs. "Institutions" such as Paris' Eiffel Tower, Seattle's Space Needle and Science Center, Munich's Olympic Stadium, and Montreal's "Man and His World Exhibit" on the Ile Saint-Ilélène were created for special events and have remained as prime tourist-resident amenities.

A paradox of tourism, however, is that the industry carries within it the seeds of its own destruction. Successful development of a resource or amenity can lead to the destruction of those very qualities which attracted visitors in the first place.

The development of tourism is occasionally undertaken in such haste and without proper planning that it simply outstrips the local infrastructure and resource base, resulting in unexpected costs which further reduce its overall economic benefit to the community. The problem here is tourism's diverse and uncoordinated structure, with numerous individual entrepreneurs striving to make a profit within their own short-term horizons.

> Examples include the construction of hotels on Majorca without proper transport and sewage linkages, the continued construction on both Ibiza and Majorca despite clear warnings of insufficient water, and the rapid and heedless construction of hotels on the coast of Keyna, which now struggle to reach 50 per cent occupancy owing to the unforeseen coincidence of the European tourist season and monsoon rains in Keyna (Dilsaver 1979, 113).

Elsewhere the tourists themselves are the prime cause of environmental damage, although the destruction is usually unintended because most visitors come to admire a scene or event and the businessman's prosperity depends on an amenity's survival. Sochor (1976) reports more than 300 mountaineering expeditions since 1949 have caused widespread deforestation, pasture destruction, and serious accumulation of litter on the slopes of Mt. Everest and other peaks in the Himalayas. Stonehenge has been placed behind a perimeter fence to protect it from the pressure of countless feet which were compacting the soil around the stores and threatening to tilt and topple the remaining inlets.

It becomes evident from this short review that tourism, as an agent of transformation, can change the social, economic, and physical relationships of communities where it has been adopted. These changes are often slow to emerge or to be appreciated because they can be both desirable and detrimental, so when the net balance is finally determined it is often too late to reverse or redirect the development process. In fact a good simile for the modern tourism industry would be that of a household fire. When the fire is contained and managed within the hearth it offers beauty and comfort to the household. When it runs out of control it can destroy the very household it was designed to support.

To maximize the benefits and minimize the disadvantages of tourism's power to transform resources and host communities, it is necessary to formulate clear planning and manage-ment policies. A logical source for such planning would be the government, because "the reasoning prevails that the environment and its resources belong to the people who inhabit an area. Given the outlook, responsibility and accountability for tourism management lie with the government empowered to represent the people" (Kaiser and Helber 1978, 12). Government involvement, however, has been slow to emerge in the *laissez-faire* economies of the west, and has only come to the fore with the development of mass tourism and its consequences on national trade accounts.

Government involvement

Government interest in tourism stemmed from concern over its economic significance, particularly its sources of revenue. According to Lickorish and Kershaw, as quoted by Middleton, this alone was sufficient reason for government intervention in the development of tourism.

> Justification of such intervention is the tremendous financial stake, taxes paid by various enterprises, indirect taxes paid by visitors and the employment

provided in areas where alternative ways of earning a living are pot usually available (Middleton 1974, 11).

Thus, it comes as no surprise that the governments at national and regional levels have been actively promoting tourism and aiding facility development through the provision of grants and subsidies. Britain's Development of Tourism Act (1969) inaugurated that government's formal involvement with tourism planning in response to a growing travel deficit. Its goals were to provide more effective promotion abroad (British Tourist Authority) and at home (Tourist Boards on a regional basis), to encourage hotel construction and to direct development to economically depressed areas. Likewise, the more recent Travel Industry Development Subsidiary Agreements (TIDSA), signed between the Canadian federal government and various provinces, were conceived as a partial response to Canada's growing travel deficit - a deficit which had reached $1.8 billion by 1978. In all these federal-provincial development plans the prime goal was to develop the attractiveness of a province and make it more appealing to forei-gners, especially United States visitors, and Canadians alike. The United States government formally joined in the promotion and stimulation of tourism with its 1981 National Tourism Policy Act, although there had been considerable local and state promotion beforehand. The newly created United States Travel and Tourism Administration's basic mission is "to promote US inbound tourism as an export" (Edgell 1983, 429), in an attempt to reduce its traditional travel budget deficit that has become an increasing burden as traditional visible exports have declined.

The most remarkable case of government involvement in tourism for economic development purposes occurred in Spain. Tourism development and promotion was used as the main financing force for the 1964 Spanish Economic and Social Development Plan. By that time tourism was the largest export sector in the country:

> Earnings covered 82 per cent of the commercial balance deficit, financed about 40 per cent of all imports and equalled 93 per cent of the total value of Spanish exports. Little wonder that a prominent banking concern has likened tourism to "manna falling from heaven, impelled by the favorable wings of stabilization". (Naylon 1967, 33).

Using the momentum of mass tourism during the 1960s, Spain invested large amounts of public and private capital in tourism infrastructure and facilities to provide employment and raise living standards in various regions. These included established tourists destinations in the Belearic Islands and Costa Brava and new developments in underutilized areas such as the Costa de la Luz and Canary Islands. The timing of this investment program was perfect. The 1960s and early 1970s were the prime growth period of international tourism, than many northern European holidaymakers ventured from the fickle weather of their traditional home resorts to seek the sun and novelty of package tours in the south. By 1971, 26 million visitors were leaving $2.2 billion in foreign currency in Spain, and the industry was employing 1.4 million people or 11 per cent of the labor force (Parsons 1973).

Spain's example of tourism-induced economic development has been emulated by Yugoslavia on its Adriatic coast. Three five-year economic and social development plans between 1955 and 1970 specified that tourism be treated as "an activity of special importance for the development of the country in general". Accordingly, facilities were developed for tourists along the Adriatic coast at sites with tourism potential and charter links with western Europe encouraged. According to Mihovilovic, by 1980 it was expected that foreign currency earnings from tourism would amount to $1.2 billion (at 1975 prices).

Over time, government involvement with the industry has extended beyond ecomomic concerns and revenue generation because with its growth came increasing evidence of its physical and social ramifications. First among these is the fact that tourism, like any other economic activity, competes for resources. Government agencies needed to accommodate tourism's growing needs with the demands of more traditional resource sectors like fishing, forestry and agriculture. Furthermore, such concerns over resource allocation had to be accommodated in an era of environmental preservation, brought about by a growing awareness of the world's resource limitations and interrelated ecosystem. In North America's western states and provinces conflicting demands for resource exploitation and recreation have become a major issue for government (Hammond and Andrus 1979; Ingram 1981; *Newsweek* 1983). Federal and state/provincial governments own considerable tracts of land within the Rocky Mountain chain where increasing user pressures have forced them to consider multiple-use and self-sustaining management strategies. Such government policies are needed if the recreation and tourist demands of a growing urban population for lake and ski resorts can be balanced with increased demands for power (hydroelectric, coal, oil sands), the needs of traditional users (forestry, fisheries), and their respon-sibilities to future generations (land reserves, including national and state/provincial parks).

In Europe, the scale of tourism movement and more intensively developed landscape has forced governments to integrate tourism into local land-use patterns and life-styles, or even become directly involved in its development. The British national parks encompass productive farmland and urban areas of considerable size, so their growing popularity as tourist destinations requires careful integration of the leisure industry into an existing economic and social system. In 1974 the Sandford Report of the National Parks Policies Review Committee recommended, and the government accepted, that landscape conservation should take precedence over recreation use. This included a duty to pay heed to the needs of agriculture and forestry, and the socio-economic well-being of local communities. Subsequent management plans of the ten National Park Authorities attempted to meet these requirements. However, not all successive governments have been wholehearted in their support for a conservation priority, and detention of traditional landscapes has come under intense pressure from the growing agribusiness farming methods.

In France the desire to develop a new area of the Mediterranean coast for tourism, to reduce the pressures on the Côte d'Azure and utilize the tourism potential of nearby coastal areas, has led the government to initiate the Languedoc-Roussillon project. Among the multiple purposes of this massive regional development plan (US$18.5 billion invested by 1979) was the creation of five tourist units. The purpose was to raise the income and employment levels of this depressed area, to provide new recreation and amenity facilities for local residents as well as visitors, and to provide an increased opportunity for social tourism projects (Willis 1977; Clarke 1981), The early experiences of the Langyuedoc-Roussillon project have not been as positive as first hoped, especially in terms of stimulating regional employ-ment and economic growth, and now the French government seems to be adopting the view that it takes time for an underdeveloped region to become an established tourist Mecca.

One problem which the French and other governments have come to appreciate is that a major obstacle to development and planning in tourism is the fragmentation of the industry. For many small businessmen tourism is the last bastion of free enterprise, where with relatively little capital but with good timing and good ideas fortunes can still be made. In this sort of atmosphere, to decide on a public policy is one thing, to communicate this goal to all the companies, businessmen, and communities affected, and coordinate their actions is another. The overall fragmentation of the industry makes it easier for development conflicts to arise and facilitates a situation where the final outcome of individual decisions can place a great strain on the natural and human resources of destination areas. As Gunn sums it up:

> the evidence of fragmentation of tourism development is mounting. As the volume of tourism expands and as development increases, many segments of tourism are running on collision courses with growing frequency. These conflicts appear to be expressed in reduced satisfactions to visitors, reduced rewards to owner-managers and erosion of basic resource assets (Gunn 1977, 92).

Acceptance of this fact has compounded government involvement with tourism, for it alone possesses the necessary financial resources and legislative power to redirect and coordinate the industry along more desirable courses of action.

Government response to this fragmented growth industry, its numerous resource demands and various impacts, has been the gradual creation of tourism departments and ministries and an evolution of policy. In most western governments tourism agencies have been linked with trade and commerce ministries, reflecting its business orientation in legislative minds. In a few national and state/provincial governments where tourism has grown into a major economic activity, often within the top three activities in terms of employment or revenue, it has been accorded its own ministry. The initial goal of many agencies was to assist in the creation of an attractive and competitive tourist product. This involved cooperation with the industry and related government departments to stimulate business and supplement facilities through promotion and physical planning. Millions of dollars were spent on the promotion of traditional and new destinations in the belied that the economic return on such "investment" would be justified. New facilities were encouraged through subsidies, tax incentives, or outright grants, especially in areas of high unemployment. This economic and plant inventory emphasis, however, has gradually been replaced by a more comprehensive planning approach as the complexity and impacts of the industry have become apparent.

Fragmentation of the industry, which has been viewed as a barrier to comprehensive development and maximization of revenue, still retains some merit if it forms the basis for local diversity and character. The joy of travel includes noting regional variations in landscape and culture, as reflected in local architecture, customs, and food. Memorable visits can be made by the personal touch of individual owners and operators. Therefore, the problems of fragmentation must not be confused with, or transposed into, the boredom of conformity and mass production.

Mings considers the tourists industry's development prospects are at a crossroads and government involvement will play a major role in its future. As he sees it:

> Rapid growth of any industry requires considerable study and planning in order to maximize its potential assets and minimize its potential liabilities. Commonly, tourism has not received the benefits of sufficient research to enable proper planning. Consequen-tly, development in most places falls short of achieving optimum impacts. Simply, too many countries have plunged headlong into an activity with inadequate and, occasionally naive understandings (Mings 1978, 2).

Governments, according to Mings, have three options in the face of this situation. First, there is the "no change" option, which consists of ignoring those problems and protests associated with the industry. Such a "hands off" approach is likely to be hazardous for both tourism and the government because the industry depends on local support and no elected government can disregard unpopular and unsuccessful activities for long. Second is the alternative course of action of withdrawing public support for tourism and even attempting to curb private promotion of tourism. In this case a danger exists that government officials under attack may react prematurely, without the benefit of adequate investigations. It may be the case that "whereas at one stage a few years ago officials jumped on to the tourism bandwagon with unwarranted haste, many are now in danger of jumping off in much the same unreasoned fashion" (Mings 1978, 3). The third option is to pursue rationalization of the industry so as to render it more beneficial. The involves an assessment of the industry's problems and prospects, followed by a plan of action to remedy weaknesses and direct the industry toward long-term goals. Underlying this option, Mings outlines two major issues:

1. Can the various objectives to tourism be remedied satisfactorily? And if the answer appears to be yes:

2. Will the contributions (economic, social and environmental) of the surviving industry be of a sufficient magnitude to warrant public support? (Mings 1978, 3)

As Mings notes, none of these three options exist in their pure form, but "most countries have borrowed some characteristics from all three options." The rapid and inadequately planned growth has created a myriad of unexpected and undesirable problems, placing tourism development at a crossroads. Either the industry's shortcomings will be attacked and its potential benefits realized, or the necessary public support will be redirected to other areas of social and economic investment.

Community Approach

The purpose is to examine the two issues raised by the Mings and offer a method by which the industry's contribution can be directed toward community goals, and thereby warrant public support. The industry possesses great potential for social and economic benefits if planning can be redirected from a pure business and development approach to a more open and community-oriented approach which views tourism as a local resource. The management of this resource for the common good and future generations should become the goal and criterion by which the industry is judged. This will involve focusing on the ecological and human qualities of a destination area in addition to business consi-derations.

A community approach to tourism management requires a complex combination of interlocking parts, leading to a general goal that can be identified and measured. The objective of this strategy is to produce a "Community Tourism Product" which like the traditional tourist product will be an amalgam of the destination's resources and facilities, but in this case it is one which the community, as a whole, wishes to present to the tourism market. To research this goal three separate stages are identified and discussed.

The prime consideration in any planning or management scheme is what components to consider. In this case environmental and acessibility considerations have been selected first because of the industry's dependence on its resource base and connectivity with tourist-generating areas. The presence of resources and a potential market, however, do not necessarily make a viable industry, so business and economic considerations need to be considered next. In addition, the fact that tourism is so dependent on local hospitality makes it mandatory that development proceeds in accord with the desires and customs of local people, thus social and cultural considerations need to be included. Finally, management of a community product provides a range of options. By placing tourism in a community perspective it becomes only one of several functions and opportunities for an area, and must be planned in accordance with its relative importance and contribution.

Within each of the four consideration areas certain major issues have been selected to illustrate the relevance of a commu-nity approach to this activity. They are not intended to represent all the issues within each area, but from past experience they are general problems and once which have persisted under the old *laissez-faire* or elementary planning strategies. These represent the objections to tourism, which Mings referred to, and need to be remedied if tourism is to have a future.

To ascertain if the problem areas can be rectified, various response strategies have been examined. They have been selected in terms of a community relevance, to demonstrate the feasibility of using this approach. Again the list is not meant to be all, inclusive but has been based on community-oriented response strategies used around the world.

Travel Management Strategy

In recent years we have been inundated with advice on how to formulate a strategy. It is something we know we should do, yet sadly we do not do it, preferring to operate via the "seats of our pants". We read books on the subject, attend strategic conferences and, in some instances, even propound our own theories. Yet somehow, true strategy never sees the light of day.

When something does emerge then, all too often, at the first setback or sign of retaliation, the strategy is either abandoned or, despite market changes, blindly adhered to. Why do we so often fail to establish a workable strategy? Is it just a question of inertia? Are we the innocent victims of an unpredictable market, or are we terrified about being first with anything new? Do we subconsciously fear the implications of strategy, hindered by too many 'ifs' and 'buts'. Have we any real idea of where we want to be? Is, for example, Hertz just a car hire company or does it knowingly use car hire as a means to earn insurance commissions?

The answer is rarely simple. It usually stems from a mixture of all these questions and the false assumption that the market will keep on growing. The pattern of economic and social life, however, is changing; calling for newer and more segmented approaches to the market and—perhaps only by the 1990s—will analyssts be able to make a more balanced judgement of where the industry has made mistakes, and where it has got it right.

In this chapter we seek to hightlight the need for strategic focus, its elements, potential obstacles and the actual process of strategy formulation. Before embarking on such a major under-staking, it is important to look at the people angle. This should not be viewed in terms of 'customer smiles', but in terms of how many potential customers for our services that actually are.

The Environment And The Need For Strategic Focus

In Europe, more than in the USA, the age tree is inverting: there are fewer productive people supporting more non-productive people. This definite trend primarily affects health and social security schemes, but it also has very significant implications for travel and leisure. Furthermore, the pattern of family life is also changing with the emergence of single parent families, a shorter working week, working mothers and a more sophisticated, experience-hungry youth segment.

Since the last war there have been dramatic changes in the economic fortunes of the industries and services making up the world economy. We have seen in manufacturing and industrial companies a disastrously slow response to change; failure to utilise resources effectively and efficiently and an inability in many instances to adjust costs and product offerings. The service industry, particularly in the travel field, could so easily fall victim to this malaise unless there is a move to re-think strategies in terms of cost structures and marketing opportunities.

The competitive pressure, no one can doubt, is on, forcing travel com-panies to tread new paths; challenging old ideas and tearing down traditional boundaries, often for the wrong reasons. In Europe we are beginning to emulate the American preoccupation with change. Change is equated with progress and progress with success. The drive is for the new. As we shall elaborate later, these beliefs originate from new competitors or existing market leaders, and lead to reactions from others, reactions which must be anticipated and evaluated. The inevitability of retaliation is fact, for most travel companies are market driven, seeking the same solution. Few like to innovate, most like to copy. This is perhaps why we are beginning to see only the enlightened few reassessing their roles and the validity of their strategies in the market. Often this reassessment originates from panic as newcomers poach market share. We cannot stress often enough that companies should identify what they want to be, against what they actually are and plan according to their objectives. Managers, according to Peter F. Drucker, live in two time-periods—that of today and tomorrow. In turbulent times, such as we are facing, no manager can assume that 'tomorrow will be an extension of today'. We must plan, if we are to grasp the advantage.

Those of us who are ready for, and accept and exploit, change will be the winners. Throughout this book our common message has rested on the need for five vital characteristics:

— Knowing what you are—leader or fast follower;
— flexibility;

- speed of response;
- assurance of continuity;
- positioning.

We can no longer think in terms of 'the usual', for rapid and abrupt change prevents that. Our strategy as managers must be 'taking advantage of new realities, and to convert turbulence into opportunity'.

Although some of the elements contained in this chapter apply more to the larger firms in the travel industry, small firms will also benefit from this approach. What we are advocating is that all companies, no matter what their size, must anticipate or even create environmental change. At the same time the companies need to move forward in a controlled and planned fashion. Unfortunately, the high degree of capital investment required increasingly makes flexibility and speed of response difficult. This automatically gives the newcomers a competitive advantage, particularly when dealing with the latest 'travel fad', or technology.

Who will Create The New Strategies?

The drive should come from within, for nothing can really replace entrepreneurs. Without their vision, drive and skills little can be achieved. However, the challenges which face them are complex, requiring core abilities to analyse the environment, see through its complexities, and to induce and pilot the organisation through the process of change. Where these entrepreneurs will come from is difficult to say; all we can ask is they are capable professionals who anticipate and utilise the external and internal potential of a company. Here there must be an understanding of the need to reduce the dominating role price plays. To avoid reduced margins and potentially damaging price wars, managers should continuously strive to differentiate their service offerings so that non-price competitive comparisons will play an increasing role.

What Must The Leader Review?

The company headed by the conductor/manager needs to review the challenges the future holds in terms of:

- changing growth patterns;
- unpredictability;
- demand life cycles;
- technology and delivery systems;
- accountability—to shareholders, employees and customers;
- core business;
- capital requirements.

Having obtained this strategic information, he needs to develop the corporate ability to create and operate a strategy. He needs also to balance the problem of getting weighty systems—controlled organisations—to move rapidly. He needs, above all, to understand his company's corporate capability.

Understanding Corporate Capability—Not Just A Philosophy But an Approach

In an attempt to create a working format for strategy, it is essential to identify, probably via a management workshop, the major areas of consideration. This is also a means of diagnosing the company's general management ability.

The workshop should use as its basis an analysis, preferably provided by an outsider, of the company's overall strengths and weaknesses and its multicapability relationship with its external and internal environment. Amongst the areas for consideration would be:

1. past and present performance;
2. competitive position;
3. life cycle balance in terms of products/ services;
4. market trends;
5. staff—in terms of synergy, resourcing, hiring, training, evaluating and rewarding;
6. long term objectives/short term objectives—assigning priorities;
7. capital requirements;
8. strategic planning;
9. timing.

The 'workshop', will obviously be the beginning of what can be described as a long, painful process. It is an opportunity to question much which has gone before, re-examining values and corporate goals. The process is dynamic rather than destructive and, through full management participation, change can be institutionalised and a strategic mentality evolved. It is also an opportunity to establish a review group who will help to keep the strategy flexible, so that corrective actions can be taken and resources swiftly reallocated.

In reality, the 'workshop' is an activity which is made up from a large number of component parts; parts which help to build a launching platform for the company's future activities. What is exciting about the workshop approach is that it is more pragmatic, more tailor-made to the real-life problems and opportunities facing the individual firm. This is in marked contrast to the US strategic models which usually assume a business system and culture which often does not exist in other countries.

The Concept Of Strategic Planning

Potential Traps—People And Their Attitudes

Most of us are aware of the hazards and pitfalls out there in the market. A major potential source of concern is the corporate culture, the beliefs and attitudes of the staff. One way to spread new values is to build a team of key opinion leaders, originating from the 'workshop', who can lead and communicate beliefs within their spheres of influence. Because corporate culture and people are difficult to change rapidly, the time span of such an activity is inevitably long.

Let us look at the typical response of most employees: they do things their way; whatever gives them the least hassle. We all recognise and know this characteristic. The travel agent will usually recommend the most accessible tour operator, where ease of response is evident and efficient. Those tour operators who complicate life or create problems will be avoided. The same applies to recommending insurance, car hire, travellers cheques and any other ancillary services.

The airlines, tour operators and hotels have to remember that it is their distributors who initially deal with customers and wield tremendous power over client choice. Thus, when creating a strategy, the entire concept of service to the customer must be marketed not just to one's own employees but also to those of the distributors. Any supplier who overlooks the key role the distribution partner plays, is creating a potential weakness in his own company's activities.

Business rationale and strategy must be clear, avoiding the need for middle managers and staff to read between the lines. Ideally, a shared vision has to be developed enabling everybody to understand why a particular strategy has emerged. By simple illustration, employees can readily see at what stage of development their organisation is at (see Table 1).

Fundamentally, we are talking about making employees understand why times are changing and what options are open.

Corporate Options—The Choice

1. Survival/Divestiture—strengths and weaknesses, life cycle problems;
2. Current Position Maintenance—inelastic market/defensive;
3. Expansion—distinctive competence competitive advantage—Successful company strategy;
4. Diversification - make/buy (often a result of analysis in point 1), within the industry/outside.

Presenting employees with the basic four options companies have, and the actions each demands, helps employees to understand the vital elements concerning strategy. They learn to realise the importance of the match between an organisation's resources and skills, and the risks and opportunities present in the environment. It helps them, too, to understand how the company actually makes its money, not always via the core business. It makes for accountability: vision is improved.

Strategies Of The Winners

Who are the winners? We hesitate to mention names because of the volatility of the market, choosing rather to look at the constituents of a winning strategy.

1. Low cost distribution—understanding the business, its development and trends;
2. Concentration on customer group and sales channel—matching them up;
3. Opportunistic use of technology;
4. Differentiating the Services/Products offered: which is done in relation to perceived value to the customers and the cost differ-entiation in relation to competitors:
   (a) Specialised services—e.g. Business Travel A/C Management, free travel to airports, frequent flyer programmes;
   (b) Ego products—Golden cards, Concord flights, Orient Express, etc;
   (c) Standard products—Package holidays, car hire;
   (d) Standard services—Luggage labels, in flight meals, terminal facilities;
5. Understanding the need for both competitor focus and market focus;
6. Avoiding competition on price alone. Constantly looking for competitive differentiation and value added;
7. Consistent management objectives;
8. Measuring performance in wealth creation and cost effective overheads;
9. Constant review of market attractiveness in relation to competitive position;
10. Ongoing search for new products/markets, understanding the importance of fringe activities;
11. Strong flexible organisation, vision and leadership.

What Must Be Reviewed?

Basically, the 'winners' maintain an ongoing review of the possible directions their strategies can go.

1. The improvement of competitive performance;
2. Changing the method of competing;
3. Establishing new products and markets.

The Losers

Let us now identify the characteristics of the losers—the ones lagging behind in strategic management, the ones who need to change to survive. What observations can we make about them?

- Lack of strategic problem solving—inflexibility;
- Limited awareness or interest in business trends;
- Too inward-looking;
- Too much emphasis on budgeting planning;
- Lack of strategic focus;
- Unclear cost and service balance;
- No real market position;
- Poor use of marketing techniques;
- Poor use of technology—lack of flexibility in systems;
- Poor leadership;
- Short term management—crisis management;
- Contradictory goals;
- Failure to monitor or evaluate changes.

The losers (or would it be better to say the potential losers) have five options:

1. Improve market position by evaluating profitability of each activity;
2. Exploit synergies;
3. Move into related businesses;
4. Diversify into new markets;
5. Leave the industry.

Each option requires some form of activity and each activity must be viewed against four basic accepted projections about the future.

1. The travel environment is changing;
2. The momentum of change will be rapid;
3. New concepts are needed in relation to products and their life cycles, distribution, cash innovation, timing;
4. The age of information and customisation.

Today, with the help of a computer and relevant data, a strategy can be formulated. However, danger looms when the strategy needs to be converted into plans and activities. Management is in many companies too thinly stretched, preventing radical and pertinent ideas being carried through.

We see decisions being taken, but, due to the multiplicity of activities and diversity of client relations, not carried out. It is too often forgotten that a main strategy creates and is dependent on mini-strategies, which need to work and develop in harmony, if the overall picture is to be achieved. When concentrating on the mini-strategy, sight should not be lost of the overall goals.

To understand this complexity, it helps to create a total framework of the strategy formulation procedure (see figure 10.2) plus a planning and execution chart. The framework should ensure systematic informed decisions are made, programmes for imple-mentation prepared, and would make for the measurement of actual results against criteria. A planning and execution chart should also be designed in such a way as to create and maintain commitment to the overall goals. It should clearly show each area of activity and responsibility, demonstrating how the mini-strategies interlock. It is important to note the way an organisation structures itself, for strategic decisions may differ from the way it operates in managing daily activities.

Additionally, it will encourage the creation of permanent and 'ad hoc' teams. By this commitment, performance expectations will be huge, with the emphasis on continuous improvements which reflect the requirements of the marketplace. If this commitment is missing, then any new strategy will flounder, leaving a company distinctly more vulnerable than before.

Below is a framework for the formulation of strategy. As a rule, during the early stages of transformation, few immediate changes can occur in the basic structure of the organisation. It is easy to attempt to change too much too soon. How rapid will be the transformation in workforce strategy? Hard facts on this subject are difficult to come by. We have observed the work done is SAS and BA, and, although these organisations have adopted a comprehensive version of the commitment approach, it is probably true to say that, to date, only the transitional stage has been reached.

The diagram shows the various stages and variables involved in the process. Each one must be identified and the role it plays understood. It must also be viewed in conjunction with a competitor analysis (see figure 10.3) in order to ascertain an even clearer picture. From all this there would evolve the strategic plan. The strategic plan is the key document which gives guidance and allocates resources. All of us associated with this book believe that not everything in the strategic plan can be based on fact. Certain assumptions about the unknown have to be made.

We have deliberately refrained in this book from discussing the strategic plan in depth because of our belief that the only advice we can extend is that of Drucker who believed it to be a document which will 'organise systematically the effort'. The plan should be designed to be ready for any contingencies should the basic assumptions on which the strategy was built change, or if the strategy fails. After the contingency element has been developed, then a mechanism must be built into the company's monitoring and control system which will bring it into action at the appropriate moment.

What Is The Message?

We think strategy is important. We advocate that its formulation should be managed and not left to chance or overlooked. We need it to identify and develop goals and objectives, to recognise strategic issues and to match them to our existing resources.

Each chapter of this book has sought to give, in a practical and realistic way, a variety of opinions for the future. Much of what we have written is experience-orientated and attempts to bridge the gap between theory and practice. That is why we offer fig. 10.4 as a practical methodology. The Strategic Tree highlights a timespan of activities which, once set in motion, will ensure the right combination of products, services and markets is selected.

We have deliberately omitted the element of capital investment in this chapter, due to the wide differences and needs for fixed assets and equipment etc. All we can stress is that strategy must take into account careful resources. The synergy between needs and capital must be absolute to harness the potential of the company in the market place. Here again each individual company, using sound research and a degree of anticipation, must create its own equation. The worth of each project must be weighed up in relation to net value and calculated risk. What must at all times be remembered is that greater stress needs to be placed on managing financial costs and risks, without crippling entrepreneurship and morale. The only limit to new kinds of financial instruments and techniques seems to be human ingenuity.

There are immense challenges facing us all, for it is a new surprising world, of which nobody is the master. As the travel industry continues to develop and newcomers bring in new dimensions, one thing will remain constant—the need for informed, hands on, heads up management. Really there is nothing else you can rely on!

Tourism Management Strategy

It's known as the "smokeless industry". It's now the world's biggest. And increasingly, tourism claims to offer a sustainable development option to countries short on cash but long on environmental riches. In fact, tourism, even ecotourism, is causing widespread environmental and cultural disruption. In this article, Sue Wheat compares the best of ecotourism with the rest.

"Wanted—an Island to buy or rent" reads an advertisement in the *Belize Review*, giving an Arizona contact address. Now that Belize has become a mecca for nature lovers—especially from its neighbour the US—such advertisements are commonplace. With its idyllic tropical island cayes, the second largest barrier reef in the world, abundant flora and fauna in spectacular rainforest and ancient Mayan ruins, this small, Central American state attracts huge interest from both pleasure seekers wanting to get away from it all and keen-eyed investors.

However, Belize is just one of many developing countries which has seen a rapid expansion in its tourist industry. Cheapter flights and increased leisure time have stimulated a dramatic increase in "long-haul" travel, in many cases to parts of the world that other industries have never touched. Thirty years ago, few peopole could have imagined the ease with which it is now possible to reach the remotest corners of the world. Today, the search for the exotic destination is on with a vengeance. The combination of palm-fringed islands, adventure, intriguingly different clutures and strong Northern currencies, has meant that international tourist arrivals in developing countries have more than doubled since 1976.

According to the World Travel and Tourism Council (WTTC), tourism is already the world's largest industry and is growing at a phenomenal rate—23 per cent faster than the overall world economy. The number of people now travelling for tourism purposes is around 500 million and is expected to rise to 937 million by 2010. For an industry which doesn't have to manufacture anything itself and simply exploits ready-made features, these are astounding figures.

But just because the tourism industry does not have factories does not mean that its impact on the world is negligible. In fact, the "smokeless industry", as it has been described, is increasingly being blamed for massive envirnmental cultural and social damage. In a 1992 report entitled "The Tourism Industry and the Environment", the Economist Intelligence Unit (EIU) aruges that a growing number of disasters such as polluted beaches, degraded corel reefs, wildlife parks without wildlife and disappearing indigenous cultures, are the result of tourism and are "part of an accelerating pattern".

Growing awareness of these problems and pressure on the tourist industry to become environmentally friendly have prompted a search for alternative froms of tourism". "Ecotourism", "responsible tourism", "sustainable tourism", and "low-impact tourism" are just some of the terms used to describe these new approaches. Ecotourism is one of the most commonly used, referring to a niche market for environmentally aware tourists who are interested in observing nature. But what started off as a small-scale, locally-owned initiative is now succumbing to overdevelopment. Ecotourism has become the fastest expanding sector in the industry.

The ecotourist mecca

Although tourism has only become an important factor in Belize's economy in the last decade, it is probably the world's most famour ecotourist destination today and has hosted two major international ecotourism conferences. Tourism revenue now accounts for 26 per cent of its gross national product (GNP) and international tourists number around 250,000—a massive increase from the average figure of 11,000 in the 1960s.

As has happened in many developing countries, Belize is caught in an economic Catch 22 and is looking to tourism for a way out. A drastie fall in world market prices for its cash crops forced the country to find other source of foreign exchange, much of it needed to meet obligations on its $103 million foreign debt.

But like other countries which have taken this route. Belize did not take account of the likely enviornmental consequences of promoting tourism. These impacts are most graphically illustrated in coastal areas where the ecosystems are particularly fragile. "Coastal development in Belize involves the clearing of mangrove swampland, drainage and infilling, using topsoil literally shaved off the wetland savanna a few miles inland. This involves the destruction of two distinctive ecosystems," explains Erlet Cater, Senior Geography Lecturer at Reading University and an expert on sustainable tourism in Belize.

Ironically, the international standard Biltmore Plaza hotel, the venue for the 1991 Caribbean Ecotourism conference, was built on land reclaimed in this way. And hotels are themselves far from benign in their effect on the environment, argues Cater. In fact, their impact can be disastrous. In catering to western standards, for instance, hotels use up large amounts of energy and generate huge quantities of waste.

Attempts to protect the environment on which Belize's national income is so dependent are now underway. There new protected marine areas have been declared and the Government is cooperating with various environmental organisations. Coral Cay Conservation, a non profit-making British marine research group, provides scientific expertise and resources to help develop management initiatives for the protection and sustainable use of the country's coastal resources. And Edinburg University's grography department is mapping the country's mangroves with satellite imagery, as part of a plan to control and coordinate tourism development, urban expansion, fisheries, coastal protection and timber use.

Coral Cay Conservation works closely with local government departments and trains local people in scientific techniques, so that the project can eventually be Belizean-run. "We are there to protect the biodiversity of Belize, but the last thing we want to do is say tourists can come and look but the fishermen can't fish," explains Samantha Flint, manager at Coral Cay Conservation.

Flint feels that the erosion of the indigenous culture and the exclusion of local people from tourism policy are storing up problems for Belize. With an estimated 90 per cent of coastal building development now under foreign ownership. Belizeans may already be permanently alienated from their own land.

Ian Munt, who has worked in Belize as an urban planner, and Egbert Higin to, from the University of West Indies in Belize, have investigated the impacts of tourism on the country and maintain that "despite some promising results, much ecotourism in Belize merely replicates the problems characteristic of traditional mass-tourism—foreign exchange leakage, foreign ownership and environmental degradation."

They point to the $50 million "sustainable tourism" development on the highly developed Ambergis Cay as an example of how ecotourism is simply being used as a marketing label. The Belizean Government bought back two-thirds of the 8,000-hectare cay from its US owner in an attempt to "reinvest in the Belizean people" and proposed "an integrated and ecologically sound resort development" for the caye. However, this includes at least one international hotel, two "all-inclusive spa hotels", three to five upscale lodges, two golf courses, 1,000 luxury homes, polo fields and stables. As Munt and Higinio point out, "it is difficult to see how this development really differs from any other".

Trickle-down effect

Belize is Certainly not alone in suffering these problems. The Western desire for the exotic has been identified by many developing country governments as the route to easy wealth and a panacea for various economic ills. However, the proverbial economic trickle-down effect invariably means just that—a trickle. While tourism employing more than 127 million people worldwide, in developing countries, the local people normally work in menial, seasonal and low-paid positions, with managerial jobs going mainly to expatriartes working for multinationals.

Transnational corporations (TNCs), such as airlines, hotel chains and building giants, now dominate the industry and much of the financial benefit. Many of these TNCs have a turnover larger than the gross domestic product of the developing countries in which they operate. According to the World Tourism Organisation (WTO), at least 55 per cent of the foreign exchange earned by tourism leaks back to developed countries through spending on imports for the tourist industry, such as fittings, foodstuffs and labour. In some Caribbean countries, this figure may be as much as 70 per cent. Although the developing world increased its share of international arrivals during the 1980s, its share of tourism revenues actually fell, according to an EIU analysis of WTO figures.

Across the world, the hidden costs of tourism are often severe. On the resort islands of Thailand, much of the indigenous population has been forced to migrate, because the price of basic necessities and land is beyond their purchasing power. In many developing countries, children skip school to sell to tourists, and traditional livelihoods are abandoned. Local farmers and landowners in tourist destinations are often harassed by developers wanting to build on their property; fishermen are prvented from using public beaches taken over by hotels.

In Tanzania, the Government forced the Masai from their centuries-old homeland in the Ngorongorn Crater, in order to open up the park for tourism. As a result, posing for photographs is one of the only ways they can avoid poverty. The indigenous Berawan in Sarawak are in a legal battle with the Royal Mulu Resort Hote, which is planning to expand and construct a gold course on their ancestral land. The Berawan stress that they welcome tourists, but they are concerned that they might loss their Native Customary Rights to land. "Although most of Mulu workers are Berawan, they do not hold any position or partake in the development process within Mulu. Is this development for us? Certainly we are left out," says a Berawan statement.

However, many local communities aronud the developing world have had enough to being exploited by the tourist industry and are trying to garner a better share of the proceeds. The Toedo Ecotourism Association (TEA)—a grassroots organisation of Mayan indigenous people in southern Belize—is organising village stays for tourists in settlements built by the Mayans with local materials. Tourists are looked after by the villagers themselves, ensuring that all the financial benefits are kept within the community. Special emphasis is put on preserving their ancient culture and fragile environment. Aware of the danger of their tourism business becoming a "monoculture", the TEA members are also developing a firm agricultural base. Their main product is cocoa, which they are selling to a UK company for organic chocolate.

Cash for conservation

Village Communities in Zimbabwe are taking a similar approach to a different tourist resource. By joining the Communal Areas Mangement Programme (Campfire), they acquire ownership of the wildlife in their area and profit from it by charging tourists who want to take part in sustainable hunting and photosafaris. "In a country where 95 per cent of the population had been forced into 30 per cent of the land mass during colonial rule and wildlife had been given 15 to 20 per cent of the land, the people had great animosity towards wildlife," explains Keith Madders. Director of the Zimbabwe Trust, which manages Campfire. Now that the wildlife has an economic value for the community their attitude has changed. As a result, Campfire has lifted many people out of poverty, often doubling their income. Many animals once under threat of extinction are also out of danger, as it is in the communities interests to deter poachers.

The maoney from tourism is paid directly to the Campfire communities and used at their discretion. The people of Mahenya have so far funded a school, a clinic and a grinding mill with their profits. In 1992, the community decided to distribute the $70,000 (£7,700) made from hunting four elephants and one buffalo between each of 391 houscholds, giving each one $180 (£20) cash after costs were deducted. In rural Zimbabwe, that is a useful sum, even if it's not a fortune. There are now 22 districts involved in Campfire—a rapid growth from the two that existed in 1987—and it is expected that similar project will start in other Africa countries.

While community-based initiatives may be more socially beneficial than mass tourism, they are not without their problems. How long will a low-impact project stay low impact once it is successful? How can such groups compete with the discount-prices of the large tour operators? The EIU concludes that "the future of tourism, therefore, must lie in the way mass tourism is conducted and not in a move to 'alternative' tourism."

The WTTC suggests environmental protection is best achieved through voluntary codes of conduct. Its Environment Research Council lists more than 100 agreements and guidelines. They also point to the "International Hotels Environment Initiative", with its manual of good environmental practice for hotels.

However, Tricia Barnett of Tourism concern maintains that the tourism industry has to go beyond cosmetic environmental changes. It must accept that " the environment" includes both the natural and social environment, she says. "While the tourism industry is patting itself on the back for recycling brochures or reducing energy consumption, the really serious social issues such as displacement of people from their homes, loss of livelihoods and lack of access to public land are being ignored."

Voluntary regulation have certainly not helped those currently fighting to save their land and livelihoods. Some 50,000 Sri Lankans demonstrated against the building of the Kandalama Hotel on an important local reservoir. Campaigners are seeking to deter European tour operators from using the hotel, which is set to open this year. In West Java, farmers have been harrassed, imprisoned and their homes burnt down after peacefully demonstrating against their illegal eviction by a company planning a tourist resort and golf course on their land. The case of one farmer imprisoned for 10 months have now been taken up by Amnesty International.

For travellers searching for the exotic, and for the industry itself, it is a psychological hurdle to accept tourism as a human rights issue. But this is what is has become. The ever-increasing number of tourists will continue to cause cultural disintegration, the marginalisation of local people and environmental degradation, unless the tourism industry, government and local communities work together. Tourism is no different to any other multibillion pound industry. Even in Paradise, profits have priority over people. One can only hope that community-based tourism initiatives will be able to prosper enough to give Paradise fack to the people who live there.

Contemporary Global Tourism Strategy

Increased affluence, leisure time and travel facilities in recent decades have made tourim a new and significant part of human experience. Here we look at what the phenomenon, couched in endless statistics, means to the geographer.

As recently as the 1950 the word 'tourism' was so little used that the average layman might have been forgiven for thinking it was some sort of eastern religion, along with Buddhism or Hinduism! Today tourism is a word on everbody's lips—both in the industralised world and, increasingly, in the Third World. According to the World Tourist

Organisation (WTO), tourism has seen a growth of 1,600 per cent over the last 40 years. That is more than 'impressive growth'; it is an explosion.

Tourism has recently been described as a $2 trillion industry, making it the largest single item of world trade. While the validity of that statistic may be questioned, all trends suggest that by the end of the century it will be the most important economic activity in the world. (The WTO's more conservative estimate has tourism accounting for 12 per cent of the world's gross national product, and over five per cent of world trade). Already tourism creates 100 million jobs, which means that it employs more people than any other industry. One in five workers is employed in tourism-related acitvity.

Fundamentally, tourism is a geographic phenomenon concerned with the movement of people from place to place. Geographers study the spatial expression of tourism as a human activity. There are three main geographical components to this movement: (1) Generating areas (where tourists come from); (2) Tourist destinations; (3) Routes travelled between locations. This last point — tourist flows between regions — is fundamental to the geography of tourism.

From a geographical point of view, tourism and tourist flows can be considered on a number of scales, from the global level, through the regional, down to the local level depending on the detail required. Despite the fact that the number of international travellers has increased sixfold since 1960, tourism remains very much a 'first world' phenomenon. Two-thirds of international visitors arrivals are concentrated in just 20 industrialist countries, and 90 per cent of the world travel markets in the developed nations. The United States is the largest single market (21 per cent), followed by Spain, France and the UK. Europe together accounts for per cent of the world travel market.

As lifestyles become more affluent so more and the people are taking holidays abroad. It is predicted international arrivals will have increased from the current level of about 360 million to 600 million by the end of the century.

But while the relative importance of domestic tourist is declining in many countries, it still remains cornerstone of the industry, particularly in the U.S. Probably 90 per cent of the total tourism flows in the world are domestic, though this is difficult to - since even a family day out in the car or a week-end at the 'in-laws' is generally classed as 'tourism'. The encompasses much more than the two-week packed tour. It also covers business and official (government) travel, which itself accounts for one-third of the total industry.

Several questions need to be addressed. Firstly, it has there been such an explosion in tourism general. Secondly, what are the factors which influence tour flows? And thirdly, what is the scope for the future of the tourism industry?

There are several reasons for the extraordinary growth of tourism? The principal determinants of tourism and leisure activities are personal income and availability leisure time. Both have grown at record reates for industrilized nations during the last 25 years. Before 1960's, half the working population of Britain had holiday entitlement of a week or less. By the late 1970 the whole working population of the European countries had paid holiday entitlement of three weeks or more— addition to bank holidays, and weekends. Never before have so many people had so much leisure time.

Another vital factor accounting for the upsurge of travel —especially overseas travel — has been technological advances made in the field of transport. Mass air transport in fuel-efficient widebody jets has to a dramatic reduction in airfares, and and increase speed and comfort of travel. Car ownership has increased dramatically. In the UK only one-in-ten of the population had use of a car in 1960; today there is an average of almost one vehicle per family. The mobility the population in the industrialized world has been increased, making travel easier and cheaper than before.

Paradise lost?

Europe may ne our favourite location but long-haul holidays are also popular as high-rise hotels and crowded beaches in Rio prove.

Relative distance reduced

Much lower airfares, coupled with increases in the speed and comfort of air travel, have opened up and attractive and fashionable way to spend leisure time. Packages tours bringing Europe within easy reach, are now affordable by most people.

UK Training and career opportunities in tourism

In the last few years the numbers of tourism related courses in the UK has mushroomed at all levels. An indicator of the interest in the field is the success of the new GCSE in the Travel and Tourism. This is believed to be the first school-level qualification which has direct industrey involvement: American Express, British Tourist Authority, Trusthouse Forte, Crest Hotels and the International Leisure Group are all working with Local Concils in a project known as the Travel & Tourism Programme. It is expected that around 120 schools will be offering the new GCSE course in September this year.

Many Colleges of Further Education now offer tourism as part of a business course or in other guises, and several Polytechnics and Universities are offering a variety of tourism options an dcourses. Undoubtedly the largest and best-known department is at Surrey University, headed by Professor Steve WAnhill. The undergraduate courses here lean towards hotel management. Three graduate courses, aimed at managerial level, are also popular: Tourism Studies is a more general course, while the planning/development and marketing courses are aimed at more specific elements of the industry.

Statistics, tourism research & planning

One of the problems which has plagued the tourism industry kis a dearth of credible staistics and information. This has resulted in a ageneral lack of planning, and masking of the importance of tourism in the eyes of policy analysts an ddecision makers . Partly because tourism has been seen as the domain ofthe private sector, and partly becayuse the industry is so diverse and segmented, development has been largely unstructured and ad hoc. Co. operative data collection efforts and data-sharing kagreements are rare in the private sector, despite the potential mutual benefits to be gained when several organizations work together.

There is, therefore, a pressing need for much more high-quality research in order to generate consistent and credible statistics. Although most countries have data-collection precedures, there is significant vaiation in the quality of the data collected. The validity of international tourism statistics is notoriously suspect. Despite the efforts of the Would Tourism Organization (WTO) and the Orgainization for Economic Cooperation and Development (OECD) variations in definitions, data-collection methods and accounting still exist between countries.

The WTO's statistics are based on and attempt to collate the record of all arrivals in all countiris. They give a useful guide to the total volume of world tourism, but at the national and regional level such figures are less than satisfactory, partly due to a failure to distinguish between short-stay, long-stay and transit visitors. The lack of standardized procedure and definitions makes comparisons between different countries difficult.

The other main source of tourism statistics in the UK is the International Passenger Survey. (Business Monitor MAC: Overseas Travel and Tourism, published annually by HMSO). This is based on sample surveys of visitors on departure and arrival, and is carried out by the Office of Population Censuses an dSurveys for the DTI. For detailed national and regional tourism statistics, this may show trends more realistically simply because the figures have the consistency of having been obtained by the same standarized procedure for many years.

Much more research also needs to be carried out at tourist destinations on host communities. Methods for estimating the impact of tourism on communities are still in their infancy. A better understanding of this topic would allow the more efficient distribution of resources between competing claims and help to ensure that the environmentally and socially unacceptable side-effects of tourism are minimized in future. "Although research is expanding all the time, there is much more to be done," said Professor Steve Wanhill, of Surrey University. "We want to ensure that host communities will get the best mix of tourists to fit in with their culture."

Quite apart from the lack of hard research results, another continuing source of frustration for tourism planners and analysts is the lack of consistent and universally-accepted definitions. For example, the very words 'tourists' and tourism have been in use since the early 19th Century yet there is still no single acceted o9perational definition for either. Such definitional inconsistency only further confuses any attempts to compare tourist flows and such related phenomena when drawing on data from diverse sources.

9. Tourism Management Policy

THE PAST few decades have seen a steady expansion of tourism activity throughout the world. International tourism flows have shown considerable growth. Arrivals at international borders rose by about 4 per cent per annum in the 1980s. They now stand at over 400 million. The reasons behind this expansion are complex but certain key influences may be identified. On the supply side, the development of wide-bodied aircraft, and the increase in fuel efficiency, have led to a fall in the real cost of air transport (Edwards (1990) estimates that real international air fares fell by about 4 per cent per annum in the mid-1980). Organizational develop-ments, most notably the package tour, have also reduced the cost of international tourism. On the demand side, the high income elasticity of demand for leisure activities has ensured that the rise in per capita incomes in the developed countries (roughly 3 per cent per annum over the past 20 years or so) has led to a more than propor-tionate increase in tourism. (For a summary of the evidence on income elasticities for foreign holidays, see Johnson and Ashworth (1990) and Colin Crouch's contribution in *Choice and Demand in Tourism*.) Furthermore, the increasing ease of international commu-nications has played a part in generating new consumer tastes in world travel. *Business* tourism, which grew at about 5 per cent per annum in the 1980s, has been stimulated by the expansion in world trade.

International tourism is of course only one element in tourism activity. Intra-country tourism and leisure day trips—the latter are usually excluded from the standard definitions of tourism used in official statistics, but are clearly very closely related to it—are quantitatively very significant. For example it is estimated that in 1989 UK residents spent $10,865 million on staying trips in the UK and around $4,500 million on day and half-day leisure trips. These figures compare with earnings from visits to the UK by overseas residents of $6,945 million and overseas expenditure by UK residents of $9,357 million. Not surprisingly, in the USA domestic tourism is over-whelmingly important, accounting for 90 per cent of all travel expenditure.

THE CASE FOR A TOURISM POLICY

The development of tourism raises substantial policy issues. Two reasons for this are that tourism may generate significant externalities and that it is of considerable economic importance as an activity. Each of these reasons is examined below. It is probably true to say that the emphasis in tourism research to date has been on the measurement and evaluation of the economic importance to tourism. This emphasis is reflected in the balance of topics dealt with in the following chapters. However, the externalities generated by tourism have recently attracted increasing attention they are therefore given relatively more weight in the following discussion. There are of course other relevant policy considerations.

EXTERNALITIES

Externalities may be positive or negative. Positive externalities may arise (for example) because tourism puts an area 'on the map'. Another reason may be that attractions that are only viable as a result of visits by tourists may satisfy the 'option demand' of those who value the existence of the attraction because it preserves their *option* to visit at some future date, even though in the event they may never exercise that option. Non-visitors may also attach a positive 'existence value' to an attraction because they derive benefit from the fact that it exists, quite apart from whether or not they have visited it or might to do so.

It is the negative aspects which have received most attention and which are therefore the main focus here. Tourism may impose costs on others that are not fully reflected in the market prices paid by tourists. The presence of such externalities means *inter alia* that, even in a competitive market, buyers of tourism services do not always pay a price that reflects the true cost of the provision of those services—because suppliers do not have to meet all the costs incurred by their activity—and that as a result 'the market' generates a socially inefficient level of tourism activity.

Negative Externalities and the Environment

A Broad View of The Environment

A key mechanism through which negative enternalities arise is the degradation of the environment. As Howard Green and Colin Hunter point out it is helpful to take a very broad view of what constitutes the 'environment'. The term may be taken as referring not only to the atmosphere and the natural environment (e.g. mountains, countryside and coast) but also to social relationships, the cultural heritage and the built environment. Thus where tourism leads to the destruction of, say, centuries-old social customs or ties, or to the wearing out of ancient buildings, it may be said to be destroying the environment. In some cases tourism may develop to such an extent that it destroys the very phenomena (e.g. uncrowded beaches, solitude in the country) from which it was originally designed to benefit; see Mishan for an early graphic treatment of this issue.

Inter-Generational Issues

The adverse environmental impact of tourism may be felt not only by the current generation, but also by future generations. Thus if this generation's tourists wear out a staircase in an ancient building, future generations will be denied *for ever* the chance of using that same staircase. Replicas may of course be used to replace the original staircase, either before it is worn out, thereby enabling it to be removed to a place of safety, or after it has reached that stage. This in turn raises questions about the relative merits of usage and observation of 'the real thing', and about how the needs of one generation of tourists are to be traded off against those of another. Such a trade-off is far from straight-forward as it is not known whether (for example) an artefact or experience valued by the current generation will in fact be similarly valued by a future generation. By the same token, something that is considered worthless today may be highly valued tomorrow. One response to this uncertainly is to preserve as much as possible *in case* it is valued later. For an example of this approach in museum collecting see Atkinson (1985). However, preservation is not a costless activity. As a result, the question that arises is: to what extent should this generation incur resource costs to preserve the environment (in its widest sense) for others? Given scarce resources some ranking of priorities is inevitable. In some cases the maintenance of the original facility may not be valued highly. Here, replacement or restoration may be an appropriate response and raise no question over which generation should benefit from the original, although it will never be certain that fashions will not change and that no subsequent generation will value the original. However, it is likely that few visitors will object to a path being resurfaced with stones brought from elsewhere, unless of course the path happens to be along Hardrian's Wall. Where restoration is an appropriate policy, questions of the generational distribution of the costs and benefits still have to be resolved.

The Sustainability of Tourism

In recent years considerable attention has focused on the *sustainability* of the environment a concept that has been applied to tourism development (English Tourist Board/Department of Employment, 1991). A key element in such sustainability is that the future enjoyment of an environmental resource should not be prejudiced by current activities, i.e. the present generation should pass on the resource intact to the next generation. Such a concept, involving as it does the notion of trusteeship, is intuitively appealing, but it does raise important issues of resource allocation: as indicated previously, it requires decisions on *what* and *how much* to preserve. The inherent attractiveness of the idea of sustainability does not of itself generate additional resources.

Externalities and Property Rights

The presence of negative externalities (and indeed of their positive counterparts) raises important questions over the allocation of property rights between tourists, local residents and other interest groups. For example, should tourists have the 'right' to impose noise and congestion on local residents when they visit a beauty spot, and should the local residents have a 'right' to an environment free of congestion and noise? Should developers be free to destroy a good skyline by the insensitive development of multi-storey hotels, or should residents have a right to the protection of their skyline? Do tourists visiting a cathedral have the 'right' to restrict the activities or access of regular worshippers or do the latter have precedence? Clearly, how property rights are allocated will determine the distribution of the gains and losses arising from tourism activity, although it may be argued, following Coase (1960), that an efficient level of tourism activity will result, whatever the allocation of rights, provided this allocation is clearly defined and bargaining between the parties is costless.

Externalities: The Policy Response

In assessing the scale of tourism externalities and what policy responses might be made towards them, it may be helpful to bear the following points in mind. Firstly, some of what may at first sight appear to be external effects may be reflected to a greater or lesser extent in market prices. For example, higher traffic congestion will tend to raise costs and hence prices. Again, if land and facilities become more scarce their prices will rise. Of course, increased congestion and more built-up areas may also reduce demand (at each price), in which case prices could *fall*.

Secondly, the existence of a negative externality may not always lead to 'free riding' on the part of those organizations and individuals who generate them, but who are not, for various reasons, contractually liable for them. They may be willing to 'pay' something towards the costs of restoring facilities that they have played a part in destroying, either by donations or by taking voluntary corrective action. Indeed the more pressure that is put on economic actors to behave 'responsibly' towards the environment, the more externalities will become internalized. It is interesting to note that the more competitive a market is, the less likely it is that any one firm in the market will be able to contribute unilaterally to the costs of restoration for which they have no legal responsibility.

Thirdly, the existence of market 'failure' arising from the existence of externalities does not of itself necessarily mean that the case for some form of government intervention has automatically been made. Such intervention itself involves resources. It may also generate further distortions because of *government* 'failure', derived, for example, from government officials pursuing their own objectives, which may not be compatible with the achievement of a socially optimal level of tourism activity, or from unanticipated side-effects of policy.

Faced with the existence of externalities, the government has a number of policy options that it could explore. Possibilities include: moral pressure; legislation which restricts certain activities, defines property rights more fully or imposes compliance costs on firms or individuals; subsidies; public ownership; or taxation. Little work has been done on the relative merits of the different options.

THE ECONOMIC IMPORTANCE

The second reason why tourism raises important policy issues is the scale and nature of the economic activity involved. There has been much debate about the appropriate boundaries for tourism employment (for a review, see Johnson and Thomas, 1990). However, if the figures presented by Gary Akehurst are taken as a broad guide, tourism is clearly a significant employer, accounting for between 5 and 10 per cent of all employ-ment in ten European Community member countries. There has also been substantial growth in recent years. Ray Hudson and Alan Townsend estimate that there was an increase of nearly a quarter in direct tourism employment in the UK between 1981 and 1989. As these authors point out, the encouragement of tourism is often seen by policy-makers as a particularly useful way of combating unemployment because many of the jobs have a relatively low skill requirement and may be especially suited to young people. Furthermore, parts of the industry are relatively labour intensive; this is likely to mean that a given amount of assistance towards capital investment in the industry will generate more jobs than elsewhere. There is a further reason why tourism appears attractive as a vehicle for alleviating unemployment. Some tourism development may be footloose in the sense that it could be located in any of a number of possible locations. It may therefore be possible to locate such development in areas where the employment effects are most beneficial. Whether the employment (or indeed any other) characteristics of tourism *justify* policy intervention is another matter.

Tourism employment is also economically important in terms of GNP and the balance of payments. Akehurst's figures suggest that in nine of the eleven European Community countries for which data are available, tourism accounts for 4 per cent or more of GNP. And in eight of these countries the percentage share of travel receipts in total export earnings is over 5 per cent (in three, it is over 15 per cent).

There is a further characteristic of tourism connected with its economic importance that deserves mention. While, as indicated earlier, the high income elasticity of demand for tourism means that such demand will grow more rapidly than incomes, it also means that tourism is likely to be relatively sensitive to economic fluctuations. This in turn will generate problems, particularly in downturns.

It is in the context of the significance of tourism for policy that Keith Hartley and Nicholas Hooper addressed a range of fundamental questions on the role of public policy in tourism. A particularly interesting question is whether market failure in the tourism field might be most appropriately dealt with via general policy measures, given that similar types of failure exist in other economic activities, rather than through a specifically *tourism* policy. They also point out that the self-interests of particular groups, including government officials and politicians, may lead to *government* failure. Their analysis is particularly refreshing in that it raises important issues that have received scant attention in the tourism literature, although they have been the subject of considerable treatment in other contexts.

Howard Green and Colin Hunter broaden the policy discussion with a detailed consideration of the relationship between tourism and the environment in its broadest sense. They also examine the way in which a formal environmental impact assessment (EIA) can be used to aid decisions over tourism developments. They apply EIA in a case study which utilizes the Delphi technique to assess 'expert' views. It would be helpful to see how a rigorous environmental evaluation of this kind could be incorporated into an *overall* appraisal of tourism developments. How, for example, might environmental factors be compared with the economic characteristics (e.g. employment and incomes) of a project?

Ray Hudson and Alan Townsend focus on the characteristic of tourism employment—a preoccupation of policy-makers—and the implications of tourism development for policy at the local level. The first part of their chapter provides a critical review of tourism employment statistics available in the UK. It shows how misleading a superficial treatment of these statistics can be. The second examines local authority decision making processes with regard to tourism and the role of employment statistics in those decisions. It is striking that many authorities are basing policies on a slim or non-existent research and database. The authors also raise the question of the extent to which tourism-promoting agencies at the local level are playing a zero sum game.

The emphasis is on different methodological approaches to the estimation of the impact of tourism. Lino Briguglio calculates tourism multipliers for the Maltese economy using both a Keynesian model of the economy and input-output data (the advantage of the latter is that it enables sectoral breakdowns to be made). This study provides policy-makers with a means of estimating the impact on the economy as a whole, and on particular sectors, of a change in the level of tourism activity. The chapter shows that considerable and painstaking effort is often required before official published statistics can be used for this purpose. Furthermore, care must be taken to bear all the limitations of the exercise firmly in mind.

Stephen Wanhill considers manpower planning in tourism and utilizes an input-output model for Nepal as a basis for such planning in that country. Interestingly, the data as far as tourism is concerned appear much richer for Nepal than for Malta. Wanhill shows how the resultant manpower forecasts can be used as an input into the formulation of an educational strategy for the sector. The results are of course only as good as the assumptions and data on which they are based. However, they are superior to the available alternatives. Provided the figures are used for guidance rather than followed slavishly, they can be of considerable value in stimulating a more rigorous approach to tourism policy.

Marion Jackson and David Bruce, is in one sense much more narrowly focused in that it examines tourism in a fairly small market town in the UK. In another sense it is more wide-ranging in its assessment of impact, since it considers the environmental and other non-economic aspects of that impact. There are two particularly distinctive features of the study reported by Jackson and Bruce, Firstly, it is part of an *ongoing* monitoring of a tourism development programme, the results of which are to be fed into the planning of subsequent phases of the programme. Such close interaction between research and policy is rare, Secondly, it pays attention to the explicit specification of the objectives behind the programme. Clearly stated objectives are an essential prerequisite for any evaluation.

These are primarily concerned with the magnitude of the economic impact of tourism in a variety of locations. Mary Fish's concern is with evaluating the impact of some university football games on the local economy (Tuscaloosa County, Alabama). Her study draws on previous work at other universities and on an established econometric model for the economy to derive employment and income estimates. These estimates are directly relevant for decisions on the future capacity of the university's stadiums, which are currently unable to cope with the demand.

James Deegan and Donal Dineen report on an impact study of three tourist attractions in Ireland. Their paper demonstrates the formidable difficulties involved in estimating the full effect of tourism at the micro level. The extent to which employment and incomes generated by expenditure *outside the boundaries* of the attractions by visitors to those attractions can be attributed to the existence of the latter is a particularly thorny problem. Another difficulty is the estimation of the extent to which demand, and hence employment, is simply diverted to the attractions from elsewhere. Two conclusions of the study are worth noting. Firstly, it shows that visitors' 'associated' spending, i.e. that taking place outside the attractions, is very significant in determining the economic impact. Thus the measurement of 'attribution' may be vital to the assessment of economic impact. Secondly, Deegan and Dineen emphasize the importance of the displacement factor. In considering whether to provide public support for a project, policy-makers must always be aware of possible negative 'knock-on' effects.

The economic impact of tourism in the Province of Antwerp is done by Dirk Yzewyn and Guido De Brabander by using a variety of approaches and data—all of which have limitations, as the authors are careful to make clear—to estimate this impact. Not surprisingly, they identify wide variations in the average daily expenditure of different categories of tourist. Their study further highlights the importance of short visits not involving an overnight stay, a category of visit often excluded from conventional definitions of tourism.

Brian Goodall and Mike Stabler, provides a detailed treatment of the policy implications of a specific recent development, that of timeshare. Their chapter shows that these implications are complex, involving a wide range of considerations, including consumer protection and care of the environment. It also raises some fundamental questions—for example in relation to why the competitive process does not itself lead to the elimination of 'sharp' practice—which need further investigation.

Steve Curry examines the way in which economic policy has affected the tourism sector in Jamaica. His particular concern is with the effects of structural adjustment policies introduced as a condition of assistance from international agencies. He is especially interested in the hotel sector. Curry's contribution provides some helpful insights into the variety to ways in which economic policy can affect the tourism industry. It also shows how the component parts of a particular sector, such as hotels, can be affected differentially by economic policy.

Gary Akehurst takes an altogether broader perspective, and looks at the development of tourism policy in the European Community. As he shows, this development has been slow. One possible reason for this has been the lack of clarity on precisely what role (if any) a supra-national organization such as the European Community has to play in this area. Akehurst is right to stress the importance of basing any policy on sound statistical information and on an intimate knowledge of the industry itself.

This provides an indication of some of the concerns of researchers working in the tourism field. It also offers a basis, albeit a partial one, for considering possible future directions for research. As far as the economic perspective is concerned, it is probably fair to say that the 'impact' literature is now reasonably well established. Economic impact studies, using a variety of methodologies and data sources, will continue to be undertaken, and in increasing numbers as tourism grows in significance. Although much more attention needs to be paid to the concepts and measurement of attribution and demand diversion in the analysis of the impact of particular attractions, it is unlikely that the basic framework for such studies will change in any dramatic way. However, this framework could be extended to deal with a number of questions which are of direct policy relevance but which have not been addressed in any sustained way. For example, relatively little is known about the way in which tourism activity is affected *at the margin* by changes in policy or public funding. Impact studies do not typically ask what would happen if, say, public assistance were to *change* by x per cent.

There are also more fundamental economic questions to be asked about tourism policy. For example, little detailed analysis has been made of the underlying economic rationale for the public funding of tourism promotion and development. It is not self-evident that governments should be involved (at least to the extent and in the way that they currently are) in this area. In this context it would be helpful to have more firm evidence on the effects of public policy and institutions, and to explore more fully the kinds of issues raised. Another area in which work could usefully be done is in the relationships between individual (publicy financed) local promoters of tourism (regional tourist broads and local authorities): to what extent are they involved in a zero sum game? The same question is relevant when relationships between local and national bodies are considered. A further issue of direct concern to the appropriateness of public assistance for tourism is the extent to which the economic actors involved do in fact utilise mechanisms other than commercial transactions to 'pay' for negative externalities that they generate.

Although the methodologies of economic impact studies of the conventional kind may be fairly well developed, the same cannot be said for studies which take a broader view of the effects of tourism. Given the growing concern with the environment (in its broadest sense), there are likely to be considerable gains from adopting a multi-, or inter-, disciplinary approach to impact analysis. Such an approach would present some major methodological challenges, not least those relating to the way in which different 'costs' and 'benefits' might be weighted in any overall assessment of the effects of tourism. Economists have made considerable strides in recent years in attempting to value costs and benefits for which appropriate market values do not exist—recreation and the arts have been an important area of study—but the perspectives of other disciplines would be vital in this kind of study.

There is clearly much policy-relevant tourism research to be undertaken, much of it involving the application of established methodologies from other disciplines, such as geography, psychology and sociology. If this has implicitly or explicitly helped to identify potentially fruitful areas for future work, it will have succeeded.

Tourism Management Policy Formulation

Tourism policy is implemented through the efforts of tourism organizations. The functions of international, regional, and national organizations are examined in regard to their role in carrying out tourism policy.

The efforts of the US public sector to establish tourism policy are traced from 1940 to the present, and problems with and primary functions of organizations at the national, state, and local levels are outlined.

Reasons for Public Sector Involvement

There are several reasons why the public sector should be involved in tourism. First, there are political reasons. Tourism by its nature involves travel across national boundaries. Government must get involved in terms of policies relating to the procedures regarding the entry and exit of travellers and nationals. The encouragement of tourism can be used for political purposes—as a means of furthering international relations between two countries, or as a means of enhancing the national and international image of a particular destination.

Second, there are environmental reasons for public-sector involvement. Tourism "sells" such things as the scenery, history, and cultural heritage of a region. One of the dangers of tourism is that in attempting to make the national environment more acceptable to a foreign market, the true nature of that environment, physical or cultural, may be lost.

Last, there are economic reasons for public sector involvement in tourism. It is an export industry. In order to maximize tourism's economic advantages to the host country, the government, to some extent, must get involved.

The type and amount of government involvement will vary from country to country. The greater the importance that the government attaches to tourism, the greater will be the involvement. The conditions existing in the country will also affect the type and amount of government involvement. The political/economic/constitutional system is an important factor. We would expect the level of involvement of a socialist government to be greater than in a country that has a predominantly free-enterprice philosophy. The level of socio-economic development is another important factor determining the level of a government's involvement. The greater the economic development of a region, the less the need for government involvement. In connection with this, the maturity and financial capabilities of the private sector will have to be considered. The greater the capabilities of the private sector, the less the need for public sector involvement.

PUBLIC SECTOR ROLES

Coordination

The public sector often plays a co-ordinating function. Coordination is necessary among the many governmental bodies concerned with different aspects of tourism. Immigration may, for example, wish to relax the frontier formalities in order to expedite the entry of tourists into a country. The obviously will aid tourism. The appropriate agency for drug enforcement may be against this proposal of relaxation, though, for fear that it will increase the flow of drugs as well as tourists into the host country. Some kind of coordination is obviously necessary. Coordination is also necessary among government at the federal, state, and local levels. To be truly effective, tourism within a country must be coordinated so that all regions are moving toward the same goals. For the same reason, coordination is necessary between the public sector and the private sector as well as between the public sector nonprofit organi-zations. Many educational and cultural organizations, although they do not have tourism as their major focus, do much to provide resources that attract tourists. The private sector is obviously very involved in tourism. To avoid duplication of effort, it is vital that goals and strategies be coordinated.

Planning

In countries such as Algeria and Israel, government gets into the planning of tourism development. National tourism development plans are drawn up in which the government decides which sectors of the various tourism-related industries will be developed, what the appropriate rate of growth will be, and who will provide the needed capital for expansion. The key is to balance the development of supply (attractions, facilities, and infrastructure) and the promotion of demand (the number of tourists).

Legislation and Regulation

An important role of government is that of legislature and regulator. Government legislation can affect the number of paid vacation days during the year and hence the amount of discretionary paid time available for vacations. Policies on passports and visas have to be determined. A visa is required for tourists from Europe entering the United States; the reverse is not true. The appropriate policy is determined by the government. Government influence may also be felt in the regulations necessary to run a tourism business. In some countries, guides must be licensed. Businesses may have safely and health regulations to abide by; they may also have to meet zoning, building, and licensing requirements. The need to protect the resources that attract tourists may result in restrictions regarding entry to and use of fragile natural resources. Tourists are no longer allowed to enter certain European monuments, and in the United States the national parks have certain areas set aside as wilder-ness, the use of which is severely limited.

Entrepreneur

The public sector will generally provide the infrastructure for tourism development in a region. In addition, however, government gets involved in owning and running attractions and services. Many countries operate state-owned airlines, and in Greece, Spain, and Portugal the government owns and operates hotels.

Stimulator

A government can stimulate tourism within a country, state, or locality in one of three ways. First, financial incentives, such as low-interest loans or nonpayment of taxes for a specified period of time, may be offered to induce private-sector investment. Second, the public sector may sponsor research that will benefit an industry in general rather than one company in particular. For instance, research may be conducted on the characteristics of a particular foreign market. The results then can be made available to those in the private sector who can develop their own plans to attract this market to use each particular facility. Last, government can stimulate tourism by spending money on promotion. The effort should be aimed at promoting the entire country or state, and it usually consists of travel promotion aimed at generating tourist demand. In some cases, it may also involve investment promotion aimed at inducing capital investment for tourism attractions and facilities.

Establishing a tourism policy

It should be clear that whether those in public sector like it or not, they are involved in tourism. To guide its actions and the actions of those in the private and nonprofit sectors, it is advisable to establish a tourism policy.

The policy acts as a set of guidelines to determine which specific objectives and actions should be pursued to meet the needs of those in the particular destination areas under consideration.

A Model for Tourism Policy

The process by which tourism policy is formulated. The many needs of a region are identified by using appropriate research techniques. Tourism goals reflect these needs, but they are constrained by the existing market and resource factors. A series of programs or strategies will flow from the overall policy that is aimed at achieving goals and satisfying previously identified needs. Also, the constraints of market and resource will be changed as a result of feedback resulting from the generated policy. The model will now be explored in greater depth.

Goals

Goals for tourism have to be set before policy can be developed. However, it is crucial that goals for the tourism sector not be set in isolation. For example, there is a very close link between tourism and recreation.

It can be argued that tourism is a form of recreation involving overnight travel or a certain distance away from home.

Tourism goals must also be formulated to agree with the broad national interest and to complement the specific objectives of national, state, and local bodies in related fields. A recent US study has identified the following principles of national public policy by which the federal government achieves a consensus for guiding federal legislation. They can be used as an expression of the US national interest:

Energy conservation
Full employment
Economic growth with minimum inflation
Improved operation of the federal government
Environmental protection
Judicious use of natural resources
Urban revitalization
Preservation of national heritage resources
Consumer protection
Equal opportunities for people in disadvantaged segments of the population
Improved physical and mental health
Reduced international trade deficits
Equitable taxation
Economic viability of small businesses
Minimum regulation of private industry
Improved international goodwill
Balanced national transportation system

Against this backdrop of national interests, tourism goals can be developed along four lines—economic, consumer, national resource/environmental, and govenment operations.

Constraints

Before specific objectives can be developed in the four above-mentioned areas, it is necessary to consider some constraining factors. Constraints may be external or internal to the host destination. External constraints are those outside the control of the host destination.

External: Because the volume of demand for vacations is closely related to levels of disposable income, policy is constrained by general economic conditions in the tourist-generating countries. A stagnant economic situation suggests that one plan for, at best, limited growth and a policy of improved quality rather than quantity of resources.

Policy is also constrained by the world energy situation. The price and supply of gasoline particularly affects destination regions that rely upon auto tourists. The overall effect of an increase in the price of gas or uncertainty over gasoline supplies may be a reduction in the number of auto-based tourists, a redistribution of tourists to more accessible areas, and a more centre-based vacation than a touring one. Such a situation will have important policy implications for the development of facilities and the encouragement of public transportation.

The travel potential of various segments of the market will also influence policy. For example, the best potential for increased package holidays to Scotland is from Southern England because of rapid access by public transportation, particularly by air. This suggests that on make policies regarding the development of public transportation.

Climatic factors constrain the types of tourism that can be developed. For example, the climate of Scotland is regarded unfavorably by many people in Britain. To a certain extent the image is not totally justified and may be remedied by promoting the seasons when the climate is conductive to vacations. If poor weather limits vacation activities, the obvious implications for policy makers is to develop more wet-weather facilities.

Internal: Internal constraints, although influencing tourism policy, can be modified as the result of the policy created.

The quality of attractions and available facilities limits, for example, the type of vacations that can reasonably be attracted. The US market is very accustomed to private bathrooms in hotels. If these are lacking, a policy implication may be to allow financial incentives to modernize existing facilities by building more rooms with private bathrooms. Facilities that have been built private bathrooms will not be eligible for such aid.

It has been noted earlier that tourism policy cannot be separated from recreation and leisure policy. The use of attractions and facilities by the local population has to be considered as a possible constraint to tourism policy. In and around urban areas to may be that only a small portion of the recreational capacity will be available for tourists, particularly on weekends. On the other hand, certain cultural and recreational facilities may be viable and available to the local community only because of support from tourist demand. The extensive theatre facilities in London are a prime example. Many of these theatres rely upon tourist traffic to make them commercially viable. If this demand were not present, many theatres would be forced to close and this resource would be lost to the local population.

The availability of both land and investment is also of concern to destination areas. Particularly in small areas, difficult decisions must be made regarding appropriate land use. In the United Stated considerable controversy has arisen over the use of public land for wilderness or recreational use. The scarcity of investment money raises particular problems for a destination country. The lack of money for investment will prevent tourism development, but the encouragement of capital from outside the area will result in a loss of local control. This problem is felt not only by countries but also by local areas within a country that seek financing from domestic sources of capital. Decisions to expand, contract, build, or close facilities—decisions that vitally affect the local community—are decided by people outside the community.

The availability of manpower also acts as a constraint to tourism policy. Tourism is a people industry. The characteristics of the tourism industry create particular employment problems. Tourism jobs are often seasonal and low-paying. In order to deal with the public form another social class and culture, it may be necessary to learn different behaviours or different ways of serving food than those used in the home. In some cases, U.S. hotel companies, prior to the opening of an overseas property, have had to support the development of a school for training local employees in methods of serving the American market.

Tourism Goals

The tourism goals set will be tempered by the constraints already discussed. Typical tourism goals are:

Economic: To optimize the contribution of tourism and recreation to economic prosperity, full employment, regional economic development, and improved international balance of payments.

Consumer: To make the opportunity for and the benefits of travel and recreation universally accessible to residents and visitors.

— To contribute to the personal growth and education of the population and encourage their appreciation of the geography, history, and ethnic diversity of the nation.

— To encourage the free and welcome entry of foreigners, while balancing this goal with the need to monitor persons and goods entering the country with laws protecting public health.

Environment and natural resource: To protect and preserve the historical and cultural foundations of the nation as a living part of community life and development, and to insure future generations an opportunity to enjoy the rich heritage of the nation.

— To insure the compatibility of tourism, secretional and activity policies with other national interests in energy development and conservation, environmental protection, and judicious use of natural resources.

Government operations: To harmonize to the maximum extent possible all federal activities supporting tourism and recreation; to support the needs of the general public and the public and private sectors of the industries involved with tourism and recreation; to take a leadership role with all those concerned with tourism, recreation and national heritage conservation.

Tourism Objectives

Once the above-stated broad goals are made, conflicts arise when specific objectives are set. Conflicts may arise between goals or within goals. For example, should casino gambling be encouraged? To do so may be consistent with an economic goal, but it may conflict with a consumer goa. Trinidad and Tobago have decided that permission will not be granted for the operation of gambling casinos. Although they recognize the earning potential of casinos, it is felt that the social cost will be too great. Similar fears for their citizens have stopped several U.S. states from allowing casino gambling. Similar conflicts can arise within goals. For example, encouraging foreigners to visit existing tourist ports of entry, the international balance of payments may be improved, thus helping achieve part of an economic goal, but it will not be compatible with a desire to maximize regional economic development.

Only when local interests weigh what is best for their community, what meets the community needs, will such conflicts be solved in the best interests of the community.

Tourism Policy

The agreed-upon objectives, formulated to meet set goals, constitute the tourism policy of a destination area. The many alternative ways to meet tourism's goals have been resolved by Trinidad and Tobago in such a way to arrive at a basic policy statement.

Because the country's resources and facilities must be directed primarily to serving the needs, comforts, and enjoyment of its own citizens, the general public is guaranteed access to all beaches in the country and no discrimination is allowed against any person on the grounds of race, colour, class or religion.

Although the likely earning potential of casinos is great, because the social

Tourism Management Policy

cost is too high a price to pay, permission will not be granted for the operation of gambling casinos.

Although the major attraction for tourism arises out of the culture of the islands, any program for tourism development must include positive measure to protect the country's art forms and the artists who perform them from wanton destruction.

Because tourism employs either directly or indirectly a large number of persons, it is important that clear evidence exist that a person of any race, class, colour, or religion be expected on merit to aspire to the highest positions of employment in the industry.

A fair share of the investment in tourism must be reserved for the small entrepreneur, either by way of participation in larger projects or by way of small hotels and guest houses.

Firms engaged in tourism development will be required to show that effective decision making is vested in citizens of the country.

The entire industry must take steps to reverse the trend of relying heavily on imports, and it must more vigorously seek to maximize the use of local goods and services, particularly in the fields of food, drink, entertainment, and professional and consulting services.

Tourism Programs

Working with the set policy, developers will set up programs to meet the stated objectives. Examples include programs establishing specific investment incentives, programs setting immigration rules, programs organizing the tax structure, and promotional campaigns aiming at a specific target market. The successful completion of these programs will result in the objectives being met. This in turn will affect the internal constraint as it moves toward meeting the agreed-upon tourism goals. As stated earlier, these goals are set in line with the needs of the community.

TOURISM ORGANIZATIONS

World Tourism Organization

Many types of organizations have formed at the international, national, and local levels to develop and implement tourism policy. The only organization that represents govern-mental tourist interests is the World Tourism Organization, which is based in Madrid. Formed in 1975 from the international Union of Official Travel Organizations, WTO is the official tourism voice to the United Nations. The organization generally aims to promote and develop tourism and specifically pays attention to the interests of developing countries. To this end, the WTO collects information and issues publications on such subjects as world tourism trends, marketing approaches, and the protection of natural and cultural resources. Training programs are conducted and work is undertaken to make foreign travel easier in such ways as reducing the number of passport and visa requirements and standardizing the travel signs.

International Civil Aviation Organization

Established in 1944, the International Civil Aviation Organization (ICAO) is make up of representatives from the governments of eighty countries. The principal task of the ICAO is to promote worldwide civil aviation. To achieve this, international standards and practices regarding air navigation have been adopted. Proposals have been developed for the construction of facilities and the reduction of frontier formalities to help ensure the growth of international civil aviation in a safe and orderly way.

Regional Organizations

Many organizations have come into being to assist in the development of tourism in different regions of the world. Some, such as the Organization for Economic Cooperation and Development (OECD) were established for reasons of general growth and stability. Within OECD a tourism committee was established to deal specifically with tourism, including the assessment of the effect of member country policies on tourism.

In other cases, organizations have been created to implement policies to develop, promote, and facilitate travel to specific regions of the world. PATA, the Pacific Area Travel to Association, was organized in 1951 promote travel in the Pacific area. Similarly, the Caribbean Tourism Organization and the European Travel Commission have been organized to assist the Caribbean islands and Europe, respectively.

National Organizations

The tourism policies of a country are developed by and implemented through a national tourism organization (NTO). An NTO is the official body responsible for the development and marketing of tourism. The functions of the official tourism organization will vary according to the governmental status it is given. First, it may be governmental part of a civil service system as either an independent ministry, such as the State Secretariat for Tourism in Maxico, or as a part of another related ministry. In France the Stage Secretariat for Tourism is part of the Ministry of Cultural Affairs and the Environment, but in Spain the Ministry of Commerce and Tourism contains the national tourism organization. Approximately 30 per cent of World Tourism Organization members have an independent ministry for tourism.

Second, the official tourism organization may be a government agency or bureau responsible for tourism and set within a larger department. Tourism Canada, formely the Canadian Government Office of Tourism, is located within the Department of Regional Industrial Expansion, but the Japanese Department of Tourism finds itself as part of the Department of Transportation. The govenment agency has, in general, less influence and status than the ministry form described above. Mexico, for example, has an independent government agency called the National Tourism Council that is responsible for international promotion but that reports to and receives policy guidance from the above-mentioned State Tourism Secretariat. Tourism bodies that have governmental status heave the broadest range of functions of NTOs.

Third, the official tourism organization may be a quasi-public government-funded corporation, board, or authority, such as the Hong Kong Tourist Association, the Irish Tourist Board, or the British Tourist Authority. A key advantage of the government-funded board is that it has greater management flexibility in dealing with the commercial aspects of tourism development and promotion. A closer liaison with the private sector and the consuming public is possible. In fact, members of the private sector are often asked to serve as board directors.

Last, the official tourism organization may be a private industry association indirectly supported by government funding, such as the Japan Tourist Association. Less than ten per cent of WTO members have a national tourism organization that has non-governmental status. A primary advantage of having a government agency as a national tourist organization is that the NTO has the authority within government to represent tourism and develop and interpret tourism policy.

Functions-supply

As the text has noted, the functions of the NTO will vary depending upon the governmental status given to it. To some extent, the NTO will be involved with the supply of and demand for tourism facilities and attractions. This involves conducting an inventory of resources prior to the formulation of a general plan for tourism development. In fewer cases, the NTO will get involved with maintaining the quality of the tourism product. This may include protecting the environment that tourists come to view or setting standards in hotels or for tour guides. NTOs in free-enterprise countries tend to have less input into any of the aspects of quality control. The input of the NTO in free-enterprise economics will probably be limited to the giving of advice on the effects of industry practices on tourism. When another agency sets policy that affects tourism, the NTO may have some advisory input into that policy.

Although the state's role in economic activities in free-market economies is generally confined to legislation and regulation, the role of the state in socialist countries is quite different. In such countries the government may actually get involved in owning and managing tourist facilities. Developing countries that lack private industry capital and expertise have often found it necessary for the state to develop, own, and manage facilities and attractions. To further ensure the proper development of supply, it may be necessary for the government to get involved in the areas of financial incentives to ensure facility development and manpower development to produce sufficient numbers of qualified personnel. Table 11.4 contains the results of a comparative study by Arthur D. Little of the tourism functions of developed countries.

Functions-demand

On the demand side, NTOs tend to get involved in matters of facilitation, promotion, market research, and representation at the international level. The role of the NTO in facilitation tends to be an advisory one, commenting on the effect of government policies regarding visas, passports, and custom formalities on tourist demand. National tourism organizations are primarily known for their role in marketing.

US INVOLVEMENT IN TOURISM

Prior to World War II the federal government of the United States had done little to involve itself with either domestic or international tourism. In 1940, however, the Domestic Travel Act was passed. This act authorized the National Park Service, a part of the Department of the Interior, to promote and administer tourism functions of the department. World War II halted any plans the NPS might have had. After the war the National Park Service was faced with restrictions of budget and a need to expand park facilities to meet the increasing numbers of park visitors. Thus, travel activities were given no attention.

At the same time, two developments led to a tourism balance of payments deficit for the United States. First, Americans were encouraged to visit Europe to help the divested European economies. This was partly justified by the argument that the inflow of US dollars would better enable Europe to purchase American goods. Second, many foreign countries, because of their need to acquire American dollars, restricted foreign travel by their own citizens in the immediate postwar years.

In 1960, President Eisenhower proclaimed a "Visit U.S.A. Year," but felt that, although government involvement in tourism could be justified on economic grounds, it was not a proper function of government to advertise and promote travel. Pushed initially by the Senate Commerce Committee, the International Travel Act, passed by Congress in 1961, established the United States Travel Service within the Department of Commerce. The USTS represented the first real attempt to promote the United States to foreigners. The office was authorized to set up overseas office and to promote and advertise US' travel destinations in foreign countries. The goals of the USTS were to:

Contribute to the maximum extent possible to the balance of payments position of the United States of America.

Contribute to the maximum extent possible to the health and well-being of the American people

Contribute to the maximum extent possible to international good-will and understanding

> Emphasis was placed on the economic goal of achieving as favourable a balance of payments position as possible.

By the mid-1960s the travel deficit had increased to $1.6 billion. In an attempt to reduce this, President Johnson proposed in 1968 the imposition of a tax on international tickets and a reduction in the duty-free allowance upon return to the United States. The proposal was not enacted because of the widespread opposition generated. Recognizing that a travel deficit could be reduced not only be discouraging American travel abroad but also by encouraging foreign travel to the United States, Congress in 1970 amended the 1961 International Travel Act to authorize matching funds to states or nonprofit organizations for projects aimed at promoting foreign travel to the United States. At the same time the position of director of the USTS was elevated to that of assistant secretary of commerce for tourism.

In 1975, the authority for domestic tourism that the secretary of the interior had agreed to transfer to the secretary of commerce was given to the United States Travel Service, which was later renamed the US Travel and Tourism Administration. Passage of the National Tourism Policy Act in 1981 ended an eight-year industry lobbying effort. The act, which survived strong objections from the executive branch including a presidential veto, has resulted in the US Travel and Tourism Administration being headed by an undersecretary of tourism, which is an elevation in status from an assistant secretary. Funding, however, has been kept at a level so low, having declined from $30 million in 1977 to a proposed $0 in 1984 (this will probably result in a compromise of about $6.5 million), that meaningful activities at the federal level have been effectively stymied.

Present Role

Problems. The tourism system is comprised of natural resources, attractions, facilities, services, transportation, facilitation, and marketing. The blend of these factors determines the effectiveness of the system. A major difficulty in the United States is that the role of the federal government in tourism is so fragmented that integration of the various tourism elements is exceedingly difficult.

There appear to be over one-hundered different programs in approximately fifty different departments or agencies that directly affect tourism, travel, or recreation. The difficulties caused by this fragmentation are obviously felt in problems of communication. A study by Arthur D. Little found a "widespread lack of understanding among Federal officials of the degree of their agencies' current involvement in and/or impacts on tourism and travel." The study team also found that the federal interagency coordination on travel and tourism was poor to nonexistent. Little or no coordination existed between those agencies viewed as influencing tourism and the USTTA. There was general agreement that there were too many federal programs involved in an aspect of tourism and no effective means of coordinating existing efforts, resulting in an ineffective federal involvement.

Marketing. The marketing aspect of tourism lies in the hands of the US Travel and Tourism Administration, which is a part of the Department of Commerce. The agency is primarily concerned with overseas promotion, although a certain amount of market research has culminated in a variety of publications being made available to the public at a nominal charge. Programs range from promotional campaigns aimed at attracting conventions and sponsorship of international trade shows, to the development of gateway reception areas to provide language assistance to the international visitor.

Natural Resources. The natural resources of the United States are the responsibility of the Department of the Interior, the Department of Agriculture, and the Department of Defence, and additional independent government offices. The primery research, development, and planning function is undertaken by the former Bureau of Outdoor Recreation, now the Heritage Conservation and Recreation Service (HCRS). HCRS has the primary responsibility of maintaining a comprehensive nationwide outdoor recreation plan. The agency can only make recommendations on recreation policy, planning, and research, and it has no authority to manage land, water, and recreation areas.

The link between tourism and recreation is again shown by the fact that of the 760 million acres of land owned by the federal government, 447 million acres have been set aside for recreation use by tourists. Federal lands repesent appronimately 85 per cent of the recreation space in the United States. The principal agencies that manage federal lands for recreation and tourism are the Corps of Engineers, the U.S. Forest Service, and the National Park Service.

The Corps of Engineers is responsible for navigation, beech erosion control, hurricane flood protection, major drainage, flood control, and water resources on both federal land waterways and improved inland and intercoastal waterways. The corps takes recreation into account in their cost/benefit analysis to determine whether or not a project should be undertaken. Although recreation sites at project sites are operated by the corps, the agency prefers to turn over operation to nonfederal unit.

The US Forest Service controls both national forest areas and national grasslands areas. Recreation is a major activity on forest land, as is timber harvesting, mining, livestock grazing, and protecting wildlife. Approximately half of the nation's ski areas operate under permit from the US Forest Service.

The original purpose of the National Park Service (NPS) was to preserve the unique natural wonders of the country for the use and pleasure of all people. Later legislation added historic preservation, intensive outdoor recreation, and cultural activities to that mandate. NPS areas serve as attractions for hundreds of thousands of visitors every year.

A major problem as far as tourism is concerned is the question of preservation versus development. The agencies mentioned above are very concerned about the resources they manage. Critics argue that a certain level of development is necessary to service the visitors that travel to the natural resource attractions. This is answered by those who are concerned that too much development will ruin the attraction of the natural resources. Although tourism is heavily dependent on the proper management of the natural resources of land and water, it also relies upon physical improvement of the base. The contraversy arises over this balance.

Facilitation. The Department of State, Transportation, Treasury, and Justice are concerned with the movement of tourists. The US Travel and Tourism Administration is authorized to encourage the simplification, reduction, or elimination of travel barriers. In reality, apart from transportation, the influence of arguments for encouraging tourism is very low.

In summary, the problem tourism faces at the federal level is that the programs of many government departments and agencies affect it, but these same departments attach little importance to tourism. Additionally, an insufficient coordinating mechanism exists to ensure a concerted federal action on behalf of tourism.

ROLE OF STATE GOVERNMENTS

Structure

Within the many states, tourism's role within each state and the corresponding role of each state in tourism is recognized to varying degrees. Essentially three types of organization structures are present:

1. A public or quasi-public travel commission or bureau
2. An independent or semi-independent travel development department
3. Travel development within another department

Hawaii and Michigan are examples of the first type of structure. In Hawaii, leadership is given by the private Hawaii Visitors Bureau. A senior vice-president and a vice-president for finance and administration report to the president who in turn is responsible to a board of directors. The vice-president for finance and adminis-tration is responsible for accounting and administrative support. He or she is also responsible for attracting conventions. This officer in addition to three directors-for special events and promotions, for information services, and for sales and service—report directly to the senior vice-president as does an outside advertising agency. The directors of visitor satisfaction and of research and marketing report directly to the president. In the case of Michigan, leadership comes from the public sector. The Michigan Travel Commission acts as the board of directors and is made up of representatives of convention bureaus, representatives of the state travel bureau, and conoumer representatives appointed by the governor. Located within the Department of Commerce, the Travel Bureau is organized into three divisions. The Marketing and Promotion Division is responsible for publicity, advertising, publications, sales offices outside the state, special projects, and information services. The Product Development Division liaises with local, state, and federal governments while it prospects for new business develop-ments. In addition it handles traveller services, consumer protection, and product satisfaction. The Programs and Administration Division is responsible for research and program development, market analysis, adminis-trative services, and the administration of grants.

This allows for a simplification of the decision-making process because of the access that the commissioner of tourism development has to the governor due to his position as a member of the governor's cabinet. Another important plus is the advantage the commission has, especially at the time of the budget, in dealing with the state legislature as a full department. Reporting to the deputy commissioner are four distinct divisions. The Fiscal Services Division regulates all fiscal and personnel management of the commission. The Travel Promotion Division is responsible for promoting tourism in Tennessee. This includes working with various intermediaries to help produce packages and selecting and placing all advertising materials, including brochures, publications, and maps. Within the Information and Media Services Division feature articles and news items are developed and placed in magazines, newspapers, and trade publications to promote the state. This division supervises the State Photographic Laboratory and liaises with Memphis State University in the development of a research program concerning relevant statistical data. The Support Services Division is responsible for upgrading hotel and restaurant facilities and educating managers about the value of tourism to the state. The division is also responsible for staffing and operating the state's welcome centers.

The State of Montana represents the third type of structure. The parent of the travel promotion unit is the Department of Highways. Three divisions exist within the unit—those of film location, tour, and photo and publicity. A major concern in this type of structure is that tourism is regarded as secondary to the main purpose of the department and may have to struggle for attention.

Those states that have the most active travel and tourism programs have certain characteristics:

1. They have the personal interest and active support of either the governor or lieutenant governor and the legislature.
2. A committee of the legislature deals specifically with travel and tourism.
3. A program of research and evaluation out to indicate the effectiveness of the marketing effort and of tourism on the state.
4. The economic development aspects of tourism are emphasized.
5. Active advisory councils or commissions are present, and the liason between the private and the public sectors is strong.
6. State travel/tourism plans are part of the planning/budgeting process.
7. Spending of promotional dollars has shifted from promoting the natural resources to promoting urban, convention, and man-made attractions.

Functions

All of the fifty states have some kind of official government agency responsible for tourism development. In recent years, at various times, California and Maine have not had a state travel office. Approximately 90 per cent of the states retain advertising agencies to handle their promotional program. In order to stretch state tourist dollars, approximately thirty states have a matching formula, usually on a fifty-fifty basis, with private businesses, regional travel organizations, and city convention and visitor bureaus. Magazines and newspapers are the preferred media to use for state travel advertising. Radio is used by approximately 10 percent of the states, and television is used even less. Most states pericipate in travel shows, and approximately one-quarter operate out-of-state information centres. Although all states have a special travel promotion or theme, less than one in six states have different themes directed to separate market segments.

Although almost 90 per cent of state travel offices have programs devoted to package-tour development, only one-third of them publish and distribute state package-tour catalogs. About two-thirds of all states operate familiarization tours for tour operators and retail travel agents.

About two-thirds of the states publish travel-oriented newsletters. They are generally distributed monthly. In slightly over half the cases the newsletter is distributed to the public.

Almost all states employ a public relations or press information officer, while about three-quarters of the states conduct press or travel writer tours.

In just over half the states there is a staff member assigned to travel research, although for more than half of the members this is a part-time responsibility. In approximately 40 per cent of the states, research is conducted by university faculty members, and in about one-quarter of the states this function is undertaken by employees in other agencies of state government. In about one-third of the states, private research organizations are hired to conduct research. In nine out of ten states, travel data is gathered on a continuous basis, usually welcome centres and/or vehicle counts.

ORGANIZING FOR TOURISM AT THE DESTINATION

Within a state it is desirable for local communities, under the umbrella of the state effort, to initiate their own policies and strategies for the effective development of tourism. This may involve regional organizations, as in Michigan, where four tourist associations are responsible for encouraging visitors to their part of the state. Funded in part by a state grant and in part by contributions form private businesses, these regional organizations supplement the effort at the state level while encouraging a joint public/private sector involvement.

At the local community level a tourism organization typically evolves in the following way:

1. A small, informal group of people (most likely a special-interest group) interested in increasing tourism in the community gets together to seek additional support and help by visiting governmental or community agencies such as the city council.

2. Once the agencies are made aware of the many things involved in the community affecting and affected by

tourism, there develops the realization that a proper community involvement is necessary; a subcommittee on tourism is formed as part of the chamber of commerce or city council.

3. When it is realized that certain jobs can best be accomplished by people who share the same priorities, an association forms either as a part of the chamber of a commerce, as a part of the local government under the city council, or as an independent entity; as the quantity of work increases, a regular office and secretary may be established to complement the volunteer leadership.

4. At the final stage a full-time executive director is hired to direct the organization's work.

The way an organization forms depends in great part upon the tradition within the community, the resources that are available, the organizational structure in the community, the strength of the local chamber of commerce, and the amount of confidence in the local elected official. At the state level, cooperation may be given to local communities in one of two ways:

1. States may assist local efforts by passing legislation enabling communities to collect taxes to support local promotional activities; this is usually in the form of a bed tax, but some cities derive support from a tax on mixed drinks, entertainment, or tickets, or from an earmarked sales tax.

2. The states may provide matching funds, either for general purposes or for activities specified by the state government; these activities are usually such things as promotion and public relations, familiarization tours for travel brokers and writers, preparation of information materials, and technical assistance and research.

Structure and Function

An organizational structure for a destination-area tourism council is suggested in Figure 10.6. The tourism council establishes the philosophy for the community and sets the overall goal for the master plan. Assisted by input from related organizations, the council develops policies that are carried out by a full-time staff. Eight primary planning committees are represented in addition to the two basic functionaries of research and data collection and promotion and public relations. The Committee on Community Involvement and Leadership is responsible for maximizing the involvement of community leaders in the work of the council. The Committee on Development of Tourist Attractions seeks to identify new attraction opportunities and develop them. Similar tasks are undertaken by the Committee on Support Facilities in regard to the need for both private and public facilities to support the goals of tourism develop-ment.

The role of the Budget and Finance Committee is to identify and evaluate the various ways of financing the operations of the council. This may be accomplished through various means. As mentioned above, a bed or transient guest tax is a common method of obtaining funding. This usually requires passage of a city ordinance after state enabling legislation has authorized such a tax. This tax is usually resisted by local lodging groups as an unfair tax on only one segment of the industry, although residents are inclined to support it since it is a tax paid by the visitor. To a lesser though rather considerable extent, communities receive allocation from the general funds of the city, county, or state. A major limitation is that cities are often reluctant to allocate general revenue funds to agencies over which they have no control—in some cases it may not even be legal. A number of states will provide matching funds for the purpose of attracting tourists from outside the state. Provisions may be placed on the use of such funds to ensure that they are used for advertising rather than for staff salaries and that they are used for specific objectives, for example, attracting out-of-state businesses that the state supports.

The most common method of financing local efforts is through membership dues. The dues may be on a sliding scale, depending upon the volume of business or the number of employees. A major responsibility of the director or president of such an organization is to convince local businesses that it is worth their time and money to belong to such an organization. Some communities will organize special events—such as races and auctions—to raise funds. These activities usually require a great deal of organization by the local staff as well as the support of many local people and businesses. It does, however, provide a focal point for galvanizing community support. It is often possible, although not often undertaken, to have property owners vote a mill levy on their real estate property to be specifically used for tourism development. Monies so collected do not reflect the pressures of inflation unless new properties are constructed.

The Research and Data Collection Committee determines the amount of research needed and what data should be collected. An important, though often overlooked function, is that of ensuring that the level of service given visitors at the destination is of sufficiently high quality. The Education and Training Committee is concerned with determining the best ways that employees in the various tourism businesses can be trained. This is usually done by the individual operation, but in some cases it may be more efficient to have a group training session on, for instance, fire safety or the importance of customer service.

The Public Relations Committee seeks to develop the best ways of communicating with the different publics of the community. This involves getting press releases and articles in newspapers and magazines, handling tourist complaints, and determining how best to promote the destination. The last committee, the Evaluations Committee, is responsible for determining how to evaluate each part of the tourism program.

Because of the economic and social importance of tourism, the public sector has, to some extent, taken a role in regaining tourism. The amount of involvement will depend upon factors such as the political philosophy of the government and the degree of maturity of the destination area. The case has been made for establishing a clear tourism policy to guide the tourism destiny of the region, and a model for establishing the policy has been suggested.

To implement tourism policy it is necessary to have an organization. A tourism organization may be the World Tourism Organization, which has a province that is worldwide, or a regional or national organization, or a mechanism at the local level. At each level, the possible functions and roles of the tourism organizations are delineated.

Without a policy and a mechanism for implementing it, tourism will increase or decline at the destination in a haphazard manner.

Tourism

Most tourism policies have been designed to expand the tourist industry—whether in a relatively infant stage, as in Spain in the 1950s, or in a more mature stage, as in the United Kingdom in the 1980s. However, the very nature of tourism—with its heavy spatial and seasonal polarization—usually requires some form of interventionism. Furthermore, the tourist product has a determinate life cycle, and ageing resorts in decline are a problem for increasing importance. Examples touched upon in this book include the spa towns of Portugal and the lakes region of Austria. In essence, however, the aim of policy has to be to influence the number of visitors that are attracted and to modify their quality (spending capacity and range of activities), the timing of their visits and their specific destinations or, indeed, some combination of these.

The study of policy formation is made more complex because the aims of the local state may diverge from those of the central state. The local state is likely to be concerned with the needs of the local community as a whole. Therefore, the economic benefits of tourism are likely to be evaluated against the requirements of other economic sectors and the interests of local residents. Consequently, social and environmental concerns may be prioritized and tourism development may not always be encouraged. In contrast, the objectives of the central state are usually those of economic maximization: they include the improvement of the balance of payments, diversification of the national economic base, increasing incomes, raising state revenues and creating new jobs (Pearce 1981). Increasingly, however, as has been shown in this volume, state policy is also likely to incorporate, at least nominally, the aims of regional equity, environmental concern and social improvement.

According to the OECD (1974, p. 3), post-1945 tourism policies can be divided into three distinct phases: in the late 1940s and 1950s 'there was a need to dismantle and streamline the many police, currency, health and customs regulations which were the legacy of a war and immediate post-war situation'; in the 1950s governments moved more into promotion as they 'became aware of the "dollar gap" and hence the need to increase their earnings of both dollars and any other hard currency'; while, latterly, governments have become concerned with the problems of tourism supply and with the link between this and regional development. By the 1970s and early 1980s broader social and environmental issues had become the dominant issues in the tourism policies, at least of northern Europe, according to Airey (1983). However, it is doubtful whether the reality of tourism policy—as measured by state expenditure—corresponds to the emphases given to these issues on paper. Instead, most of the contributors in this book have highlighted the continuing preoccupation of most governments with increasing or redistributing demand.

The prime attraction of tourism for national policymakers is as an agent of economic change and, especially in the face of global recession in the 1980s, as a source of employment creation. Furthermore, tourism may be prioritised because of the rapidity with which economic growth can be generated, even—or especially—in previously, virtually uncommercialized regions, such as the South of Tenerife or particular Greek islands; As a minimum, the development of tourism has only two prerequisites: the generation of demand, and the provision of food and accommodation for tourists. Beyond this, investment may be necessary to create or open up particular attractions; examples are the provision of ski lifts or the construction of beaches and/or swimming pools. Much of the post-war boom in mass tourism has been based on such minimalist provision. In this context, and bearing in mind the mixed economies prevalent in Western Europe, the lead role in the development of tourism has been taken by the private sector. The role of the state has mainly been that of providing a regulatory framework or, in particular instances, providing investment (such as in leisure centres or airports) where the private sector has been unable to guarantee the minimalist provisions. Therefore, although state intervention is relatively limited in scope, it is often highly influential in the development of tourism.

THE INTERNATIONAL FRAMEWORK FOR TOURISM SERVICES

There is very little in the way of supranational regulation of tourism services, except for the major controls which exist over air transport. Tourism—along with the service sector in general—has rarely been prominent in the discussions of the General Agreement on Trade and Tariffs (GATT) and has only recently attracted the attention of the European Community, as the move to a single market gains pace. This was highlighted in a position paper by the Commission of the European Community (1982, p.5):

Article 2 of the Treaty of Rome assigns to the European Community the task of promoting closer relations between the States which belong to it. Tourism can assist the Community to achieve this goal and, by bringing the people of Europe into contact, it buttresses the edifice of European integration.

Tourism is also an important economic activity in the spirit of Article 2 of the Treaty. It provides jobs for 4 million people in the Community and its indirect effect on employment is considerably greater. It contributes to balance of payments stability between the northern European countries and those of the south and assists in the development of the poorest regions of the Community. Special attention should therefore be paid to promoting its harmonious development throughout the Community.

A further measure of the importance of tourism to the Community is the large number of Community policies which, directly or indirectly, have a bearing on it. These range from the free movement of persons and the freedom to provide tourist services, through passenger transport to regional development and the protection of the environment. To give further stimulation to tourism within the Community, a 'tourist dimension' should be given to these so that the needs of tourism are taken into account when decisions are taken and Community actions implemented."

In practice, European Community policy for tourism has had little impact, precisely because it is located in an area of very weak common policy, that is, the production and delivery of services. Tourist-related policies can be broadly subdivided into five categories (see Table 11.14). The first of these is freedom of movement and the protection of EC tourists. Only in 1986 have any real advances been made in this and, even then, they have been minimal. They include guidance on classification of hotels and standard EC signs (but not procedures!) at international frontiers. A second area of EC policy covers working conditions but, other than small-scale training and Social Fund expenditures, these have also been of limited importance. However, the free movement of labour required by the Treaty of Rome has influenced the supply of labour for the tourist industry. Transport, which is the third area, presents an equally dismal picture. This is probably the least developed of all the 'common' policies specified in the Treaty of Rome. The only real advance, apart from some harmonization of inter-national motorway construction, has been the attempt by the Commission during 1986-7 to deregulate and liberalize air traffic, which is likely to lead to some reduction in air fares. Similarly, measures to promote the environment have had more symbolic than real effects on tourism.

Probably the most significant contribution of the EC to tourism has been through expenditure by two of its 'structural' funds, the European Regional Development Fund (ERDF) and the European Agricultural Guidance and Guarantee Fund (EAGGF). ERDF expenditure is divided between quota (for individual countries) and non-quota funds. Under the quota scheme the EC contributed some 69 million ECU, in 1975-81, to tourist projects jointly financed with member states, having a total value of 481 million ECU. Under its operating rules the EC provides up to 20 per cent of the costs of new or modernised accommodation (subject to not exceeding 50 per cent of the aid provided by the national government, and up to 30 per cetn of the costs of infrastructure projects. In practice most (59 million ECU) resources have been granted to infrastructural development. Non-quota funds have largely been channelled into a few selected projects, especially in the frontier region between Ireland and Northern Ireland, in Aquitaine, Rousillon-Languedoc, Midi-Pyreneées and the Mezzogiorno. EAGGF funds have mainly been used to train farmers for tourist-related jobs, and to promote farm tourism and rural craft industries. Compared to the funds provided for other EC expenditure, tourism still appears marginal to the central interests of Community policy.

While there has been relatively little supranational regulation of tourism, national governments have placed a number of constraints on the internationalization of tourism services. These include exchange controls, customs regulations, and travel-documentation requirements for travellers, and limits on profits remittances and local equity participation for firms. However, national policies have mostly been concerned with the development and promotion of the tourist industry rather than with regulation.

National context

Not all states have equal interests in tourism. This depends on their capacity for developing tourism, the current state of the industry (whether it is perceived as prospering or struggling), and the dictates of wider economic considerations, rich as the pressure to create jobs in times of recession. With respect to the capacity for developing tourism, Wolfson (1964) recognizes four main types of country: where tourism is limited and is likely to remain so; it has limited possibilities of being developed; it exists and, with proper handling, could become a very important factor in the national economy; it is highly advanced and the problem is how to maintain the industry. In Western Europe all countries (if not all regions) fall into the latter two categories. Indeed, as the case studies in this volume have shown, most countries are faced with the need for policies both to help traditional tourist regions and to develop new regions. The precise form of the policies, however, depends on a number of broader considerations, including the division of power and finance among the national, regional and local levels. Thus federal Switzerland and the Federal Republic of Germany have quite different tourism policy structures to those which have evolved in more centralized France or Portugal. Even so, the general shift to local economic initiatives as part of a broader emphasis on self-reliance and indigenous resources in development strategies (Bassand et al. 1986), has meant that increasing numbers of municipal authorities have become involved in tourism policies. Virtually every rural region has a strategy for rural tourism, while all major (and most minor) cities have urban tourism projects. While the domestic and foreign market segments are still distinctive in many respects, the growing internationalization of tourism means that, increasingly, all local areas are tending to compete for the same limited (if expanding) market.

National policies for the development of tourism are broadly similar, even if these vary considerably in detail. They are considered here under the following headings: promotion; direct investment; subsidies; labour market intervention; and regulation.

The promotion of tourism

The promotion of tourism, especially in foreign markets, has been favoured by virtually every national tourist board. One of the first ventures in this field was the establishment of the Travel Association of Great Britain and Northern Ireland in the 1920s to attract foreign visitors. There has been a rapid expansion in the number of tourist boards subsequently and, according to Ascher (1983), more than 170 governments have foreign travel promotion offices. This is but the tip of the iceberg, for most regions and tourist resorts have their own tourism promotion services. There are two main ways in which the tourist industry to any one country can be prompted: encouraging foreign tourism, and redirecting the holidays of nationals from foreign to domestic destinations.

The promotion of tourism in foreign markets in mainly based on advertising campaigns aimed either directly at the public or at travel agents and tour companies. These campaigns can take a variety of forms, including advertisements in general newspapers or public spaces, free distribution of brochures, and representation at trade or holiday exhibitions. National tourist boards may either seek to promote the whole country or specific regions. Spain provides notable examples of both approaches in its 'Everything under the sun' and 'So you think you know Spain' campaigns. Balancing diverse regional interests poses particular problems for any national tourist board and, for example, the British Tourist Authority is frequently cirticized for giving too much emphasis to London in its campaigns. This is a particularly difficult problem which can be resolved into two separate questions: how best to attract foreign visitors initially; and how, subsequently, to ensure that there is some geographical spread in their visits and spending. Another major consideration is the identification of the market segments to be targeted in the promotion campaign. Most tourist authorities are aware of the advantages of higher-income tourism and, indeed, some tourist boards have strategies to attract the higher spenders. However, in other case—such as Spain—the existence of large numbers of hotels in mass tourist resorts makes it difficult to achieve any significant shift from mass to elite tourism.

The domestic tourist industry can also be assisted by measures aimed at reducing the numbers of foreign holidays taken by nationals. This may involved restrictions on foreign travel, such as the exchange controls in operation in the United Kingdom in 1966-70, and in France in 1983. Alternatively, the attractions of domestic tourism can be promoted. Recent examples include Belgium's *Vacances au pays*' campaign and Finland's 'Ski cheaply' campaign (OECD 1986). Many such domestic campaigns emphasize the neglected cultural heritage and landscape beauty of the home country in contrast to the discomfort of foreign travel and the grosser attributes of (foreign) mass tourist resorts. A related aspect of domestic promotion campaigns has been the attempt to extend the tourist season and reduce the considerable seasonal peaking in demand. This may involve the promotion of 'shoulder-season' or 'out-of-season' lower-cost short breaks, or it may involve attempts to stagger holidays. For example, in France the tourist authorities grant *Aménagmement du temps* prizes to the projects which have been most successful in this respect.

Domestic tourism can also be assisted through measures to assist social tourism, that is, tourism for economically weak groups, such as single-parent families or handicapped persons. The assistance, which may be provided by the state or by voluntary bodies, can either involve payments of grants (which will probably be spent on domestic tourism) or provision of free or subsidised accommodation or holiday packages. Social tourism has long-roots and one of the earliest organizations was the Co-operative Holidays Association founded in the United Kingdom in 1893. At present, the state-financed Swiss Travel Saving Fund is one of the more highly developed forms of social tourism. It secures price reductions in holidays, helps low-income families to save and publicises details of low-price holidays. In addition, individuals may be granted a 'tourism cheque' to be used—as they wish—to purchase a holiday. Social tourism is a more recent innovation in other countries but even in Greece, where such schemes only date from 1982, some 400,000 individuals (especially the disabled, the unemployed and pensioners) had been assisted in taking vacations by 1985.

State investment in tourism

State investment has become widespread in most modern economies as a means to support the private sector. This may involve state subsidies to the private sector or direct state investment where there are market gaps which are not filled by the private sector. Such a process has been labelled 'the devalorization of capital', whereby the state socialises part of the cost of production; examples include subsidies for hotel construction, investment in infrastructure or investment in tourist attractions. The reasons for such state interventionism were outlined earlier. In recent years there has been a tendency for the tourist industry to become more capital-intensive—with the requirement for new airports, marinas, theme parks.

Hotel swimming pools, etc.—and this has increased the pressure on government intervention.

Infrastructural investment usually depends on the state and this can be crucial in opening up regions to tourism. For example, the construction of the M5 motorway greatly assisted the continuing development of tourism in southwest England, while the construction of Málaga airport was critical in opening up Spain's Gosta del Sol. In addition, the development of greenfield sites or substantial (non-incremental) additions to existing resorts will require large-scale investment in water and energy supplies and sewage and waste disposal. It is, invariably, the state which takes the lead role in such investments. In addition, the state may invest in tourist addictions such as conferences centres or the conservation of historic sites, as non-profit-making poles of attraction; a notable example is the Vienna Conference Centre.

The accommodation sector has not usually been the object of direct state investment. There are examples of this, notably the *pousadas* of Portugal and the *paradores* of Spain which were designed to attract tourists away from the seaside resorts: however, these are the exceptions and most government intervention has been limited to providing subsidies to the accommodation sector. Examples include the English Tourist Board grants for upgrading hotel rooms, and the low-cost loans made by Spain's Industrial Credit Bank and by Greece's Organization for the Financing of Economic Development for hotel construction. This system of subsidies can be critical both in opening up new tourist zones (as in parts of the Algarve in the 1960s) and in assisting hotels in existing resorts to upgrade their facilities in line with rising consumer expectations (as in the United Kingdom in the 1980s).

State investment in tourism may often be linked to particular regional development strategies. For example, tourism featured in the development programmes of Italy's Cassa per il Mezzogiorno and 7-10 per cent of its budget was spent on this in the 1960s. Other examples include France's regional plan to open up the Languedoc-Roussillon area to tourism, and the 1973 Swiss plan to spend 500 million francs opening up the mountain regions to tourism. While tourism does offer some advantages for regional development strategies, it is appropriate to repeat Middleton's (1997) view on this: 'Unfortunately, in the current state of knowledge one must conclude that tourism, in practice, is a rather blunt instrument for achieving regional objectives and carries with it dangers arising from the difficulties of control.'

Labour-market intervention

There is far less specific state intervention in tourism labour markets than in the provision of capital. This is not to say that tourism is unaffected by the general regulation of labour markets. Minimum wages, hours and conditions of work regulations, and restrictions on immigration, all affect the supply of and the price of labour. For example, Switzerland's immigrant labour laws contribute to the existence of a cheap, flexible and seasonal labour force for tourism. However, these are secondary effects from legislation which usually has not been primarily or specifically designed for the tourist industry.

Most direct intervfention is limited to specific minimum wages regulations for the accommodation and catering sectors, and to the provision of training courses. Most European countries provide some training course either in tourism in general or in specific skills such as catering or hotel work. In some countries training is relatively well organized and, in France, for example, all firms with more than ten employees have to pay 1.1 per cent of their wage bill as a training levy. However, as most surveys of tourist firms have shown, the majority of employers and employees have had little formal training. Most have only a minimal amount of on-the-job training or learn to run their businesses from practice. This tends to reinforce the casual nature of and the rapid turnover which is characteristic of tourism labour markets.

Environmental regulation

Large-scale tourist developments produce considerable pressures on the environment and on the local population. These include destruction of the traditional landscape, congestion in the transport system, and air, land and water pollution. Such problems are usually most acute in the rapidly developed mass tourist resorts. In contrast, rural tourism, business tourism and elite tourism tend to be more incremental in nature and the tourists are more easily integrated within existing economic, social and built-environment structures. Their is linked to the concept of 'the capacity to absorb tourism' (see Getz 1983) but it is clear that this can be evaluated from several different perspectives. Different sectors of the local community—depending on their economic interests and precise place of residence—may be affected in strongly contrasting ways by tourism development. Furthermore, while municipal authorities may decide to limit further tourist development for social or environmental reasons, this may bring them into conflict with the economic interests of central or regional governments wishing to promote tourism. Ultimately, environmental controls have to be enforced, otherwise uncontrolled tourist development may lead to the attraction of the tourist area being severely reduced.

All municipal authorities in areas of large-scale tourism are likely to come under pressure to limit tourism development for environmental reasons. Their ability to do so depends on the precise distribution of powers between central, regional and local government in each country. In the United Kingdom, for example, development-control powers give local authorities considerable scope to refuse planning permission for new tourist developments but little power to modify existing tourist activities. The Netherlands has an even stronger system of land use regulation. There are also strong controls at the commune level in Switzerland but the considerable degree of decentralization means that neighbouring municipalities may pursue conflicting tourism policies. Environmental regulation is least developed in southern Europe (see Wynn 1984) because of the traditions of centralism and the weakness of municipal finances in these countries. As these are also the countries where the rate of tourist development has been greatest in recent decades, they tend to have experienced the greatest amount of environmental degradation as a result of tourism development. In contrast, all provinces in the Netherlands have to produce a Tourism and Recreation Development Plan which provides both an inventory of existing facilities and an assessment of the potential for future development. By the late 1980s most European countries has begun to discuss the ways in which tourism development could be harmoniously integrated with environmental conservation and, for example, this was the specific aim of France's 1985

'Mountains Act' However, in most countries, this still remains an elusive goal rather than common practice.

TOURISM AND DEVELOPMENT

The diverse range of experiences reported in this volume underline the central fact that tourism does not offer a single model for development. Consequently, it is neither a curse nor a blessing in itself. Any evaluation of the role of tourism—and of the jobs, income and value added which it produces—must depend on particular national and local circumstances. Tourism can bring jobs and can revive stagnating local economies, but it can also be detrimental to other economic activities, destroy the environment and contribute to the informalization of labour markets. There is a need, therefore, to look not just at tourism but at the opportunity costs of its development, and the alternative strategies which could be pursued by a region or community. As de Kadt emphasized, almost a decade ago:

> tourism projects are often developed without being tested within the framework of a sectroal plan, while their costs and benefits may not even be compared with those of alternative projects in the same sector. Most seriously, although the sectoral plan should establish the place of tourism within the development strategy for the whole economy, in many cases such a plan is nonexistent or not decisively implemented.

The increased emphasis by almost all European governments on tourism development as a source of jobs in the 1980s, makes it imperative that this fuller evaluation of tourism is not neglected.

Tourism does offer economic benefits, but the total market for tourism is still limited, if expanding. Most communities, therefore, can only hope for small-scale economic advantages and in such areas tourism can be no more than one element in a wider development strategy. However, some areas may attract or generate large-scale developments for there is no reason why the mass tourist resorts of the present will continue to dominate in the future. As tastes, incomes and mobility change, new European resorts may emerge and, with the likely shift away from minimalist provision, these may create new types of jobs and investment. However, the greatest challenge for decisionmakers in the future concerns the renewal of the mass tourist resorts of the post-war period. As the product cycle reaches maturity and their facilities age, potentially they will present enormous redevelopment problems. If they do not attract new rounds of investments in tourist facilities, how is the built environment to be maintained and what will be the impact on local labour markets? It is not inconceivable that, in future decades, some tourist resorts will replace steel or textile communities as the major concern of regional economic policies.

10. Conclusion

THE ROLE of the public sector in regulating tourism is regarded by many as essential and by most as controversial. This chapter explores the many ways in which tourism is regulated by the public sector. Tourism legislation and regulation in the United States is examined in depth. The role of regulatory agencies is discussed, and arguments for and against regulation from the viewpoints of consumers, government, and industry are given. Legislation and regulation in Canada is described in full, and the situation is compared with that in the United States.

Beyond the national level, there are a number of international regulations that affect tourism. The most significant of these involve air travel between countries. The specifics of how such agreements are reached are discussed.

The chapter concludes that governments act primarily to protect the resources of the destination area as well as the visiting tourist. Thus, their role in tourism is a positive one. However, the lack of cooperation and coordination between the government agencies that directly or indirectly affect tourism means that the public sector is too often unable to react with the speed desired by the private sector.

CONTROLLING THE TRAVEL INDUSTRY

One of the public sector's roles in tourism was that of setting and enforcing various forms of legislation and regulations. This role is at the same time essential and controversial in most free-enterprise-system destination areas. It is thought to be essential because governments cannot totally rely upon the private sector to effectively control and regulate its activities; it is often controversial because the private sector feels that the public sector goes too far in enforcing its regulations. For example, in Canada in major private-sector task force has reached the following conclusions on government regulations:

> The tourism industry... could optimize its contribution to the Canadian economy if there were less intervention from all levels of government. Regulations have largely impeded the growth of tourism, rather than hastened its growth. There is a requirement to modernize these regulatory processes and have them respond to needs of the industry and the market rather than as a policing function.

In the United States as well as in Canada a multitude of government agencies have programs and regulations that directly or indirectly affect tourism. Other countries, especially those with socialist or communist governments, regulate tourism even more comprehensively. The complexity of the tourism regulatory framework in most destination areas is a direct reflection of tourism itself; tourists cross international borders, are exposed to all of the cultural, historic, man-made, and natural resources of the destination area, and must be catered to in a safe, secure, and hygienic fashion. It follows, therefore, that a variety of government agencies have tourism-related programs and regulations and not just one.

Those in the public sector generally get involved in tourism for political, environmental, and economic reasons. The specific functions of governments normally encompass coordination, planning, legislation/regulation, entrepreneurial ventures, and tourism-industry stimulation. The degree of emphasis given to each of these five principal roles varies from destination to destination, but it is usually directly related to the importance attached to tourism as an economic activity. It is important to realize that the actions of those in the public sector have to be supported by various bodies of law (legislation) and specific regulations to have legitimacy in democratic societies. It is with the actual enforcement of the laws and with the structuring of regulations that the most controversy and conflict occurs between the private and public sectors of the tourism system.

Tourism Legislation and Regulations

Before the specific types of legislation and regulations that have been introduced in the United States, Canada, and elsewhere are described, it will be useful to classify them as they are commonly found in most destination areas. One method of classification is to group the tourism legislation and regulations into functional areas, such as those related to the protection of the environment, those related to economic development, those related to frontier controls, and so on. The material on the United States is organized in this way. Another means of classification is to group on an industry sector basis by identifying the legislation and regulations that relate to airlines, hotels, travel agents, and so on. In this respect, "horizontal" legislation or regulations are those items that affect every industrial sector, whether it be a tourism or nontourism one, such as income tax and labor legislation. "Specific" legislation or regulations are those items that relate directly to an industrial sector. An example of this is a grading system for hotels. The following chart illustrates commonly found legislation and regulations classified on a sector-by-sector basis in tourism:

Accommodation Establishments

Classification and grading-rating of hotels and other establishment types
Fire safety regulations and codes
Health safety regulations and codes
Building and zoning codes
Issuance of operating and liquor licenses and other regulations of the terms and conditions of operation
Liability laws with respect to guests and their belongings
Labour and taxation legislation

Travel Agents, Tour Wholesalers, and Operators

Regulations and licensing of travel agents, tour wholesalers, and operators
Definition of responsibilities and limitations
Regulations of promotions
Labour and taxation legislation

Airlines, Railways, Buses, Ships, and other Carriers

Control of fares and tariffs
Licensing of carriers
Regulation of safety procedures

Control of route entry and exit
Limitation of weights and capacities
Negotiations of services
Subsidization of routes
Labour and taxation legislation

Other sectors of the tourism industry, including retailers, car rental agencies, commercial attractions operators, and other businesses, have their own specific legislation and regulations in addition to the horizontal laws and regulations that apply to all.

The role taken by the US federal government in preparing legislation and regulations relative to tourism reflects the country's national interests in tourism and tourism's interrelationship with other aspects of US society and business. The US Senate Committee on Commerce has identified these national interests related to tourism as follows:

1. Health and other aspects of the quality of life:
   (a) The national interest in public health
   (b) Other aspects of the quality of life
   (c) Protection of the quality of the tourism experience
   (d) Ensuring opportunities for participation in tourism
2. Tourism as an economic activity
   (a) The efficient satisfaction of consumer demand
   (b) Increasing employment, income, and regional development
3. Meeting business travel demand
4. Facilitation of international tourism
5. Tourism's impact on publicly-owned lands

In addition to recognizing tourism's direct impact and interrelationship with these five factors, the committee has also recognized that tourism interacts with the national economy, the functioning of the transportation system, the system of social and economic statistics, the forms of environmental protection, the clearance of international visitors, the public revenues, and the forms of consumer protection.

It is obvious from these expressed national interests and interactions that tourism is perceived as having a broad-scale and pervasive impact of US society, as in most destination areas that have embraced it as an important economic activity. The broad scope of these impacts is mirrored by a diverse range of legislation and regulations that directly and indirectly affect tourism within the United States.

The most comprehensive analysis of federal legislation in the United States was completed in 1976 as part of the National Tourism Policy Study. One of the major conclusions emerging from this analysis was that "Federal legislation has seldom been addressed explicitly to national interests in travel or tourism..." The Senate Commerce Committee separated the existing tourism legislation in the United States into two main categories, namely federal tourism legislation and federal tourism-related legislation. The committee also identified the following nine sub-categories of federal legislation:

Federal Tourism Legislation

1. Tourism promotion and development legislation
2. Tourism resources legislation

Federal Tourism-Related Legislation

3. Interstate transport investment and regulation
4. Nonimmigrant visa and customs legislation

5. Economic development legislation
6. Environmental quality control legislation
7. Energy legislation
8. Land-use legislation
9. Tax legislation

Within these subcategories, there are forty-five existing or proposed acts that have had some impact on tourism within the United States.

It is quite obvious, and the US Senate Commerce Committee has confirmed it, that the major direct pieces of tourism legislation in the United States, that is, the domestic and international travel acts, have been structured without sufficient regard to other legislation and the programs of affected federal agencies. The reverse is also true, since the programs and legislated manadates of other agencies have not given sufficient attention to tourism. This situation is not uncommon among those at destination areas, as few of them have systematically developed legislation on an effectively coordinated fashion. As is discussed later in this chapter, Canada for example, has moved to ease its regulatory and legislative overlaps and conflicts by forming an Inter-departmental Committee on Tourism.

We turn our attention now to regulation as opposed to legislation. Governments have two common methods of enforcing regulations, namely by establishing regulatory agencies and by utilizing regulatory techniques. In the United States, the regulatory agencies currently include the Civil Aeronauties Board (CAB), the Federal Aviation Administration (FAA), the Interstate Commerce Commission (ICC), the Federal Highway Adminis-tration (FHWA), the National Highway Traffic Safety Administration (NHTSA), the Federal Maritime Commission (FMC), the United States Coast Guard (USCG), and the Federal Trade Commission (FTC). The CAB is scheduled to be completely phased out by the end of 1984 and represents the federal government's first attempt to drastically deregulate a once closely regulated business sector. The regulatory techni-ques used by governments include, among others, establishing land-use controls, setting admission policies, and withholding government funds.

Many of the regulatory agencies in existence in the United States have been created as a result of the passage of federal tourism-related legislation. For example, the CAB was established in 1938 through the Civil Aeronautics Act. Its mandate was to protect the safety of the public and to maintain the viability of the US airline industry. The CAB was given the authority to determine which airlines could operate in the United States, which routes they could operate on, and what fares they could charge. It was given powers over airline schedules, airline profit margins, and the types of working relationships permissible. Since its inception, the CAB has probably been the most influential regulatory agency in the United States with respect to its impact on tourism within the nation. The successful passage of the Airline Deregulation Act in October 1978 was, therefore, a most significant event in terms of US tourism. This act was historically unique since it was the first time ever that the federal government virtually abolished its role in the economic regulation of an industry. The decision to wind up the powerful CAB came after much public criticism of the agency and of its perceived over-regulation of the airline industry. The general concern was that the CAB had gone too far in trying to maintain the viability of the airline industry and was beginning to engage in activities that were not beneficial to the travelling public. The following statement succinctly expressed the paradox that the CAB represented:

> The CAB in recent months has been accused of sheltering the airline industry, stifling compassion, flueling inflation, discriminating against the charter of the marketplace.
>
> It has also been praised for presiding over the development of one of the finest and most efficient air transportation networks anywhere in the world.

Another major problem with the CAB was its tardiness in responding to proposals presented by individual airline companies. During the long lag time, airlines often changed their minds about their proposals or they lost the benefit of the marketing opportunity they were seeking. Because of the apparent inability of government regulatory agencies to react with the speed which the private sector requires, a great deal of friction has existed within the tourism system. Thus, as has been the case with the CAB, it is often not a question of regulations being good *or* bad for the industry, but of their being good *and* bad. In other words, the private sector sometimes may agree wholeheartedly with the underlying principles behind the regulations, but often they will be opposed to the manner and to the degree with which the regulations are enforced.

The Airline Deregulation Act of 1978 envisaged that the CAB would be completely phased out by January 1985. The CAB "sunset" timetable included the loss of its authority over route entry in 1982 and its jurisdiction over tariffs and pricing in 1983.

The air travel experiment in the United States, which was motivated by the desire to let the marketplace operate more freely to the ultimate benefit of traders, has had its advantages and disadvantages. George James of the Air Transport Association has identified these advantages and disadvantages in the context of the three parties affected, namely consumers, government, and airline companies.

As a result of the deregulation of the airline industry, several new airline companies have emerged and have been certified by the CAB. More discounted fares have become available and the existing airline companies have been better able to rationalize their route systems. Overcrowded planes and airports, and the overbooking of flights were the most frequent criticisms of the results of deregulation.

The roles of other US regulatory agencies are as follows:

Federal Aviation Administration (FAA)

Regulates the manufacturing, operation, and maintenance of aircraft
Determines and certifies the technical proficiency and physical fitness of flight crews
Certifies airports
Inspects air navigation facilities

Interstate Commerce Commission (ICC)

Regulates railroads, but lines, water carriers, and express agencies in interstate and foreign commerce

Federal Highway Administration (FHWA)

Develops highway safety standards
Identifies and monitors locations where serious accidents have occurred
Involves itself in highway design, construction, and maintenance

Investigates common carrier accidents

Reviews commercial driver qualifications

Inspects common carrier terminals and vehicles for safety

Runs safety education programs

National Highway Traffic Safety Administration (NHTSA)

Regulates vehicle safety standards

Federal Maritime Commission (FMC)

Regulates common carriers in domestic offshore commerce and US flagships in foreign commerce

United States Coast Guard (USCG)

Policies coastal and inland waters and navigable rivers of the United States for water pollution by ships and boats

Sets uniform standards for safety and inspects recreational boats for compliance with these

Educates small boat operators in safe operation

Controls traffic

Federal Trade Commission (FTC)

Has authority to prevent deceptive advertising

The other method that the public sector uses to enforce its regulations is regulatory technique. Normally these techniques are concerned with the use of land. They include setting access or user quotas based upon a resource's carrying capacity, establishing reservation systems, making restrictive convenants on property ownership transfers, and in the United States using "eminent domain" that enables the federal government to take over endangered lands and historic sites. In the United States these techniques are exercised mainly in lands owned by the federal government.

State, regional/county, and municipal governments in the United States also have legislation and regulations that affect tourism either directly or indirectly. Although the US Constitution provides the federal government with specific powers, state governments automatically have the responsibility for all areas left unspecified. These responsibilities include the authority to regulate land uses and to acquire land within the state. Historically, these powers have been passed on to local governments at the city, town, and county levels. Cities, towns, and counties within the United States exercise these powers through zoning and the structuring of municipal plans.

Like the federal government, state governments have legislation and regulations specifically dealing with state-owned lands, including state parks. Certain states have also enacted legislation that deals specifically with sectors of the tourism industry. A common characteristic of this sectoral legislation is that it has been motivated by a desire to protect the interests of consumers. Rhode Island, for example, passed a Travel Agency Act in 1977 giving the state the power to licence retail travel agencies. The law was passed as a result of serious complaints from consumers about their experiences with certain agencies. Rhode Island was the first state in the United States to introduce such legislation, while Puerto Rico had done so earlier in 1974. Several Canadian provinces did likewise during the 1970s. Another part of the tourism industries that has received considerable attention has been the condominium real estate developments within resort areas, particularly timesharing projects. Nebraska was the first state to introduce a timesharing act to protect its citizens against any misleading claims of

Conclusion

timesharing resort developers in Nebraska and elsewhere.

Like its larger neighbour to the south, Canada has a myriad of legislation and regulations at both the federal, provincial, and municipal levels that directly or indirectly impinge upon tourism. As mentioned at the beginning of this chapter, the Sector Task Force on the Canadian Tourism Industry concluded in 1978 that the industry would be more effective economically if some of these laws and regulations were dismantled or updated. In response to this suggestion, the Canadian government established the Interdepartmental Committee on Tourism (IDCT). In addition Canada's national tourism office, Tourism Canada, has accepted as one of its basic goals the improvement in levels of cooperation and coordination between government agencies and the private sector. It has established its own coordination secretariat to liaise and consult with other federal agencies through the IDCT. It should also be noted that the Conference of Canadian Tourism Officials (CCTO) and the Federal/Provincial Conference of Tourism Ministers have been formed to improve federal/provincial government coor-dination and cooperation relative to tourism.

Tourism Canada has recognized that due to the diversity of the tourism system within Canada many federal agencies have established regulations, policies, and programs that affect tourism. In their tourism sector strategy of 1981. Tourism Canada stated that the activities of these agencies.

> In some cases. . . address the particular needs of the tourism industry. In others, the pursuit of goals different from those of the tourism industry exacerbate current industry problems or constrain the industry's ability to respond to opportunities. Tourism industry concerns have focussed on several government horizontal policy measures. . . namely labor legislation, man power policy, taxation policy, transportation regulations, environ-mental control, and the myriad of regulations at the federal, provincial, and municipal levels affecting facilities development.[6]

As in the United States, Canada's tourism legislation and regulations have their roots in the late nineteenth century. The Rocky Mountain Parks Act of 1887 established the first national park surrounding Banff, Alberta. This was the parallel in history to the Yellow-stone National Park Act of 1872 in the United States. The National Parks Act followed in Canada in 1930, and in 1953 the Historic Sites and Monuments Act was passed. The 1930 act stated that only such uses would be permitted within national parks that would "leave them unimpaired for the enjoyment of future generations." This clause has been quite controversial since certain of Canada's national parks, such as Banff and Jasper, are clearly among the nation's major tourist attractions and most favoured destinations, particularly with respect to the desires of foreign visitors. The private sector of the Canadian tourism industry via the Sector Task Force on the Canadian Tourism Industry stated that these visitor needs and potentials were not being satisfied to unnecessarily stringent development controls on the part of Parks Canada. This is a classic case of conservation versus development in tourism and of the unavoidable, inherent conflicts between the private sector and certain parts of the public sector of the tourism system.

In addition to Parks Canada, located within the Department of the Environment, at least sixteen other federal departments have tourism-related legislation and regulations. These include Regional Industrial Expansion (that includes Tourism Canada), Energy, Mines and Resources, External Affairs, Finance, Indian and Northern Affairs, Employment and Immigration, Health and Welfare, the Secretary of State, Transport, Agriculture, Consumer and Corporate Affairs, National Defence, Labour, Public Works, and Fisheries and Oceans.

There are several regulatory agencies within Canada whose mandates impact upon tourism. Principal among these is the Canadian Transport Commission (CTC), which is Canada's parallel organization to the CAB. The Air Transport Committee (ATC) is the specific group within CTC that makes airline regulatory decisions. The history of airline regulations within Canada has been quite different from that of the United States, primarily due to the existence of a nationally owned airline, Air Canada. The Canadian government established Air Canada through an act of Parliament which gave the authority for its operation to a crown corporation. Although regulations were eased over the years to allow private airline companies to provide scheduled services within Canada, Air Canada (originally established as Trans Canada Airlines) has always been pre eminent, and the scheduled air service market could therefore be described as being one of "regulated competion." This is in sharp contrast to the open market situation that has developed in the United States as a result of airline deregulation. The CTC is also responsible for the regulation of railways and merchant shipping in Canada. The Canadian Coast Guard, located within Transport Canada, regulates nonmerchant boats and ships travelling in Canadian waters, including recreational crafts and cruise/sightseeing vessels.

As in the United States, the ten Canadian provinces and two territories have legislation and regulations that affect tourism directly and indirectly. Several of the provinces have specific tourism acts that give them the authority to license and, in some cases, to inspect tourism businesses. The province of Quebec, for example, has the power through its tourism act to inspect and grade commercial accommodation facilities. Additionally, certain provinces, including Ontario and Quibec, have legislation that permits them to license and regulate retail travel agencies. All of the provinces and territories have considerable legislation governing the use of their parks and other natural resource areas.

Multinational Regulations Affecting the Travel Industry

In addition to the layers of national, state/provincial, regional/county, and city/town legislation and regulations affecting tourism, there are certain agreements that have been reached between foreign countries which have a direct impact upon travel.

Perhaps the most significant of these agreements are those which relate to air travel between countries. The embryonic period for these air travel agreements was during World War II. The "five freedom" of international air travel were first discussed at an international civil aviation conference in Chicago in 1944. These five freedoms were:

1. Right of transit—The freedom to fly over another country without stopping

2. Right of technical stop—The right to stop at another country's airport for fuel and servicing

3. Right to discharge passengers at another country's airport

4. Right to pick up passengers from another country's airport and return them to their homes

5. Right to discharge passengers at another country's airport and to then load passengers for countries further on

Althouth these freedoms had considerable support, especially from the United States, they were never agreed to universally. This meant that there was a need to establish bilateral agreements between countries. The Bermuda Agreement of 1946 was the first of these, and it dealt with air travel between the United States and Britain. The formation of the International Civil Aviation Organization (ICAO) in 1944 and the International Air Transport Association (IATA) in 1945 paved the way for these types of agreements. ICAO is an organization of national governments; IATA represents the airlines. Approximately eighty countries including the United States, Canada, and the United Kingdom belong to ICAO. Its objectives are

1. To adopt international standards and recommended practices for regulating air navigation

2. To recommend installation of navigation facilities by member countries

3. To set forth proposals for the reduction of customs and immigration formalities

4. To plan for the safe and orderly growth of international civil aviation throughout the world

5. To encourage the improvement of the art of aircraft design and operation for peaceful purposes

6. To seek the development of airways, airports, and air navigation facilities for international civil aviation

7. To provide for safe, regular, efficient, and economical air transportation

8. To discourage unreasonable competition

9. To insure that the rights of contracting countries are fully respected and that every member country has a fair opportunity to operate international airlines

10. To discourage discrimination between contracting countries

11. To promote the development of all aspects of international civil aeronautics

More than 110 scheduled airline companies belong to IATA, some of which are nationally owned airlines such as Air Canada and British Airways. Any company offering a scheduled international air service may belong to IATA. The association's purpose is basically to resolve problems that the airline companies would not be able to resolve if they acted individually. Its objectives are to encourage safe, regular, and economical international air services, to encourage international air commerce, and to research problems and issues affecting the industry.

One of IATA's key roles is that of setting rates on international routes to which all member airlines agree. It also acts as a clearing house for air-ticket coupons that allow passengers to fly internationally on several airlines while requiring only one flight coupon. It acts in an advisory capacity on mutual problems, such as fuel shortages, hijacking, navigation, and safety. Also, IATA is an important source of statistics on international air travel. Unlike the national regulatory agencies such as the Civil Aeronautics Board (CAB) in the United States and the Canadian Transport Commission (CTC), IATA does not certify airlines, award routes, or act on market exit decisions. These powers remain with the national governments and their regulatory authorities, such as the CAB and the CTC. Bilateral air agreements are struck between governments addressing these matters; the United Kingdom-United States Bermuda agreement of 1946 is the forerunner of these.

These bilateral agreements are frequently somewhat loose and often mask ongoing disputes between two countries over transborder air services. The 1973 bilateral agreement between the United States and Canada is a good example of this latter point. It is indicative of the inherent problems of a tourism system in which the market or political philosophies of nations are quite different. Since 1977 the United States has deregulated its airline industry and has been a strong proponent of an "open skies" airline policy internationally. In contrast, Canada has maintained a highly protectionist stance with respect to its airline companies. Canada's refusal to completely open up the international air border between itself and the United States led in 1983 to a serious dispute over a proposed package of heavily discounted fares to be offered by Air Canada to several cities in the southern United States. The CAB's obstinacy in not allowing these fare schedules caused many Canadians prebooked on these flights to cancel their trips. Quite obviously the destination areas within the southern United States suffered because of the loss of potential income from the Canadian travellers.

Before leaving the subject of international air travel regulations and agreements, mention must be made of the many pacts that have been made between countries with respect to airlines' liabilities for passenger injuries and damage or loss of baggage. Historically, there have been three such major agreements—the Warasaw Convention, the Hague Protocol, and the Montreal Agreement. The Warsaw Convention dates back to 1929 and constitutes the main body of international rules in this respect. The United States accepted the Warsaw Convention regulations in 1934; Canada and the United Kingdom are other adherents to it. Several Central American and South American countries are not members of the treaty. The Hague Protocol and the Montreal Agreement represent international agreements that have raised the dollar limit on an airline's liability to an individual passenger.

Hotel classification on an international level also represents a tacit attempt by several nations to regulate standards within another important component of the tourism system. The World Tourism Organization (WTO) has taken the lead role in this regard. It was given this authority in 1963 when the United Nations Conference on International Travel and Tourism asked it to draft these standards. The main rationale for setting these was as follows:

> Travelling problems can be eased to a considerable extent if hotels of a particular category in all countries were to present more or less the same characteristics of comfort and service.

Although many countries appear to agree in principle with the classification method and criteria that the WTO has developed, many have chosen to create their own classification and grading/

rating systems since they have found the WTO guidelines to be too broad for their purposes.

In addition to these specific agreements, there are a plethora of treaties and agreements governing trade and travel/customs procedures between nations and groups of nations. Although they are too numerous to mention, they also play a key role in the tourism regulatory framework of destination areas.

The Need for Government Regulation of Tourism

A close analysis of the legislation and regulations described above would clearly show that governments are acting in the general interests of their citizens. They do so primarily to protect and conserve their destination area's natural, historical, and cultural resources, to ensure the health and safety of visitors, and to protect the visitors from unscrupulous business practices. In these respects, the value of a government's role cannot be questioned.

From time to time, however, governments are accused of being overly bureaucratic, of developing unnecessary "red tape," and of going too far in their policing efforts. This is especially true when the political pendulum and public sentiment swing more toward the free-enterprise approach, as they have in the US airline industry. It is also true of Canada where those in the tourism industry have sharply criticized governments for hindering the development of tourism destination areas because of their lengthy and complex project approval processes. Certainly, government agencies seldom appear to act or react with the speed with which the private sector requires.

The lack of coordination and cooperation between government agencies in their policies and programs is often quite prevalent in tourism. This is a reflection of the diversity of the tourism system itself and of the inherent and unavoidable conflicts between the goals of some agencies, such as natural resource conservation versus tourism promotion and developments agencies. Any destination area with a vital interest in tourism should undertake steps to bring about the highest amount of coordination and cooperation among its government agencies. It seems logical that the national and state/provincial offices should take the lead role in this respect.